# OUT THE OTHER SIDE

## Contemporary Lesbian Writing

### Edited by Christian McEwen and Sue O'Sullivan

The Crossing Press
Freedom, California

For Irena Klepfisz, whose piece included here was the inspiration
for this book

**Library of Congress Cataloging-in-Publication Data**

Out the other side :  contemporary lesbian writing / edited by
    Christian McEwen and Sue O'Sullivan.
        p.  cm.
        "British edition 1988 by Virago Press Limited"—T.p. verso
        Includes bibliographical references
        ISBN 0-89594-364-6 — ISBN 0-89594-363-8 (pbk.)
        1. Lesbianism. 2. Feminism. 3. Identity (Psychology)
4. Lesbians' writings.        I. McEwen, Christian, 1956-
II. O'Sullivan, Sue.
HQ75.5.O94  1988
306.76′63—dc20
                                                            89-17304
                                                            CIP

# Contents 🖋

# PART FOUR: Speaking Actions, Living Words

# PART FIVE: Recovery

# PART SIX: Power and Coalition

# Acknowledgements ✍

## from Christian McEwen

Many people have helped me in the preparation of this book. I would especially like to thank Jane Winter, who has remained a steadfast friend throughout, and who, for six months in New York, paid my share of the rent, leaving me free to work part time. On the east coast I was advised by Julie Abraham, Malaga Baldi, Nancy Bereano, Jan Clausen, Deborah Edel and Tucker Farley, by Marilyn Hacker, Joan Larkin, Joan Nestle, Susan Sherman and Catharine Stimpson; on the west coast by Gloria Anzaldúa; and in London by Ruthie Petrie, Alison Read and, of course, Sue O'Sullivan. Laetitia Bermejo, Sharon Franklet, Janice Gould, Andrea Freud Loewenstein, Maia, Isabella McEwen, Aurora Levins Morales, Elizabeth Tallent and Anne Witten, sent, as always, love and mail from places far away. In daily life there was Naomi Dodds, Deborah di Meglio, Deborah Kaufmann, Maria Margaronis, Donna Masini and Anne Twitty, all of whom I knew I could always call. At work I was encouraged by Mary Allgier, Millie Aronoff, Cynthia Isaacs, Alice Hamers, Jean Olsen and Winsome Pryce. And then there were the writings and the writers themselves. Many, many thanks.

## from Sue O'Sullivan

I was a latecomer to this book, slipping with pleasure and trepidation into a co-editor's role when the project was already underway. Thanks are due to Ruthie Petrie and Christian McEwen for persuading me out of my trepidation. Friendships – old and new, close and long distance – sustain me through thick and thin, and I thank Susan Ardill, Sona Osman, Alice Henry, Ruthie, Jean Smith, Diane Hamer, Pratibha Parmar, Janet Hadley, Loretta Loach, Karen Goldman, Fiona Cooper, Nancy Jonas, Karen Slaney and Vicki Breitbart for being there. Thanks also to the Sheba collective, Araba Mercer, Michelle McKenzie and RaeAnn Robertson for being sympathetic to the rest of my hectic life. My freelance group was the perfect place to get a regular moan in about approaching and left behind deadlines . . . thanks girls. The best part of all about this book was receiving the drafts of work in progress and seeing it all come together in the end. Thanks to all the writers.

Many of the pieces in this collection have not been published previously; we are grateful to each of the authors for agreeing to have her work printed here.

For permission to reprint material that has appeared elsewhere, grateful acknowledgements are as follows:

'Notes on Racism Among Women', © 1982 by Donna Allegra, first appeared in *Heresies 15: A Feminist Publication of Art and Politics*; 'How to Tame a Wild Tongue', © 1987 by Gloria Anzaldúa, *Borderlands/La Frontera* (Spinsters/Aunt Lute Press); 'Upsetting an Applecart: Difference, Desire and Lesbian Sadomasochism' © 1986 by Ardill and O'Sullivan, *Feminist Review 23*; 'Letters between Raven and Beth' © 1983 by Beth Brant, 'A Gathering of Spirit', *Sinister Wisdom 22/23* (Sinister Wisdom Books); 'Lesbians of (Writing) Lore' © 1988 by Nicole Brossard, *The Aerial Letter* (The Women's Press, Canada); 'Making Common Cause: Diversity and Coalition' © 1985 by Charlotte Bunch, *Passionate Politics: Feminist Theory in Action, 1968–86* (St Martin's Press); 'Reverberations: dialogue', © 1986 By Sandra Butler and Barbara Rosenblum, first appeared in *The Tribe of Dina: A Jewish Women's Anthology, Sinister Wisdom 29/30* (Sinister Wisdom Books); 'Traveling Fat', © 1984 by Elana Dykewomon, from *Shadow on a Tightrope* (Aunt Lute Press); 'Dyke-tactics for Difficult Times', © 1988 by Franklin and Stacey, *Feminist Review* No. 29, 'A Woman's Right to Cruise – disability and lesbian sexuality', © 1986 by Kirsten Hearn *Trouble and Strife* No. 9; 'The Gap She Fostered', © 1983 by Amber Hollibaugh, first appeared in *The New York Native*; 'A Fem's Own Story: An Interview with Joan Nestle', © 1987 by Margaret Hunt, first appeared in *Gay Community News*; 'To Be a Radical Jew in the Late 20th Century', © 1986 by Melanie Kay/Kantrowitz, *The Tribe of Dina: A Jewish Women's Anthology, Sinister Wisdom 29/30* (Sinister Wisdom Books); 'The Distances Between Us: Feminism, Consciousness and the Girls at the Office', © 1985 by Irena Klepfisz, *Sinister Wisdom 28* (Sinister Wisdom Books); 'Age, Race, Class and Sex: Women Redefining Difference', © 1980 by Audre Lorde, *Sister Outsider: Essays and Speeches by Audre Lorde* (The Crossing Press, 1984); 'Both Feet In life: Interview with Barbara Macdonald and Cynthia Rich', © 1986 by Jean Swallow, *Women and Aging; An Anthology by Women* (Calyx Books); 'Rage and Desire: Confronting Pornography', © 1988 Pratibha Parmar in *Feminism and Censorship – The Current Debate* (Prism); 'Power and Helplessness in the Women's Movement', © 1985 by Joanna Russ, *Magic Mommas, Trembling Sisters, Puritans and Perverts* (The Crossing Press); 'Sex and Danger: Feminism and Aids', ©1987 by Sara Scott, *Trouble and Strife* No. 11; 'Philosophy and the Big Exception: Why I Write Fiction', © 1983 by Ellen Shapiro, first appeared in *Ikon: Creativity and Change, Second Series, No. 2*; 'The Shower', © 1985 by Linda Smukler, first appeared in *Conditions 11/12, 1985*; 'Class/Act: Defining a Translation from Privilege', © 1986 by Susanna J. Sturgis, first appeared in *Women: A Journal of Liberation, Vol. 8, No. 3 (1983)*; 'Recovery, the Story of an ACA', © 1984 by Jean Swallow, *Out from Under: Sober Dykes & Our Friends* (Spinsters Ink); 'Transformations', © 1986 by Sunna, *Through the Break* (Sheba).

# Introduction by Christian McEwen

In January 1986, Virago asked if I would like to edit a collection of lesbian poetry. 'Yes,' I told them. 'Absolutely yes. But can I do a prose collection too?'

'Prose?' people asked me, then and later. 'Non-fiction prose,' I always hastened to explain. 'You know, those thinking pieces, the kind of thing Adrienne Rich does so beautifully – or Audre Lorde.' They nodded doubtfully, and I could see they didn't, quite. After all, both those writers were American. And 'lesbian non-fiction prose' did not sound like such a draw. In fact, it sounded difficult and theoretical, the kind of 'ought to' that most of us would happily avoid. 'But really it's worth looking at,' I tried to say. 'Some of those writers are extraordinary. Just let me find a piece that I can show –'

*Out the Other Side* has been compiled by Sue O'Sullivan and myself in an attempt to do just that: to show the reader (in particular the unconvinced-but-interested reader), just how rich and varied and accessible lesbian writing has become. In the United States especially, there is something of a secret Renaissance going on. More women are writing and being published than ever before, and with each story, each essay, each article, lesbian culture defines itself more fully. For all the barriers of age and race and class and economics, a common language – and something of a common value system – is increasingly being established.

Such excitement and openness in relationship to lesbianism is of course extremely recent. For most of our lives, and the lives of our grandmothers and great-grandmothers, it was not an issue that could properly be raised. The degree of tolerance varied, as Lillian Faderman has shown,[1] but in general, though journals might be kept and letters sent, memoirs and autobiographies compiled, the lesbian dimension of a woman's life was very rarely given its full due. Most writers passed over such details of their daily lives in silence (see, for example, the gaping absences in Margaret Anderson's fat, three-volume autobiography),[2] others altered emphasis and pronouns (Willa Cather, Amy Lowell), still others resorted to code or invented locutions (Stein's famous use of 'cow' for orgasm or the private meaning of her 'lifting belly' with Alice).[3]

If this was the paranoia of the literary intelligentsia, the relatively well-heeled, relatively well-protected, what could life have been like for the ordinary lesbians? Far from the Paris salons, the easygoing camaraderie of Greenwich Village, they were very much left to fend for themselves. Some managed courageously and well, inventing a support system and a culture, relying on scraps of lesbian or gay lore passed down from one lover to the next.[4] Others, less fortunate, accepted the views of the dominant society, and lived lives of great fear and isolation. For comfort they turned to trashy dimestore novels (often written by men), or sought out the advice of experts (for example in the professional columns of *The Ladder*)[5] in the bleak hope that they might be helped to change, to become different, more 'normal' sorts of people.

Lest this speedy paraphrase of the bad old days set them too safely in the distant past, it needs to be said that as late as 1961, Judy Grahn was expelled from the Armed Services for being homosexual,[6] and that similar incidents continued through the late seventies and well into the eighties. In the face of such mistreatment, there were many who felt unable to tell the whole truth of who they were. Here, for example, is the young Joan Nestle, marching from Selma in support of Civil Rights:

> I did not put the word Lesbian on my card. I put Jewish and feminist. I wrote about SANE[7] and CORE.[8] I did not talk about the bars I went to, or the knowledge about bigotry I had gained by being a queer.[9]

In the end of course, it was that same Civil Rights Movement, in conjunction with the Women's Liberation Movement, that gave the lesbian issue its first real push into the limelight. By the early seventies, the first Women's Studies programs were introduced (one of them headed by an avowed lesbian),[10] and the first women's bookstores and publishing houses were being established. *Amazon Quarterly* appeared, and in its wake a host of other journals. Kate Millett published *Sexual Politics* and *Flying*, Jill Johnston published *Lesbian Nation*, Alma Routsong, under the pseudonym of Isabel Miller, published *Patience and Sarah*.[11] These were some of the starting points, the early texts, the first claimings of lesbian identity. With them came the makings of an entire lesbian culture: poets and playwrights, therapists and health-care workers, lesbian carpenters, lesbian organizers, lesbian business-women.

*

In describing this, I am, obviously, referring to the United States. The British experience was very different. Although British women got the vote earlier than their American equivalents, and had in many ways a more open attitude towards lesbianism, their liberation movement came about more slowly. *Arena 3*, the first British lesbian magazine, appeared only in 1964, eight years later than *The Ladder*, and movement lesbians were at first identified with the Gay Liberation Front, with its well-publicised weekly meetings, think-ins, Gay Days and people's dances. They separated from the men in 1971, but it was the spring of 1974 before they had a conference of their own, and in cultural matters they continued to lag behind the States.[12] Self-conscious lesbians wishing to keep abreast of their newly defined identity might rescue *The Well of Loneliness* from their local second-hand bookshop, but most of their reading matter had to be imported from abroad. Presses were founded, and, very gradually, some Women's Studies courses were introduced, but a thorough-going grass roots lesbian culture took far longer to establish.

Given all this, it is perhaps not so surprising that British and American writing should develop along such different paths, as indeed they can be seen to have done. I experienced this at first hand when I came to gather material for this book. Where in the States I was able to do much of my research at the Lesbian Herstory Archives in New York, going through the papers which had been deposited there, and reading my way through stacks of periodicals, similar research at London's Feminist Library yielded almost nothing. Gradually I saw that if I wanted to include British lesbian non-fiction prose, I would have to solicit it myself. Since I was living in the States by then, this would have been almost impossible to accomplish. Luckily Virago introduced me to Sue O'Sullivan, an expatriate American living in London, with strong experience in both politics and publishing, and she agreed to take over the British half of the book. I could not have had a better partner and co-editor.

*

Back in the States, still trying to make sense of Anglo/American differences, I called the local library and the National Council for Research on Women, and came up with a few statistics. Britain is not only a far smaller country than the States (54 million to the States' 241 million), but of those who go on to higher education, a far smaller number are women (some 40.9 per cent in Britain as opposed to 51 per cent in the States). There are, proportionally, far fewer female academics and Women's Studies Programs,[13] and (not, I think, unconnected to this), fewer lesbian-only publishers and magazines.[14] In addition, the States has a far larger number of alternative magazines open to publishing work by women, and women's magazines open to publishing work by lesbians.[15] There is, in fact, no doubt that a lesbian writer living in Britain is likely to have a far smaller chance of being published than her American equivalent – as well as far less cultural encouragement (in the form of readings, grants, workshops and role models).

This being so, it was a joy to see how at Sue's urging, piece after piece emerged out of that initial silence. If the work was in some ways 'younger' than its American counterpart, that made it no less valuable. I think here of Charlotte Bunch's account of the four stages of activism: description, analysis, vision and strategy.[16] British descriptions are as necessary as American. In fact, both are fundamental. As lesbians, our stories have all too often been told for us by other people (psychologists, sociologists, 'experts' of various stripes). It is essential that we take what time we need to tell them for ourselves – and to listen to each other too – before we go on to analysis, vision and revision, and some form of constructive strategy.

*

For those initial stages of description and analysis, the essay is a wonderfully generous and capacious form. In this particular collection, its identity has been stretched to include letters and journals, dialogues and speeches, autobiographical fiction and political meditations. Length varies considerably, and tone and angle and intention vary with it, from the high rhetoric of speech-making to the easygoing emphases of conversation, from the self-consciously formal and argumentative to the deliberate collage. Because the essay is, in a sense, everybody's first form (second only, perhaps, to poetry), it secures a wide range of possible practitioners, from beginning writers to well-established professionals. No other form offers such large-hearted welcome.

When I began to gather material for this collection, first alone and then with Sue, I was not aware of all these things. I was operating from a strong gut feeling about the interest and excitement of recent lesbian writing, and I thought too, along with Joan Nestle, that the 'knowledge of bigotry gained by being a queer' was a good place from which to understand other forms of social oppression. There had, I thought, been enough coming-out stories. And so I began to look for writing which came 'out the other side', writing which had as base a 'lesbian presumption' that could be put to use in analysing other issues.

The catalyst for this was a piece by Irena Klepfisz called 'The Distances Between Us: Feminism, Consciousness and the Girls at the Office'. In this piece, Klepfisz makes use of her own very specific background (as a writer, teacher, lesbian and Jew), to make sense of the way in which women office-workers are mistreated and misunderstood, both by their immediate bosses, and by their so-called sisters in the women's movement. She writes of what it is to be 'an alert, thinking human being absorbed, assaulted by mindless unintelligent work. The fragmentation. The sense of being robbed.' It is an issue which the bosses cannot allow themselves to recognise. To do so would be to meet their workers head on as human beings. Easier, far easier to see them as a class of drones who are actually happy to do the work that everyone else rejects. Easier to provide the musak and the self-erasing typewriter, the comfortable swivel-chair, to dismiss the office-work as 'very boring' and the office-workers along with it.

But it is here that Irena Klepfisz makes her stand. Her essay is itself an argument, a refusal to take such treatment lightly, to be persuaded that it is less than utterly inhumane. If the situation cannot be changed immediately, at least, she says, let us face it among ourselves. Let us 'put an end to the shame and guilt surrounding both power and powerlessness', and, as women and as activists, find some way that we can work together.

\*

In the same way that Klepfisz uses her politics and feminism in 'Girls at the Office', choosing specific lived details to emphasise much larger points, so too the other writers in this book make use of their experience. They come from Britain and the States and Canada, from Australia and India. They are Black and white and Asian and Chicana, Jewish and

Chinese. But for all their background differences, their underlying philosophies have much in common. They are lesbians and speech-makers, they are moralists and thinkers, and their aim is a shared aim: to describe a difficult, often taboo piece of experience, and in so doing, to alter its quality: to make of the snake's venom the cure for the snake's bite. To this end, the subjects chosen are by no means easy: incest and alcoholism, age and race and class and sex, disability, menopause. But however painful or potentially embarrassing, the intention remains firm: to name the taboo, not to luxuriate in it, but to make sense of it and so to get beyond it: to forgive the self and rediscover self-respect. With this comes a new expansiveness, a stronger coalition, a richer and more complicated sense of identity.

If this sounds just a touch too good to be true, it probably is. Facing up to taboo subjects takes time and persistence, both on paper and in life. As Chrystos says in her piece 'Perhaps', 'We see ourselves as "better" because we have to, in order to survive the mainstream opinion of us. But we're not better.' Being lesbians may give us some sort of handle on our complicated pasts, but it can hardly give us a foolproof method for solving them.

This becomes very clear in *Beginnings*, the first section of the book, where both Amber Hollibaugh and Susanna J. Sturgis deal with the issue of class in their families. Hollibaugh grew up poor and working-class; she was the first in her family to finish high school. Sturgis grew up upper-middle class, sure of her own importance in the world. Neither has found it easy to deal with her inheritance. Hollibaugh writes that in order to give her a chance, her parents had to 'create a child they did not understand, they had to endure [her] shame of them'. Sturgis had the opposite situation to make sense of. She had to teach herself that 'there [was] evil in the soil that nourished [her], that gave [her her] voice'. She had to 'learn to listen to voices [she] was never meant to hear'. As so often (there is a parallel, though very different example in the self-interview of the two Jewish lovers, Sandra Butler and Barbara Rosenblum), writing about such things is only the beginning. The rest is patience, self-love and forgiveness, watching and waiting, allowing room for change.

*Inside the Body* takes the theme of difference and self-acceptance from another angle, this time drawing on the testimony of a fat woman and a disabled woman, as well as including pieces on menopause and AIDS. Because of our position in society, lesbians often feel that we know exactly what it is like to feel 'different'. *Inside the Body* draws attention to the areas where our knowing fails us: it is information that could only be got from those we have hurt or misunderstood. In 'Traveling Fat', for example, Elana Dykewomon writes of what it is like to be a fat woman, and, as such, continually discounted or left out. She describes the way in which dieting has been institutionalised, and how efficiently this connects with race and class oppression. 'How well the hope of class mobility keeps every mother dieting and handing the diets down to her daughter, hoping the daughter may do even better.' Dykewomon points out the insult of this, since 'the vast majority of women will never be thin enough'.

With the same clarity, and the same focussed anger, Kirsten Hearn writes of her own situation as a disabled blind woman. She herself celebrates her disability, though she notes how utterly surprising this is to most 'severely abled' people. In her case, she says, being blind 'is a positive part of me, and a part of which I am intensely proud'.

The third section, *Family and Relationships*, covers a number of different issues, among them lesbians and family, life without a lover, self-insemination and lesbian single motherhood. In her piece, Sigrid Nielsen notes that when she 'was dating a presentable young man, the university became a different place . . . full of subtle welcome and encouragement. Once that phase was over' – ie, once she had gone back to being a lesbian – 'the scene dissolved into the usual genteel wasteland.' It is a familiar story. More troubling and insidious is the point made by Lorna Hardy, that 'the pressure to have a lover or lovers – to be known to have *someone* to have sex with – is at least as great in lesbian feminist circles'. As lesbians, we would like to set up different rules, but don't entirely know how. 'Although it is fine for women to complain about their lovers, it is much rarer for any of us to break down in public and say. "I'm fed up because I haven't slept with anyone for eighteen months –" ' As always with the really painful issues, much of the silencing is self-silencing.

Given this, it is fitting that the next section should be *Speaking Actions, Living Words*. As a Chicana,[17] Gloria Anzaldúa speaks with the 'forked tongue' of both English and Spanish, flickering into combinations of eight different language-dialects. For years she has been forced to accommodate the dominant language (mainly English), rather than speak and write in Spanglish as she herself prefers.[18] Now at last she has started to refuse this accommodation:

I will no longer be made ashamed of existing. I will have my tongue: Indian, Spanish, white. I will have my serpent's tongue, my woman's voice, my sexual voice, my poet's voice . . . Until I can take pride in my language, I cannot take pride in myself.

For Nicole Brossard and Ellen Shapiro, taking pride in ourselves and writing from that pride, have much to do with the physical body. Brossard writes of taking to the letter 'our bodies, our skin, our sweat, our pleasure, sensuality, sexuality, sexual bliss'. And Shapiro, in explaining why she is now a fiction writer rather than a student of philosophy, tells of the faith she has 'that her body will find its gravity' and 'the voice that says "Trust me, I know the things you have forgotten." '

In the exchange of letters between Native American Beth Brant and her friend Raven, that 'Trust me' echoes again, not about the body this time, but about the power of writing itself, the sustenance each finds in their correspondence. 'I admire you greatly,' writes Raven. 'You are of freedom.

I seek friendship of those who know and accept themselves, and stand in truth without plastic covers.'

To 'stand in truth without plastic covers' is of course the aim of every writer in this book, but this is especially true of those in the section on recovery. There is a courage here, a nakedness and a sense of risk, as each one reaches out for help in whatever direction seems best to her. Therapy, exercise, acupuncture, psychic guidance, good nutrition: all these things are recognised as valuable. But behind them too is the strength drawn from the act of writing itself (letters, journals, the very work included here), and, again, behind that, the love and support provided by the lesbian community.

It is in *Power and Coalition*, the last and longest section of the book, that this initial reaching out comes fully into its own. Joanna Russ writes painfully and wittily on all the forces ranged against us, in particular the notion that all 'really good women, really "nice" women, really sisterly women, are dead women'. She is teasing us, of course, but not entirely. We have all been well-trained in the self-defeating roles of 'Magic Mommas and Trembling Sisters'. Russ reminds us that self-love and self-assertiveness are not evil, and that what matters is not our inflated notion of someone else's power, but a fierce and thorough claiming of our own.

Someone who has definitely claimed her power many times over is the activist Barbara Macdonald, author, with Cynthia Rich, of *Look Me in the Eye: Old Women, Aging and Ageism.*[19] Like Kirsten Hearn, the degree to which she enjoys her life probably comes as a surprise to most people. But her explanation for this rings wonderfully true: 'Part of the reason I say I get real pleasure out of growing old is because I'm a dyke. I'm not facing otherness for the first time . . . And now I have this brand new chance to find out who I am, facing another kind of otherness'. She says too, that she has really almost no desire left to please, 'and there is power in that'.

The power of that 'not needing to please' is of course the power of self acceptance, of being able to take pride in ourselves and our inheritance, however contradictory and divided it may seem. Audre Lorde writes very beautifully of this in 'Age, Race, Class and Sex':

My fullest concentration of energy is available to me only when I integrate all the parts of who I am, openly, allowing power from particular sources of my living to flow back and forth freely through all my different selves.

It is a call for wholeness and completion, for self-celebration and delight, a difficult message for this wizened western culture to hear. And yet, as Charlotte Bunch makes plain, 'Successful coalitions are not built around feeling sorry for others or being apologetic about one's own existence'. One of the best first steps in reaching out to other people is to take a sturdy working pride in who we are. And it is here, in this reaching out, this hard-earned pride, that lesbian non-fiction prose most truly comes into its own. Here, among the contributors to this book, are the 'one-woman coalitions' that Bunch writes about, here are the visionaries and the strategists, the stylists and the speechmakers. And here, less than two decades after the first consciousness-raising sessions, is the point where they explode, through dividedness and difference, and 'out the other side'.

## Notes

1. Lillian Faderman, *Surpassing the Love of Men: Romantic Friendship and Love Between Women from the Renaissance to the Present*, Junction Books Ltd., 1981; Women's Press, 1987.
2. Margaret Anderson, *My Thirty Years War*, Covinci, Friedge, 1930, The Fiery Fountain, Hermitage House, 1951, and *The Strange Necessity*, Horizon Press, 1969.
3. See Lillian Faderman, op. cit., p. 401. Compare too, *I Know My Own Heart: The Diaries of Anne Lister*, ed. Helena Whitbread, Virago, 1987.
4. See Judy Grahn, *Another Mother Tongue: Gay Words, Gay Worlds*, pp. 3–6, Beacon Press, 1984.
5. Pioneering lesbian magazine, published in the States between 1956 and 1972. See Elly Bulkin's introduction to *Lesbian Fiction: an anthology*, Persephone Press, 1981.
6. See Judy Grahn, op. cit., p. 28.
7. SANE: Committee for a Sane Nuclear Policy.
8. CORE: Congress of Racial Equality.
9. See Joan Nestle, *A Restricted Country*, p. 61, Firebrand Books, 1987.
10. Tucker Farley, who for a long time administered the Women's Studies Program at Brooklyn College (personal communication).
11. *Amazon Quarterly* was founded by Audre Lorde in 1972. *Sexual Politics* appeared in 1969, *Flying* in 1974, *Lesbian Nation* in 1973, and *Patience and Sarah* in 1967.
12. Early movement newsletters included the Rev/Rad newsletter, WIRES, and the Leeds Revolutionary Feminist Newsletter, but these were local and political, as opposed to the broad range of literary periodicals enjoyed by feminists in the States.
13. There are thirty Women's Studies Programmes in England and Wales, and none at all in Scotland, in comparison with 30,000 courses in the States, given in over 500 degree-granting institutions. Many thanks to Kate Stimpson and Florence Howe for this information, and also for referring me to Mariam Chamberlain at the National Council for Research on Women, 47–49 East 69th Street, New York, NY 10021.
14. Where Britain has only Onlywomen Press (founded 1974), American lesbian publishers include Naiad Press Inc. (founded in 1974), L.F.R. (founded 1978), Word Weavers (founded 1981) and Firebrand Books (founded in 1984).
    Where Britain can claim only *Gossip* (founded 1986), American lesbian magazines include *Feminary* (founded in 1969), *Sinister Wisdom* (founded in 1976), *Common Lives/Lesbian Lives* (founded in 1981), and *Lesbian Ethics* (founded in 1984).
15. British periodicals include *Outwrite* (founded 1982), *Trouble and Strife* (founded 1983), *Spare Rib* (founded 1972), and *Feminist Review* (founded 1979). In the States there is still a far wider range of options. See, for

example, such magazines as *Conditions* (founded in 1976), *Calyx* (founded in 1976), *Heresies* (founded in 1976), and *Ikon: Creativity and Change* (re-established in 1982–83), all concentrating on original literary work.

16. See Charlotte Bunch, *Passionate Politics: Feminist Theory in Action 1968–86*, pp. 244–246, St Martin's Press, 1987.

17. Mexican American, but see Gloria Anzaldúa on the difficulty of giving any quick and easy definition.

18. I would like to thank Gloria Anzaldúa for agreeing to translate the Spanish phrases in her article. I felt it necessary for a British audience, but obviously it went very much against her principles.

19. Cynthia Rich and Barbara Macdonald, *Look Me in the Eye: Old Women, Aging and Ageism*, Spinsters/Aunt Lute Press, 1983.

# PART ONE
## Beginnings

---

## The Gap She Fostered
Amber Hollibaugh

I have lived in New York for two years, and this weekend I finally set up my office. It terrifies me to put together my own space, to set up the books, construct the desk, arrange the files and papers I collect with such greed. It seems pretentious and outlandish, a crazy fantasy gotten out of hand. In the hours between midnight and dawn, it is exhilarating to imagine myself a writer, to dream myself a passionate, creative figure in the privacy of my own imagination; in daylight, it seems preposterous. It makes me sick to my stomach when I try.

I am the first in my family to finish high school. Two of my cousins got their high school equivalency in the Marines and my father has now gone back and finished, but I was the first. Growing up, I read *Readers Digest Condensed Novels* and love comics. There was a copy of *The Prophet* by Khalil Gibran and a full set of encyclopedias. My father read *Hamlet* and loved it. There were a million auto mechanic books, carpentry manuals, and issues of *Popular Mechanics*. The bathroom held a book called *Jokes For The Pot*, and there were *Family Circles* and cookbooks. But it is fair to say that respect for books is not the same as possessing them, and we had only a few at that.

As a child I was the 'bookworm' of my family; everybody talked about it. I read everything in sight: milk bottles and mayonnaise jars, *The Bobbsey Twins* and the *Cherry Ames* series. I was as passionate about books as my family was about cars, motorcycles, and Friday night pinochle. It was through books that I first began to see a world different from my home town – it was not so pretty where I come from. The magic of books took me away from the fights and the dirt, the cars in the front yard, the too little money and the worry which filled the rooms we lived in. Nothing about my life seemed so bad when I had a book to read. Books

1

could be borrowed from the library or stolen from the drugstore. I never cared whether I had 'taste.' I read them all.

It was the opening up of a novel that brought extraordinary people and events into my orbit; it was in books that I found people who felt things no one in my family admitted feeling: emotions and conflicts, sex, wrong-headed passions. People in books talked differently and scrambled my notions of normal or right. Books held promise. I was an addict at an early age and I fought for the right to read more desperately than I struggled for anything else in my life.

No one in my family could figure out where this love of books had come from, and what had given me a craving for words. It was their considered opinion that it happened because I had been a sick child, premature at birth, not even walking until my second birthday. I had asthma and colds more than I didn't. I was badly cross-eyed and would run sideways when I caught adults watching me play. They looked in my direction first when they heard a child fall and were always shaking their heads over my clumsiness.

But, I also scared the hell out of them. To them, I was emotionally out of control. I lived in the world of feelings; they in the silent world of work. I wanted to talk; they wanted to do. I said out loud what everyone had agreed not to notice. I was dangerous to them and to the place I was to inhabit as a grown woman. They held that my moods were caused by reading too much, 'getting ideas,' and 'living in a dream world.' They thought it was crazy, unsafe and dead end. They did not want to see me disappointed and there was no way to make a living from my passion for books.

Back then, my mother did not have abstract concepts like class, but she damn well understood what was possible and what would break my heart. I was her baby and, proud as she was of my reading and dreaming, she could not afford to encourage a fantasy which would leave me unprepared to face what she knew awaited me. A survivor herself, she meant me to be one too. Truth is, I was as afraid as my parents were when I tried to see where it was leading. They were right; it didn't make any sense for me. I could be the best-read waitress in Roseville, the best-read wife, the best-read biker, the best-read teenage mother.

I was queer and I wanted a 'better' life. In books, I met people who had both. I read the whole encyclopedia many times over, fascinated by the wheat crop figures in the USSR, the kind of snakes in Japan, the reason for the speed of light. I tried out new places to live and other languages. I was a child in the Himalayas and I first met lesbians in the soft-core porn I was stealing from the place next to Woolworths; books gave me ideas.

Meanwhile, my mother and I were at war. I was at an age where I would brook no interference from her. She didn't agree. In my senior year, I was sent away on scholarship to an upper class school to create some peace for us both. I returned home without many clothes and a suitcase of books. I brought them all back, including the most pretentious I had read that year. I had been introduced to 'good' books and I took to them with the same stubborn determination which had kept me reading bad ones.

That year in boarding school had been terrible for me. I was different and stupid seeming to most of the students, and most of the time, I agreed with them. I felt ignorant and unpractised in all they took for granted. But the one thing they had that I could figure out was books. I was being introduced to a literature which I could never have discovered or understood in my home town. Night after night I stayed up after curfew trying to catch up. I tried to span the distance between the other kids and myself in eight months – a difference created by the years when they had been surrounded by literature, poetry, and music alien to my world. In the end, I couldn't cross that distance, but the race between me and words set in motion a flight from the deadening effects of too much hard work and a rush towards learning which I had been fearing and desiring all my life.

I came home awkward and bitter towards my parents. I saw that they couldn't give me ever, what those kids' parents could grant effortlessly in a month's allowance or a well-placed phone call. Humiliating as the year had been, it made it impossible for me to stay in my home town for good, impossible to forget the other ways I could be in the world. I had been AWAY. I had been a learner, a student of great ideas and powerful thinkers. I had taken the trip outside and was forever changed by it. Now, I had to leave.

In that first strange month of my return home my parents built me a desk and shelves for all the books. They framed a map I brought back of the Parthenon and got me bookends and a study light. None of us knew what I was to do with these things, it just seemed required now that I was the owner of such large, impressive-looking books. They were awed by them, held them in reverence and dread just as I did – though I wouldn't admit to it. These were my trophies, the stuffed animal heads on my wall. This was the proof that their sacrifice to send me away from the place where I was raised had been worth it.

We all circled those bookcases like hounds after an animal we had never come upon before. I, as their owner, would shut the door to my room and open their pages again and again. They were proof to me that I had been 'somewhere,' and to my parents they were a sign of how I had become different and unknown to them, how I had traveled without them to places they could not imagine. It was a sign of how we had changed and grown apart.

I was not duplicating the motions of the women in my family, each female child moving slightly away from the woman who birthed her, though less than it seemed initially, once she became an adult and settled in. I would rechart the map my family and I had propped up in our minds. I had been born to grow up to have children, marry and live out my life as a modern version of the women who had come before me. Now it was clear, I would not. I was becoming another kind of survivor.

A week after the shelves were put up and the books in place I returned home in the middle of the day to find my mother in my room, surrounded by them. They were spread all around her, some half open, some sprawled across the bed as though they'd been thrown. She was crying – my mother who never cried in front of me. I stood at the door of my room, too stunned to speak. We stared at each other and those books, not talking, her crying. And finally, she turned toward me and said, 'I don't understand any of these books, nothing that's in them, nothing they say. How can you read them, understand them, if I can't? How can you still be my daughter and have these on your walls? Who do you think you are to have these in my house?' And then, she left.

I have never put together an office when I haven't fought against the sense of betraying my family. My mother's terrible pain when she sat on the edge of my bed envelopes me whenever I try to start. I see her grand intelligence and the terrible price she was forced to pay to offer me hope. I feel her wounds at being so cheated of any chances of her own. Her only hope had to rest in me and what her determination could wrest from a poor start. I see her face, the slope of her shoulders, as she cried and touched the books around her and faced the difference she had helped foster between us. It is a terrible thing that the world is so weighted on the side of wealth and privilege.

This is a pain I cannot avoid each time I sit at my typewriter or assemble my office. The ghost of her narrowed options and all the dreams she had to defer to me, the confusions and bitter separation between us are shapes which hang in my house now and live with me. In order to give me a chance, my parents had to create a child they did not understand, they had to endure my shame of them. The pride we carry about each other is surrounded by a sadness none of us can dissolve.

☙

# Spinsterhood and the Chinese Lesbian Group: A Visit to My Aunts

Alice Lee  ☙

I would like to look at the idea of Spinsterhood as a way of life, seeing as how some of us strong, independent women, sometimes known as lesbians, face the reality of living on the so-called fringes. We get by with, or without, the blessing of our families and much to the disgust of our various communities who quietly ignore us, or actively deny us.

What started me thinking about Spinsterhood in relation to the Chinese Lesbian group[1] was a visit to my two aunts, both of whom are spinsters in their mid-70s. They live quietly in a council flat in Liverpool. My aunts are sprightly women, born in the West Indies. Their grandparents came originally from Canton by ship at the end of the last century and settled in the Caribbean. The visit to my aunts was the first I had made in sixteen years. We talked of marriage, families, and life back home. They told me they had never wanted to marry and were satisfied with the way their lives had gone. They talked of my great aunts, also spinsters, who lived in the Caribbean.

Talking to my aunts made me realise that I came from a strong tradition of marriage-resisting women. I'm thinking now of the popular spinsterhood associations that existed in and around the Canton Delta. These associations were closely linked to the silk-weaving industry that flourished at the end of the last century right up to the 1930s. Women's labour was important in all stages of silk production. The sisterhood associations that formed around the industry were already part of village life. They became more organised with the advent of mechanisation and wage labour in the industry.

I first came across the sisterhood in an account by Agnes Smedley, an American journalist.[2] She visited Canton in 1930 and wrote about the women silk workers who allegedly organised themselves to demand better wages and who formed 'sister societies'. The person that Agnes travelled with told her that the spinners were notorious throughout China as lesbians because they refused to marry. If they were forced to do so by their families, they would bribe their husbands with part of their wages. Some even formed suicide pacts.

After she had met the women in question, Agnes declared that she could understand why they were seen as lesbians as their independence seemed an affront to officialdom.

Han Suyin also refers to this lesbian society in her book, *My House has Two Doors*:

There is a famous district in the province of Kuangtung (Canton Province), in which all the nurseries where the silkworms are reared, and the mulberry trees which provide the leaves for their food, are owned by women. And so that this wealth of silk and its labour should not fall into the hands of men, who would exploit the labour of women and their adroit fingers and reap the profit, the women live in sororities, and form their own couples, vowing love and sisterhood to each other. They wear their hair long in a virgin pigtail all their lives. This lesbian society, which is also an economic system, is accepted and respected.[3]

Han Suyin goes on to describe how some women organised resistance to marriage, going as far as finding substitutes. Girl children born to the 'substitutes' were adopted by the marriage resisters. (Hurray! I thought, not all the girl children were thrown down the well.) Moreover, it was a way of perpetuating the sisterhood.

Curious about these lesbians, I searched around and came across a biographical account of a Chinese nun, Jing Sih Sifu, which turned out to be most comprehensive.[4] Jing Sih Sifu speaks of her early life in the village of Lungsan (Guangzhou Province). She helped her family raise mulberry bushes, the leaves of which were fed to the silk worms. Sifu talks of becoming a spinner in the 1920s and of resisting marriage at the age of nineteen. She says the custom was practised by her grandmother and by generations before her – even before the advent of the factories. Sifu talks of the special ceremony that went with the spinsterhood vow: a hair combing ceremony and a dinner banquet rather like the wedding ceremony. In the wedding ceremony, a young woman would change her hair from that of a girl (two long braids) to that of a woman (hair knotted in a bun); in the spinsterhood ceremony, the woman's hair would be plaited in a single braid. After the ceremony, as she could no longer live at home, the woman would go to live in a spinster house in another section of the village. In Sifu's case, she is helped by her 'sisters' and her godmother to build her own spinster house. These 'spinster societies' that formed seemed a cross between an association and a guild, through which the women gave each other practical and emotional support. Even after the silk-weaving industry collapsed, the women helped each other to retrain and to find jobs. Some became servants, amahs, or cooks, travelling as far as Hong Kong, Malaysia and Singapore.

Sifu herself became a domestic. She worked as a cook, travelled to Hong Kong and then much later, became a Buddhist nun and helped to set up a vegetarian food hall in Hong Kong. Throughout all this she kept in touch with other sisters, eventually giving over her spinster house in the village to a younger woman.

What I like about these spinsterhood associations is the fact that the women supported each other emotionally, as well as financially; they even set up house together. I would like to think that our Chinese Lesbian group has such a widespread and organised antecedent. As Chinese lesbians, we have very few role models to go by. Just knowing about the sisterhood is a kind of validation in itself. We need to find out more about them as a way of preserving our history and we need to learn from them.

When I visited Hong Kong and travelled on Landau Island, I saw many nuns such as Sifu with shaved heads living in vegetarian food halls. I can only compare them to my aunts in Liverpool and my great aunt in the West Indies, her hair plaited into a long queue at the back. Somehow, they had worked out their alternative choices and had slipped into the true rhythm of living.

Many of us in the Chinese Lesbian group put distance between ourselves and our families because of how we have chosen to live. As a result we have only ourselves to fall back on; all the more reason for valuing each other and for organising ourselves, particularly in the way we have children and take care of them. Moreover, at least we have the security of knowing that we are not the first, or by any means the last.

After I left my aunts' flat a good many questions buzzed in my head; all of them of direct relevance to us.

Given another time, might they have chosen to be lesbians? Was spinsterhood their choice as lesbianism is ours? How did they feel about not having children?

I had to contain myself until the next visit.

6

# Notes

1.  The Chinese Lesbian group came about after three of us met at a Lesbian Sexuality conference in London in 1983. We called ourselves the Chinese Lesbian group even though there was only three of us – you have to begin somewhere. Having had enough of the white lesbians, it was wonderful to be able to say exactly what you wanted to without having to explain a whole history of colonialism and racism and so on. After about six months we were joined by another two women and the group became a closed one. The sorts of issues we discussed were: our experience of racism in this country, our families, our lesbianism, how we fit into the emerging Black lesbian network. Over the past eighteen months, other women have joined, some have stayed, some have left. We keep in contact, informally with a wider set of women in the UK, New Zealand, San Francisco, and Japan.
    Contact address: Box 47, 190 Upper Street, London N1 1RQ.
2.  For more details see Agnes Smedley, *Portraits of Chinese women in Revolution*, Feminist Press, 1976.
3.  Han Suyin, *My House has Two Doors*, Jonathan Cape Ltd, 1980.
4.  M. Sheridan and Janet Salaff (eds.), *Lives: Chinese Working Women*, Indiana University Press. Sifu's life history is recorded by Andrea Sankar in 'Spinster Sisterhoods'.

# Class/Act: Beginning a Translation from Privilege

Susanna J. Sturgis

> And yes I am completely self-referenced right now because it is the only translation I can trust, and I do believe not until every woman traces her weave back strand by bloody self-referenced strand will we begin to alter the whole pattern.
>
> *Audre Lorde*, The Cancer Journals

I have used the ambiguities of class in the United States to downplay my own birthclass: I sometimes say facetiously that I come from upper-class values, an upper-middle-class life-style, and a middle-class income. As many women have 'passed' – for men, for straight, for white, for middle class, for members of a group less oppressed than their own – so have I. I have obscured some details of my life and emphasized others, to give the impression that I have always been part of the anonymous American white middle class which is supposed to mean nearly everyone but doesn't. No. I was born and brought up an upper-class white Anglo-Saxon Protestant (Episcopalian) New Englander. The history and literature taught in U.S. schools are my class and cultural tradition.

Yet I cannot leave it there: the particulars of a woman's experience are not fully conveyed by the words that describe her class, race, ethnic background, or sexuality. To some, 'upper class' means simply 'rich' – having servants, summering in Europe, living in a house that could pass for a museum. By such a standard, the details of my life are upper middle class: prestigious private girls' school, a degree from an Ivy League university, not having to work for my education, a family summer place on Martha's Vineyard, dancing school, music lessons, and horse shows. But all the separate privileges don't add up to the privilege I know I had.

Being upper class is more than a matter of money, though money counts. One would say that economically my family is downwardly mobile, though my father and his brothers inherited enough money to make a big difference in how they lived: they could live on the interest of their inheritance rather than spend the substance of it. I identify myself as a daughter of the upper class even though I had friends and neighbors whose families were wealthier than mine.

Upper class means a certainty of belonging, an assumption of one's importance in the world. It is said that in the United States there is no aristocracy, but of course there is. Like the European aristocracies, it has fallen on hard times: its sons are working for a living not because meaningful work is a moral imperative but because otherwise they won't eat. Still, they go into the world with the best of tools: degrees from the élite prep schools and universities that their fathers and fathers' fathers attended, degrees that mean not only an education but a network of connections – advanced standing in the highest levels of the 'old boy network.'

It has been centuries since 'aristocratic' was synonymous with 'wealthiest.' Rich merchants married their daughters to men who had more titles and prestige than money; royalty conferred estates and peerages on the wealthy men who bailed them out of debt. Nobility and wealth were separate, though complementary and often overlapping, indications of access to power. The U.S. aristocracy is not identified by titles or land ownership, but is institutionalized. Clues can be found in the 'social registers' of various, mostly northeastern, U.S. cities, or in the rosters of those who have documented their descent from Mayflower passengers or pre-Revolutionary colonials.

Most powerfully, though, the U.S. aristocracy is institutionalized in U.S. history and in the mythology that transcends it. Take away black studies, women's studies, ethnic studies, Jewish studies, labor history, Chicano studies, Native American studies: what is left is what has passed for 'history' with no qualifying adjective, the story of those whose belonging was never disputed. White, heterosexual, affluent, overwhelmingly WASP men. Presidents, congressmen, generals, explorers, intellectuals, diplomats, 'captains of industry.' Men whose decisions affected the lives of thousands of people that they never saw or seriously considered.

8

I come from one 'old Boston family' and am related to most of the others. When I learned in elementary school that some men had wanted George Washington for a king, I already knew enough of my place to think immediately, 'I could have been a princess!' Now I look around at everything that enrages me, at every institution that destroys human beings and ruins the earth, that decides who is expendable and what is worth noticing, and I know from history and the newspapers that it has been created by my male ancestors and cousins and by those who act in their names. There is evil in the soil that nourished me, that gave me my voice. *Whole cultures have been destroyed.* So many people, nations, and countries that once grew according to their own ways have been bent and distorted for the master's pleasure and nourishment.

I suspect that my strong separatist inclinations, and maybe my lesbianism itself, are my way of reconciling these fundamental, and irreconcilable, contradictions. It was not hard to give up the men of my class; by declaring myself independent, unmarryable, lesbian, I took myself out of the upper class. A woman on her own can be working class, middle class, even upper middle class; she can certainly be poor, but very rarely can she continue to be upper class. Upper class implies a degree of money, power, and certainty to which only a few women have access, and then generally only through fathers and husbands.

When I was a college student, existing uneasily between the New Left and the antiwar movement, I knew many men and women from the upper classes who prided themselves on their 'downward mobility,' their lack of possessions, their identification with the oppressed. We joked about the campus radical who drove off to every picket line in the white Mustang that his father had given him. It was the working-class and poor radicals (and, later, feminists) who pointed out that this kind of separation, of denial, was itself a function of class privilege, and – more to the point – a delusion. The most conspicuous of the downwardly mobile, particularly the men, went on to law or medical or graduate school and, presumably the professions. Privilege cannot be disowned.

Audre Lorde is quite right, and on many levels, when she writes that 'the master's tools will never dismantle the master's house.' Neither the master's flunkies, nor the master's theories, nor the master's machines, nor especially the master's sons will ever dismantle the master's house, though they may paint the exterior or landscape the grounds. It is like defusing a bomb, to make with upper-class tools the tools that a lesbian-feminist can use. As an anarchist and a feminist, I know and deeply respect the power of *means*. Yet, uneasily, aware of the paradox, I must assert this: that I grew up in the master's house, that I learned to use many of the master's tools, that with those tools I have made the tools I am using now. *And I have learned to listen to voices I was never meant to hear.*

I am split: how can I be otherwise? I turn Michelle Cliff's title, 'claiming an identity they taught me to despise,' upside down: part of my identity, which I was taught to value, is despicable, and I have learned to despise it; I have learned to dissociate myself from it, but I cannot deny it. To deny this in me or to despise it. For many women, feminism is a movement toward becoming whole; for an upper-class (or white or heterosexual or otherwise privileged) woman, it must be a movement toward coming apart, toward embracing some facets of self while repudiating, leaving behind, or changing others.

My womanhood has been the wedge between myself and my class. When I was growing up, a voracious reader of history and politics, there was very little to suggest that most Americans weren't much like me – and so they were, in the places where their lives touched mine. I saw my family names in the history books, and it never seemed inappropriate to think that my name might someday be there too. My assumptions about the world, fostered by my ethnic and class background, collided with the world's assumptions about my womanself. There is an intuition, an initiating spark, that comes from my womanhood that gives me a chance of hearing the words of women from other white ethnic groups, of women of color and Third World women, of working-class and poor women. It is because I am a woman that I first realized that the whole story was not being told.

It was as a woman that I understood the horrors of the U.S. 'melting pot,' held up to us in school textbooks as both accomplishment and ideal. By force or persuasion, the melting pot was supposed to make everyone over in the middle-to-upper class WASP mold and convince us that we shared one culture, one language, one history. The cost, needless to say, was never mentioned. Names deemed unpronounceable by English-speaking immigration officials were changed at the border. Native peoples were massacred. African peoples were robbed of names, languages, cultures, and often lives. There is a vast difference in degree, but I believe that there is an important connection: I do not know who the lesbians were in my home town, and I do not know the birth names of my great-grandmothers.

It is easy to get sucked into a relentless guilt by what has been, is being, done in one's name. I have been waiting for years for feminists from privileged backgrounds – including myself – to begin speaking about their/our specific experiences. Few of us have spoken. Certainly it isn't that there is a shortage of feminists from the upper-middle and upper classes. It isn't that we are inarticulate, illiterate, or unable to get our work published in the feminist and lesbian-feminist press; our lifelong training in 'standard' English may be, for us as a group, our single most important privilege, the one we can rely on regardless of our income level.

Nevertheless, and ironically, some of the deepest, most powerful insights about privilege have come from women of color and/or working-class women who have discussed the relative privilege of lighter skin color, being able to 'pass'; of being the first in one's family to go to college or to be a writer; of not having to be on welfare. I should not be surprised: was sexism first exposed by men, or homophobia by heterosexuals? Yet I have waited for other women of privilege to explore their own experiences, using these insights and adding their own – I have waited *for other women*. I have waited, who am in the habit of writing. Why?

Because privileged women have already done too much of the talking? Because everyone else has already heard, already knows, enough? Because when you identify yourself with an oppressor class, some people will see nothing else about you? Because while you cannot disguise your white skin or your educated speech, no one knows the extent of your privilege until you claim it? Because exploring the details of your life is self-indulgence, and you were taught to deal in generalities? There are a hundred reasons/excuses, all of which can be at least partially refuted, most of which are at least partially true.

For me, it was finally because I write that I had to write about and discuss my privileged background. As a proficient user of words, a committed radical feminist, and a woman from privilege, I live at the tense intersection of conflicting identities. Facility with the written or spoken language can be a source of great power, and power is something about which the feminist movement has had a sometimes healthy, destructive ambivalence. The writers develop theory – structure the way we see things – in poetry, fiction, and nonfiction; they interpret and communicate the essential and long-hidden knowledge of women. In local communities and in the national and international networks, it is often the writers who are the most widely known. Being known; being heard: these are the native privileges of our community, the roots of a possible feminist élite.

It is our command of English that gives us access to this privilege and power; our command of English is a function of class, culture, education, personal priorities. 'Standard' English is the construct of white, upper-class men; it expresses and shapes their view of the world. Still, I love what I can do with the language I grew up with. I love to read and hear English when it is used well, clearly, playfully, gracefully, eloquently, sensually, grittily, angrily. It is surely the master's most powerful and insidious tool; yet it enables lesbians and other feminists in English-speaking cultures to learn each other's lives. Sometimes I feel like a child with a loaded gun: I have learned to use this language not only to explore and to share, but to silence and conceal. Sometimes it seems to exercise a will of its own.

About half of my writing blocks stem from sheer, unadulterated laziness; the rest are from failures of courage. I am afraid of going too deep. I am afraid of using the master's tool in the master's way. I am afraid of the terrifying personal demands of being a feminist writer; I would like to fall back on my school-taught ability to be glib and/or detached. When I write, I long for the security, the certainty, the self-affirmation, of my class and ethnic traditions. It is then that I am most tempted to reject my lesbian consciousness, to be re-absorbed on any terms into my privileged birthclass, to bolt back over the bridge I cannot burn. Even when I stand my ground, I hear echoes of *noblesse oblige*[1] in my own feminist head: 'Look what I have sacrificed to be here with you; you ought to be *grateful*.'

11

There is shame in the hearing; my commitment to honor demands that I listen. I do not trust privileged white men who are radical or gay because it is too easy for them to pass from outsider to insider at the first sign of trouble. There are women who do not trust me for the same reasons, who would not trust me if they knew where I came from. The more I know of myself, the better I know that their reservations are well-founded and necessary for their own self-protection. To write honestly, I must know myself in all my complexity, my temptation to give up or sell out as well as the depth of my commitment. To deny the pull of my class is self-delusion.

I ask of other privileged women, especially those privileged by color and class, that we begin to explore and to reveal to each other the particulars of our experience; often our most serious handicap is the assumption that other women are just, or almost, like us, or that they would be like us if they could. I ask that we not exaggerate our oppression as women or (if applicable) as lesbians; among women we are *privileged*. I ask that we not overestimate the extent to which we can dissociate ourselves from what the men of our class and culture have done; though we and our foresisters haven't had male power, our attitudes and actions have been extremely oppressive.

For each of us, regardless of our privileges, recognizing and acknowledging the specifics of our lives is a first step toward determining the details of our struggle against complexly intertwined oppressions.

## Notes

1. *Noblesse oblige* is the aristocratic notion, by no means universally shared, that rank imposes obligations. The lord, in other words, is supposed to be civil to his underlings.

   This essay was written in summer 1981 and revised the following winter. Continuing reading, discussion, and reflection have enabled me to challenge some of its insights and to deepen others; particularly important to this process was a CR group on class in which I participated with several other lesbians from privileged backgrounds. Yet 'Class/Act' stands, I think, as what it was meant to be: a 'beginning translation from privilege.' Deep thanks to the past and present members of Hallowmas Women Writers for their support and especially to Toni White, who first suggested that we explore the influence of our class backgrounds on our writing.

# The Shower

Linda Smukler

my voice is thin    I stand in the shower    what's that?    I ask
I am at the level of that    what is it?    a penis    he says    men
have them    I stand there watching it    I don't have one    girls

12

don't have one   he holds it for me   touch it   can I touch it?
long and skin   thick over something hard   thicker than all my
fingers   it moves under them   it's not a part of him   does he
take it off when he puts on his clothes?   we are taking a shower
he is holding it to show me underneath   this is the scrotum   he
says   like two eggs   what's all that raised over them?   touch it
veins he says   hairy   he is very black hairy there   I am pink
it feels like a lie   what does it do?   it's something men do
my face is no taller   I am pink and he is hairy black hair
against the wall are knobs to make the water go hot and cold   my
back is against them   he tells me not to be scared and rubs his
fingers through my hair   curly head   he says   it's just the
difference between boys and girls   he is not a boy   he is my
father   boys are on t.v.   a boy is a friend of Lassie and
rescues things   boys are me   smooth like me   he is still
showing me   the shower walls are there   knobs like a gate I
can't go through   I have to stand in the middle   I have to see
him   the water protects me   falling between us like rain falls
make it hotter   I tell him   scared makes me cold   time to wash
he says   no I say   first I'll wash you then you can wash me   he
says   no   I don't want to wash   I want to sit down in the
water   the hot makes my heart beat too fast   he has the wash
cloth   he is washing me anyway   soaping my back   the thing
hangs down on me as he bends over to scrub   it's sticking up
brushing back and forth along my shoulder   I pull away   I'm
almost done   he says   stand still and let me wash your legs   I
have to pee   his legs are hairy too   I've seen them before
what's wrong?   he tickles me in the ribs with the wash cloth
it is rough and orange   more will come if I pull away   my
serious little girl   what's wrong?   he tickles more   I am
laughing   no   I try to pull away   be careful or you'll slip
he holds me and tickles me all over   I can't get past the water
or the walls   he drops the soap   my feet lift off the ground
he holds me by the shoulder   I laugh and cry   he can't tell if
I am laughing or crying   I am going to pee   he pokes me in the
stomach   he is laughing   that penis   thing   shaking as he
laughs   had enough?   now let me wash you   I can't hold it   I
am peeing   I bend down to get the soap to hide that I am peeing
he doesn't notice   the water runs too hard   I hand him the soap
I am done peeing   he washes up my legs   feet first   up into my
crotch   washing me because I am dirty   washing the pee away
he washes me a long time   moving the washcloth and soap back and
forth   I stand on my own   staring at the dark tiles   at the
water beading and falling by its own weight   far away I hear him
whistling   he echoes in the walls   o.k.   you're done   he says
it's my turn   I tell him to turn the water hotter   I'm getting
cold   it's not cold he says   yes it is   he turns the water

13

hotter to please me   he hands me the wash cloth and points to
his stomach   here first   he says   I wash his stomach   reaching
out and above the thing below   good he says   and pulls me to him
my arms around him   the thing is in my face   my neck   he tells
me to wash his back   he holds me there   I am choking   I can
barely move my arms   you have to wash harder than that to get me
clean   I try to wash harder   his legs are shaking   his knees
around my own   I am choking   I try to say I'm done   he calls
down to me   what?   not letting go   I drop the washcloth and grab
his hips and push away   the thing springs out after me   it's
following me   I turn away and try to open the door handle   I
can't reach it   I look at him   I'm done I say again   you're
done?   but I'm not half as clean as you he says   I have to go
I'm cold   he stares at me and says   I guess your daddy is just
going to have to get clean himself   there's a towel for you
outside on the rack   be careful and don't slip   he opens the
shower door for me and closes it when I'm out   outside I am
surprised the rest of the bathroom is still there   it is white
and steamy   the mirror is covered with fog   I pretend I am
hidden in the steam   I pull the towel to me and hold it to my
belly   it is tired from the pee being forced out of me   I hear
my daddy singing and look through the glass door of the shower to
see his shadow washing himself   he sounds happy   he stops
singing   I can see the pink outline of his hands   not hairy now
washing the thing   penis   he washes and is silent   it must
take a long time to get it clean   then I hear his breath and
suddenly he shouts like he has hurt himself   his breath is fast
like he is getting mad   he will come after me   I made him turn
it up   I throw the towel up over my head and run out of the room
the water got too hot   I made him turn it up

# Reverberations

## Sandra Butler and Barbara Rosenblum

We both thought that our joining would represent 'coming home.' A
place to rest where we didn't have to explain everything, where we
would be understood, where our samenesses would balance (somehow)
our differences. But instead we found that our homes were furnished
differently. I found myself living in overheated and overstuffed rooms
filled with silent others and unfinished dreams. The mirrors that were to
reflect us in each other are cloudy and scratched and we cannot always see
where we are going and remember where we have been.

*I know she will say it's like a mirror, like looking at yourself in a mirror. It is not that way for me. It is more like two diamonds each of which is spinning around. Maybe like a* dreydl *or* dice, *and I don't know which side will be up when it topples over. Sometimes, only sometimes, does my Jewish or lesbian side match her Jewish or lesbian side. More often, it is a mismatch; my lower class facet faces her maternal side or my spare, tight, conceptual academic side faces her dramatic, flamboyant, emotional side. The same rubbing against, the same reaching out and not connecting, the same as in all other relationships. Is it like coming home? Only sometimes.*

*But when it is, it is powerful, rich, sustaining, fulfilling. It is a connection of a sort unlike any other. A* mekhaye! *When other girls were reading* Sweet Sixteen *and anticipating their seventeenth summer, I was reading Mark Twain and Thomas Wolfe. They had imprinted in me the stories of American injustice, the inherent wrongness of slavery and a passionate sense of the possibilities of human freedom. I had learned that being a Jew meant seeing those injustices and doing something about them. My parents first sent me to Hebrew School but I rebelled at once. A year later I was sent to a Jewish cultural school (shule). The teacher was a progressive Jewish man, a survivor, making a living in America by teaching. How I hated it! The room was dark and smelled wet. Not enough electric lighting, one or two bare bulbs on the ceiling. We had to learn Jewish culture and some Yiddish songs. I could not bear the smell. Each day as I passed those I wanted to be my friends in the school playground, the girls laughing together watching the boys play football, I was dressed like a poor immigrant kid in hand-me-downs. We were then still very poor. I wore funny colored leggings and they pointed and laughed at me. That was to shape my sense of myself as an outsider. As marginal. A sense of myself that remains still central.*

It was different in my house. We were scrubbing to erase all traces of the *shtetl*. An elaborate training to be with 'my own kind.' A search that has taken nearly half my lifetime. Admonitions that still ring in my ears hissed nervously for fear/of fear. Don't holler out the window. Don't draw attention to yourself in a public place. Don't talk with your hands. (The irony now is that one daughter is a dancer and talks with her entire body.) But always it was a struggle to keep balance. Being Jewish but not 'too Jewish.' Everyone in my suburb was Jewish, of course. We were to go to school together, to temple together, to marry together. But it was all to be muted. Well-behaved. Not to be like those 'others.' Gangsters, entertainers, *shysters*, communists, troublemakers. Not our sort.

There was always emphasis on good manners and an admonition about passion of all sorts. Intellectual passion was unseemly for a girl since it might frighten off the smart boys. 'It is hard enough to get a boyfriend without being too smart.' Words my mother's mother had told her a generation before. The legacy handed down as truths from mother to daughter and again to daughter. Instead the skills valued were those of 'drawing the other out.' Listening, nodding, smiling, feigning interest in others. Not the impassioned and heated arguments about Poland, Stalin, Israel, the Bolsheviks that she remembers. Never. The rules were lengthy but consistent. Never to interrupt. Never to talk too loudly. Never to be too strident. Never to have a different opinion unless it was couched carefully in a warm smiling voice. Not to be Jewish (in the bad way). I did understand that there was something dangerous about being Jewish, but during the first dozen years of my life, except for muttered conversations abruptly ended when I entered the room about the 'camps,' I didn't know what it was.

*When I read* The Painted Bird, *I was not shocked. I was not even surprised. These horrendous grotesque stories straight out of the ignorance of the Middle Ages were familiar to me. Did I not grow up hearing about the dumb Polish villagers? My mother laughingly told me how she would ridicule their believing in the sanctified birth of Jesus Christ. 'A bastid. They believe in a bastid,' she would laugh. Her own syphillitic brother, in the state of paresis and fully delusional, used to roam the streets of the village, talking to ghosts. The villagers laughed at him, the town fool and idiot; they taunted her: 'There she goes, the sister of the idiot.' When he became unmanageable, my mother remembers, they locked him in the closet where he withered, shriveled and soon died.*

*Is this a story from the 20th century?*

*I remember now another story. When my mother was a girl in her village and someone got sick, you went to a witch, what we would probably call now an herbalist, perhaps a midwife or a barber. They would burn your back with* bankes *(hot cups), collect odd things and make potions. When I was a young girl and got sick, my back was badly burned with* bankes. *These were my growing up stories.*

When I was 13, I had a jukebox in our fully decorated 'gameroom.' I used to listen to the music of Nat 'King' Cole and sway with (my boyfriend) a broom, preparing myself for the popularity and social success I hoped was awaiting me.

*When she was 13 and dancing to popular American music, I was 8 and still listening to the Yiddish radio. But I made it. Upward mobility was my way out. My parents wanted the job security of the civil service for me, a postal clerk I should become. But I went up through the City College system in New York, that free university that permitted thousands of first and second generation Jews to become professionals. I did it too.*

*Often the difference between us is expressed through food. I order fancy wines, exotic cuisines. It is a way of marking how far I have come. We ate poor. Jewish people's poor food: chicken fat stew, beef, lung and heart soup. And pitcha: calf's foot jelly smeared on rye bread with a piece of garlic and* schmalts *was often supper. Beef flanken soup packed with bones. When she is out of town on business, I buy a bag of bones in the supermarket and make soup. I call my mother and tell her I made soup. She seems pleased. I still remember the first time I had steak. I was eleven years old. It was a sign we were beginning to become more American. Beginning to assimilate. Steak.*

We did not eat with our fingers. We did not talk with our mouths full. We did not have 'seconds' until all our 'firsts' were eaten. We ate roast beef, steak, lamb chops and mashed potatoes. Every Sunday we went to the Abner Wheeler House for dinner after my mother finished listening to Milton Cross and the opera. I always ordered roast beef and popovers. My brother had steak and mashed potatoes. My mother had breast of chicken, very well done and with the skin removed please. My father drank and nibbled at whatever was put before him. WASP food. A WASP restaurant. One Sunday my brother loudly told us about the woman at the adjoining table who had a noticeable moustache. Horrified, my mother muttered that now the entire restaurant was staring at us. We were drawing attention to ourselves. Now, thirty years later, I know that we were the only Jews in the restaurant all those Sundays. We sat and were careful not to spill, not to talk too loudly, not to make 'them' stare at us. The outsiders. The unwelcome ones. I still don't know why we always went.

And smells – another admonition of my middle-class Jewish catechism. There was always airwick on the counter, fans spinning, windows open to remove 'smells' of cooking. A house that smells of cooking is a poor house, I was repeatedly told. I remember my grandmother's apartment lobby and hallway being the best smelling place in the world to me. Welcoming, thickly textured smells all mingling: cabbage, beets, potted meat, baking bread. I didn't understand why fresh air was nearly as good. Oilcloth I didn't have to worry about spilling on. No lace cloths, no centerpieces unless you counted the bits and pieces of projects she was always beginning. Snippets of crepe paper, bits of wire, pots of paste all jumbled in a clutter that drew me. I remember once realizing delightedly that she probably never even dusted! And now when I step off the elevator to visit my lover's family who live on the 22nd floor (not in a private home), the smells surround me again. The same smell of my grandmother's lobby. The smell that welcomes. The house full of food and smells and the house that welcomes.

Entering her parents' house I see the walls filled with *shtetl* pictures, memories of the loss of a way of life. A home with history in it. Books about the Holocaust. Stories still to be repeated. To be remembered. For me, the Holocaust was an intellectual and emotional immersion into a period of my history that served as a guide for me in formulating my moral, ethical and political posture in the world. A way to understand what it is, what it means to be a Jew. What the nature of evil is. What the imminent dangers are. What my relationship to the state of Israel, that 'sorry miracle,' has become. It was an immersion that was both connection and warning. Work that led me directly to engage in the political issues of my own decades. School busing. Civil rights. Vietnam. A sense of the urgency of a principled life. It was a period of heightening the sense of myself as 'other.' As outsider. As hated Jew. (Not yet woman.) And understanding that even if the *goyim* saw me as a troublemaker, a Zionist scourge, a dirty, aggressive, shrill kike ... I began to see myself in community with other Jews and a sense of pride emerged. Those of us actively involved in political work during the 60s were the bearers of the torch of freedom and righteousness with other oppressed people. I was an oppressed person. It was a huge leap from the well-behaved, well-modulated young girl. My immersion in the Holocaust was the beginning of my bonding with all Jews.

*I know there are many ways to understand the Holocaust but they all come down to one of two ways: from the outside and from the inside. How come an American Jew like me looks at it (and feels justified to look at it) from the inside? It wasn't until I was in my 30s that I could look at it from the outside, in terms of scholarship, of genocide, or the origins of totalitarianism. Most of my life, I saw it from the inside, from my family, hearing the stories of those who had survived. In the early 50s, my mother spent almost all of her time in the courthouse, signing sworn statements about the character of all her relatives who were coming to America. One by one, I met them. Emaciated bodies, toothless mouths, metal teeth. I met each one as they came through our house. I went to the beach with them and saw their scarred bodies, Hitler's experiments. One uncle had no ribs on one side of his body. It was an experiment so the German doctors could see how someone might live without ribs. Another woman had no insides. They excavated the flesh of my living relatives. They wrote numbers on their arms. I met each one and learned their stories. Who among them did not almost die. And saw their families die?*

*Each morning before leaving for school, I heard the announcements on the Yiddish radio. A man, Moishe Schwartz from the town of Czecknova, has just arrived. Does anyone remember him? Does anyone know someone from his village? Does he have any living relatives? If you know, please call the radio station. Can anyone please locate a* lantsman *for Mr. Schwartz? Tombstones of the living on the airwaves.*

And together we go now to Sh'aar Za'av. A congregation in San Francisco for homosexual Jews. We attend the Rosh Hashonah services eagerly without knowing exactly what to expect. Only knowing that a conservative and traditional temple has no room for us. There is no place for us to pray together, to be in community with Jews together. We go hoping that this place will be another dimension of our coming home. And as we enter the basketball court of a community center where the services are to be held, there is good feeling. We see many we know. Separately and as a couple. We are greeted, hugged, we smile, nod, acknowledge, squeeze hands and lower ourselves into the folding chairs with a sense of possibility. Perhaps a resting place.

*After my grandmother died, I went to services every year but felt so alien in those elegant surroundings, velour seats, well-dressed congregations. I go now with eagerness. A place. The pulse of excitement animates the spare room. 'How nice to see you here.' 'Take my new phone number.' 'Call me soon, so we can catch up.' Shhh. Sha shtil. The service begins. I look around feeling something is wrong. This group is too young. Where are the old ones? The bobes and the zeydes, the tantes and uncles, the cousins? Where are the children shifting around impatiently? This is no shul. The illusion cannot be sustained. There are too many blondes. Too many goyim. Some even sit and watch as we rise for responsive reading. 'Get out you goyim,' I hiss to myself. 'Get out. You don't belong here. I don't want you here.' I ache with disappointment. Where do I go to say the prayer for my grandmother?*

I sit alongside her and hear the voice of my grandmother. 'Give a little. Take a little. Before you know it, it all evens out.' It is just what I need to do to find a place here. Our grandmothers are both so present. Not dear and departed, but alongside us in our lives. But my temple had an organ, a choir, maroon upholstered seats, donated prayer books with inscriptions 'in the memory of' carefully typed inside. Not the poorly xeroxed sheets I hold in my hand. But was the congregation of Temple Ohabei Shalom 'my own kind'? Are they in this room now? Why does it still all feel so alien? There are moments when I feel full of the possibility of this new

18

experiment. But then the sense of marginality intrudes. A room full of 30ish queers and many with their gentile lovers. Do these people carry the ghosts of the murdered dead with the same urgency? I know that just beyond this small room is a world that hates us. Hates me. As a Jew. As a woman. As a queer. And I know that finally there is no safety except that which we provide for ourselves and each other. And the fragility of it overwhelms me in this moment.

*For me, I suppose, there has always been the loss. My mother thinks she is lucky because she lives in an apartment with indoor hot and cold running water. She never feels safe and has a recurring dream that she will have no place to sleep at night and awakens with the same terrified feeling she had as a girl. So there is nothing more to lose. Just to continue to regain. Recapture. Build. And always understand we live on the margin. Always.*

*And as we walk the streets of San Francisco together we see many of the same things. While we each come to this moment with so many differences, we see so much of the same thing. Hardships etched into a face. A child looking frightened. A mother trembling with frustration. A window advertising Irish sweaters decorated with sacks of rotten potatoes. Bag ladies. Those who are alone. Marginal, lost, anxious, angry. We turn to each other and silently acknowledge that 'Yes, I see. Yes. We are them too. Yes.' It is a very big consolation in a very disorderly world.*

We have become mother, lover, friend, confidante, partner, playmate, it is too much. And yet, beyond each other is the danger. We use each other to represent our 'own kind.' There is always the sense of thin ice upon which we walk as confidently as we can, holding tightly to each other's hand.

We ease the passage for each other now. I steer her through the labyrinth of social rules I have memorized since girlhood. She is patient with me in my intellectual hungers. We open doors for each other and allow our arms to circle the other's waist. Just for a moment. I am here with you. Don't worry. I'm on your side. It isn't finally coming home but making the home we always hungered for.

# PART TWO
## Inside the Body

---

## Traveling Fat

Elana Dykewomon

*Some notes from 1982 on fat and: public spaces, community, friendship, politics, class, sex, and ethnic identity.*

I was hanging out in america and there are lots of ways to do it.
I was a fat womon traveling around alone with a dog.
I was a lesbian who had made her contacts ahead and the homes
spread out in welcome like a net.
I was a Jew who hungered for other Jews in the wide spaces
of the midwest.
I was a poet who put on a shiny tie & a silk vest twenty times.
The vest was made special, by a friend, to fit.
And I said what I thought was good to be said, and mostly
it was good, but sometimes I was wrong.
I was strong and tough enough and charming.

How else is a fat Jew lesbian poet gonna get by?
Listening to the radio, staying home, staying alone, like
they mean us to.

Who means you to be left out?
Who don't?

Who doesn't mean for fat womyn to be left out? Don't answer too quick
now. A womon gathers a lot of scenes as she goes. Here she records a bunch
of them, to show something about what it means, fat womyn trying to be
a part of community, fat travels in the country.
    For the sake of definition, we'll say here that a fat womon is a womon
who weights over 200 pounds at an 'average' height, or is a womon who
endures one or more of these things: access problems in public places,
job discrimination, random and frequent attempts at humiliation from

strangers (or family & friends), having to go to special stores or catalogs to find clothes that might fit. Who endures these things in the present. You might not expect that there would be womyn who aren't fat womyn, really fat womyn, who would want to join this group; who would, themselves, feel left out if asked to leave, but there are. That's what I mean about not answering too quick. It's a complex group of scenes.

Scene: The first Fat Womyn Only performance anyone remembers. Fat Lip, May 1982, in Berkeley. Let's say there are at least 20,000 fat womyn in the S.F. Bay area. Thirty or forty come, some from out of state. A thin womon gets turned away, much to her surprise. Some not very big womyn get in, making it a little uncomfortable for some of the others. It's a good night. This is not to reproduce their script, which covers too much of the body and spirit to paraphrase. But to let you know it happened. Afterwards womyn talk, coming from many different feelings about their bodies and the bodies of other fat womyn. There are a lot of challenges and different, important, recognitions. It was not a safe place for every fat womon there, but it was an important place.

The next night, Fat Lip gave a performance in S.F. open to all womyn. There was a big difference in the 'feel' of it. There were fewer fat womyn among the 150 who were there. The laughter of thin womyn was suspect, but not questioned. Sitting among thin womyn, you could feel them go blank when a huge womon shook her booty in their faces. You could feel them thinking they understood, now, what it's about, the lifetime humiliation, the daily figuring it out, how to fit, how not to be left out without being noticed, how to live. You could hear some of the thin womyn thinking they had done their political duty, and they were glad it was going to be over soon. And you could hear decades of silences breaking in the faces of fat womyn, you could hear that too. These are first times. If they didn't give every fat womon all she needed, or gave thin womyn too much, they were still wonderful, rare gifts.

Scene: The Jewish Feminist Conference, S.F., late May 1982. Some of the Fat Lip womyn were advisors to the coordinators. The coordinators provided for fat womyn in ways that I never experienced at a conference. At the beginning, statements were read on behalf of womyn whose needs and presences are most often ignored – older womyn, mothers, working class womyn, Sephardic Jews, disabled womyn, lesbians, fat womyn. Of course some statements were carried out better than others. But even the statements made a tremendous difference. There were no diet drinks or foods, there was accessible seating provided for fat and disabled womyn and their friends. There was a fat affinity group, fat workshops, and theatre by the Jewish womyn in Fat Lip. There was, among others, a printed statement on Fat Liberation, written by Judith Stein. So thin womyn attending the conference got told. We didn't have to tell them, or to figure they didn't know.

It's hard to convey exactly what this meant. Meant to me. And of course part of it was being among so many Jews, so many Jewish Lesbians. But at the dance Saturday night, I danced with a fat womon whom I love, and I felt safer, prouder of my body, than I have any other time in any other public place, certainly in any other group of mixed thin and fat womyn. I felt like it had been said, 'if you out there who normally own the dance floor are having a problem, tough shit.' I felt that the thin womyn there had heard it, and although their hearing it didn't necessarily change how they felt, they were keeping their vibes to themselves. That joy, that ability to move, to finally move, that moment of feeling like we, together, were a proof, proof positive of everything that had been said and done, that was a gift.

But you never really know the value of a gift until you come to expect it as part of life, as part of the awareness of the womyn's community, and it isn't.

The scenes changed. I've been living in the americas for over thirty years, I shouldn't have been surprised, but I was. The surprises taught me.

Scene: The National Women's Studies Conference, in Arcata, California, June 1982. The organizers of this conference had not seen fit to waive the registration fee for two womyn who were coming only to lead a fat liberation workshop – so they couldn't come. The organizers did, however, leave the workshop on the schedule. That was more like the conferences I remembered. The group of womyn who met to discuss fat liberation without facilitators spent an hour or so struggling with the old myths about fat womyn, especially that fat womyn aren't healthy, and couldn't expect to have enjoyable sexual relationships with anyone. I mean, that's what the fat womyn said. The fat womyn who said different (me and one other) were the clear minority. The thin womyn were either insulting or quiet. I wasn't ready, then, to do what had been done for me. Expecting someone else there to articulate what I believe, I suddenly found that I had to speak about it for myself. Which made me pissed and scared. For the first time in years, in a room full of womyn, I said something about my lovers, and heard – you know how you can hear, sometimes, exactly what's going through women's minds, even if they don't say it? – heard half the womyn in the room, fat and thin, think: who does she think she's kidding? She doesn't have lovers, probably doesn't have even one. She's just trying to make up for being fat, poor thing. Boasting to feel better. Hmph.

Well, hmph. Later at this same conference, a womon, Max Dashu, was giving a slide presentation about the suppressed womyn's histories in the Sahara and Sudan, and China. She was talking about foot-binding – now this may seem out of place here, but it got to me, it seemed like the link and the key. She was talking about the transition times, when men were taking power from womyn, and how one of the things they did in taking over was to invent class, subject and divide women along class lines. And one of the ways they helped class work was to impose the most hideous restrictions on the bodies of upper-class women. So that if women wanted class mobility, which meant some access to power, or sometimes simple survival (if not for themselves, for their children), they could prove themselves desirable only by being successful at self-mutilation. They had to reach for the very things

23

that crippled them, in order to maintain or better their class positions, and pass that crippling on to their daughters.

Hmm, I thought, that's just like dieting.

There in that classroom I got a flash of how it's all set up – set up one generation after another – what it means, now, 'you can't be too rich or too thin.' How well it works, will keep on working, because the vast majority of women will never be thin. Thin enough. How well the hope of class mobility keeps every mother dieting, and handing the diets down to her daughter, hoping the daughter may do even better. When you combine this with the fact that many non-white peoples tend to be heavier than white folks, dieting becomes a tool not only in enforcing class but in encouraging assimilation. The more you are successful in looking like the ruling class, the more your mother thinks you may succeed, even if you have to leave your mother behind to do it. This has been working well a long time.

Later, in the discussion, some white woman was trying to bring up clitorectomies, in a patronizing, 'isn't it horrible what they do' way. Max pointed out that it's easy for us in this culture to focus on a custom in another, thinking it's so grim – and that that's one of the ways racism works, thinking that a particular practice is the province of a 'lesser' people, never your own. The same womon would never have brought up stomach-stapling. Or even thought of it in the same way.

I was talking about this, months later, with Judy Freespirit, and about the flash I had had about dieting having the same class function as foot-binding. She asked if that had been said in the discussion. No, I said. I didn't think so, she said.

All of that at a conference I just went to to sell books.

So I should have known a little better about what it was going to be like, when I was on the road, a fat womon traveling alone. But I didn't get it.

Until: I went out to dinner in Eugene with my lover Dolphin, who's small, and two friends. Real good friends, long-time friends. One of them is skinny, and one a little *zaftig*, but a very medium size. The friend who's *zaftig* was talking about going to see her family. We were eating Greek food outside, under the trees. She was talking about how she and her sisters had been comparing themselves in the mirror recently, how they had done that as kids, as teenagers, competing in that danger-ous country, mirror-land. But this time, she said, she looked at them, now they were straight and married, they didn't look so happy, so gorgeous. She found herself surprised to like how she looked. My friend said she thought she looked good, looked better than any of them, even if she was fat.

Even if. I lay down my fork and stared at the cold fish. Right there it broke, I felt wrong to be eating in front of these thin womyn, ashamed and angry. Dolphin kept trying to get my eye. When she finally did, I shook my head – No, I was trying to say to her, don't say anything.

I feel bad enough, this is humiliating, and so far only I know how it is that I'm humiliated, even if you can see it; even if you can see it, even if you can understand it, you don't know how it feels, keep your mouth shut. – But she didn't.

My *zaftig* friend saw something going on, but she didn't see my face, because she was sitting next to me, only Dolphin's. Dolphin said something like: 'If you sit here and say you thought you looked good "even if" you were fat, imagine how Elana must feel. Not even in the discussion. A creature from another planet.' Words to that effect.

It was how I felt then. Transformed from one of the gang into a creature from outer space whose body is beyond all normal sense of proportion so simply isn't included in the spectrum of relationships. It was different from something I could be either angry about or repress, the way I had felt at that Women's Studies Conference. I was ashamed, and isolated, among womyn I love, and it was a shock. A Big Deal. My friend, she got it quick, said, 'O shit, it's like when someone said I'm pretty even though I'm Jewish.' 'Yes, something like that,' I said. She apologized and was sincerely sorry. And that's life. I mean, we all walk around not looking at what's in front of us, since we don't have any way to recognize it, even when we've been told we should be able to. We learn stuff from each other's pain at our mistakes. Later, in another city, she 'made it up to me,' and that's more than most of us get, even from our intimates, let alone our friends.

But that's when I figured it out. Traveling around the country as a fat woman was not going to be a bed of roses. Being in other womyn's houses. I had thought I had prepared myself for being sociable, for being likable enough to get through the rough spots, to meet the womyn who thought what I was about was neat as well as those who thought I was full of shit. But I had forgotten to prepare myself for what they were gonna think when they looked at me.

That night after dinner, we went to a lesbian video show. For the first hour, all I could think about was how I was the fattest woman in the room, something that I couldn't remember worrying about in the last two years, having been in rooms where size had changed, where the proportions of womyn had begun to feel different. And besides, having a 'rep' clears space ahead of you, it tends to give a legitimacy – or notoriety – before you speak, so you don't have to worry that no one's paying attention to the fat girl.

But there I was, a 'fat girl' again – the one nobody knows, the one whose clothes don't fit right, who keeps tugging at herself hoping that this or that roll of fat will be less noticeable, maybe she won't be noticed at all, maybe no one will know she was even there (but why does she keep overhearing conversations about dieting during intermission?), she just wants to see the picture show like the rest of the girls, maybe if she tries hard, no one will mind her being there, or worse, make fun of her for being there, when obviously fat girls don't go to those things, don't go to anything, they don't belong, they don't even fit in the seats, they're wrong to try.

I had this figured out before. But each time you get it, it stuns you more. At each level, it's hard to separate the reasons for the way you've learned to present yourself in the world. You try to follow yourself in the best of conscience, not because you're trying to prove stuff to your mother or somebody, not because you're trying to get even, not because you're trying to make up for what other people might find wrong about you, but because you're trying, simply, to be honest. But there are moments when you're bound to have very extreme doubts about your own motives, and quite some suffering and rage. Even simple confusion, doubting what you know you know.

Out there on the road, womyn were not going to necessarily be my allies. They wouldn't have seen Fat Lip or been to the Jewish Feminist Conference, they could pass over the articles about fat liberation in the feminist and lesbian papers – or not believe them. They could think stomach-stapling, like psychosurgery, doesn't happen anymore. Certainly not to lesbians, not their friends, or peers. Womyn who might say in a discussion of dieting: Is this the new thing we have to be p.c. (politically correct) about? What has dieting got to do with anything? –

What does it.


But even then, I held onto this fantasy. I thought that out there in america there were groups of fat dykes everywhere who, if not always together, were at least giving each other support, encouragement to love their own and each other's bodies, who were doing the work they could in the womyn's communities, and who were being met by an at least accepting, if not always responsive, community. I'd heard about a couple of fat womyn's conferences (was it only two in five years, and I just thought there were more?), seen a centerfold of fat dyke photos in the *Inciter* and had been spoiled by the handful of fat womyn doing this work in the Bay Area and Seattle. It was just a fantasy.

In some of the cities I went to I did meet fat dykes. One or two. Who felt isolated, and in pain. Who felt that no one took them seriously when they talked about fat politics, that it still doesn't qualify as real political thought, it's viewed as a leisure pursuit of the bourgeoise who want to be left alone to be self-indulgent in peace; or that it's 'cashing in' on the political groundwork done by other groups (even if fat womyn are members of the 'other groups'). Mostly it's just too hard. To be one womon, going against the grain.

I was in a lot of thin womyn's houses. I can't begin to tell you how many refrigerators were full of diet soda, light beer, lo-cal salad dressing. Among womyn who were quick to eat brownies, or go out for pizza. Among womyn who otherwise ate 'health food' and womyn who ate 'junk food,' vegetarians and omnivores. (The need of diabetic womyn to have access to sweet-tasting things without using sugar is not in question here – I'm talking about the ways womyn buy into the institution of dieting, not the

26

need some womyn have to keep careful watch over their blood sugar levels in order to stay alive.)

When I left Oregon alone, the first city I went to was Minneapolis. I expected Minneapolis to be a place with a high consciousness about fat politics. I was there for a week before I met another fat woman, who had come to the coffeehouse on Friday night on the rumor that she might meet another fat dyke and separatist there, who was me.

The Minneapolis coffeehouse is well known for being a good, chemically free alternative to the bar scene. I had old friends who thought it was a wonderful place. When I went there, I was still in the middle of my fantasy. I walked out of my fantasy, down unramped steps, through a corridor of posters offering this or that therapy, into a room of young, thin, predominantly able-bodied, white and light-skinned womyn drinking a lot of diet soda, with a big display of T-shirts that only went up to x-large. I hadn't been in a mostly lesbian-run space that didn't have T-shirts going up to 4x for some time. I felt like somebody had dumped a glass of water on my head. OK, kid, you're back in the world again.

The woman who had been waiting for me introduced herself – she and a friend of hers were the only other fat womyn in a large crowd, and her friend was the only fat woman dancing. It's another story, the things we said, or how the three of us ended up dancing together, what that meant to us, how long it took. I'm just describing a scene, where fat womyn recognize each other with a raw and pulsing nerve exposed, and no one around them notices.

Later, I had to tell my friends, the womyn I was with, what I felt, why I was so upset. I also had to read in the coffeehouse in two days. It was hard telling my friends. Asking them what message they thought a thin woman gives, going around with a diet soda in her hand. What a fat woman swallows, drinking it too. They got the point, though. They did good, and that was its own kind of gift. They negotiated with the coffeehouse womyn, who were responsive and said they would not sell diet drinks at the reading, provided I made a statement about it.

So there I was, I had to do what had been done for me. This was the statement I came up with:

'The coffeehouse has agreed not to sell diet drinks at this performance, at the request of myself and other concerned lesbians. Usually I just start reading, but they asked me to make a statement about that request. There's lots of good written material about Fat Oppression, and I encourage you all to read, or reread, what's been published, so I'm not going over that ground now.

'I assume that this community intends for its spaces to be safe and accessible for all the lesbians in them. When you sell or buy diet drinks, you make it unsafe for fat womyn to be with you. When you sell T-shirts that only go up to x-large, you are defining that as the size limit for womyn who come here. Dieting, not unlike foot-binding, is a male-created institution which obsesses, weakens, sickens and kills womyn; enforces class oppression and the assimilation of ethnic peoples. It's easy for us in this

27

country to condemn cultures which practice clitorectomies – and not so easy for us to look at how we participate with our "own" patriarchy in defining a natural condition among womyn as a disgusting sickness. I hope next time I read in Minneapolis there'll be no need to make this statement. All our bodies should be all our joy.'

It seemed like at least some of the womyn that night appreciated the statement – I never really got feedback about it stirring anything up. Like I did when I made a similar statement in the Chicago coffeehouse – there, having no close friends in the city and arriving only a couple hours before I was supposed to work, the coffeehouse womyn did not agree to stop selling diet drinks for the duration of the reading. That's where the complaint 'is this the new thing we're going to have to be p.c. about?' came back to me.

This isn't to trash the coffeehouses in those cities – a lot of work is being done by a lot of womyn trying to make space for womyn as best as they can figure out, starting from their first identifiable needs. And as usual, the womyn who do the most get criticized the most. But the almost universal physical inaccessibility of most womyn's spaces, for instance, came as a tremendous shock to me, traveling. I may not be able to tolerate the arguments about dieting, but I know where they come from, how pervasively they're 'socially sanctioned.' I can't imagine a case for inaccessibility, although I've heard lots of excuses. Which is to say, we have done a very little bit, we need to do a lot more, there's work we need to get down to.

But I felt like I couldn't just write down the statement that I read in the coffeehouse, because it's incomplete without the contexts from which it comes. Without your knowing how I stayed up all night that first Friday in Minneapolis, writing in my journal, calling back to Oakland to talk with an intimate, how hurt I felt, and how unexpected that hurt was.

Later I was used to it. I wasn't surprised anymore when I found the diet shit in womyn's houses, and I had the ability then to choose what, and when, to say about that. The second half of the trip I ended up staying in fat womyn's houses, or the houses of friends, more often than not, and that helped. Because for the first three weeks I found I could barely eat in front of anyone, which is an old problem, something I had forgotten, a self-consciousness and discomfort, a sense that other womyn are watching. I waited it out; it wasn't, you know, a terrible hardship. I just remembered who wasn't there, saw who didn't come to the readings, who did not feel safe to leave their homes, who would not assume that I would try to make the spaces safe for them, who couldn't believe that the womyn in their communities would make the spaces safe for them.

A womon in one city where I read wrote to another, in a city in which I was going to read, that I didn't look like what she had expected. I didn't look like a star. Susanjill said, 'She meant you were fat.' I said, 'I'm glad you said that, that's what I thought too.' But it was a correspondence between thin womyn, I was in a thin womon's house, I wasn't about to risk telling her that that's what I thought her friend meant.

There were a lot of other scenes. In Lincoln, there was a brunch of fat lesbians, five of us, we talked, but we never talked about being fat. We acknowledged that. It was good to be together though.

Not quite as good as it was the last reading I did, in San Francisco, for the last 'Fat Friday' event at the Women's Building. Zoe Mosko had put up an exhibit of photographs of fat lesbians, for the month of October. I was on the road, nervous in midwest cities, while the first three 'Fat Fridays' went on – Fridays where fat womyn shared their arts in the photo gallery, surrounded by pictures of fat lesbians, with full houses of all-sized womyn. I got reports on how great the events were, Fat Lip doing theatre, Judy Freespirit showing a videotape, 'Freespirit in the Flesh,' Ruth Jovel, Ronda Slater, Sylvia Kohan doing a night of theatre, comedy, and music.

For my turn, I had intended to read a story I had written, 'Speaking of Fat Out Loud At Last,' among other things. But I had never read the story out loud. In Denver, on my way west, I spent a day preparing for Fat Friday. As I started to reread the story (for the first time in six months), I realized I was terrified. There, toward the end of the journey, with the diet vibes of the womyn's community deep in me. I couldn't believe how many times I had written the word 'fat' in eight pages, I couldn't picture standing in front of a group of lesbians anywhere and saying 'fat' that many times.

I called up Susanjill in Oakland, I said, 'I can't do this.' She said, 'I've been trying to tell you that for months. You hadn't reread the story when you told me you were going to perform it, had you?' 'No,' I said, 'and I don't think I can do this.' 'But you're going to, aren't you?' 'Yes,' I said.

And I did.

I did something else, too. I told about a dream I'd had, the night before that first reading in Minneapolis. I dreamt that I got up in the womyn's coffeehouse and said: I've put away the reading I was going to do. Instead, I'm going to spend the next two hours telling you in graphic detail every food I ever used while making love, how I used it, where it was put, how it tasted on her, how it felt on me, how we ate in bed . . . In Minneapolis I had seen it as a kind of revenge, making an audience of mostly thin womyn squirm in their seats.

But on Fat Friday, in a room of eighty lesbians, half of whom were fat, I wished that I had it to tell.

But that's another story, isn't it?

After all, this was just to record the basic statement and its contexts, to try to talk about an understanding of how the fear of fat works. It works because it's being manipulated in us to enforce class divisions, racisms, womyn-hatred. And we give it the room to work because it's so close to us, it's our own bodies, that we don't see it as coming from outside ourselves, we don't name it for the weapon it is.

And it works because so many of us are so often afraid of how we might please each other, of how beautiful the body is, in every moment of her size and age.

# A Cruel Trick: Menopause/Aging

Berta Freistadt and Marg Yeo

*Berta Freistadt and Marg Yeo have been friends for ten years, and have accumulated sixty-five years of bleeding between them. They are both approaching the menopause with anticipation and relief. After a decade of gossiping, when asked to do an article on this subject, they felt a conversation might be more up their street. They set out with five questions for each other, and a tape recorder, and this is the (slightly edited) result.*

BF: I wanted to talk first of all about the actual bleeding process. I wore tampons for years and years and years, and then when the tampon scare happened, about three or four years ago, I stopped wearing them, and I started wearing towels again. I was absolutely amazed, the first time I used the towel, and then took it away from my body and there was the blood, I remembered being fifteen! I've always been very lucky. My periods have always been trouble-free, and I've felt a sort of superiority, (over men), about bleeding, that it makes me a bit different, special, that it means I'm a real woman, and I know that when I stop bleeding I shall be really sorry about that. I know it seems crazy, and women will laugh when I say I actually like bleeding. So my question to you is, will you miss bleeding? Not the pain and the inconvenience, but the blood itself, which makes us women and not men or children.

MY: My experience has been completely different. My periods were always very painful and irregular. They've only been regular for about the last four years, and that's been on a twenty-one day cycle.

BF: Oh god.

MY: Yes, exactly. They've also been incredibly heavy, so it's not so clear for me. I think in some ways I will miss it, because of some of the feelings I attach to it, which I think are similar to yours. It is symbolic of being a woman, but in lots of ways I'll be just delighted to see the end of it.

BF: But I feel that while we're bleeding, it means that we're still young women. What do you say to that? I mean, when you stop bleeding, it appears that you're going into old age.

MY: That's one of the things that makes it more complicated. I'm really aware of a whole set of conflicting feelings that I've got about

30

age. I'm very glad to be the age that I am. I wouldn't want to be my younger self again at all! No way! But there's so much about aging that *is* frightening. It makes you start to think about pensions, and the old dykes' home.

BF: What about the symbolic side of having periods?

MY: To me, that's connected with youth again, the fertile symbolism.

BF: I don't see it as that so much. At least, I don't think I do.

MY: It's hard to be sure.

BF: It is hard to be sure, but I've never wanted children and I've never really been into that fertile, mother-earth thing. I suppose for me it's a badge of adulthood.

MY: I don't know that I've seen it quite like that, because I actually feel that menopause is the real badge of adulthood. I feel like I'm being admitted to a closed society, since I've been menopausal. The second that I've mentioned being menopausal, a lot of the older women that I know, who've never ever mentioned one single word about menopause until now, though some of them are very good friends, have opened the doors and let me in. I've been gifted with a whole wealth of information and experience that just wasn't available to me before, which is one of the things that makes me feel very positive about it, even though it's complicated.

The first thing that I wanted to ask you was about what seems to be the two sides of menopause, the physical and the emotional. While they're obviously connected in some ways, their appearance isn't necessarily connected. What I wanted to know was how long it took you to identify those two sides as menopausal, because it took me a long time, and what was your first reaction to recognising that.

BF: Well, I think this is the most difficult of your questions for me, because I still don't know, really, whether I am menopausal. My periods are still regular; they've just gone into another phase. I've had three phases of different bleeding patterns in my life, and I've just in the last two years gone into what seem to be the final ones. Certainly, within the last two years, I've been aware of having periods of very serious depression, but when I look back over my life, I've always had those periods of depression. I can certainly remember when I was about twenty-five, I was literally banging my head on the wall in despair. So it's not a sudden thing for me. Although this doesn't quite answer your question, I suppose what I'm doing here, claiming space among the menopausal women, is that I know it's going to happen and I want to be ready for it.

MY: One of the things that my reading around the subject and my talking to other women about menopause has led me to suspect is that a lot of women find it a difficult thing to claim without the evidence of having stopped bleeding. I haven't either, and I've been depressed at other points in my life too, but I've felt about the kind of depressions that

31

I've had recently that they were different, that always before during depressions I could eventually find my way through to a cause, a real concrete, physical, wide awake alive cause. It might not be simple, like a single person or one event, but there would be something recognisable. In the depressions that I've had in the last year, that wasn't true. Whatever causes there were around were insufficient to have produced the depth of depression and anxiety that I was feeling, which was really enormous. And at the same time I was having a set of physical symptoms, like incredibly sore breasts for a long time before each period, all of which are associated with menopause, and I went through fears like thinking I had breast cancer or that I was a lunatic. That was coupled with the fact that it was very hard to find anybody who would talk to me about it. My lover at the time, who was a lot younger than I was, just didn't want to know anything about any of it at all. It was awfully scary, and when I actually sat down and read the Rosetta Reitz book,[1] as I turned each page I said 'Ah!' in recognition. What was exciting, for me personally, was that recognising that I was menopausal was an enormous relief, because I finally had an explanation for a whole lot of physical and emotional things, the sore breasts and the causeless depressions, that had just seemed over the edge. I knew I didn't have breast cancer, however painful my breasts were, and the depressions faded to the normal level of ups and downs that I expect to experience. All of that has settled down now, partly because I've tried to alter my diet to include foods that are high in Vitamin B, but also because I feel a lot calmer about it. So however mixed my feelings are about aging and menopause, I still feel relief. I don't mind, as long as I know what the reason for it is. It's the not knowing that's terrifying.

One of the things that really shocked me about being menopausal and wanting to explore what that meant for me, was how many of my friends just didn't want to know. I found it really upsetting, and what I want to know next is whether that happened to you.

BF: I presume you're talking about your younger friends.

MY: No. I mean friends who are close to my age.

BF: Well, most of my close friends are younger than I am, and I don't know whether it's a sense of self-preservation that I've automatically assumed, but I haven't actually talked a lot to most of my close friends about it. I might have made some sort of remark, like 'Oh god, I feel menopausal today,' but I'm afraid I do assume that lack of interest, or that fear, that you're talking about, and I have, automatically, sought out people like yourself, and other friends who maybe I'm not so close to but who I know are my age and who I know have gone through it, are going through it. I want to turn your question on its head, actually. Rather than take risks with close friends of mine, I can think of one in particular who I know would make a joke of it, I've almost approached people who I'm not very close to and have, with those people, found an instant rapport. There's a woman who's

32

about five years older than me, who's always made it very clear that she's menopausal, and I have no close dealings with her at all. Yet the moment that I said just half a syllable of the word, she said, 'Oh, borrow this book,' and it was the Rosetta Reitz book. I kept it for months before she asked for it back. In a way, it's a question of this secret society that you're talking about again. It's as though women who are coming into the menopause are so grateful for each other's sufferings that it tends to lighten your own a little, that other women are going through the same.

I've read the Rosetta Reitz book. I can't remember what my reactions were. I certainly, this last month, have had a very sore left breast and had thought of breast cancer. I don't know whether I'm resisting the thought of the menopause. Maybe I am.

MY: I don't think it would be surprising for anyone to resist it. We're all different, so we're bound to have a whole range of different feelings around it, but that resistance must be very common, because of all the symbolism around aging, like that common notion that we lose our sexuality with the arrival of menopause.

BF: Yes, you don't like to think that you're not prepared to face the truth.

MY: But what I don't understand is how *any* woman is prepared to face the truth, because nobody talks to you about it till you've already gone through it! I mean, I knew less than nothing about the menopause until I started reading about it. One friend of mine had a horrific menopause, ten or fifteen years ago, and that scared me witless, but it didn't do a lot to increase my practical knowledge. I think it's ridiculous. At least, when we start bleeding, most of us know about it, and are prepared for it in some sense.

BF: But menopause is different.

MY: Yeah, this time you're on your own. Nobody wants to talk about it because nobody wants to admit to it, or something like that.

BF: How old are you, Marg?

MY: Forty. I'm comparatively young to be menopausal. And I'm really angry that nobody's talked to me about it! I'm furious!

BF: My next question for you is, that since youth is so painful and periods are so inconvenient, why do we regret the relief of maturity and the cessation of bleeding?

MY: It must be partly social conditioning. We're led to believe that being young has it all, and it's not true! I wouldn't go back to being twenty-one for anything in the world. I was a total mess then. I'm not saying I'm perfect now, but at least I've got my shit a little bit together.

BF: At least you know you're not perfect. Do you think this has always been the case, or do you think maybe it's just in the last couple of decades, because when I was a little girl, to be a teenager in Britain was nothing, and to be a woman of thirty was what everybody aimed at. While I was young, while I was still thirteen and fourteen, all that started to change and the American teenage idea happened, and I wonder if it's always been the same . . .

33

MY: But it's never been a woman of fifty that everybody wanted to be, or has it? Thirty, from my point of view, is comparatively young.

BF: Also, thirty's a nice age.

MY: Um. I still wouldn't want to be thirty again, either.

BF: No . . .

MY: That was wistful! Go on, you wouldn't, would you?

BF: Well, only if . . . God, this is dreadful, isn't it? It sounds really old. Only if we could be thirty, knowing what we know now. It's so corny.

MY: But there's no chance for that, it just doesn't work like that.

BF: When you're mature, presumably forty upwards, you do know so much more about yourself and about how to behave in the world and how to deal with what the world expects of you. Life is so much easier than when you're say, twenty-three. I know that today's young women of twenty-three, at least some of the ones that I know, seem to be so mature and know it all, but they can't, you can't know in twenty-three years what you know in forty-three. There is so much more to learn. It seems like an evil trick, that your twenties are spent thinking you know everything, and yet somehow dying little deaths every day, because it's so dreadful, and yet when you reach the age of forty-five, the world around you begins to despise you merely, presumably, because of how you look. That just seems such a cruel joke.

MY: Do you think that you're editing yourself, for example with younger women? Do you think that might be at least partly a product of that mistaken idea that people have about menopause, about a woman's sexuality, that you cease to be sexual when you stop bleeding?

BF: No. I see those two things as really separate, sexualness and the menopause. Being sexual or not being sexual has relatively little to do with the menopause, for me. For example, there are women who I feel constantly oppressed by, in terms of sexuality, who are always burgeoning with lust and desire, and some of them are menopausal women. Whereas, if I'm not in a sexual relationship, I can quite easily become disinterested in sexual matters. My hesitation here is not to do with being an old maid . . .

MY: Or with being seen as being . . . ?

BF: I don't see that there's anything wrong in being seen as, in being, an old maid. Women would be quite happy to be old maids, as long as other people let them get on and be that, without trying to put them down for it.

MY: It also worries me that there's so much mythology attached to ceasing to be able to bear children.

BF: But since some of us have never been in that league, as it were, then there must be a separation between what we are, what we have chosen to be, and what the world expects of us and therefore sees us to be. There must be even less sympathy for lesbians than for heterosexual women around the time of the menopause, since as far

34

as the world is concerned as soon as we become lesbian we might as well all have hysterectomies. In the heterosexual world, the greatest pervert must be a lesbian with a womb, or a lesbian with children. So when it comes to the menopause, because many of us are seen to have no use for our wombs, to grieve the loss of bleeding is seen as making a fuss about nothing.

MY: I made a clear decision, quite a long time ago, not to have children, but I found that, with menopause, came an odd kind of grief that I hadn't expected. I wonder if you've experienced anything similar, and if you have, why you think that sort of thing happens?

BF: I've only regretted it twice, I think. Once when I was about twenty-eight, and then when I was about thirty-five, I had a week's depression, and everybody said, 'Why are you so depressed?' and I couldn't tell them, but it was because I knew that I wasn't going to have children. But on the whole, for one reason or another, it's been a decision that I haven't regretted. I always used to think I'd be a very bad mother [though I've recently come to think that I would be just as good as anybody else]. No, what I grieve about is being alone, very often. This is a very big, and very complicated question. It does seem that if you're a single woman, rather than just if you're a single lesbian, you're bound to be very lonely, quite a lot of the time. I suppose it becomes like toothache really, you get on and stick a clove in your jaw, or you have a good cry, but you just have to get on with it. You rely a lot on friends, don't you? But friends can't always be there, especially if they are married, however they're married, and if they have children themselves, then they're not always available.

I must say I do worry about what's going to happen to me. I visit my mother, who is eighty-seven, every week, and she often cracks a joke about what people said to her when she was pregnant with me. Everybody wanted her to have an abortion, and she says she has the last laugh now, because here I am checking up on her every week. But who's going to check up on me? That's what I want to know.

MY: Maybe that's what it is. Maybe that's what it is in me . . .

BF: It's the ultimate aloneness.

MY: You're right, and I think that lesbians are especially vulnerable to exactly that. It would be nice to think that when we're eighty, we'll all still be able to support each other, but my fear is that we'll be divided, separated, from each other by the infirmities that come with age and further disabled by the way our society treats the elderly. It's not age itself I fear. What I fear are the consequences.

BF: I've been reading about hormone replacement therapy. Tell me what you think of it, and would you do it?

MY: I wouldn't touch it with a barge pole! My one excursion into anything vaguely hormonal was taking steroids. I took them for three days and had virtually every side-effect in the book for the next three months. Also, certainly for me, changing my diet has helped to alleviate the symptoms enormously, and when that's true, there's no point in even considering hormone replacement. It's just not worth it. I read what Rosetta Reitz had to say about it, that it increases the risk of cancer, of heart disease, and that she sees it as largely a socially conditioned attempt to postpone the natural process of aging, and I said, 'Right on!' and never let it cross my mind again.

BF: I must say I agree with you about that. I feel very resistant to the idea of hormone replacement, although I don't think I know nearly enough about it, but obviously for some women it's a very useful approach, as long as GPs don't make it out to be the solution to the 'problem' of aging.

Here's a question. What do you say to women who would flatter you with 'But you don't look your age!' Because I always want to say, 'Well, fuck you, lady! Thank you very much. I *am* forty-five, and I look how I look how I look.' How can I not look forty-five, because this is what I am? In a way I don't want all those years of pain and turmoil to be translated into an invisibility. I want the world to know; they should know. Each grey hair was a tear!

MY: Well, questions like that are really to do with conforming to people's stereotypes, aren't they? It's ridiculous to say, 'You don't look your age', when in fact we all show our ages differently and in different ways. I think it's quite insulting to say that, in fact.

That's a good lead in to the next thing I had down to ask you. One of the positive sides of menopause, and something else I hadn't expected, is that I feel I've finally grown up. Do you feel that there are positive aspects to it for you, as if doors are opening, even though others might be closing?

BF: Yes. Again, I'm not sure whether or not it's the menopause, but certainly with getting older, yes, I feel that to a certain extent I can dump a lot of things that have been concerning me since I was fourteen. Since I was fourteen, I've been worrying about love and who was going to love me. Despite what I've said in the earlier question about who's going to look after me when I'm eighty-seven, I think I'm much more concerned now with things like work, and what I want to do, rather than am I beautiful and am I lovable. Yes, I feel grown up as well. But of course, what I resent very much is that very few people treat me as if I'm grown up. I don't know if that's something to do with my manner, or if it's something to do with them, or whether it's just to do with our lesbian circles. I do not feel as venerated as I think I deserve.

MY: But indeed, I think that may be a consequence of living an alternative lifestyle. That may be for us the kind of thing we have to expect. I know I'm not just more prepared but more able to take certain things, arguments, and so on, on board that twenty years ago I wouldn't have dreamed of trying to cope with. I feel a lot tougher. I think I also feel that one of the effects of recognising I was menopausal was feeling that half my life is over: now, what's important and what isn't, where do I actually want to put my energy?

I've been looking at the time I've wasted on things that I don't really think are important, even though some of them might have been learning experiences. I don't want to waste any more time, but I feel much more able, now, to drop things that aren't going in the directions I want to go, or things that are other people's ideas and not mine. I need to follow my own ideas, what I know from my own experience to be true.

BF: What are the signs of aging in your body, if that's not too personal?

MY: I've been thinking about that, and in many respects, I've aged less visibly than a lot of women that I know. I'm aware, certainly, of physical changes, like I've put on weight and find it impossible to lose, no matter what I do, and it's not particularly that I want to be slim, which is a physical impossibility for me anyway, but I need to take off weight because I've got arthritis in my spine – there's another thing which is a direct product of aging! Of course, the arthritis is a sign of aging which is not visible, except to me because I have a direct experience of the pain. My hair is quite white, but because I'm blond it's not visible except in certain lights. A friend said to me this week, 'My god, you've got a lot of white hair!' Well, I've been saying that to people for ages, and they aren't convinced because they can't see it. I find it irritating – I would prefer it to show, because then people might not take for granted things about me which they do.

BF: Yes, I got my first grey hairs when I was twenty-five. I can remember being quite amused at the time. Just before Christmas, I had an x-ray on my spine, and the results are that I have 'the normal arthritic deterioration for a woman my age'.

MY: I know. I said to my doctor, 'So, what do I do about it?' and she said, 'Nothing!' Well, there are exercises I do, but that doesn't stop it from happening, it just makes the effects less painful.

That brings up a need for the theory about this, the discussions, to help us deal with it. I think that just now a whole generation of women, and particularly a whole generation of lesbian feminists, are coming to maturity. Do you think menopause and aging can be a different experience for us, because of our lesbianism and our feminism?

BF: Well, I must say that I always imagined that because I was a single woman, I wouldn't get the menopause! I always firmly believed that the menopause happened because your husband went off with a younger woman and your children left home, so you felt lonely and suicidal, which seems a perfectly sensible reaction. So I cannot explain my disastrous depressions nor my friend's dreadful migraines nor your whatever. It would appear that there is such a thing as menopause, after all! I'm sure, though, that what we're talking about a lot of the time is physical symptoms and certainly that is enough to put up with. I'm very glad I don't have a husband who's going to go off with a younger woman, and I'm very glad that I don't have to say goodbye to my young and beautiful children who have the rest of their lives before them, leaving me at home to hoover the cat and fold away the duvets. So I think being a lesbian and a feminist, with all the 'glorious perspectives' that those two lifestyles offer us, does make it a little easier. But I do certainly think that there needs to be some talk about this, otherwise we're not going to have a particular lesbian perspective on the subject. But, as with most things lesbian, I can't see it as separate. I can't see us having a perspective on the menopause without – going back to my earlier complaint – without having a perspective on sexuality that allows me to be, if I want to be, a passionless old maid, and yet allows my forty-eight year-old friend to be rampantly full of desire, if she wants to be. I think it's very important that we allow each other to be menopausal lesbians, however we want to do that. And I also think we do need to consider what our situations are going to be – again, we've already spoken about what's going to happen to us when we're eighty-seven. How can we do that, if we are so against individualism, capitalism, maybe being landladies to make some money to put aside for our old age? We're against all that, so what are we going to do? I'm having a hard enough time now, even to pay the rent, let alone to put money aside for my old age.

MY: And when we're all eighty, and in that same position, we're not going to be able to support each other. That's what terrifies me, I think. That's why we need to start talking about it and planning for it coherently, now, and not as individuals. We need to plan for it together.

BF: It's not us who need to plan for it, we're there already. It's all the young women who should be planning for it.

MY: But you don't realise, till you reach our age, that you *do* need to plan for it. We're talking, I think, about all of us, the women who are now in our forties, looking at the fact that in another twenty years, we're going to be retiring. Where are we going to retire to, on what, in what kind of social groupings? We need to look at how we can actually set ourselves up to maintain the independence that we want to have, and still not end up dependent on the vast heterosexual community out there who are going to give us zilch.

BF: We're talking about money, aren't we?

MY: Yes, I reckon we are. Where it's going to come from, and how we're going to get it, I don't know. I'm sure it's why a lot of women our age are taking up fulltime work that they don't necessarily want to do, because they're recognising that while it's possible to survive on part-time work and political activity up to a point, a time will come when we'll no longer be able to do that, we'll be destitute, and we'll be unable to fight any more battles because we won't be able to function as independent women. The only way we can get around that is, first, to make some money – there's no way round that, it's an economic fact of life – but second, to put our heads together and recognise that if we can work together, we've got a far better chance

38

of succeeding, and maintaining our politics, than if each one of us ends up staggering on in isolation.

BF: Let's hope that the menopause is going to bring us together.

MY: Surely, we're old enough and wise enough by now to manage it. That's a thought I'd like to finish with.

BF: Oh dear! I wanted to say something about how forgetful I've become over the last few years – but I forgot!

## Notes

1 Rosetta Reitz, *Menopause: A Positive Approach*, Penguin, 1979.

# Both Feet in Life: Interviews with Barbara Macdonald and Cynthia Rich

Jean Swallow

*I interviewed Barbara Macdonald and Cynthia Rich after their essays and narratives were published together in the book* Look Me in the Eye: Old Women, Aging and Ageism. *Barbara is a small, solid seventy-one-year-old white-haired woman. Cynthia is taller than Barbara, and her gray hair contrasts to Barbara's white. Cynthia is in her early fifties. In part because of the difference in their ages, they have come at the issues of age and ageism from different perspectives. They now live together in a small trailer on the Anza-Borrego desert in Southern California, writing and producing the crucial conversations which inform the book.* Look Me in the Eye *is the first book on aging, ageism and old women to come out of the lesbian-feminist sensibility, and it is intense, intelligent, angry, and hopeful, as are both these women.*

## Talking with Barbara Macdonald:

JEAN SWALLOW: Tell me why you wrote this book.

BARBARA MACDONALD: I wrote the essays in *Look Me in the Eye* because I was taking in aging and ageism and I was so angry, I had to deal with it.

I put the essays together because they have a sequence. When I went to live in Cambridge I couldn't figure out what was going on. I had come from a place where everybody knew me and all of a sudden nobody knew me except as an old woman; that was all they could see. It was a matter of shock. When I wrote the first essay, I began to see that there was something operating; there was a politic; it was not just my personal experience. So then I wanted to put the essays together so that other women could start from where I was and go through the experience with me.

S: *Tell me how you see yourself.*

M: I think of myself as a woman who survived the Depression. One of the differences between women of certain ages is whether or not they lived through the Depression. Once you have lived through that experience in which there were literally no jobs, no money, there are certain things that you just can't take for granted.

For example, prosperity. I never really trust it. I'm not a consumer. If I decide to spend $50, I think of everything I had to do in the thirties to earn that much, or I think of the last ten years before my retirement, when I earned more but I had to waste years of my life just waiting to live. I guess I'm saying that money represents years of my life, so that even if I had a lot of money now, I couldn't throw it away, spend it casually, because of what it represents. I paid too much for it in order to survive.

I am a radical feminist. I think I really didn't know that I was always a radical feminist until I read Joan Nestle's work. When I read her description of the dykes of the fifties, it helped me understand who I was in the thirties. A lot of what earlier felt shameful to me in terms of the pain of being so different, I see now in just a very different way.

I define myself as an old woman. I think young lesbians define me as an old dyke, but I define myself as an old woman. The dyke is a given – doesn't need explaining, not that I want to minimize it. Part of the reason I say I get real pleasure out of growing old is because I'm a dyke. I'm not facing otherness for the first time, with all that discomfort that I once felt about being other. And now I have this brand new chance to find out who I am, facing now another kind of otherness. Almost in some ways I welcome it as a chance to know myself.

S: *What else do you like about growing old?*

M: I spent a lot of my life, as I think most women have, wondering, 'Am I even going to really make it, will I make it through life?' I see now that I'm going to. I have that answer.

Some women I talk to are so frightened of growing old. I sense their desperation. They say things to me like, 'I'm not going to live to be old. I'm not going to live to be dependent.' The message young women get from the youth culture is that it's wonderful to be young and terrible to grow old. If you think about it, it's an impossible dilemma – how can you make a good start in life if you are being told at the same time how terrible the finish is? And this ageism encourages a sort of carelessness with life – fast cars, fast foods, drugs. There's a kind of toying with death. This is reinforced by the violence constantly portrayed, saying life is cheap – and for men, life *is* cheap, they don't produce it. These are male values, destructive to women.

Because of ageism, many women don't fully commit themselves to living life out until they can no longer pass as young. They live their lives with one foot in life and one foot outside it. With age you resolve that. I know the value of each day and I'm living with both feet in life. I'm living much more fully.

I like taking the measure of my own death – it was always part of my life. We miss a lot by not taking in the real jeopardy we are in. Every ,moment is important. We don't talk about the fact that you and I, despite the differences in our ages, may not live our lives out; that between what we are eating, breathing, and the risks of chemicals all around us, and the possibility of dying by nuclear bombs, your chances of dying in the next few years may be as great as mine. And if we are both going to go out by a nuclear bomb tomorrow or if I'm going to go out in the process of old age and dying, we ought to know the reality of our lives every day. To be conscious.

There is something about taking in the ending that changes your values – you are empowered by it. You are less willing to compromise. You are more determined to make your life meaningful and to refuse to distort in any way who you are in order to please. I have really almost no desire left to please and there is power in that. The power of the old woman is not being afraid to die, being conscious of all of her life, being in charge of her life, and these are in addition to the ways she is empowered by being less useful to men.

I was never useful to men, though I had to work for a living and so I had to work for men. But the message that I sent out was that I would not serve men, I would not be available to men for any kind of exploitation and to the degree that I could do that and earn a living and survive, I did. Now, I am out of the labor market and it is an understatement to say that I am not useful to men. I will thwart their purposes every way I can for the rest of my life.

And I think that in one sense, I can't say they are afraid of me, because they can't see me. I am invisible to them. But when I make myself visible, then they are afraid. The power of the old woman is that because she is outside the system, she can attack it. And I am determined to attack it.

One of the ways in which I am particularly conscious of this stance is when I go down the street. People expect me to move over. I noticed it particularly in Cambridge, where there is the University and there are groups of young people, and they are coming down the street in groups of two, three, or four and they expect me to move over, which means to step on the grass or on the curb. I just woke up one day to the fact that I was moving over. I have no idea for how many years I had been doing that. Now I never move over.

I simply keep walking. And we hit full force, because the other person is so sure that I am going to move that he isn't even paying any attention and we simply ram each other. If it's a man with a woman, he shows embarrassment, because he just about knocked down a five-foot seventy-year-old woman and so he quickly apologizes. But he's startled, he doesn't understand why I didn't move over, he doesn't even know how I got there, where I came from. I am invisible to him, despite the fact that I am on my own side of the street, simply refusing to give him that space that he assumes is his.

Another example. I have always liked to fix things. When Cynthia and I go to a hardware store to get something, the hardware man will only discuss it with Cynthia. It is inconceivable to him that I could use a screwdriver, whereas when I was younger they would talk to me. Sometimes in a store, I just make a great big scene. 'What the hell do you mean,' I shout. And they are kind of stunned.

By the very way that they shut me out, I have found my power. I've gotten a hold of my rage and I speak out and I define it for them. I go to women's department stores and I say, 'What do you mean that there is not a thing in this store for me to wear? Don't send me over to that rack when you know there is not a thing for me on that rack.' And I say so in a loud voice and I don't care if a crowd gathers. It's infuriating.

Clothes have been designed to separate women. Over here we have the young who are bonded with males. And the clothes are dykey; the pants have pockets; they are well-made. At least superficially, they are made to empower women. Then you have another set of clothes that are made to disempower. They have no pockets, are made of polyester, flouncy. They define you as other; they define you as mother.

When I can't go into a store and buy clothes, I want young women to know that I am angry. I know you have heard this before from me, and I am not through. I hope other old women will not give up their anger until young women walk into a store (and I don't care if they can wear a size 13, size 18, or a size 40) and say, 'I will not purchase from this store if I do not know that *all* women can come in here and buy clothes that are comfortable, that allow for body movement, and that you do not have hanging on your racks Mother Hubbards, or any other clothes designed by men to set women apart.'

I expect to see young women marching in front of those stores before I'll be satisfied. Young women really don't seem to take in that I and other old women are turned away at the door and that this is outrageous.

S: *Is this what you want me to do? What you want women my age to do?*

M: I want you first to form consciousness-raising groups and workshops to examine your own ageism, and I want that process to be ongoing. I think that out of that process women's collectives – publishers, activists – will see that they have not included old women. I want such groups to study the publications coming out and be sensitive to what is ageist. But yes – I want you to quit going into clothing stores that pretend I don't exist. Why would you go into a store that turns me away? Why aren't you out in front of those stores marching? If you were, you would be surprised at how many old women would come out of the closet to join you around other issues.

42

S: *Now this brings me to a question that I have not asked because I was embarrassed and shy.*

M: I understand shyness – believe it or not.

S: *As a lesbian, I don't feel I have a history. I have a desperate desire to know that you were a lesbian in the thirties. I have a desperate need to know that there have always been lesbians. And because you are here now, I think that the tendency of myself and of my contemporaries, who also have that need for place and time and continuity, is to treat you as justification. If someone was one before me, then I can't be unnatural. I take immense delight in knowing that there are queer seagulls. I think that I, and my contemporaries, need to know that lesbians have always been. Except what happens is we don't want to deal with, maybe we even can't see, old women, women like you. And so we make up stories about who you are (and those stories are certainly published by a number of presses and magazines) rather than talk with you.*

M: If you dealt with old women as equals, you would already know our stories. You would have already heard our stories, as you have heard all this morning around this breakfast table because you have engaged with us on a real level and know what the pain is like. And so I don't feel as though you are staring at us as though we were an animal in a cage. I feel as though you want to know who I am, that you see me as a woman in process.

S: *And to not make it up, not to have some thirty-five-year-old out there making it up. I mean, it strikes me as obscene, in a way that Henry Miller is obscene, in that it is somebody else telling me what my story is.*

*But the other thing that occurs to me is that I want to know how you made it through your life. I want you to be my parent. I don't have a gay parent, and I have had some negative parenting in some areas. I think I want to go to you and say, 'What do I do now?' Which is probably okay if we are friends. But when I go to you as an old woman and say 'Give me your wisdom' then I've trapped you, haven't I?*

M: I haven't got any wisdom. I wish I did. I would love to be able to tell you how great I was and how I had this powerful stance and how I made it through and tell you I never had anything to do with men and I had a clear vision.

But I just muddled my way through as best I could and I am filled with shame at the compromises I had to make. It's a curious kind of reversal. When I was young, I was filled with shame at my difference and I tried to hide it, and now that I try to write about my past, my shame is in the way I did not reveal it, the ways I compromised myself. It is not easy. It is not easy for an old dyke to tell you about the early years of being a dyke. For me at least, it is filled with shame and now I begin to feel that I may be able to write about those early years, but only since Joan Nestle has helped me out.

Anyone can ask me, but I have no answers. I just muddled through. And I never thought I'd make it. Half the fun of old age is that I made it. And there is no magical way.

S: *What becomes clear to me is that out of my need, I am putting you in a slot. And I am separating you from me. It seems to me that the pain of ageism is about separating us. That you become this, and I become that, and we no longer are able to be together.*

M: That's right. And I think Cynthia describes that so well in the book: if we sit down to have coffee with each other, as long as we are two women talking together everything goes well, but at the point where one of us thinks this woman could be my daughter or my mother, the conversation is really over. We've gotten into roles that are part of the patriarchal caste system. We need to change the ways women talk to each other across generations if we are going to change the world.

## Talking with Cynthia Rich:

S: *How do you see age and ageism being dealt with in the women's movement?*

R: When I began to consider myself a feminist and first thought about 'women's' issues, the image that came to my mind was of women in their twenties or thirties or maybe, like myself, just coming into middle age. In my mind's eye, I simply did not see old women. I think that wasn't unusual in 1970. It's painful to say, but – fifteen years later in the movement – it seems as if younger women still don't see old women as real women whose lives are ongoing, who face many of the issues and problems that younger women face, but also the women's issue of ageism.

When younger women are aware of old women at all, it's usually as women who *used* to be somebody. So from time to time we'll seek out some old woman to tell us how it was back in the days when she was still a young woman.

But our level of awareness of how things *are* for old women now is very, very low in the women's movement. We've treated ageism as a luxury issue, or even a non-issue. The National Women's Studies Association has knocked ageism off its list of serious oppressions.

S: *It was on, and now it's off?*

R: At one point, NWSA at least gave lip-service to it. It's not as if ageism was ever significantly integrated into women's studies. You can go to conference after conference where it's simply not seen as important. Yet it seems to me that you can't really have a feminist politic without looking at ageism, that ageism connects to every other issue that affects women's lives.

Barbara and I attended the National Association of Lesbian and Gay Gerontologists recently, and there was not a single workshop on ageism. The issue wasn't discussed. Here were younger lesbians planning social services for old lesbians without feeling any need to examine their own ageism.

S: *Talk to me about social services, and how that relates to ageism.*

R: It's a question of who defines whom. Old women are not the ones defining aging, old women are not listened to about aging and ageism. Right now, aging is being defined by all sorts of people who make a living from inventing goods and services for old women. So we get stereotypes that serve the purposes of profit-making, and we're left with no real insight into either the process of aging or what old women have to confront in the world every day of their lives.

Social agencies are one of the ways by which old women are defined for profit. They raise money by assuring the public of how capable service workers are and how needy and incapable the women they serve are. Of course they're not out to insist on changes in the economic and social system that is the source of their clients' problems.

So we have organizations like the United Way of Massachusetts raising funds with an ad that shows an old woman in a room alone, staring out the window. The caption reads: 'One day you wake up old and all your friends are gone.' The advertisement goes on to feed the idea that – naturally – as you grow old, your friends will all be old like yourself, and when they die – naturally – no younger women are going to be interested in you. The message is that an old woman shouldn't even expect friendship or companionship from a younger woman. Who says that's natural? It's insulting and it's a self-fulfilling prophesy. It's also self-serving – only United Way is willing to be friends with an old woman.

Just as bad is the stereotype developed by advertisers of consumer products. Because the numbers of old women are growing so rapidly, manufacturers see there are profits to be made off those old women who aren't yet divorced or widowed, and who still have access to some of their husband's money. These aren't most old women, but there's a market there. So advertising has begun to portray the old woman as the sensuous grandmother, as the woman who gets off the plane in her little tennis suit and puts on her Oil of Olay. She is a white woman, of course, and she is very comfortably off. Unlike most old women, she's not worried about whether to pay the gas bill or buy groceries – she just wants to bring out her beauty.

Another way old women – both Black and white – are stereotyped for exploitation is by always showing them as grandmothers. Here the message is that the only real joy or meaning in an old woman's life comes from being with children. So we have all sorts of programs like Foster Grandparents. It's another way of cashing in on more of women's unpaid work. The most blatant example of that is an agency in Orlando, Florida, called 'Dial-a-Grandma, Hire-a-Grandpa.' Most old women worked hard raising their own family of children, and didn't have many other choices. Now they're expected to go on and raise another generation. Why are old women supposed to be interested only in 'future generations' and not in themselves or each other? Why is it that kids on the street call Barbara 'Grandma' – as in 'Move along, Grandma'? Who's making these definitions?

The central issue here is that it's only old women who can define what it means to be an old woman in America. Statistics tell us something, though, about the extent to which ageism is a woman's issue, not to be covered up by the term 'elderly.' Old women who are single or widowed or divorced – that is, women who are not at that moment by the warm side of a man – are four times as likely to live at poverty levels of income. And two-thirds of all old women aren't living with a husband. More than twice as many old women as men live in poverty.

Almost all the residents of public housing for the elderly are women. Over two-thirds of nursing home beds are occupied by women. So when we read about cutbacks in Social Security or shocking stories about nursing homes, we have to see that these are women's problems.

S: *You've said that as soon as a woman ceases to be useful to a man in terms of bearing his children or taking care of him, she is no longer valuable. Also, my understanding of your essays in the book is that if she doesn't play the role of grandmother, she may be seen as a witch.*

R: Historically, and as far as I can tell cross-culturally, men have been afraid of what they perceived as old women's power. There is this kind of mythic thing that men have done with women in their heads – a splitting-off of woman into the 'good' woman and the 'bad' woman. In many cultures, it's the old woman who has been the mythic image of what men most fear in women, which is the woman who claims her own self. And so we have the old woman, the terrible witch, who actually devours children, who is the opposite of the good woman, the good mother. All old women have to carry that.

The woman who no longer serves men is potentially powerful and potentially dangerous. In some cultures, she's bought off – they let her into the boy's club as a token woman. In this culture, in the United States of America of 1984, the way this fear is dealt with is by making the old woman invisible, and by pushing her back into family again – or if that doesn't work, then portraying her as crazy, incompetent, overexcitable, and childlike.

S: *What about women who really are that way? I think of my grandmother who died of one of the dementia diseases. My head tells me that one of the ways these stereotypes work is that they have some part that is true, and that the balance is off, but my heart knows what I saw. What do you think?*

R: I think we can't possibly know what the natural processes of aging are until we understand ageism – just as we can't know what is natural to womanhood without understanding sexism and patriarchy. We know that women of all ages seek therapy or are institutionalized much more often than men. But how do we interpret that statistic?

You need only look at the ads in our feminist publications to see that younger women are out of our minds. We have therapy to survive our incest and rape, therapy for our drinking and our parents' drinking, therapy for eating problems and therapy for non-eating problems, therapy for stress, therapy for handling victimization, therapy for ex-mental patients – the list is endless. If it takes that much therapy to get through our twenties and thirties and forties, and we have not included old women in this liberation process, what do you expect to find at the far end of a life of oppression? Actually, what you find is a lot of strong survivors. This isn't to deny that old women suffer from burn-out, breakdowns, and disorientation, as other women do.

We've never used our feminist political framework to look at what happens to old women. It's as if suddenly, after sixty or sixty-five everything that happens to a woman is just 'natural.' Right now a huge amount of attention and money is going toward Alzheimer's disease. I'm not saying that there's no such thing as Alzheimer's, no diseases that are specific to people over fifty. But nowhere near as much attention has gone to the recent revelations that many, many old women have been diagnosed as having senile dementia who in fact have brain tumors, or, more often, are overdosed with drugs or – even more often – are severely depressed. Loss of memory, poor concentration, fatigue, apathy, are classic symptoms of depression in a twenty- or an eighty-year-old. What does it mean to be depressed because people's attitudes towards you are so annihilating, and then to have your depression diagnosed as hopeless senility?

Younger women need to know the issues in old women's lives. Many of these issues connect directly with issues younger women face, so it is crazy that we are not facing them together.

For example, male violence. Old women are even less safe on the street than younger women – many old women won't leave the house after sundown, or only go out while school is in session. Enforced heterosexuality controls the lives of both lesbian and non-lesbian old women, since the 'solution' to the issues for old women is always seen as a heterosexual-family solution.

It's really odd that infirmity is so much the stereotype of old age, and yet when we discuss questions of disability and access for younger women, issues for physically challenged old women are essentially never raised. The connections just aren't seen; it's as if these were two different worlds.

Women who take seriously the issue of women's unpaid work don't hesitate to use their mothers for babysitting. When the old woman is grandmother, her continuing labor of childcare without any kind of compensation is seen as just part of her nature.

The connections between ageism, sexism and racism become clear when we learn that 44 percent of old Black women – but only 7 per cent of old white men – are poor.

And yet the women's movement has not seemed to feel that the issues facing women in the last thirty years of our lives are critical to an understanding of sexism. Even when we talk about women's poverty, we rarely mention old women – although worldwide, in both industrial and agricultural countries, old women are the poorest of the poor. I think we have to ask ourselves how this can be, since we are all headed in this direction.

S: *I see that I have asked you about ageism in the women's movement and ageism in our social agencies, but I haven't asked you about what this experience is like for you.*

R: It changes for me all the time. When I wrote the essays in the book, I still identified as a younger woman, and much less as a woman who would have to face ageism herself. At first, ageism was my problem only because I am Barbara's lover and attitudes in the outside world were bringing a lot of pain into our lives. Later I became increasingly aware of how the lives of other old women I knew were controlled by ageism. But I didn't really believe I'd ever be old myself – I'd had to face the possibility of death at forty-one, but I'd never had to take in my own aging in a deep, life-changing way. When I re-read the ending of [the essay] 'The Women in the Tower,' I can see that what I was really doing was pushing myself to take that next step. I knew it would be freeing, and it has been.

Now more and more I feel connected to the woman I'll be in my eighties or nineties if Im lucky enough to live that long. I don't know her, but I know more about her, and I like her values. I feel much closer to her than I do to that woman I used to be in my twenties and thirties.

I didn't come out to myself as a lesbian until I was in my late thirties. I feel the same excitement about growing old that I've felt about being a lesbian – we can't believe what they tell us so we have to create it every step of the way, discover for ourselves what it means to be an old woman. It's a frontier.

# A Woman's Right to Cruise

Kirsten Hearn

Six hundred lesbians attended the eighth International Lesbian Information Service (ILIS) conference in Geneva in 1986. The overwhelming majority of them were white, European, gentile, middle-class, employed, educationally privileged, aged 25 to 35, childless, symmetrical, slim and severely able-bodied. Some Black, Jewish, Irish, working class and disabled sisters and lesbian mothers were to be found if you searched hard enough.

Conflict was the order of the day. The agenda reflected only marginally the lives of Black, Jewish, non-European, Third World, working class and disabled lesbians and those of lesbian mothers. Racism, anti-semitism, classism and ableism were greatly in evidence.

Here, I want to talk about my experience as a disabled lesbian and those of other disabled lesbians I have talked to or who have written about their experiences. I am a middle-class, childless, high-waged, thirty-year-old, blind lesbian WASP (white anglo-saxon protestant) who lives independently. As usual, lesbians with disabilities were forced to talk about issues concerning the access and participation at the conference. Our frustrations forced us to take time at the final plenary to outline these, which meant that there was no time to talk about the real reasons why we are excluded from the International Lesbian Movement.

Since I was not given an opportunity at the conference, I would now like to take the space here to talk briefly about the issues we had originally wanted to raise at the conference in Geneva.

Ableism is the label given to a set of assumptions, stereotypes, oppressive ideologies and practices which deliberately seek to totally exclude lesbians who do not adhere to the accepted lesbian identity. In this case, this means physically and/or mentally functioning 'differently' from the accepted norm, e.g. not having the full use of some or all senses, parts or all of one or more limbs, parts or all of one or more organs or body systems, the conventional use of the powers of memory, reason or comprehension, etc.

Ableism defines the lack of or immobility or different use of one or more of these functions as personal to the individual and therefore of no concern to the so-called majority of 'normal' people. This de-politicises the exclusion of lesbians with disabilities from the lesbian movement and its other struggles.

Unlike other struggles, disability is seen as a personal tragedy and as a Bad Thing, whilst it is now accepted (hopefully) in the women's movement that being a lesbian is positive. No one would ever dare to suggest to a lesbian that they might prefer to be heterosexual and therefore, should seek a cure. It is impossible to change one's sexuality by having a physical operation, though psychological methods have been used: it lies at the root of the oppression that heterosexual people assume that lesbians and gay men would want to.

One of the bases of ableism is the assumption that as lesbians with disabilities we would want to be cured. I astound many lesbians by stating that I neither seek a cure nor would ever want to be able-bodied because I not only enjoy my life as a blind lesbian, but feel that it is a positive part of me and a part of which I am intensely proud. I celebrate my culture in all its non-visual ways as proudly as Black women, Jewish women and lesbians celebrate theirs.

Part of the oppression I face in my attempts not just to exist but also to participate in the lesbian movement is the fact that not only am I defined as a fat woman, but I move differently too. I use a white stick and touch and listen instead of look. I feel forced to change my body size, but even if I were able-bodied I probably couldn't. If I found myself thinking that I should, which I do from time to time when I'm depressed, I know that I'm acting out the oppression which says that dykes should not be fat. I have a hard time trying to work out which is the reason for my feeling excluded from the lesbian movement and have decided that even if I were thin I still would not pass as acceptable because of my disability. I can hide it, when I'm sitting, but not when I move. I can hide it when I am talking to someone, but only for short periods because I cannot make eye contact and respond visually to body language. I am often thought to be rude, drunk or not interested. Other lesbians with disabilities can't even hide their 'different' bodies even when they are seated.

Severely able-bodied lesbians look at us and go, 'Urgh, what's *wrong* with her?' You only have to go to a disco to realise to what extent lesbians have bought the image of the slim, agile, symmetrical body.

I thought cruising was something sailors did before I joined the lesbian movement. I would go to discos and bars with sighted friends and they would get talking to women whilst I got drunk. (Well, what else can you do when they've left you in a corner and gone off dancing?) If women ever talked to me it was always because of my disability.

I always thought that going to bars and discos was the way you got to know lesbians. Now I know that this might be the case for some severely able-bodied dykes. A 'straight', 'non-political' lesbian friend recently gave me a lesson on cruising. She said I should look around the room, trying to catch women's eyes, exchange looks, follow their movements, then go across and stand near them, exchange a few more looks, then go and ask them for a dance etc, etc. My reply was, 'A nod is as good as a wink . . .' I pondered the possibility of cruising tactilely, but decided that since this was a mixed gay disco, I might find myself touching up a short gay man.

Whether lesbians have ever tried cruising me I do not know because they have never made it verbal. Recently I have been thinking of a new design for a badge: 'Don't eye me up, proposition me.'

Whilst lesbians with different disabilities who are sighted may be able to do some of this 'eyeing-up stuff', the possibility of them being able to *swagger* suavely across the dance floor in their wheelchairs or on their crutches, with their sticks or calipers, is pretty remote.

From my experience of talking with other disabled lesbians and through reading the *Gemma* newsletter, our experience demonstrates that the reaction of severely able-bodied dykes when being cruised by one of us is likely to be embarrassment or terror. We are generally not taken seriously in these situations, since we are not supposed to have any sexual feelings whatsoever, let alone the ability to carry them out. In my experience, making relationships with lesbians with or without disabilities has always happened when the other woman has known me first.

Once again, it is a pre-requisite of getting to know dykes and forming relationships that we must behave, look and move as the so-called majority does. And it's just tough if we can't.

Different women with different disabilities have different needs and abilities before, during and after sex. Some of us can only lie in certain positions or may have to use different parts of our bodies. Some of us have more strength and energy than others.

A previous sighted lover once said to me that we were equal in bed because the lights were out. Whether or not sight was necessary during the sexual act, she was ignoring my disability and its effects on my self-confidence. Many lesbians with disabilities, taking in the oppressive ideologies that we do not deserve, wanting and needing to be loved, will find ourselves under-confident, over-anxious to please and willing to submit to almost anything the other woman wishes us to do or have done to us. This often spills over into our behaviour outside our sexual practice with each other.

Some of us feel we need to demand monogamy for fear that we will not have the choices our able-bodied lovers have and therefore should hold on to what we've got. Sometimes, by having several lovers ourselves, we are able to hold on to more positive relationships because our needs are met by them individually and differently. Some of us are forced into accepting our partners' non-monogamy, again for fear of losing what little we have of them.

The monogamy versus non-monogamy argument and the choices open to us are very much dependent on the power imbalances in our relationships. As lesbians with disabilities we often experience great powerlessness within our relationships. This power imbalance exists whether our lovers are able-bodied or disabled.

Two of my previous lovers have been fully sighted. One of them had a mobility disability. The severely able-bodied one had both the power of mobility and sight. She was independent and could socialize freely. When we went away together I was dependent on her, because we were in a strange environment. This also happened, to a lesser degree but equally painfully, when I had a partially sighted lover.

The lover with the mobility disability needed me to help her up and down steps and help her carry things. I believe that this relationship worked better because we could trade off our needs. However, another power imbalance came into play here, because she was bisexual.

When a lover is needed to do other things outside the sexual relationship, such as reading print to a blind lesbian or helping a woman with a mobility disability get around, these needs may be used as payment for something else. For example, 'I will do your washing if you agree that I can be non-monogamous'. There is also a tendency for able-bodied lovers of lesbians with disabilities to think of forgetting the disabled lover's disability as a compliment when it is vital that she remembers it.

All this results in many of us feeling increasingly isolated within and outside the lesbian movement. Because we have disabilities, we are not thought to have any sexuality at all, therefore how can we possibly be lesbians? Whilst many of us are out in the movement, our participation is not made easier by all the things that have been mentioned in this article. Lesbian activists such as myself often totally lack confidence and believe that we are unloveable. We may be able to function in meetings or write in magazines but many of us have much more difficulty in functioning socially within the movement, let alone making relationships.

Whilst we know what we are missing, what of our isolated lesbian sisters in the institutions and the residential homes? What, too, of those lesbians with multiple disabilities or less acceptable ones such as learning disabilities? Whilst some of us have the ability/power to get to meetings, bars and discos, others have to rely on Dial-a-Rides or relatives. Even heterosexual life in institutions and in our families is often a no-go area. Coming out as a lesbian to carers, relatives and the Social Services (which the obtaining of a Lesbian book or magazine or going to a meeting or disco requires) often means the withdrawal of these services and support systems and, in some cases, incarceration in mental hospitals. Until the lesbian movement recognises that all lesbians with disabilities have a right to full participation and starts organising differently, none of us, not even the most out activists such as myself, are welcome in the movement. By this we don't mean just pity or embarrassment, or just plain access as outlined by us in the past, but an acceptance that we are viable, loveable, and totally worthy members of the lesbian sisterhood.

## Notes

*Gemma*, Box 5700, London WC1 N3XX Books.
Susan Browne et al., *With the Power of Each Breath*, Cleis Press, 1985.
Jo Campling, *Images of Ourselves: Women With Disabilities Talking*, Routledge & Kegan Paul, 1981.

# Sex and Danger: Feminism and Aids

Sara Scott

Aids is a feminist issue. It is no longer, if it ever was, simply the name of a medically recognised syndrome; it is a social disease. Aids brings with it an enormous range of politically loaded questions; for the Right it has become a metaphor of corruption, retribution and moral decay. For the media, the government and the medical profession, the questions it raises are divided into the moral and the practical, with the former frequently disguised as the latter. Organising media-linked Aids advice lines during the last few months has provided me with plenty of food for feminist thought, but little space for discussing the sexual politics of Aids. At the very least, such a politics would deny the division between practical and moral questions and could argue for changes in sexual practice which would be in the interests of women.

It strikes me as bizarre that through all the sound and fury of the Aids debate, feminists in Britain have remained so quiet. Aids has created the biggest public debate on sexuality, sexual practice and sexual morality since the media recovered from the shock of the sixties;

yet it is one to which feminists have yet to make a particular contribution. Our silence seems bizarre because the issues raised by Aids are very much on our political patch. I believe we ought to be thinking fast about the implications of Aids as a health issue for women and the implications for feminism of all the things other people are saying. I'll return later to why I think feminists have failed to get involved in the Aids debate to date and I'll examine what the few who have written on the subject have had to say. But first I want to look at the meanings for women of non-feminist public thought on the Aids crisis.

The idea that there might be other reasons for criticising male heterosexual practice, apart from catching or spreading disease has not entered public debates. Instead, the liberal establishments are seeing the past (their own male youth perhaps) through rose-tinted spectacles, building a myth of a pre-Aids golden age of sexual liberation. At the same time as bemoaning the loss of wilder days, they appear to be uncritically accepting a monogamous, condom-bound solution to the present crisis. Meanwhile, the Right are regarding the whole affair if not as the wrath of god, then certainly as a gift of the gods in providing an argument 'from nature' in support of their views on 'promiscuity', the sanctity of the family and the evils of homosexuality. The Left has had very little to say about Aids except to criticise the government campaign. It certainly cannot be assumed that they have listened to feminist insistence that sexuality is socially constructed any harder than other men.

The ways of curtailing the Aids crisis pushed by the government, media and medical profession are by no means the ones that feminists would promote, but they still raise interesting contradictions. For example, a government opposed to sex education in schools is now obliged to promote the most explicit sexual information for young people. It is being advocated that women carry condoms – previously the prerogative of prostitutes and men alone. This suggestion is itself full of ambiguities. In accepting uncritically that women are more responsible than men, it fails to challenge male behaviour and puts the burden of changing their acts and attitudes on to individual women within personal relationships. It takes as 'natural' men's resistance to self control, and falls far short of promoting what an earlier generation of feminists referred to as 'male continence'. At the same time, public permission for women to carry condoms urges us to declare an interest in and preparedness for heterosexual penetrative sex, which women have always been supposed to deny. Most women on the pill, for example, have chosen this form of contraception in part for its invisibility. Young women's only approved role in relation to sex has been to be 'overwhelmed' – an attitude which fits uncomfortably with having a packet of Featherlight in their handbags.

There is a major contradiction for those who use Aids to advocate a return to 'old fashioned' values, which is that the act which is most acceptable to them is, in Aids terms, the most dangerous. Women's health campaigners have recognised this for generations – hence the campaigns for male continence in relation to venereal disease in the early part of the century.[1] Feminists have understood that penetrative sex has never been free of fear for women: the fear of pregnancy, in or out of marriage; fear of contraceptive failure or side-effects, many of which are life threatening; as well as fear of disease. Our solution has been to promote changes in men's sexual practices. We should advocate non-penetrative sex, with all its positive implications for women's sexual pleasure, as the best way of combating the spread of Aids. It's too contradictory for men in general and the Right in particular to advocate 'non-normal' sex because of a health crisis – which is why they're trying to get away with condoms as the solution. We shouldn't be letting them.

The thing I find most frustrating is that because Aids is such a new problem it is possible to get radical ideas through to places they would never normally reach, but there is no-one pushing feminist ideas through these channels. Gay men active around Aids have had unprecedented success in encouraging the media and others to talk about high risk practices in relation to Aids, rather than high risk groups. This has been argued on the basis that not all men who engage in homosexual sex identify as homosexual and they will not therefore 'hear' advice aimed at high risk groups. When some people are identified as 'high risk', it is possible for others to disassociate themselves from the problem as they do from the group. At the same time, this argument is an attempt to use a philosophical idea about the historical construction of sexuality (Michel Foucault, Jeffrey Weeks), in a political present tense. Jeffrey Weeks has argued that the concept of a homosexual person is an extremely recent one and that until fairly late in the nineteenth century, homosexuality was identified solely in terms of acts not identities. The law encoded only a series of non-procreative sexual acts, in which buggery appeared alongside bestiality.[2]

What are the implications if gay men are successful in using this argument as a health education tack, an argument which also aims to reduce the homophobia which Aids has been used to stir up?

For example, is this kind of intervention part of a continued retreat from identity amongst gay men, with the demise of a gender conscious gay liberation movement? In the context of a 'queer bashing' media, the interventions of gay men are a step forward, but we need to be talking about the wider sexual politics.

I come across some wonderfully contradictory things in the course of my work. I hear gay men counselling straight men about non-penetrative sex. I hear women telling women they have the right not just to insist that men wear condoms, but to sex they like. And I come across terrible things like the woman co-ordinator of a local Aids line giving her support to the re-licensing of a sex shop on the grounds that fantasy equals 'safe sex'. I want to be part of a feminist discussion of these contradictions.

Some parts of the media Aids campaign have been targetted at women, and frequently emphasise women's supposedly natural inclination towards monogamous relationships.

The solution proposed for men's non-monogamy and their unwillingness to use condoms was for women to put pressure on them. No attention was paid to the respective difference between men's and women's commitment to monogamy, or to how women are meant to persuade their long-term and supposedly monogamous partners to use condoms as a precaution against Aids. How many women could admit, even to themselves that their husbands might visit prostitutes or have affairs? The media made it quite plain during Aids week on TV that they were not prepared to advocate monogamy for men outright. Instead they landed responsibility on women, saying that women are 'good girls' naturally and can look after the other half of the population.

Just as the 'naturalness' of women's monogamy is assumed, so is the necessity of heterosexual intercourse. I found the nearest to a feminist media statement in the following from a Channel 4 update to its *Well Being* booklet on sexually transmitted diseases: 'Many people have found that sexual pleasure does not have to depend on penetration; mutual masturbation, for instance, is completely without risk and can give great satisfaction to couples who are worried about the risks of infecting each other.' No comment.

Most of the women's magazines have now carried articles on Aids and their approach is best summed up by the *Good Housekeeping* headline: 'Aids: is all the hysteria a blessing in disguise?' Emanating from article to article is a sense of relief, a current of 'we told you so' satisfaction presented as the view of middle-aged, middle-class married women. Celebrating the death of the permissive society, they suggest smugly: 'If you tend to "sleep around", be sensible and aim to settle down with one partner over the next few years.'

It's sad that so many women felt conned, exploited or threatened by sexual 'liberation' but never developed a feminist critique of it. The line taken by these magazines is not anti-women, but it takes for granted that women prefer monogamy – by nature rather than because of the social options available to them, and it takes a cheerfully moral view of the joys of less sex.

On the implications of Aids for relationships between the sexes, Philip Hodson in *She* magazine wrote: 'Men who don't look bisexual (even though they may be) will stand in greatest demand. Women will dress to attract the masculine male, paradoxically appearing more seductive, alluring and sexy . . . while others will become practically celibate, with all the sex appeal of boiler suits and bags . . .'

In this scenario a return to 'old fashioned' moral standards and earlier marriage is to be accompanied by a return to old fashioned sex roles and stereotypes.

The more I hear about Aids and the new morality, the more puzzled I become about feminist silence on the subject.

I don't think that as feminists we are immune to the attitudes of the population at large. A recent Gallup poll showed that 80 per cent of people interviewed see themselves at no risk from Aids, and that 48 per cent agreed that 'most people with Aids have only themselves to blame'. The idea of Aids as a gay men's problem has been a slow one to die. This, coupled with the immunity many of us have felt so far as lesbians plus our political criticism of many gay male lifestyles means we have been slow to regard Aids as having much personal meaning for us. Certainly Vada Hart's article in *Gossip 2* was an extreme example of burying one's head in the sand. Her argument that lesbians and gay men have nothing in common, only the media insists on lumping us together is fair enough. But the directive that we therefore reject anything to do with Aids seems positively callous in the face of the biggest surge in 'queer bashing' that the streets or the press have ever seen. It is also incredibly shortsighted.

As lesbians we are associated with male homosexuality, like it or not. *We* may not regard homosexuality as a unitary concept – believing that in a society where men have power over women, loving your own sex has completely different meanings depending on which sex you are – but attacks on gay men do not leave us untouched. Attitudes towards homosexuality and the position of women are often closely linked. What distresses me most about the article is that it regards lesbians as unconcerned and unaffected by something of major importance in the lives of non-lesbian/celibate women. I find this hermetically sealed concept of the lesbian community deeply shocking.

Another explanation for feminist silence is that WLM debates about heterosexual practice have been few and far between in recent years. Few public feminist agendas include responsibility for contraception, non-penetrative sex, non-monogamy or even marriage. In *Marxism Today* (April 1987), Melissa Benn observes that heterosexual socialist feminists do not talk about sexuality any more: 'If the debate about sexuality has taken place anywhere in the 1980s it has taken place within lesbian feminism. It is almost as if the subject of sexuality has returned to a pre-1970 situation for women on the Left: the unspeakable clothed as the irrelevant, the disruptive dismissed as the merely embarrassing.'

For these reasons we were ill-equipped to raise feminist issues in the context of Aids. If we don't rebuild our critique of heterosexuality and the nitty-gritty of heterosexual practice our position will be defined for us *within* the parameters of the present debate. This is what I feel Lynne Segal in *New Socialist* (April 1987) is already doing. She claims that feminists have failed to distance themselves from the mainstream anti-sex response to Aids and, even suggests that the anti-sex scare tactics of the popular press, equating casual sex and death, are following the lead set by some feminist positions on sex: 'They convey a message women have been hearing for some years from a small, but vocal, feminist minority. Sex with men is always and inevitably dangerous. "A woman needs a man like a fish needs a bisexual" they might say today.'

If only it were so easy to persuade the popular press to promote feminist messages. Actually, the sex and danger line is a lot older than us and has done very nicely without our help.

Lynne Segal is trying to associate feminist critiques of heterosexuality with right-wing morality, obviously believing that we have a secret attachment to the nuclear family, will do anything to reduce heterosexual sex in the world or we are simply too stupid to see where our criticisms lead. Feminists, she feels, are liable 'to join the chorus condemning the "permissive" sixties and heralding a new confining morality'. In her fear that political lesbians are going to forge alliances with the 'moral majority', Segal omits to recognise that if the formation of the WLM owes anything to the sexual liberation movement, it is as much to feminist criticisms of its philosophies as to the opening up of sexual mores it created. This acceptance that the sixties did represent the freeing of sexuality from 'policing and punishment', rather than the construction of new codes for social control, suggests a dangerous forgetfulness of the lessons of the early 1970s in the face of the quite different problems of the mid 1980s.

We have to find a fuller way of discussing sexual liberation and sexual morality. In Melissa Benn's recent article on feminism in the eighties, she dances on the grave of political lesbianism (a little disconcertingly for those of us yet unburied) and the possibility of a feminist sexual 'morality': 'There has been a growth in the refusal of feminism to accept any idea of a "correct" or "incorrect" kind of sexual practice.'

She claims the lesbian S/M debate was about 'a rejection by some lesbian feminists of a prescriptive public morality about sex'. I do not believe that our views on sex have become so liberal, nor do I believe we are about to fall into the lap of the Right, but I fear we will be allocated to one side or another unless we get our act together.

Some of Lynne Segal's points are important – for example, that the media campaign has consistently reduced sex to the 'activity of the penis' and that the government campaign has fostered anxiety and guilt about sex in men and women (witness thousands of helpline calls from people frantic about oral sex – a comparatively low risk practice, but one that is not seen as 'normal'). She argues that given the power imbalance between the sexes, Aids can only be countered by 'honesty', 'openness' and more 'imaginative' (women-centred?) sexual habits, which 'necessitates more equal relationships between men and women' (women's liberation?). What concerns me is her lack of anger at men's sexual exploitation of women in 'normal' heterosexual sex; her association of feminists who are critical on this score with the anti-sex lobby and her nostalgia for a 'joint sexual politics with men', which she sees as having been part of the WLM of the early 1970s.

In contrast to Lynne Segal's, Ros Coward's contribution is a well-argued case for feminist engagement in discussions about Aids (*New Internationalist*, March 1987). She states that Aids is going to create a 'sexual revolution' of one sort or another, so we may as well use the opportunity to push our vision of what that revolution should look like. It's an optimistic article which suggests that women may have something to gain from the Aids tragedy:

Men and women have different interests at stake in any possible sexual revolution and the crisis produced by Aids may well have different implications for men and women . . . women have been bearing the brunt of making sex safe for men in the past . . . But now, suddenly, it's a matter of life and death to *men* that they abandon their historical privilege of spontaneous sex and assume personal responsibility for their actions ... sexuality could be redefined as something other than male discharge into any kind of receptacle. In this new context where penetration might literally spell death, there is a chance for a massive relearning about sexuality.

It's a long shot, and condoms are far more likely to catch on, but given the personal terrors and dilemmas many heterosexual women are facing at the moment, we really must be saying something. The explicit discussions of sexual practice which Aids has caused have got to be regarded positively, and the necessity for a new kind of sex education for young people is pressing. Youth workers and feminist teachers around the country are using the Aids crisis as a way into discussing responsibility and the rights of women to define their own sexuality. As a movement we should be making as much public noise as possible in support of them.

Friends have bemoaned the fact that no-one has listened to feminists when we've tackled the very issues which Aids is getting everyone in a spin about. As Ros Coward puts it:

There are some especially cruel ironies for feminism in the current situation. We have to watch general pressure mounting to transform sexual innuendo in advertising yet feminist campaigns against sexism in advertising have largely failed. Especially cruel is the conclusion of the British Government Aids leaflet: 'Ultimately defence against the disease depends on all of us taking responsibility for our own actions.' The feminist call for men to do just that has been something of a voice in the wilderness in the past.

Feminists could be exploiting the numerous contradictions in the Right and Left positions. Like how the Right's 'sex is dangerous' position rests incongruously with their advocacy of 'normal' heterosexual practice. Or the Left's espousal of an outdated liberation politics which substituted one form of women's sexual oppression for another. Perhaps the most satisfying exploitable contradiction is that of a government who, within the space of weeks, moved from attempting to ban sex education in schools, to having to promote frank and detailed information about sexual practice for the entire population!

Ironically, Aids has promoted the open discussion of sexual practice on an unprecedented scale. We should seize the opportunity to get into the debate, proposing alternatives to a penetrative heterosexual morality and place a radical, feminist analysis of sexuality firmly on the agenda.

## Notes

1. Sheila Jeffreys, *The Spinster and her Enemies*, Pandora Press, 1986.
2. Jeffrey Weeks, *Coming Out*, Quartet Books, 1977.

Thank you for ideas to: Al Dickens, Sue Scott, Harriet Wistrich and the National Advisory Service of Aids.

# PART THREE
## Family and Relationships

---

## Perhaps
Chrystos

I begin this to avoid my impulse to write her an invitation to dinner. We've muttered & mumbled greetings in the press of public gatherings, completely refusing eye contact, for two years. We were lovers for five. She might reduce this figure. This is my side. We've clung to our anger, rags of pride, to the wound two women who have loved so deeply create when they fling themselves apart. I loved her passionately when I left, clear only that if I stayed I'd end up dead or back in the looney bin. She taught me to recognize every variety of emotional abuse. Guns that are words. A special shredder for self-respect. Tortures to reduce the spirit. She would deny this. Even when I hated her most passionately, I could be made to agree that it had not been malicious on her part. That is to say, she did not know what she was doing. We both called it love. That's what you do call it, even when you know that you haven't got it right, that under the veneer of daily tolerance, the bones are sour & collapsing. I wanted a relationship that lasted the rest of my life. So did she. We were weary of bars, one-night stands, devastatingly inadequate affairs & polite feminist arrangements. I continue to miss our long rambling conversations late at night which went out to the sun & back catching all the light on the way. I console myself that she must also miss that gathering we did, especially as her current lover is stupid. I say this without malice although no one would believe me unless they met the new lover & secretly agreed, 'Yes, she IS stupid. Safe, no doubt though.' Of course, not even my closest friends will agree to this out loud, where it might be heard & criticized as a non-feminist statement. I'll describe her stupidity. It's an artificial creation, bolstered by years of avoiding confrontations with herself and others, denying, lying, refusing responsibility for her actions, seasoned with more varieties of drugs & liquor than one body should be required to

59

process. She doesn't remember what she does. This is a literal fact, called alcohol-induced brain damage. Cruel to call her stupid. Perhaps soon we will have an acceptable euphemism. I make enemies because I have such a bad habit of telling the truth. It's been made clear to me countless times that most people would rather hear about the emperess' new clothes, or at least find a more acceptable word to describe her than, 'naked'. Perhaps my ex-lover finds her new lover comforting. It would seem that she could not be a dangerous opponent, as I certainly was, in the struggle for love.

Why would I want to take this ex-lover to dinner? This is a question which would take me several novels to answer. I'm sure you've taken someone to lunch or dinner in the same spirit. Driven by obscure obsession. The need to understand what happened. To change what happened. To have the last word. Last bite. Last gasp.

This is not an impulse which attacks me from the blue. The poor blue which is blamed for so many of our more indiscreet & brutal actions. She happened to have dinner last night with my new lover. During dinner, she was of the opinion that she was ready to see me, but doubted that I was ready to see her. I internally disagreed vehemently the moment this was repeated to me. I've firmly believed SHE is the one not ready to see me for at least the last six months. Her opinion is interesting, particularly if you have the view of our relationship which is so clear to me now. During our entire life together, she regularly assigned me feelings (not necessarily with my consent or awareness), which she proposed to me, to friends, to strangers. This is what her mother did to her as a child. Control was the dominating theme of what we were doing but I wasn't to see that until long afterward. She decided what I felt, what should be done about what I felt. I was so hungry to be loved that I willingly went along with the program. Control was not important to me. If she wanted it, needed it so badly, I was willing to give mine up. She could run everything. I would do the laundry, wash the dishes, bolster her ego, cook, rub her neck or her head or her back & iron her shirts. There is much of heterosexual role-playing evident in this division of responsibility. I'm a child of my time (almost forty), a lesbian who came out in the butch/femme bar life at seventeen. The scars remain, no matter how many feminist pamphlets I read about becoming a carpenter. Probably as a result of this relationship, I've become obsessed with 'control'.

I debate about taking her to the fanciest restaurant on this island, which I cannot afford, but would do in the spirit of revenge. I work as a maid. She earns $40,000 a year at a computer desk job during which she primarily writes fifteen-page letters to my friends (who in the course of five years, also became her friends, as friends do). They've all maintained strict neutrality, which was a problem when I was at the height of my ravings about her Charles Manson character. I gracefully left her friends alone. I raged that she was not as courteous. I became obsessed with ethics. I'd quite naively assumed that my ethics were general policy. After hitting numerous very painful brick walls, I've discovered that ethics is a dirty word for the most part. I can't tell you how many women have righteously

60

denounced my clothes or hair (which is long) or my indifference to Marx. Responsible behavior toward others arouses no such interest. Indeed, it has seemed to me that the more a woman behaved like Attila the Hun (ravishing women left & right, including the lovers of her best friends, & denouncing everyone who doesn't agree with her), the more she was respected. Or enjoyed. Lesbianism clings so desperately to its outlaw status, with much the same atmosphere in bars as in an old MGM movie about frontier towns in the American West. Everybody wants to be the Jack of Diamonds.

I'd take her to the fanciest restaurant to prove that I could. That her money no longer controlled me. That I'm as good as she is. Money was a hand grenade we tossed back & forth. She came from an uppermiddle class background. She sulked when she could not afford to buy anything she wanted & she often went ahead & bought it via plastic card. She frequently showered expensive presents on me, which in the beginning I enjoyed, having been poor for the most part of my life. Later I resented the presents & now refuse expensive presents from lovers. They terrify me. 'What is the price?' my heart beats in a frantic rhythm. 'What are you trying to put over on me or take away from me?' She was an excellent fomentor of paranoia. The presents were meant, I think, to shut me up or keep me there or to prove that she loved me. Perhaps to prove it to herself more than to me, for I was absorbed in loving her in the ways I knew how. Her behavior was not loving. I can forgive myself for this or make the excuse that none of my early life was loving. Violence, rape, the peculiar lessons of the streets. My idea of love was shaped by Hallmark cards & sappy pictures of roses, as we all were. Loving behavior was not something I was aware of. I threw my heart after women (it seems now completely mysterious as to WHY I chose those particular women, but often I was not doing the choosing). I waved goodbye to myself. Pleasing. I have pleased my lovers to the point of hating them. The point was to get SOME ONE to love me & then I wouldn't hurt so badly. Love was going to heal the bag of scars I was. It has. & hasn't. When the idea of loving myself was first proposed to me, it had a bizarre ring. More of that UFO stuff.

Taking her to the Pleasant Beach Oyster Grill is a sign that I'm her equal. That she can no longer buy me. That any relationship between us must be based on mutual respect. That my need to be controlled and/or rescued by her is dead. She has consistently refused to come to the funeral. It's so difficult to make others change the way they see you. If you have been 'crazy', you remain 'weird', even when your behavior is impeccably boring. If you have been rich, you are still treated with respect, even if you end up on Skid Row. I'm reminded of an antique boyfriend from my smack days who had come from southern gentility. Everyone always gave him the first hit without noticing that they were.

I wonder if she has changed in two years. Her voice has sounded phony everytime I've had to hear it. Brittle. Perhaps she is so uncomfortable at the sight of me that she retreats behind her lady bountiful routine as defense. I wonder if it is possible to have a genuine friendship with an ex-lover. I'm always being told about them but I've never seen one I'd like to be a part of. Perhaps I expect too much of friendship. Yes, I do.

I realize as I'm writing that wasting money on a fancy restaurant is falling into the trap of living inside of her dimensions. We lived on this island long enough to have eaten at every one of the restaurants. Memories on the floors. Most of them have changed names at least once since we sat opposite one another as lovers. The floors are the same. How often in those years did I look at the floor while she pontificated on some subject or other? They taught her that in graduate school. Sometimes she was able to talk, particularly after getting stoned. In public, she lectured me. I don't remember a thing from all those meals. She needed to impress the other diners, the waitress or waiter, possibly the cook, impress upon them her intelligence, her distance from 'menial' labor, her education. She was terrified of being boring. I continuously reassured her that she was not boring until exasperated at the end I screamed at her that *everyone* was boring sometimes & she should go fuck herself. Perhaps this is why she has been reluctant to speak to me. We hate to have our dearest notions ridiculed. It has to be important whether she is boring or not. The importance of this issue is probably a disguise for some deeper & more painful issue. Only she could tell you what that might be. She doesn't want to know, however, & so none of us will. After devoting five years of gratis therapy to heal her of this & that, I can assure you that she prefers the surface of all things. Change is a dirty word. Perhaps intimacy is. It took me quite a long time to figure out that I was wasting my time, which probably makes me a fool. Perhaps it taught me to stop thinking I could heal the afflicted. I make such good meals you see. It's become a habit.

I'm a better cook than any of the restaurants here. I also set a more beautiful table & have exquisite music. I didn't consider having her here. An invasion. I don't trust her enough to cook for her. I don't want her to look at my plain glasses with her appraising eye. In the separation, she took the cut crystal her liberal mother gave us as a 'wedding present'. I miss their rainbows but would never spend $20 to buy a glass. They are probably much more expensive than that.

She'd probably refuse an invitation to come here. She's afraid of intimacy. I am her opposite in that I'm a junkie for intimacy, perhaps just as dangerous a disease. I don't want her in my home. Perhaps not for a long time. It is very odd to think of seeing someone in public as acceptable (as opposed to privately), when you've slept with them for five years. Slept is usually a euphemism for sex. In this case, it is not. Our fiercest, nastiest battles concerned my claim that she never wanted to have sex. She claimed that my demands turned her off. It was my fault. Perhaps it was. I think I can safely say, with her approval even, that we equally devastated one another on the subject of sex. I still see the blood around our ankles when we startle one another at the grocery store or the pow wow or in someone's living room or at a concert. She has told the grapevine that I am a sex maniac. I've told the grapevine that she couldn't get it up. Both of these statements are false, hateful, cruel &

true. The grapevine should be named after a more bitter fruit. It should be called the grapefruit tree.

In any case, it didn't occur to me until I'd written three pages of this, that I could invite her here. Dangerous ideas are the ones that surface after you've mulled something over. Perhaps they arise from the boredom of mulling. I need an anti-mull pill rather than an anti-depressant. Depression is a very sensible reaction to just about everything we live in now. But mulling makes me want to strip my brain out of my skull. I can mull for forty minutes on what to buy at the grocery store, which sheets to put on the bed, whether I want to clean the kitchen or go for a walk. I suspect mulling covers something deeper which I'm afraid to face. Perhaps you could tell me what it is. If we were friends. We must be friends or you wouldn't know all this. The floor goes out from under me as I recognize writing as a kind of pen pal system for discovering kindred souls. Perhaps you'll find the convolutions of this relationship illuminating to your own. Perhaps this thinly disguised pain will cause you to sigh with relief. Because there are no lesbian relationship ethics. We're free to treat one another as badly as we please. There is no community without shared ethics, which is why I refer to the 'lesbian gang' instead. Most of us were given very garbled versions of 'love'. There is certainly no graduate degree program in it. It is 'women's work'. We're supposed to know how to do it by instinct & we firmly believe that we do. I've known women in lesbian relationships as appalling as anything I've observed in heterosexuality (including partner rape, battering & murder). We see ourselves as 'better' because we have to, in order to survive the mainstream opinion of us. But we're not better.

I can't use her name in this writing. She's in the closet at work. Although no one from her work would ever read this. Not ethical to use her name because everything I've said could be hotly disputed. Perhaps even by my friends who are not hers also. I'm looking for the plot in this. I want to understand our motives, our lessons. I want to heal myself of this bitterness & even, though paranoia tells me I'm a fool, to heal her of the bitterness that I caused. I don't pretend to be innocent. During the relationship I concealed much of my distress in my journal. I didn't demand that she be more reciprocal. I let her use me. I thought, quite sincerely at the time, that using me was loving me. When I discovered my error, my rage was a razor. She continued to betray me in various ways. I could not see then that betrayal was her last weapon to get my attention. She was clinging to me, doing exactly what she knew would throw me into a rage in order to preserve *some*thing. If I was furious with her, at least I was focused in her direction.

Once in a moment of coherency during the fights of the final days, she said, 'I can't bear to lose you. I feel as if all the joy is going out of my life.' That sentence has echoed so often in these months, the words always colored with poignancy. She's probably forgotten she ever said them. Her consistent story, through the grapefruit tree, is that she left me, that I used her financially & drained her, that life with me was unbearable, better that it was over. For a while, I bothered to argue that I was the one with $4,000 saved when we met & I was the one who paid off her debts with it & I was the one who left & that she consistently used me as a domestic convenience. I stopped arguing when I realized two facts. One is that the listeners absolutely didn't care one way or the other. They were simply waiting for their chance to air their woes. Or they were sympathetic with the hope of taking her place. Some did. The other fact is that IT didn't matter. The fact of the breakup & terrible pain were aspects we were both forced to deal with, each in our contradictory ways. I spent the year obsessing about running my motor-cycle into any nearest tree, getting drunk & arrested & various other dramatic activities. She maintained that she was just fine, went to work, started new relationships, was above it all. The fact we both had to face was the same. We had failed as deeply as we had loved. Blame is irrelevant. Now we talk, through the grapefruit tree, of meeting for dinner. I could possibly send back through the tree, without actually committing myself to dangerous & vulnerable paper, that I was amiable to dinner or coffee somewhere neutral. We could spend several more months negotiating when, at whose convenience, where, with or without seconds (i.e., our new lovers), etc. I have my own car now (not as new as hers) so I avoid the humility of having to be picked up on this busless island. She nagged me the entire five years to learn to drive which I did as we were breaking up. A sour fruit I'm sure she clings to as desperately as I do to the one where she became lovers with the only woman here with whom I could talk about art. My new lover thinks I should go ahead & ask her to dinner. This seemed for an hour or two to be the 'solution'. Slowly I realized that this ex-lover whom I hate & love for knowing me so well, is right. I am not ready for dinner. I am barely ready to see her back in the parking lot. It is a back I know so well.

Feminism had high hopes that this sort of garbage between people was burnable, discardable. We could overcome it because we were women. It is exactly because we are women that we cling to it. This is our realm. Romance novels. No matter that our unrequited loves have breasts. This is what we are trained for. To love. To suffer in the claws of need & fear. It doesn't have to be this way we all say. Each new lover is an improvement over the last mistakes. We won't be fooled by this or that again. We fail to recognize that we are still playing the game we have been assigned – even if we play only with women.

I want us to create ethics, community, pay attention to ourselves (rather than the candy striper routine of saving El Salvador), stop using love to bludgeon one another. We cannot do much about a country where we don't live & the majority of us don't speak the language. We can do a lot about how we treat one another. We could ax the grapefruit tree. We could stop trashing one another. We could maybe find out a little something about this thing we're supposed to be expert at. Love.

# 'But of course I wouldn't want my friends to know you were a Lesbian': Lesbians and the Family

## Lis Whitelaw

I began writing this the day after I became an aunt for the second time. My nephew was born on my grandfather's birthday which pleased everyone very much; it made me think about families. Where do I, as a lesbian, fit into the structure of my family? Can I? Do I want to?

Ever since I began to think seriously about such things I have regarded the family as destructive; a battleground where struggles for power and individual identity leave all the participants permanently scarred and exhausted and where the best anyone can hope for is a wary armed truce. This belief was nurtured by the pop psychologists of the sixties – the time when my own struggle was just beginning – and in a film like *Family Life* one saw all the horror in action. Later, when I joined consciousness-raising groups, I noticed how often women talked about their relationships with their parents, and especially with their mothers, and how often understanding those relationships helped them to understand their oppression as women. But now, well into my thirties, I accept that relationships with parents are going to continue to be difficult and that, except in a very few, very exceptional cases it's too late to change anything. Most parents find it very hard to distance themselves sufficiently from their children to accept them as truly autonomous beings; the fact that their daughter is a lesbian reflects unfavourably on them and that is usually impossible to forgive. The parents who have the honesty finally to acknowledge that a lesbian relationship has been a source of strength are rare indeed. Not many mothers would have the grace of the woman who at her eightieth birthday party thanked her daughter's lover publicly, acknowledging that she was leaving her in safe hands. Now when I think constructively about families I think about my own generation and their children.

When my brother told me about the birth of his son and mentioned that a cousin had also had a son the previous day, I realised very forcefully how different my world is from theirs. And as we all get older the gap between our experience will widen and I will seem to be more different from them than I have done up to now. Up to now my unmarried, childless state has been contained within the acceptable possibilities for a woman of my age; soon my real non-conformity will become apparent. My immediate family know that I am a lesbian; soon, if they haven't done so already, the rest of them will start speculating. So why, if I am so aware of the gulf between me and my family, don't I just cut loose and enjoy my life as it is? After all, a great many people have nothing to do with their families.

There are a number of reasons, both personal and political, why I believe it's important to give the family another try. Britain's present government has politicised the family and homosexuals are being written out of the scenario. Clause 28 in the Local Government Bill which prohibits the 'promotion' of homosexuality mentions 'pretended family relationships' as something homosexuals should not claim to have. Does that mean that gay parents do *not* have a family relationship with their children or that those of us who are not parents are to be denied contact with our families? It is, of course, the very absurdity of this which shows how little those who drafted the Bill have really thought about who homosexuals are and how we fit into society. To them we are alien, beyond the pale and we must be suppressed. Those engaged in the current outbreak of officially sanctioned gay-bashing find it convenient to cling to stereotypes; it is easier for them to persecute us if they avoid knowing who we are. But how ridiculous not to realise our diversity and to insist that families can *only* be the most restricted unit – parents and children, and presumably from one marriage only – when so many people, straight as well as gay, live in much more complex and enriching networks of relationship. Recently a friend, a lesbian, working in local government and involved in a range of activities which are currently presented as worthless or, worse still, as subversive – CND, socialism, conservation – said, 'It's time to stand up and say, "We live here too."' She is right, we must assert our right to our beliefs and politics in the face of a state which seems increasingly intent upon eliminating dissent by controlling what people think.

But while we must confront the present we must also try to educate the future; and the family seems to me an important place to start. In one way the Right is correct about the importance of the family; it has enormous power to shape the way people see the world. That saying of the Jesuits – give me a child until he is seven years old and he is mine for life – may be a cliché, but like so many clichés it is also true. If we as lesbians cut ourselves off from the next generation where are they going to learn about our lives? If this government has its way they will not be allowed to discuss such matters with their teachers and there will be no helpful books left on the shelves of libraries. We will be back in a world where playground rumour and the caricatures of the gutter press will be all that is available to them – unless they hear the truth at home. And I want to be there to tell them that truth.

Recently, watching a film in which lesbians told their coming out stories, I was struck by one woman's statement that although she knew she was a lesbian herself she still thought of lesbians as 'sleazy'. That, I thought, is the problem: deep down that's what everyone thinks, even when they know lesbians who aren't. I want to do something to change that within my own family – for my own sake certainly, but also because I believe that my niece and nephew will actually benefit from knowing the truth. I want to shake off that 'sleazy' image which haunts us all, a convenient image for those who want to see us as an alien underclass. Only when you are perceived as a member of an underclass, as not fully a person, can you be told that

66

the disease that is killing you horribly is no more than you deserve. Most lesbians do not live in the twilight world depicted in the grimmer kind of lesbian fiction and it is about time that the straight world was reminded forcibly that we are not pseudo-men, child-molesters or sex-crazed neurotics. If those nearest to me become aware that while my way of life may be different from theirs it is, most of the time, no less humdrum and ordinary, then when my niece reads in a tabloid that 'disgusted husband unmasks so and so (name of well-known woman) in lesbian sex scandal' or finds that it is illegal for her teachers or librarians to help her find out more about lesbian lives, with the implied corollary that such information is 'immoral', she will have some experience of her own against which to measure the 'facts'. I am not, of course, so naive or so optimistic as to believe that I and those of my friends whom she may come to know can alone resist the tide of homophobia in which she will be swamped, but I do have proof that attitudes can change, quite spontaneously. In the past few weeks, while my lover has been seriously ill in hospital, my brother has been visiting and has had a chance to see our relationship in action; it has come as a surprise to him to see the level of support and commitment which we give to each other and which we receive from our friends. He readily admits that it all compares very favourably with what he sees in many heterosexual relationships under the same kind of stress. I think he has been most surprised by the discovery that instead of the isolation and unhappiness which he expected there is community and a community which can be relied upon. I am glad that for the first time he has seen my life as it really is and has been prepared to be a part of it. I am optimistic that his understanding will affect his children too, that he will encourage them to be honest enough to acknowledge successful lesbian and gay relationships for what they are rather than hanging on to the stereotypes.

One excuse that many parents give for objecting to the fact that their daughters are lesbians is that 'lesbian relationships are so unstable, you'll never be happy'. Leaving aside the many, well-documented monuments to lesbian fidelity, or perhaps tenacity, it seems to me that the family is a crucial, if potentially explosive, place in which to attack this notion. While it would be both foolish and dishonest to gloss over the problems that do beset lesbian relationships, we have to question the many false assumptions which make it possible for that statement to sound like an expression of caring. 'All right,' I want to say to my niece, 'are all the heterosexual couples you know happy? And what about the causes of instability, don't you think that other people's attitudes, their hostility and the need to lie, to live secret lives, don't you think that they may make it harder to sustain a relationship?' And then the big heresy: 'Maybe all relationships have a finite span and it's just that lesbians are more honest about calling a halt. Would it really be better to struggle on in misery for forty years, poisoning everything around you? Don't you think it's better to be honest about relationships? Has it ever occurred to you that instability is just another word for flexibility and that flexibility gives you genuine freedom? Maybe it's our freedom which makes us such a threat. Don't you think that a lot of people would like to be like us if they were honest about it?' If I say all that to my niece perhaps her definition of a lesbian will be more accurate than the one I grew up with: 'Well, you see, dear, there are some women who'd really rather be men.'

But these are not the only reasons why I want to be involved in the lives of my niece and nephew. Until recently, except for my work, I lived my life almost entirely among people of my own age. I now have a lover very much older than myself and that has meant that I spend time with her older friends, but it has also made me aware of how segregated by age the lesbian community is. At a recent meeting of twenty women no one was younger than her mid-twenties and no one older than her late forties. It seems to me a great pity to restrict the range of experience in which one shares, and while everyone tends to have friends of roughly their own age, families are a useful short cut into the warp and weft of society as a whole, a way of cutting across age differences. When I first became a lesbian I believed that the lesbian community offered an alternative, a complete world; that once I found my way in, I would need no other sanctuary. I know better now. Having, reluctantly, given up the idea of all-embracing lesbian sisterhood, I find that my own small community provides much of what I had hoped for from the 'lesbian nation' and much more than anyone can hope for from their family. Friends, lovers can provide far better than the family intimacy, acceptance and love. And, if you are lucky, with few of the preconceived patterns which dog family relations. For the really close relationships, friends and lovers undoubtedly provide far more than the family. Oddly, it's on a more superficial level that they fail, in providing those loose interconnections which I am beginning to value more than I would have expected. Your friends can't provide the sense of connection to the past and the future which the family offers effortlessly. Individuals both much older and much younger than oneself can provide strands reaching back and forward, but I detect in myself now a desire to be part of a web, stretching in all directions, connecting me, regardless of what I do or what I think, to my own history. I am surprised, but not dismayed, to find that I am pleased to be told that my niece looks like me or is showing signs of developing some of my interests or abilities. Five years ago I would have dismissed such ideas as unsound, inappropriate; now I can admit that I value such connections. There are some parts of my life which only members of my family have shared in and I am not prepared to discard those parts as unimportant just because I do not live in a conventional family myself. At the same time, in order to share that part of myself with my family, I am not willing to disguise my lesbianism; it is my past as well as theirs and I need to claim it on my own terms. As a writer and biographer I am more and more interested in tracing the connections and networks that bind people together; as I get older I am prepared to acknowledge the importance of that web for myself.

At one stage of my life I was prepared to reject the *theory* of the family while maintaining close and often painful contact with the reality of my own. The family was a symbol of conformity and an agent of social control which I saw as dangerous to my development both as a lesbian and as a feminist. For women to be free the family had to be destroyed. It is perhaps significant that when we talked like that we were talking primarily about the small, nuclear family. All of us who lived through the sixties and early seventies know about the alternatives to the family, the communities which sought to replace the destructiveness of the nuclear family with the benevolence of the extended one. All the communities I knew failed and I am now convinced that the reason they failed was that ultimately people cannot live solely in the context of their own generation; they have to move into wider networks of involvement. A few, a very few, manage to manufacture these networks independent of any blood ties, but the people involved are very unusual.

When I first became a lesbian I was rather excited by the image of myself as an outlaw and saw no objection to the idea of living a large part of my life in a ghetto; now I want to connect, as myself, with a wider range of people of all generations. Of course I recognise the appalling effects of the family; I am fully aware of how it always oppresses women and often betrays children. It is just because I do recognise all this that I don't believe that the family should be left to the heterosexuals. This is especially true now, when the idea of the family is being manipulated by the political Right for its own purposes: presented as a repository of all acceptable morality and expressly offered as a bastion against the 'perversion' and 'evil' of a homosexual way of life. We must acknowledge, and force others to acknowledge, that we, as lesbians, have a legitimate and particular place within the family, not hiding behind euphemism and fictitious heterosexually broken hearts, but presenting an authentic and viable alternative of women living their lives with and for other women which is readily available to all generations of women within our own families. As Cicely Hamilton put it as long ago as 1909: 'Those women who are proving by their lives that marriage is not a necessity for them, that maternity is not a necessity for them, are preparing a heritage of fuller humanity for the daughters of others – who will be daughters of their own in the spirit if not in the flesh.'[1]

# Notes

1.   Cicely Hamilton, *Marriage as a Trade*, reprinted 1981, p. 144.

# The Hard Part of Mothering

Lisa Saffron 🖋

The answer is yes, I did know and no, I don't regret it. If I were perfectly honest, I would have to admit that there are times when I wished I'd never done self insemination. These are the times I'm stuck in rush-hour traffic with my blood sugar level plummeting to zero and a self inseminated baby screaming that I'm not a good enough mother. Luckily those times are rare. Usually, I either remember to bring crisps, coca cola and sweeties to keep her quiet and raise my blood sugar level, or I manage to grab the edge of her car seat and shake it with rage. Sometimes I stop the car and scream with her. Then we both laugh and I think, Nu, so what's so hard about being a mother!

It is bloody hard in many ways. I have lived with Dena for nearly three years and there are great times – times of real pleasure in her, intense love and good fun. But the things that make it hard are sometimes overwhelming. Here I'm writing about what I find hard about being a mother and my attempts to make it easier.

The hardest part for me is that Dena refuses to let me be a Good Mother. I keep trying – I read the childcare books, I listen to advice from all and sundry – and I realise I'm constantly doing it all wrong. I know very well how a Good Mother should act and I'm a total failure.

Good Mothers have children who are cooperative and clear up after themselves. When my daughter at two and a half years spills her yoghurt, I hand her a cloth and say calmly and assertively, 'I want you to mop up the yoghurt.' She replies just as calmly and assertively, 'No thanks!' and walks out of the room to attend to more important business. I proceed to have a full-scale tantrum. I want to be the one in control.

Good Mothers are always patient no matter how demanding their toddlers are. I can't tell you how many times I've shrieked at, slapped and shaken mine. I've even called Parents Anonymous in utter despair at my uncontrollable rages, only to be told that it's very bad to shake a child. I tried to explain that I wasn't doing it because I thought it was good for her. However, the volunteer on the other end of the phone had no further advice when I complained that I couldn't be patient when I felt exhausted, lonely and desperate.

Good Mothers respect and validate their children's feelings but limit their actions. They have such a good relationship with their children that once they let the child know that his or her feelings are understood, the child is eager to please. Dena at two has a favourite toy monkey which she wants to bring with her to the childminder's. I know that only Bad Mothers cause full-scale tantrums by grabbing favourite toy monkeys out of the determined clutches of a two-year-old. So I squat down at her level, look her in the eye and say with authority, 'Monkey can't come with you to the childminder. You have to leave it here though I know how much you'd like to bring it with you.' She tightens her grip and utters the one word she practises daily: 'NO!' 'I see you really feel strongly about that monkey,' I say with empathy. She nods vigorously. 'You wish you could bring the monkey with you to the childminder.' I'm oozing with understanding. She nods again and marches towards the car with the monkey in a vice-like grip. I rush back into the house, find the parenting book that got me into this mess in the first place and re-read Step 4 'IF THEY DO NOT OBEY, REPEAT THE COMMAND. When the child discovers that you do not give up, give an entertaining minor nervous breakdown, or get sidetracked, then he simply gives in.' I go out and repeat the command. 'Leave the monkey in the house.' She screams, 'NO.' I re-read Step 1: 'BE CLEAR IN YOUR MIND. IT'S NOT A REQUEST, IT'S A DEMAND WHICH YOU HAVE A RIGHT TO MAKE.' I decide to opt for the entertaining minor nervous breakdown and be done with it. I wrench the monkey out of her arms, jump up and down and scream, 'I don't know why you want to take that god damn stupid monkey anyway.'

Good Mothers are everything I'm not. I have a Good Mother demon inside my head who constantly tells me I'm doing it wrong. If I get on with the housework, leaving Dena to play on her own, the Good Mother demon chides me for being neglectful and failing to stimulate her with educational toys. If I encourage Dena to learn the names of the animals in her zoo book, the Good Mother demon accuses me of overstimulating her and of not letting her learn in her own time and way. If I give her junk food, the Good Mother demon is horrified. If she doesn't eat the wholesome food I put in front of her, the Good Mother demon claims that's my fault as well. If she won't clean up after herself, the Good Mother demon demands to know who is in control, the adult or the child. But if Dena wipes her mouth and bib with a cloth after every spoonful, the Good Mother demon wonders anxiously whether I have created a neurotically obsessive personality.

I have gradually learned that I can never please this demon. To all observers, Dena is a happy, strong willed, self sufficient, adaptable, sociable child. But according to the Good Mother demon, this has nothing to do with mothering. It is entirely due to Dena's innate personality. I know that the only way I can win is to forget about trying to be a Good Mother. My challenge is to accept both myself and Dena for who we are. Basically, we're okay. Knowing and believing that is the hard part.

I knew before I decided to get pregnant that mothers suffer from exhaustion, isolation, loneliness and invisibility in what seems like a child-hating society. I'd also been around enough children to be aware of the problems that arise in each stage of the child's development. But it's one thing to know about it and another to live with it. When I was exhausted, I was irritable, prone to violent outbursts, constantly sick with flus and often despairing. Having lived with exhaustion for several years, I now don't think anything is more important than being rested and well. I can cope with anything on a good night's sleep.

Isolation and loneliness is another hard part of being a single mother which I thought I could handle better than I have done. It is still almost impossible for me to sort out how much is my paranoia and how much is objective reality. I live on my own but for most of Dena's second year, I couldn't spend time by myself without panicking. I felt abandoned and desperate, convinced that I wasn't important in anyone's life. I 'knew' that I ceased to exist in the minds of my friends as soon as a visit ended. I felt that I was forced into solitary confinement because no one would 'allow' me to spend time in their company. It seemed like a wilful conscious act on their part not to contact me. I would sit by the phone every evening after Dena went to bed waiting for it to ring. When it didn't ring, my worst fears were confirmed. It *was* true that I had no friends. When the phone did ring, I felt resentful. Just when I'd be settling down to a good solid evening of misery and pain, a friend would call. I often caught myself moaning. 'No one ever calls me except X and Y and Z.' At one point, I got myself in such a state that I unplugged the phone and hid it in a cupboard for several weeks. I only told one friend what I was doing and she came by every day to check on us. No one else seemed to realise that I was sulking. It wasn't a particularly useful exercise and I wouldn't recommend it.

I decided I had to keep time alone to a minimum so I spent hours trying to make arrangements for the weekends and evenings. It took tremendous courage and emotional energy to ring my friends and remind them of my existence. I was certain they didn't welcome my calls and I tried to spare them the burden of my company by not calling very often.

My visits with them did not make me feel less alone. When I was with friends who had children, I felt jealous of the attention the children received. I wanted to drag the mothers off for an adult chat and leave the kids to play together. But most of my friends are Good Mothers who believe in stimulating and instructing their children at every opportunity. I never admitted that I got bored playing with stickle bricks and reading *Meg and Mog* stories. I also found that talking about children with other mothers wasn't the best way to get support (unless they were having as hard a time as I was). When I tried to share the rages I felt toward Dena with my lesbian friends, they stared at me in pity. One woman clucked sympathetically and said that she too had felt rage towards her daughter about six weeks earlier and had even raised her voice. This was at a time when my throat was sore every day from screaming at Dena and I was close to strangling her several times a week. Luckily for me, quite a few of the heterosexual mothers I'm friends with are also Bad Mothers like me.

It has taken me a long time to realise that it's not possible for me as a single woman to have close friendships with mothers in couples. They will never need a friendship with me the way I need them. When I'm around couples who are raising their children in nuclear families, whether lesbian or not, I feel an outsider, excluded, peripheral, an illegitimate family. I can't hold on to my own sense of validity. I listen to them complain about the weekend their partner was away – how difficult it was to spend all that time with a small child, how they filled up the time with activities and visits to friends and how they could never do it all the time like I do. I feel perplexed and wonder why that awareness doesn't cause them to invite me over more often – to realise that I'm just the same. Sometimes I think scornfully, 'You spent a weekend alone in the company of a two-year-old – big fucking deal!'

It seems as if it's just as hard for a couple to raise one child as it is for me. I certainly envy the sharing and caring that members of a couple give each other but it doesn't seem to make childcare that much easier for the individuals involved. Once when our babies were all younger than four months, I went with a lesbian couple and another single mother on holiday. We set up a rota for cooking dinners but although there were four adults, the couple acted as a single unit, claiming it took both of them to cook and care for their baby. The two of us who were single mothers could manage both feats because we had to, and because we expected to be able to cook with one arm and carry a baby in the other.

My expectation of lesbian mothers is probably a big reason for my feeling isolated. I am part of a lesbian community. I know lesbians with children and I have been to various Lesbian Mothers Support Groups. I wanted and still want the lesbian community to be like family for me, especially since I have no family in this country. I thought our children could grow up together like cousins, that we'd be in and out of each other's homes, that we could call on each other when things got tough. But it hasn't worked out like that for me. Perhaps I attach too much significance to the label 'lesbian mother'. I thought I fitted into that category until I had a frank discussion with a friend who is in a lesbian couple. She told me that it's more important for her and her lover to be visible as lesbians than for me. She felt that she has no choice but to be out whereas I can pass as a single mother like thousands of others in this neighbourhood. I have never denied or hidden my lesbianism and I don't cease being a lesbian when I'm not having a sexual relationship. She left me feeling invisible even in the lesbian community. But just because we are all lesbians, with young children, living in the same neighbourhood, it does not mean we're going to be friends.

I finally decided that what I found hard about parenting was being a single mother. Being a lesbian mother hadn't created any special problems for me. At a particularly desperate time in my parenting career, I came across a poster advertising a workshop entitled Parenting Alone. It was run by an organisation called Exploring Parenthood which described its workshops as 'a chance for parents to learn about and exchange ideas and worries about bringing up their children with each other and with members of the EP team of child and family therapists, doctors and psychologists'. It sounded promising despite the fact that there was more emphasis on professional involvement than I am used to. I went along to a workshop.

We divided into small groups, each with a professional as group leader. I wasn't sure if there would be any other lesbian mothers there but I felt that I would have enough in common with heterosexual single mothers to make the day worthwhile. Until the word lesbian passed my lips, we had been openly and honestly talking about our different situations and how we were coping. Then suddenly they were no longer able to make eye contact and the subject matter shifted to my sexuality:

'Did your parents have a particularly bad relationship?' (No)

'Were your parents heterosexual?' (Yes)

'Were they real heterosexuals? Are you sure they weren't closet gays?' (I'm sure)

'Are you going to tell your daughter that you're a lesbian?' (Of course)

'Do you want your daughter to be one?' (I have no preference. At least she'll grow up knowing there's a valid choice)

'Are your friends who have children in normal couples?' (Yes, they're normal lesbian couples)

'You mean there are others like you?' (Indeed)

While I was being forced to defend lesbian motherhood, the workshop leader made no attempt to focus the discussion on to what we had in common as single parents. After lunch (during which I was pointedly ignored), the final blow was struck by a woman who still called her youngest child a bastard and had just divorced her third husband because he had attacked her son and had a record for paedophilia.

'Your reasons for having a child are purely selfish. You did it out of your own insecurity. The only valid reason for having a child is if it grows out of the love between a man and a woman. What you are doing is AGAINST NATURE!'

I was shaking too badly to speak and spent the next half hour trying to breathe myself into a calm enough state to walk out. During that time the conversation moved on as if nothing had happened.

The next day I phoned the workshop leader and expressed my anger at her for allowing the anti-lesbian abuse to continue unchallenged and for not making the workshop a safe place for me to share my troubles. She simply repeated over and over that she could see how distressed I had been and that Exploring Parenthood would provide free counselling for me to talk about the parenting problems I face. She never accepted responsibility for her role as workshop leader nor apologised for the distress she had caused me by her total lack of awareness. In fact, she asked why I had said I was a lesbian in the first place, since I had volunteered the information myself. I got the message that if I wasn't prepared to deny my identity, I had better be prepared to justify it. Some support group!

When I wrote to the director of Exploring Parenthood, I received a revealing but totally unsatisfactory reply. 'We would state at all times, and if you had stayed for the final session you would have heard the assertion, that Exploring Parenthood is an organisation for all parents in whatever situation they find themselves, or choose to be.' I doubt whether I would have found this reassuring since their assertions had already been contradicted by their actions. They went on to say in the letter that 'it would be worth discussing the provocative position you took up with the group. We believe it is fine for people to press for their positions but manner and style can affect the response of others, and lead to rigid and hostile stances being assumed, negating any chance of adjustment and exchange.' I wonder what in particular constituted provocative behaviour – the simple statement 'I am a lesbian' or my assertive response to the barrage of questions about my sexuality. I also feel overwhelmed by the responsibility they placed upon me. Not only did I provoke the group but I caused the others to assume rigid and hostile stances and I made exchange impossible.

Luckily, the letter went on to explain what they meant. 'Indeed, Exploring Parenthood may not be right for all parents, as a reflective rather than didactic (teaching) style cannot possibly suit everyone.' Yes, that was true, Exploring Parenthood workshops are certainly reflective, not didactic. In the workshop I attended, they reflected anti-lesbianism very effectively. Black women attending their workshops will undoubtedly discover how well they reflect racist attitudes. Jewish women who don't hide their Jewishness will experience the reflection of anti-semitism. In fact, any woman who doesn't fit the 'norm' will experience the reflective style of Exploring Parenthood. However, we won't be labelling it reflective. We'll call it oppressive.

I published my account of the workshop in *Spare Rib*, a feminist magazine. To my surprise and delight, several feminist organisations responded by writing letters of protest to Exploring Parenthood. The Rights of Women Lesbian Custody Group arranged a meeting with the directors. They came away with the impression that the directors, at least, were open to learning and did support my right to be a lesbian mother. They said that there had been an 'energetic and wholehearted challenge of the homophobic hostility shown by some workshop members'. Unfortunately this didn't begin until after I had left. The directors also accepted that this was not good enough. I was encouraged by the apparent success of these tactics and am willing to re-open my mind about Exploring Parenthood. So, if another lesbian mother wants to try out one of their workshops, I wouldn't put her off. I just won't go with her.

Sometimes it's necessary to try a completely new angle. My latest 'new angle' has nothing to do with humans at all. I decided to take Dena to the City Farm once a week to feed the rabbits – a good way to fill up time during the long weekends, putting no unrealistic expectations on friends, and doing something socially worthwhile and educational in the process. However, the animals have not been properly grateful and have refused to provide the kind of education I had in mind for Dena. The geese took one look at us coming, hissed viciously and charged straight for Dena who by this time was clinging to my head. The rabbits produce a powerful spray of piss for such cute cuddly creatures. Dena got hit in the eye by one such spray and hasn't been overly fond of rabbits since. The donkey marched over apparently to say hello and bit Dena on the leg, leaving a huge bruise. I don't know what the chickens have done but she leapt up the nearest ladder as soon as they came into view. Our original enthusiasm for the farm has waned somewhat.

I haven't given up on getting support from friends, lesbian mothers, couples, single mothers or farm animals. I keep struggling with it in my own fashion. I like to think that I'm gradually growing in awareness and self acceptance. I still have moments when I have to withdraw from certain people because I find the relationship painful. Sometimes I regress into bitterness and loneliness. But there are times when I can see that I am not alone, that there are people in my life who do care about me. And Dena herself is one of them. She's nearly three now and finally talking. Today I came home from work exhausted and irritable. Before long we were both screaming at each other and sobbing. I was too tired to do anything but snap and snarl. Eventually I collapsed crying with weariness. She climbed into my lap and said, 'Let's calm down. I love you.'

# Exposure

Lorna Hardy

> I walk in the garden
> the rain is wet on my head
> every twig, every leaf, drips
> low clouds drape about me
> but high in the sky
> the light vibrates
>
> I feel like a rose bush
> pruned beyond recognition
> I have been promised midsummer profusion
> but at present I look austere,
> my bark is toughening
> I have big thorns
>
> my feet dig deep in the wet black earth
> seeking my source
> the sap rises,
> throbs through me
>
> let me be soaked with love

I wrote this poem in March 1984 when I was twenty-nine. I had not had a lover since July 1981, and I was feeling lonely and desolate, though determined not to give up hope altogether. I had realised with a sudden horrible jolt that the best part of my twenties had been spent on my own. Ever since splitting up with a boyfriend of four years standing when I was twenty-one, I had never been lovers with anyone for more than two or three months, with increasingly long gaps in between. The pages of my diary are filled with a procession of women I was obsessed with, but, every time I fell in love, it either came to nothing, or the woman would decide, after a brief experiment, that she did not want to be lovers after all. She would explain, kindly, but firmly, that she was very fond of me, but that she just wanted to be friends. . .

I'm writing this piece because I've never read anything about what it is like to be a loverless lesbian. I'm not using the word 'celibate' because for me that implies a deliberate decision not to have a lover, and that's not what I'm talking about. However, I suspect that this article may ring some bells with any women who have gone for long periods without lovers, whether by 'choice' or not. I know I'm not the only woman who has been in this situation, and I wanted to break the taboo surrounding the subject. It's very difficult to talk or write about, because you can't help feeling people will think you must be 'inadequate' in some way if your relationships with lovers don't usually get off the ground. The pressure to have a lover or lovers – to be known to have *someone* to have sex with – is at least as great in lesbian feminist circles as it is in straight heterosexual society. Most of us would die sooner than admit to sexual disappointment or defeat. I probably wouldn't even be writing this now if my long-term plight of loverlessness were not – for the time being at least! – in abeyance.

Lesbians and feminists are supposed to have challenged oppressive notions about sex and sexuality, love and romance: yet the imperative 'Thou shalt have a lover' is one that almost all of us have internalised. So if, for whatever reason, we don't have one, we feel that we have failed, and that others are likely to look on us with either pity or scorn. It is acceptable, in lesbian feminist circles, for women to grouse about their lovers, or to cry about their broken hearts: much more rare for any of us to break down in public and say, 'I'm fed up because I haven't slept with anyone for eighteen months. I'm feeling really lonely and deprived, and I'm frightened that I'll never manage to make a lasting relationship.' The fear of being perceived as sexually or emotionally inadequate by our lesbian feminist peers must have condemned many of us to suffer in silence when, as always, sharing our experiences could ease the burden and give individual women the comfort of knowing that their own situation is not all that unusual.

For me, being on my own for such long stretches has meant a great deal of anguish, though only my nearest and dearest, at least until recently, have known quite how much I have suffered.

How did it all come about? I have interrogated myself over and over again about what it is in me that puts people off. I've got lots of friends so I can't be a totally obnoxious personality, yet I am certainly lacking in the sort of magnetism which attracts potential lovers.

Like most people, I suppose, I am a bundle of contradictions. I am sociable, but I also like solitude. I am very affectionate, but fiercely independent. I am passionate, but extremely reserved; articulate, but find it hard to talk about my feelings. I am quite conceited, I admit, but incredibly self-critical. I think of myself as very strong, but I cry easily, and am often deeply afraid. I am bold, but I lack self-confidence. A common complaint about me is that despite my friendliness, I seem to remain aloof. I have kept a diary for years in which I have scrutinised my every feeling, action and motivation – and yet there are things about my personality which remain as much a mystery to me as ever!

I fell head over heels in love four times between 1977 and 1981, but in every case my feelings were thwarted and I felt I had to dam up a torrent of emotion that had nowhere to go. The women were all quite different, and I felt that I approached each relationship in a different way: the only common denominator was that none of them wanted to pursue the affair. I was enthusiastic, affectionate, considerate – so what was I doing wrong?

A poem I wrote about one of these relationships shows all my yearning, all my hesitation, and above all, my fear of imposing myself on someone else. It is noticeable that I bend over backwards to be fair to the other woman. I strive to be reasonable; and significantly, I all but silence my anger and resentment at being let down:

## I sent a letter to my love and on the way I lost it

hello you
you, who shall be nameless
for the time being
you keep getting into my dreams
which is unfair
because it's there that I have least resistance

it must be your animal magnetism my darling
which makes my body go on hoping
long after my brain has accepted your indifference

I think you thought I was trying to sew us together
needle and thread taut and tearing our fingertips
so you put your hands behind your back

you who wooed me under the moon in June
phoned every night to croon and make jokes
I had all the power then
I was circumspect as usual
fearful for my little heartbud
keeping control
we made no promises
I had no expectations
better that way in case they get dashed
you said you loved me and I was pleased
but I never said I loved you
in case it wasn't true

you were demonstrative
in the heat of your glee
I decided to let myself go
I unfurled my fist of feeling

till it was open and trembling
I wanted to stroke you
I wanted you to cuddle me

but you put your hands behind your back
and you had all the power then
my love came pulsing through
but what had that to do with you, you asked
incurious
so I felt obsolete

I remonstrated with you
(I was remonstrative)
but you were unimpressed
and so I remonstrated with myself:
to go on loving where love is not wanted
is a waste of energy and a humiliation
it's also trespassing
so stop it
and so I've tried to stop
I've clenched my fist again in self-defence

but now I fear
(because it's not the first time that I've had to do this)
I fear the damage I have done:
I might stop feeling altogether
I might not ever ache again, with pleasure or with pain

and yet I know that can't be strictly true
I know because my heart still leaps up
every time I see you
and at the party we danced womb to womb
and mine caved in

and as I said
you keep getting into my dreams:
I dreamt I was wearing my slinky black dress
you grasped me under my arms
your hands in my perfumed sweat
and I succumbed again to your demand

then my dream came true
you were really in my bed once more
laughing me out of my pyjamas
and caressing me to sleep
(you call that 'acting naturally':
I could not come to you without an invitation)
I kissed you, kept my mouth shut

I cannot trust you, and it's hard to like you much
but when the moon is full I hanker for your touch


I can remember that when I wrote this poem I did not want to
come across as harsh, or spiteful, or petty, or weak. I was prepared

to allow myself to express longing and disappointment (good romantic qualities), but not base emotions such as resentment or vindictiveness. I think it has always been very important to me to be seen to be *generous*: even if someone hurt me I would not stoop so low as to try to get my own back. I even changed the second-to-last line from 'I do not like you much' to 'It's hard to like you much,' in case I hurt the feelings of the woman concerned! I was much harder on myself than I was on her. In the original version, the last few lines of the seventh verse read:

> *to go on loving where love is not wanted*
> *is a waste of energy and a humiliation*
> *it's also a rape and an imperialism*
> *no wonder it's not wanted*
> *so stop it*

I changed these lines when a friend objected to me characterising myself in such vicious terms.

Yet at some level I must have sensed the violence I was doing to myself by denying my anger a voice. The first draft continued:

> *and now I fear*
> *(because it's not the first time that I've had to do this)*
> *I fear I might stop feeling altogether*
> *as if I'd given myself a massive dose of ECT*
> *wiped out the nerve cells that were troubling me*
> *so they could never ache again, with pleasure or with pain*

The same friend objected to the reference to ECT, on the grounds that it trivialised the experience of women who had actually been subjected to shock treatment. Perhaps this is true, but nevertheless this image does give a vivid picture of what my intuition told me I was doing to myself. And the implied connection between anger and madness is very striking.

Anger, hatred, envy, malice – I don't allow myself the luxury of any of these emotions. They are nasty, cruel, selfish, wrong: at some very deep level I still consider them to be *sins*. I received my earliest moral education from my mother, an agnostic pacifist, deeply influenced by her Scottish Presbyterian forebears, and at the age of twelve I became an evangelical Christian. The overriding principle I imbibed from my mother, and found attractive in some versions of Christianity, is that it is wrong, in almost any circumstances, to cause anyone pain. The hidden message behind this is that given a choice between hurting someone else and hurting yourself, you should choose the latter. I gave up Christianity when I decided that God himself didn't match up to this principle if he was prepared to torture millions of souls for ever and ever in hell. But when I adopted feminism, I think I simply transferred many of my Christian values into my new faith. The general principle of loving thy neighbour and obeying certain commandments was very similar. It was now all right to hate men, but *on no account* to hate women. Women were to be supported unconditionally (as long as they weren't racists, or Mrs Thatcher herself) and their faults, if any, were to be explained away with reference to their oppression. In effect, I still believed in turning the other cheek. Ironically, with my particular background and personality, some of the basic tenets of white middle-class feminism actually served to *prevent* me from really asserting my own needs.

I now realise that I have swallowed mountains of anger over the years. When lovers vacillated and hurt my feelings and deserted me, I always thought that I was in the wrong for wanting something that they couldn't give.

It is noticeable that on several occasions I have got involved with working-class women which, because I am middle class, has exacerbated the situation even more. Whereas I felt that I never had any right to be angry in the first place, I could see very well that they had *every* right to be angry. If they let me down I felt that was just something I had to bear.

What I didn't realise, of course, is that not everyone has grown up with the same taboo on anger as I did. Within my family, conflict was always to be avoided at any cost. I must have grown up believing that if I got angry, I was no longer lovable. I now suspect that some of my lovers must have found my very reasonableness and endless accommodation to their whims infuriatingly insipid, but because I was always so 'nice', they couldn't get angry with me. I can't help wondering if I didn't drive some of these lovers away by my very inability to lose my temper once in a while.

In all these early, unsuccessful relationships, then, as soon as the other woman showed any sign of doubt or withdrawal, I never allowed myself to assert any claim of my own, and was always cautioning myself about being too importunate, as this tortuous extract from my diary shows:

*I don't know what is going to happen with our relationship. I don't know what I want and I don't know what she wants. I am actually quite suspicious about my own feelings. I have this awful fear that I want to possess her, make her mine in some way, rather than that I really desire her. The fact is that although I like her so much and think she is so attractive and really want her to be my lover, I cannot testify to any great feelings of sexual arousal ... The question is, am I really just hell bent on getting a lover, by hook or by crook? Is that my motivation? Or do I really and truly want a relationship with A, for herself? There is no doubt about it, I do feel ever so fond of her and admiring of her and drawn to her. So perhaps my negative feelings/anxieties/inhibitions are coming from my fear of rejection: I cannot allow myself to feel too strongly, to let myself go, in case I get hurt yet again.*

*It is uneven, because it seems that I do want to see her more than she wants to see me. Am I going to get impatient? Is she right when she says she is apprehensive because she doesn't think she can give me as much as I want? Am I going to find myself breathing down her neck, or trying desperately not to breathe down her neck, always self-conscious, insecure, frustrated, unsatisfied?*

*It wouldn't be so bad if I didn't have such strong ideological objections to the whole concept of wooing, because to me, wooing implies drawing someone beyond where they would go voluntarily, and possibly the concept of knowing better than they do what their own feelings are (or might be).*

*What I would like more than anything else in the world at the moment would be to be mutually in love, with someone wanting me as much as I wanted her. I haven't experienced that since the first few weeks with B. It would be lovely to be loved, so long as it was someone I was also in love with, and not to feel, as I always do, that I am the one with all the love on my side, and I am only an irritation and a bit of a problem for my lover . . .*

It is possible, of course, that my moral/political objection to the idea of putting a lover under any pressure whatsoever (which I thought stemmed from my determination not to treat women as men have treated us), was in fact really a rationalisation of my own ambivalence, if on a deeper level I was actually scared of becoming involved. The effect of my measured, almost fanatically honourable approach may well have been that despite my protestations I came across to my lovers as less than 100 per cent enthusiastic. I may have seemed to be saying: 'I want you madly – but don't worry, I don't expect you to respond – and don't think I can't get along without you . . .'

It has been suggested to me more than once that at some unconscious level I do not really want a lover. It could be fear of sex, fear of getting too dependent on someone or of someone getting too dependent on me, fear of feeling invaded or feeling trapped . . . Women whom I have fallen in love with may well have picked up on this ambivalence: the message I allegedly give out which says, 'Don't get too close to me!' It's a plausible theory, and it may very well be true, but all I can say is, that is certainly not what it *feels* like: if I am in love with a particular woman, it feels like I desire her passionately and she does not desire me. If I have no one in particular in mind, it feels like I desperately want a lover, but nobody wants to be lovers with me.

So if I *am* warding other women off, it is certainly at a much deeper level than I am aware of, or can consciously control!

However, I have to admit that there probably is something in this theory.

As far back as my teens, I was lamenting the same problem, and in remarkably similar terms. I craved a soulmate, who at that time I envisaged as male, but the boys I fell for never seemed to fancy me, even if they thought I was an interesting person.

For some months when I was sixteen or seventeen, I was infatuated with an arrogant and self-centred boy whom I endowed with all the qualities of intellectual brilliance and romantic sensibility that I thought would befit my partner. I was baffled that despite his apparent regard for me, he persistently chose to go out with girls who I saw as 'flighty' or 'scatterbrained'. How could there be a marriage of true minds in such circumstances? I tried very hard to win his interest, and was mortified when he split up with one girlfriend and started going out with someone else, and once again it wasn't me:

*I am in a quandary, not knowing the reason why he didn't choose me – because to me at least (!) I was the obvious choice!!! ... The trouble with me is that I exude no animal urges. I am so proud and so shy that I keep my feelings tightly pent up inside me. Oh how I wanted to scream my feelings at him, storm him, take him by surprise, say, 'This is me! Do you want me?' But no, I wouldn't let myself, in case I discovered that he didn't want me ... I have never had any physical contact with him, and perhaps this is partly the trouble ... Oh how I want that boy! (And yet I can't help thinking – typical me – that because I am so infatuated, I will probably go off him if and when he becomes mine!!)*

Between the lines of this self-conscious angst, I can detect the same patterns which continued to dog me in my twenties, as a lesbian: I fall in love with someone who wants to be my friend, but not my lover. I try to woo them with my mind, and am aware of being inhibited physically. Inside I am a seething cauldron of longing, but outwardly I appear detached and unruffled. And finally, despite all my desire, I suspect that I might 'go off' my beloved once my wishes are fulfilled!

This hesitancy, I think, is very significant. 'Exposure', a poem I wrote in 1982, captures my continuing ambivalence. Although I express my sincere desire for a lover, it is clear that there are things I like about being on my own:

# Exposure

I live as Artemis the virgin
hunting the truth
with my bending bow
and fearsome arrows

I live in a cave
high in the pointy mountains
gulping the icy water

On the slithering pebbles
I stand in the stream
and my feet ache

It is best under the moon and stars
when the brilliant face of the night
smiles down on me

I have feasts of my own
wine and nectar from my own source
until my bowels howl with keen delight

But I am not content
I crave another huntress
fierce and tender as myself
to wrestle with
her breasts as sweet as fruit
our honey and our cream to stir and mingle

Sixteen lines celebrate a rarefied and even ecstatic solitary existence; six lines cry out for a sense of connection with someone else (and even she is to be my mirror image).

As far back as I can remember, I have had a passionate, almost loverlike relationship with my own self, and perhaps it is this characteristic which others find off-putting.

It's double-edged! It's a vicious circle! Because how could I have survived for so many years without lovers if I did not love myself, if I did not have resources of my own on which to draw, if I did not enjoy my own company, if I could not pleasure myself sexually? And on the other hand, perhaps I would not have had to go it alone for so long if I had not given off an air of self-sufficiency.

And I know that this air of self-sufficiency, though partly unconscious, has also been partly deliberately cultivated. I am ridiculously proud; I cannot bear to be thought of as a failure, in any aspect of my life. No wonder I have not wanted to appear to be a failure at sexual relationships, which have such high status in this society.

So I have put on a brave face and probably given the impression that although I don't have a lover *at the moment*, I am getting along quite nicely thank you, and am certainly not desperately seeking Susan! Cool, you know, and competent; not hankering and yearning. After all, I have my friends, my work, my writing, my political activism . . . I'm always busy, never bored. Never have to spend an evening on my own if I don't want to. And only those closest to me, my sister, some of my friends, and some of the women with whom I have had these fleeting relationships, have heard me express my loneliness, frustration and lack of fulfilment.

Many women in this society grow up with very low self-esteem, doubting their own judgement and their own worth as human beings. My own dilemma, however, stems from virtually the opposite experience.

When I plumbed the depths of distress a couple of years ago, I turned to *Dealing with Depression* by Kathy Nairne and Gerrilyn Smith (Women's Press, 1984). I found some things in the book very helpful, but on the whole I felt that the advice given did not address itself to my particular predicament. I wrote in my diary:

*I would have found it more helpful if the section on 'Images' had included more about the conflicts you go through if you grew up believing yourself strong and powerful, rather than useless and worthless. I have not personally experienced much of the stuff which is described about growing up with a 'feminine' identity, and I am unmarried, not a housewife, have no children, etc., and do not rely on men for approval. But that doesn't mean I am conflict-free.*

My self-confidence clearly derives in part from my origins: I am white, middle class, English, born and brought up in London – but that is not the whole story. I was a good deal younger than my brother and sister, and soon learnt that people would be impressed if I seemed very 'grown-up' for my age. My ideas were always listened to and valued by my family and my teachers, and so I felt respected as a person. At school I was outstandingly successful academically. This might seem like an advantage, but in reality it's a tremendous burden: the older you get, the more vital it becomes not to slip from your pedestal. I liked to think of myself as creative and talented, but it was my *intellect*, above all, that I relied on. I scoffed at the notion of male superiority; but I wasn't interested in feminist ideas at first, because I did not feel personally oppressed. I knew that I was a match intellectually for any male, and there was never any doubt in my mind that women were as valuable as men. Up till the age of sixteen, anything that I set my mind on, I achieved, by a combination of native wit and sheer determination. But when it came to finding lovers, I had to learn that these aren't particularly relevant qualities. Intelligence and willpower did not bring lovers queuing up at my door – in fact they had quite the opposite effect. This made me feel very powerless.

I did make one successful long-term relationship, with a young man, at the end of my teens. Even then it is probably significant that he was away a lot of the time at college, and that when he finally returned to London, we split up. My new-found feminism dictated that I should not 'get into a rut' with any one person, however cosy that might be. I had also begun to experience the first stirrings of desire for women. I wanted complete freedom for sexual and emotional adventures. I think I imagined a life-style where I would have numerous lovers and together we would explore all the possibilities of totally non-possessive sex, love and friendship.

For a short time perhaps it seemed that this fantasy might be realisable. In the next couple of years I slept with a handful of women without any expectation of long-term commitment. But these encounters did not happen often enough to provide me with much sustenance. And then, in the instances where my heart did become involved, I suffered all the agony of rejection.

Gradually the fantasy of the wandering lover faded; I simply did not end up in bed with women often enough! But it had never been my intention to be celibate. I began to want *a lover*, not monogamous necessarily, and certainly not as a prospective life-partner, but someone to share the present with. But time and again, as the years went on, the women I wanted to be lovers with were not interested, or soon lost interest, in being lovers with me. If this happens once, or even twice, you feel disappointed; but if it goes on happening you begin to lose all confidence, in yourself, your feelings and your judgement. Women who slip easily from one relationship to another or who have never been turned down by anyone they have proposed to can scarcely imagine what it is like to meet a series of rejections. I found it totally undermining. After my second disappointment of 1981, things went from bad to worse, and I entered my Desert Period.

After five years of intermittent, abortive relationships, I spent three years without getting involved with anyone at all. My longing for a lover had not gone away, but I didn't seem to fall in love with anyone any more. I became very confused about what I wanted. I made a rather half-hearted proposal to a friend of mine which, not surprisingly, was turned down. I did not feel any of the romantic passion I had experienced on previous occasions, and was even more beset by doubt and hesitation than usual. My diary account of the episode reads like a parody of former entries:

*On my way home the tears began to fall. Not because I am madly in love with her – I am not mad enough to let myself fall in love with anyone any more before they have begun to fall in love with me – but because I am so lonely and I do so want a lover and I like C very much and think we could have a nice time together. I have got my fingers burnt so many times that I am really reluctant to make the first move with anybody, yet in a way perhaps I ought to, just to put myself out of my misery. I don't want to work myself up into a state about her if it's going to be another non-starter. On the other hand, since I really do want a relationship, is the slender chance of success worth the big risk of another rejection? Certainly I think that rejection at this stage would be better than vague and tentative hopes sprawling out for heaven knows how long and then a rejection!*

*A phone call seems very brazen and my success rate with letters has not been spectacular, but I do seem incapable of bringing things to a head in personal conversation. So I shall have to think more . . .*

*In the end I decided I would phone her . . . I didn't really have much hope because I did feel that if she was going to make a move she would have made it by now . . . Anyway, I spent about twenty minutes plucking up the courage and rehearsing my lines, forced myself to be bold, and phoned her.*

*She went very quiet once I had told her, which certainly does not bode well, and she said she was taken aback and that it hadn't crossed her mind and she had just thought of being friends really. I said to her not to panic and I didn't expect her to answer straight away and whatever her decision was I would accept it with equanimity. That was the difficult part: to indicate (so that she wouldn't feel unduly pressured) that if she says no I won't be heartbroken, without making it look as if I am completely indifferent . . .*

My confidence sank lower and lower, and I began to fear that I would never be able to climb out of the rut:

*The terrible thing is that I have got so used to not having a lover, and so used to sexual rejection, that I don't see how I am ever going to break out of it. And whereas I used to see my loverlessness as temporary setbacks, it now begins to feel like permanent reality.*

I became even more tongue-tied than ever, finding it even harder to confide in anyone about what I was feeling. My friendships began to suffer from this exaggerated reserve:

*I know that what I do is be superficially friendly and jokey and have stimulating discussions but hardly ever confide in people or speak frankly about my emotional life.*

*There's a lot involved. For one thing, one reason I am reticent about my 'emotional life' is because I never have a lover, or never for long enough to begin to feel secure in it, and I always feel shy and ashamed about this, and left out when other people are talking about sex or relationships.*

*On the other hand, if I wasn't so reserved I would probably have a lot more sexual relationships to talk about!*

Sexually, I was not totally frustrated, because I had always been able to reach more delicious and earth-shattering orgasms on my own than with anyone else. (A fact which is probably not unconnected to the overall predicament I am describing! I am aware that it could be seen as symptomatic or symbolic of my self-love and my difficulty in opening up to other people.) But of course I missed the sensation of sharing and exchanging sexual pleasure with someone else, and the sheer sensual delight of flesh upon flesh. Also, I wanted to feel that others found my body desirable.

But the real deprivation I was subject to was emotional rather than sexual. I felt I was missing out on a very important dimension of life, that I had a lot of feelings that had nowhere to go, despite the intensity of my involvement in other things. For, even when I am not in love with anyone, I still experience strong passions: powerful emotions towards my friends and family; exhilaration when I write; passionate involvement in my work as a teacher; and a very strong emotional response – anger, grief, urgency, ardour – to what's going on in the world at large. So I tend to live keyed up to quite a high pitch emotionally; yet, if I don't have a lover, I still feel that I am missing out. There is always the wish to be more central in someone's life; to have someone to share all these emotions and ideas with, and to build up a stronger sense of intimacy and continuity, development and commitment than seems possible even with very close friends.

I went to Greece for five weeks in the summer of '83, and once again lamented my sorry plight:

*My desperation does not ease off, it grows, as time flies past, and still nobody wants me. It's over two years since I had a relationship, and all my relationships have been so very unsatisfactory. I honestly do not know how other people slip in and out of relationships so easily, or hang on to them when they've got them.*

*I also feel worried because it's not even as if I have come into contact for ages with any women with whom a relationship would be remotely feasible. At least before I was falling in love with women from time to time, but for so long it has been a virtual blank. . . And so I fear I have lost my capacity to feel sexual for someone. Which doesn't make my wish to have a lover subside in the least, but it probably makes the appearance of one much less likely, as I simply won't be giving off the vibes.*

*And all the time, this feels really wrong. I am an affectionate person, I cannot live without love, even though I am strong and independent. My youth is going past. It just seems so unfair. And I just don't understand why so many people are fond of me, which I know they are, and yet no one who I fall in love with ever falls in love with me.*

*I dreamt last night that Mum was telling me again that I ought to get a boyfriend. I was resisting her but I know that in the dream as in real life Mum's concern is for me to be fulfilled and though she doesn't know the details of my relationships with women, she does know that I am not fulfilled. And of course she sees it in terms of getting a man.*

*And in fact I think that loneliness and desperation could drive me into the arms of a man, except that I have never been good at catching men either – I think I repel them by my pride. And I don't think I would feel fulfilled with a man, I think I would feel askew. Yet I could get some relief, I think, if only of a transitory nature, just to be cuddled and held by another of my fellow beings . . .*

Strange to relate, about two days after writing that entry in my diary, I slept with a man – for the first time in seven years. No one could have been more surprised than myself, though in retrospect perhaps it isn't so amazing. In Greece, on my own, far away from my normal social circles – where I would feel inhibited, to say the least, about sleeping with a man! – I found I could be that much more playful. It didn't mean anything, so there wasn't anything at stake. He was a very nice man, and though he made it clear that he was keen to sleep with me he didn't put me under any pressure at all. (If he had, I would have rejected him without a second thought.) However, although I liked him personally, his love-making left a lot to be desired, to put it mildly. I was quite astonished at his incredible sexual selfishness and insensitivity. My verdict in my diary?

*At no time, neither before, during nor after last night's adventure, have I felt that my lesbianism was in the least bit threatened by my fling. It remains my ardent desire to establish a passionate relationship with a woman, and I am convinced that is the only way I will find emotional and sexual satisfaction. I don't think my lesbianism is endangered by sleeping with the odd man, but I do think it is endangered by not sleeping with any women. It is excruciatingly difficult to maintain a lesbian identity, against all the odds anyway, when all you are getting is the disadvantages, and none of the pleasures of being a lesbian.*

*I do not regret last night for one moment . . . I think I needed it, to restore my confidence in my own attractiveness as well as for the sheer physical contact . . . This escapade has made it seem that getting a lover is not so totally impossible.*

However, it was to be over a year before I did find a lover, and when I did, the experience was absolutely traumatic.

When we first slept together, I was thrilled that at long, long last, a woman who I regarded as so fascinating, witty, charming and beautiful wanted me as much as I wanted her. I suspected that we were not compatible on a deeper level, but what the hell, I thought – if I always insist on these strict criteria, no wonder I never have a lover! So I took the risk. 'I'm So Excited!', by the Pointer Sisters, became our theme tune.

After my years in the Desert, I would have been prepared to take a lover on virtually whatever terms she named, just so long as there was mutual desire. If all this woman had wanted was a casual fling, I think I would have been quite content with that, and probably wouldn't have got so hurt. As it happened, what she seemed to offer was a more 'meaningful', committed relationship. Within a few days, she was talking of living together and having children together, and although to me this seemed like a far-fetched fantasy, I found it very alluring. It was as if she had reached in and turned on the tap that I had been keeping so tightly screwed up all these years, and out gushed all my longing and need, the need to be loved and cherished and desired and appreciated, the longing to build a sexual relationship which would last and develop and grow.

What to other women might have been a fairly insignificant affair – it lasted just under six months, and we were patently unsuited to each other – was of enormous significance to me. My years of loneliness made me so much more vulnerable; the fact that I was thirty years of age and had been a feminist for the last ten years, armed with a hard-hitting critique of romantic love, turned out to be no protection at all.

We were deliriously happy together for about six weeks, but after that things began to go wrong. We were divided by race and class, by my lover's bisexuality and by our fundamentally different approach to everything from politics to social life. We had soon utterly disappointed each other, and lost all trust.

One of the difficulties was that I found it hard to make the transition from being 'single' to having a partner. The whole structure of my social life, and to some extent even my identity, was based on the fact that I had been single for so long. I had numerous commitments, which I wanted to honour, but which my lover was jealous of. I did make enormous efforts to adapt to my new circumstances, but I couldn't go far enough to meet her needs. I was held back partly by the genuine wish and need to see my friends and participate in lesbian and anti-racist politics; partly by the feminist tenet (which I still largely subscribe to) which says it is wrong/unwise/dangerous to immerse yourself in a sexual relationship at the expense of everything else; and partly, no doubt, by my own fear of losing my identity, or as my mother would put it, 'getting too wrapped up' in somebody else. I was also struggling with a job which I found at best extremely demanding, and at worst tremendously stressful and exhausting, and which drained me of much of my energy. The consequence of all this was that my lover felt neglected, which is supremely ironic, since I was totally and utterly obsessed with her and with our relationship, and wrote of nothing else in my diary for months.

The more frustrated my lover became at what she saw as my inflexibility, the more unreliable she grew. The more she let me down, the more dependent I became, until I could hardly recognise my own personality. What had happened to the free and independent spirit I had always prided myself on? I felt cruelly ill-treated and rejected by the woman who, only a few months before, had promised to love me forever.

As usual, I tried to see things from the other woman's point of view. I strove to be patient, reasonable and just, even when I felt that my lover was being blatantly selfish, unreasonable and unjust. My forbearance must have irritated her no end. Her behaviour was increasingly provocative, but since I was still incapable of giving vent to my anger, I responded mainly with tearful reproaches, which of course alienated her even more.

The last three months of this relationship were absolute hell, but I didn't tell even my closest friends the details of what I was going through, because I knew they would advise me to break it off, and I was determined to keep it going, whatever happened. I couldn't bear it to be just another flash in the pan, like all my other affairs.

My dreams warned me that my integrity was in danger, but I refused to listen to my own intuition.

Paradoxically, because I was aware that inflexibility is one of my faults, I was doing my utmost to be flexible, and I lost all sense of where to draw the line. I seem to find it very hard to set the boundaries: to know how to preserve my own identity, without warding everyone else off; how to open up sufficiently to be loved, without laying myself open to abuse. At first this lover had experienced me as too stand-offish, but now she seemed to fear being drowned in my bottomless need. The more she withdrew, the more desperately I clutched at her for reassurance: but all this brought forth was her contempt. And I was so used to being criticised for having standards so high that no one could ever live up to them, that I over-compensated, and did not insist on being treated even with simple courtesy. In other words, I let her walk all over me. For months afterwards, I had nightmares in which I was robbed, captured or held hostage, forced to involve myself in crimes against my will. In reality this period lasted about six weeks, at the end of which I admitted to myself that the relationship was bringing me more pain than pleasure and (to my lover's great relief, I think), I told her that I didn't want to go on.

When we split up, we tried at first to remain friends, but we just couldn't manage it. My grief at losing my love was like a giant, and I think it terrified and repelled her. She was disappointed that things hadn't worked out between us, but she wasn't devastated, as I was, and she did not accept any responsibility for my feelings. My anguish seemed out of all proportion to her. Within a matter of days, she had started a new relationship, with a man; she wanted to look to the future, not harp on the past. I was aghast at her casualness, her callousness. I had been addicted to her, as to a drug, and was now going through all the agonies of withdrawal. I had to cry myself to sleep all alone, while she could snuggle up in bed with someone else, and if she did feel any pangs of regret (which I doubted), he could comfort her and make her feel she was still lovable.

I sank into the deepest, most prolonged depression I have ever known. The depression, in fact, lasted a good deal longer than the actual relationship. For months, I cried almost daily. All it took was for someone to ask me how I was, to set me off into floods of tears. I, who had weathered all previous heartbreaks with a brave face, was unable to do so this time, and I kept breaking down in public. I usually eat a lot, but for once I lost my appetite: food literally stuck in my throat. I started waking up much too early in the morning. Rather pale and thin at the best of times, I got even paler and thinner.

I felt bereaved. Clearly I was mourning not only the loss of this particular lover and the death of this particular relationship. What I was grieving for, really, was all the lost years, all the failed relationships, all the hunger and yearning that had gone unsatisfied for so long. It was like wanting a baby for years on end, getting pregnant, and then having a miscarriage.

I never want to go through such suffering again: and perhaps I won't have to, because I do feel that I was transformed by the experience. It may be that I needed an explosive relationship like that to blast me out of the rut I had slumped into.

One positive side effect was that whether I liked it or not, I had to open up much more to my family and friends. I couldn't pretend that nothing was wrong when I kept bursting into tears all over the place. I received heaps of love and kindness and support, sometimes from sources where I would never have thought to ask for it. I was comforted not only by those close to me but also by women who I would not in 'normal circumstances' have confided in. I think the quality of my friendships has been enriched, now that I am no longer so afraid to reveal my own vulnerability.

I also made three new friends in this period, all women suffering from broken hearts and delinquent lovers, and gained great strength from sharing the experience of battling with grief and recurring depression. So many times I thought I had finally 'recovered', and then I would find myself plummetting back down into the abyss. I would feel I 'ought to be better by now', two or three or six or eight months, perhaps, after the event. Seeing these other three women also going up and down, taking a long, long time to heal, reassured me that I was not the only one.

The other significant result of my disastrous affair was that it propelled me into psycho-therapy, which not only helped me survive the immediate crisis, but also enabled me to identify and explore certain long-term patterns. In fact, I doubt I would have been able to write this article, if I had not had the experience of therapy.

I am currently involved in a very different kind of relationship: not as passionate or dramatic; much more soothing and supportive. And it has already lasted longer than any previous lesbian relationship I have had. So the future does not look so bleak after all.


Not having a lover for a long time must be a difficult experience for anyone in this society, whatever their sexual orientation. If you are a lesbian, however, there are certain specific additional pressures: the most obvious example being the crucial issue of identity.

Lesbians have had to fight tooth and nail, not only to defend our right to exist, but even to prove that we exist at all. We have had to make a song and dance about the fact that we love other women, and that we express that love sexually. And even though being a lesbian is to do with much more than just sex, sex between women remains the distinguishing factor, as well as being the vital element which provokes the horror of our enemies. Until the rest of the world becomes indifferent to the thought of women making love with each other, we are going to have to assert our right to do just that. Inevitably, however, lesbians are seen simply as 'women who sleep with other women'. So if you have hardly slept with any other women at all, or at least, not lately, you don't feel like a 'real' lesbian. (Just as, if you are a writer who hasn't written anything for the last year or so, you begin to wonder if you are still entitled to call yourself a writer.) The lesbian without a lover is doubly invisible, and sometimes it's hard just to keep on keeping on.

In my own case, being without lovers so much has also greatly prolonged the process of coming out within my family. It took me about seven years to come out to my mother, mainly because for ages I didn't feel I had anything positive to show for my lesbianism. Since she lives very near, I see her very often, and we are very fond of each other, this put our relationship, at times, under an extraordinary strain. I did partially come out to her on several occasions, and made it pretty clear that I was no longer interested in men, but I found it hard to talk to her about being a lesbian with a great deal of conviction, when not one of my relationships had flourished. And of course, my silence on the issue made it easier for her to cherish hopes that eventually I would find a nice man to settle down with.

Thus in 1983 I recorded the following conversation in my diary:

*When I went to see Mum the other day she asked if D (my sister) had a boyfriend at the moment, and I said no, and then she said, 'What about you? Have you got a boyfriend?' (which she so rarely enquires into) and I just said, 'No, there isn't anybody,' and I felt quite weird not saying anything more, not saying, 'I don't want a boyfriend, I want a girlfriend.'*

*How can you assert your lesbianism when you never have a lover? It doesn't make sense, and I didn't see the point in making an issue out of it. If and when I get a lover, then there might be a reason.*

At the same time as being evasive with my mother, however, I was increasingly outspoken both in my writing and amongst my colleagues at work. This put me on the front line in a way, and made me feel quite vulnerable and exposed. This is why it felt as if I was getting all the disadvantages of being a lesbian and none of the advantages. I was laying myself open to increased anti-lesbianism, without either experiencing the satisfaction of sexual fulfilment or enjoying the reassurance which a supportive relationship can provide against the homophobia of the world at large.

On the other hand, of course, it isn't true that I have experienced none of the benefits of being a lesbian during my periods of loverlessness. I may have missed out on the sexual side of things, but at the same time I have drawn great strength and comfort from all my lesbian friends and acquaintances. In this respect I feel I have been luckier than many heterosexual women, or isolated lesbians, who have not been successful in their relationships, and have no such supportive community around them. The peculiar intensity of lesbian friendships, the shared experience of oppression and struggle, and the shared perspective on the world, are some of the things which have most sustained me in difficult times.

In my teens I thought that romance was a hoax but that love was real, and that the essence of love was commitment. In my early twenties I thought that love was a hoax but that desire was real, and that commitment was just a euphemism for dependence. Then I spent a lot of time on my own. In my late twenties, I learnt that desire was socially constructed, and that independence wasn't all that it's cracked up to be. In my early thirties, I recognise that knowing desire to be socially constructed hasn't lessened its grip on me: and what I desire at the moment, for better or worse, is love with commitment. So I seem to have come full circle.

This article is dedicated with love and thanks to Shameem Kabir, Peg Jennes and all the friends and relations who helped me through a difficult time.

# Strange Days

## Sigrid Nielsen

1.

*Strange Days* is the title of an album by a rock band called the Doors. I first heard it in 1968, at university. *Strange* was a word that had followed me through the small towns and suburbs where I had grown up; it was still with me at age 20, though, now that I had fallen in love with a woman friend, I was beginning to be aware of other, more precise words as well. I walked around the campus in short-cropped hair, woollen trousers, and boots; it was as much of a statement as I dared to make. People who were too strange, or were strange together, had a way of receiving headed letters from the university and not being seen again. Everyone else was polite and cheerful, like radio voices from the other side of the world. It was 1968, and students were said to be changing society, and in a vague sort of way I agreed with the idea; I tried on the newspaper stereotypes of youth and power in my fantasies, shrugged, and got on with everyday life. At the back of my mind there was just the suggestion that things could, somehow, be different in the future. That was the story I told myself about the cover of *Strange Days*.

The cover showed the Doors wandering through a drab street: they looked lonely, tired, and dazed. They were all wearing outlandish costumes, but they were facing in different directions and none seemed to have noticed the others. One was juggling wooden pins in the middle of the street; his strangeness was on show for other people's amusement. But the picture was a subtle piece of work; something about the scene suggested its exact opposite. In another moment, the Doors would notice each other; they couldn't miss each other in those absurd clothes. They would get together; they would be the Doors, the interpreters of wonderful and bizarre realities, a group. And they would leave the street for a better place.

I haven't seen the cover of *Strange Days* since the sixties, while the story has been with me for a very long time; the memory may or

93

may not be accurate, but the story is still clear. Years later, I read an essay by Joan Didion, an American writer, who was assessing the Doors and other figures of sixties culture. *We tell ourselves stories in order to live*, she wrote. Put so baldly, I thought this was a sentimental idea; we tell ourselves stories in order to feel alive, not to live. But as I look back on my time at university, I realise how much I needed the story. It told me who I was and where I was going, something other people were only willing to do on certain conditions. During a period when I was dating a presentable young man, the university became a different place, a place full of subtle welcome and encouragement. Once that phase was over, the scene dissolved into the usual genteel wasteland. The story told me not to worry. Someday, things would be different. Someday, I wouldn't be so strange. Someday, everyone would be strange. I did not wonder what would happen to bring this imaginary future into the present. In the late sixties some unknown future always seemed to be about to land on top of us; everything was a surprise. I believed in the strange days precisely because they were so unlikely. Perhaps I would move to Paris and become the subject of sonnets by violet-scented women in tuxedos. Or perhaps it would be a matter of gradual change, and in a few more years old ladies would greet me with warm smiles as I stomped along the pavements. I couldn't afford to think about what I wanted realistically; I needed my story of a different future too badly to be able to consider the possibility that it might only be a story. And in fact, there was no serious reason to think I would not live the rest of my life just as I was already living, with a secret which was not a secret and created a magic circle of fixed smiles and silences wherever I went.

That was one way of looking at my dilemma. Another, simpler way was that I lacked the vocabulary to describe what I was hoping to do. I had never heard of *coming out*. Above all, I lacked the concept of a *community*. 'When you're strange, people come out of the rain,' sang the Doors, and as it turned out, they were right.

But they didn't tell me what was meant to happen next.

## 2.

Saturday night some of us from the bookstall were walking in Inverleith Park. The castle looked so clear it was almost on top of us. We started serious, then the jokes got sillier. Almost like a family. I thought of walking with my father in the evenings years ago when I was growing up, all of a sudden for no reason.

Life seems to have a track, a base.

The interview with M [a woman playwright] yesterday was good. We were anticipating each other. Almost reading each other's minds. I felt free to speak. I wanted to be her friend, but I lack the feel for involvement with many people, even as friends. They pull me in complex ways, I feel off balance.

By the time the strange days arrived for me, it was the early eighties. I was living in Edinburgh: at the time I wrote the [reworked] journal entry above, I had just taken my first job in a radical bookshop. I was also working with a feminist publisher, a lesbian group, a women's writing group, a mixed gay bookstall, and others.

94

One of the habits of thought which belongs to unpopular minorities is the belief that you can see the truth of things more clearly than other people. A great deal of lesbian writing is founded on this assumption – which, I think, grows out of the experience of having a secret for many years. You, of course, always understand the secret, while others stare the evidence in the face time after time and see only what they expect to see.

In this journal entry I showed that I, too, had selective vision, just like any normal human being. I looked forward to a future in the lesbian and gay communities; I was already writing and thinking about myself as someone who had a right to a certain kind of acceptance, a place in a certain scheme. In those days, only a few years ago, my claim made a kind of sense which is hard to recapture now. The demand for all our groups' services was growing all the time and we took that as a guarantee that the community would also grow. And not only grow: deepen, establish itself, change our old ways of living and thinking.

Yet, as the journal clearly showed, I was still a person who lacked the feel for anything but isolation. And most of us in the lesbian community were in precisely the same dilemma. We were not used to other lesbians; especially not to twenty, thirty, fifty other lesbians; least of all, to telling them anything. For us, belonging came out of smoothing and sanding the truth, making it acceptable. 'I kept my real feelings from my mother,' one woman told me around the same time. 'I kept them from my workmates. I kept them from my children. After a bit I wasn't all that sure what I felt myself.'

Somehow the lesbian community would change all this. Not gradually, but quickly, to judge by the way I wrote about it in the journal. My wished-for future was so vivid that it made the present look theoretical and lifeless. In this land of someday-now, I had roots, a place, 'freedom to speak'. And somewhere in the background of the picture, distant yet magically clear as Edinburgh Castle looked from the park on that summer evening, was the idea of a family. A group which would accept each woman exactly as she was, because of what she was, because she was a lesbian.

It seems almost simple-minded to describe any of this as an *ideal* or an *illusion*. Those of us who worked as open lesbians or gay men did our best to live it out, unselfconsciously and unobtrusively, in our everyday working practise. To me, the point of the exercise, and the proof that the community could exist, was that I was getting on with my life without The Great Secret, without being The Only One. We often talked as if our shared identity were a stage of development which any gay person would naturally reach, given a little perseverance; looked back on the days each of us had believed herself or himself to be 'the only one in the world'; occasionally realised that it was very hard to remember what things had been like when you were 'still in the closet'.

It was hard to remember. But as time passed I began to realise that it was harder still to see the community as it really was, in the present, uncoloured by the promised future or the memory of life in isolation. Now and then it would strike me that we all talked constantly about work. Even at parties and in the pub, we talked in the rhythm of work talk, quick and concise, always moving on. Occasionally I would realise how little I knew of my friends' own points of view; all our stories were stories about each other, and ultimately about our group, not about ourselves.

A friend of mine, a woman outside the community, told us once that she thought we spoke in code: she had known us for months, but she literally could not understand us. Later, in private, a few other friends let me know they had serious misgivings about the idea of a women's community. They were, in fact, disillusioned. The disillusioned were mostly refugees from split collectives; they lived alone, and made excuses when other women asked them to join new groups. They seemed to hope I was not really listening to their doubts; I felt they were saying that the failure was theirs, not the community's. But the implication was clear: someday, I would be there with them.

I began to realise that openness and isolation were not simple; it was not enough to decide that one was good and one was bad and to say so whenever possible. But I could not accept that there might be isolation built into the idea of the community. I don't think any of us could. It was too much like saying that the idea itself was unworkable. Even the disillusioned never tried to explain how they had become disillusioned; I asked one woman, and realised the next minute that it was a brutally tactless question, and one she could not answer. As time passed, and just as she had predicted, I also acquired a set of questions I could not answer. It is only now, a few years later, that I can look back and try to understand why the strange days were so much stranger than anything I had imagined.

3.
We went into the trendy cafe and sat down. A woman in a huge black coat, *Guardian* under her arm, was arguing with a weedy young man.

On our right was a group of dykes talking about motherhood and turkey basters. On our left was a thirtyish woman on her own, leafing comfortably through the papers after a long day at work.

I thought how rare it was to have a scene like this actually in front of my eyes; there must only be a few cities where you could go somewhere and expect to see people like these. We all made fun of the trendiness of the place, before we went in, while we were there, and as we walked out. We were covering for ourselves. We needed that place, and didn't want each other to know.

In becoming active as a lesbian, I took on a role I had never heard described in any detail; it lacked even a name. No one seriously calls herself a lesbian activist. One friend of mine (another worker in the mixed gay booktrades) suggested 'professional lesbian', one night in the pub. It was a good joke, and we all laughed.

None of us discussed what we thought we were doing. We spoke as if it were very ordinary, something which looked a little odd but shouldn't have done, like being a female printer. We called ourselves 'bookshop worker' or 'collective member'; what counted with us, we seemed to be saying, was day-to-day work, nothing more.

As time passed, I became more and more involved with the work, to the exclusion of whatever else there was in the role. I am still not sure how that happened. The commonsense explanation probably accounts for a great deal; as the eighties wore on, there was less money and less energy to draw on, but even more demand for our services, so that it took that much more work to keep a small group or business alive.

I worked full time, first for Edinburgh's radical bookshop and then for Lavender Menace, the lesbian and gay bookshop I had helped to found, and which had grown out of the mixed gay bookstall. I worked with other groups as well, held down a part-time job in order to support myself, co-edited a book of short pieces, and struggled to keep up my own writing. Most women I knew were working just as hard or harder. One friend apologised when I arrived for a weekend visit just before midnight on a Saturday, to find her in a meeting which had already lasted for eight hours.

Many more people than we generally realise, work hard. I have read about 96-hour weeks in industry and 36-hour days on gay publications. Some government officials, according to stories, regularly go without sleep for days, except what they can snatch in taxis or during sessions of Parliament. And housewives, of course, are said to work a 99-hour week without pay. What work means to most of these people is hard to say, since few talk or write about the effect of their jobs on the rest of their lives. I would not like to claim that lesbians, or feminists, are unique in overworking. But I had never seen anything like it in any other job I had done.

At the beginning, when I first joined the community, I had what seemed endless energy. The world had never seemed so large, but I had never been able to live on so little. Perhaps many of us had had that experience, and perhaps we made it the standard for all our work afterwards. Whatever the reason, many of us seemed to go around in a state of permanent exhaustion. At times I worked for days without a break and grew used to seeing afterimages around every moving object. Sometimes I would be so tired that my mind would go comfortably blank whenever no one was speaking to me; I called that 'the white noise stage'.

The more I worked, the more I became absorbed in the work, and that led to isolation. The work was interesting; the booktrades have their own awful and wonderful jargon, and their own skills; and lesbian books were a new field which opened a great many possibilities. But although this work was done for the community, its focus was no longer squarely on the community. It would not have been very different in an ordinary bookshop, except that it would have been for some purpose other than reaching lesbians. And having reached them, it did not necessarily bring them into anyone's personal acquaintance. There were very few places for any women to meet other women, even if they were convinced they should go out in search of the community.

As a result, my work as a bookseller seemed abstract; far away from the immediate concerns of the other women I knew. It was isolating. It was not, however, as I think back, the only thing that was isolating; a certain kind of isolation had been there all along. Because there were so few places or reasons to meet other lesbians, we used voluntary work as a kind of social life; but though we worked for the community, we did not work as a community. Each of us was solely responsible for meeting her own deadlines: 'unreliable' was the most damning term in our vocabulary. Each person in a group was expected, not only to pull her weight, but to guess, and guess correctly, how much weight was enough. Many women contributed more than their share (and if they didn't, it was almost always because they had other commitments). But it was difficult to know exactly what your share was or when you had given it. The sense of living up to expectations, being needed, connecting with other women, was elusive; though not by anyone's choice, or for any reason we knew.

Every now and then I would meet women from 'outside' the community and realise how great the resistance to joining was; and what a high price other women felt they would have to pay. One woman confessed that she admired the novels of Graham Greene and stood waiting for me to try to make her feel ridiculous. When I told her that I agreed, she looked alarmed; this wasn't in the script; I must be planning something even worse than usual for her. Another woman did a bookstall for a voluntary group, spent the entire time telling me that 'women novelists haven't got it right yet', and vanished when a newspaper photographer appeared with a camera; she never returned. For these women, our community meant surrender: of identity, of personal taste, of privacy.

At the time, I did not know what to make of such views. I simply thought they were mistaken. The women were afraid, it seemed to me; but, looking back, I wonder if we were not still afraid as well, and if the isolation we could never quite dispel was our way to hold part of ourselves back; to avoid admitting our dependence on each other, to let go of our secrets without letting go of the habits of living which had developed around them. Perhaps a younger generation of lesbians, who have grown up with one another, will be able to live the idea of openness in a different way from the way it sometimes seemed to me I lived it: as something between a pose and a hope.


4.
But there were always exceptions.

She walks into the shop. She has long black hair, a slim white face, and slim hands. She is wearing a red beret, a green-blue blouse, a silver necklace. She asks me to recommend a good book, and we start talking. She is on visitors' time, slowed down and open. The Edinburgh Festival Fringe is about to start, and she is here for three weeks. I take a deep breath and ask her out to lunch. She agrees.

Everyone wanted relationships. We discussed them a good deal, though always a bit apologetically; and we kept to specifics: who, what she said, when we were meant to see her again. We did not say too much about what we wanted from relationships: we felt, I think, that they should be able to take care of themselves in the community we were trying to be.

As I look back now, I realise we were going through a time of change in our views. In the seventies, before I arrived, there had apparently been a lot of feeling against monogamy, against the whole idea of exclusive relationships, romance, or any sort of intense and elaborate 'private' life. The ideal was to be open, 'free', making choices as they came up; how this worked in practice is not always easy to discover.

Now, things were changing. Romance and relationships had never really died, and at some point women had decided to leave them in peace. No one I knew was ever criticised for being monogamous or possessive, though we seemed to agree, tacitly, that it was probably wiser not to live with a lover or insist on introducing her to all your friends.

But, in spite of this sort of compromise, there was a very real way in which relationships cut across the life we were living as (unacknowledged) activists. Once I interviewed an actress who talked about the difficulties of keeping relationships together in her job. The hours, she said, were a problem; the intensity of the work, when there was work, made things still harder. In practice, most of the actresses and actors she knew found their lovers in their own profession; nothing else lasted.

There were not enough of us to try to apply this advice to our own lives with any great success; and we had another problem as well. For many women, being seen with one of us was dangerous to their cover. Coming out was difficult for those with children, and there were few (if any) professions in Edinburgh which were likely to treat an open lesbian with much respect. Even if she were allowed to keep her job, she could hardly hope for promotion.

I had not really expected to find deep and lasting intimacy as a result of being active in politics. It was not only my friends I thought I could rely on, but a sense I had had in the beginning, of being able to find other women through the world I thought I could help to create. This was, I suppose, part of the meaning of sisterhood, an ideal which seems remote now, but was much closer in those days of large conferences: one attracted, so they said, a thousand lesbians. A thousand lesbians: it was a phrase with a ring. I talked to some strangers at that conference as if I had always known them; and there were some I did know years later. It didn't always take a thousand: there were the meetings of the Scottish Gay Activists Alliance, and the six women who got us down the road when the pub closed, chanting, 'We are the DYKES frae A – ber – deen!' But as the mid-eighties arrived, the conferences faded away. The last national lesbian conference in Scotland was held in 1980.

The conferences had taken tremendous effort to organise, and sometimes they were fraught occasions. I don't think we ever realised, nor did anyone ever point out, how important they were to our sense of the world. They were a public space for lesbians, the only space large enough to give us any sense of what things might be like if we were not oppressed. They gave us a chance to meet women from outside our own communities, women with very different backgrounds who could open up in a larger, freer environment. They were crucial for those of us who were used to isolation, who needed all the practice we could find in order to lose the reserve we no longer wanted, but which was habitual.

Meanwhile, we went on hoping for relationships, whatever the difficulties. As far as we let on, our dreams were modest enough. If we ever wished the handsome stranger would walk through the door, we made a joke out of it. Those things never really happened, did they? Of course not. And we probably wouldn't know what to do if they did.

Adrienne and I take a taxi to Tollcross to hear Esther talk about women and nonviolence. We are late and miss her bit and end up in the discussion, which moves round and round, exposes minor points of conflict – then the subject is changed, nervously. Adrienne has to go to her performance, so I stand up and say, 'We're leaving because we have to, not because we disagree with anyone.'

We stop in a grotty chippy and A buys her first fish supper. She is an American musician, musical director of a Festival Fringe production. She stands in the chippy, wearing her cape, silver necklace, and beret, taking it all in. Then we walk down in the wind, eating and talking excitedly, and get to the venue for her show.

She plays the piano. She is wearing a long black satin gown which leaves her arms bare. I ought to be carried away by this, I think, but I have been working for fourteen days without a break and it all seems a little unreal. She plays Broadway musical numbers and I start to drift off about halfway through each one and then wake up when the audience applauds. 'I hope you don't hate Broadway musicals,' she says as she sweeps up to me in her floor-length gown during the interval. I have just realised that the performance is not one Broadway musical, but a series of unconnected songs. 'There's more to them than you realise,' I say.

Then the performance is over. Adrienne comes back in her trousers.

'Would you like to go somewhere?'

I can't see her at the disco. She must want to go for coffee.

'Where?'

'Well, there's a Scottish ceidleidh at the university . . .'

I am speechless. Even if I knew how to do Scottish dancing, just getting up the hill without tripping over the kerbs would be problematic.

'That sounds like fun,' I say.

We go up to the ceidleidh. It is taking place in a searingly lit hall full of men in cotton shirts and women in frocks. The punch is gone. I wonder how I am going to do this. Adrienne wades fearlessly into squares and circles. I trip, get stepped on, and am thrown back and forth like somebody trying to get through a rioting mob. But eventually I get a sort of second wind and stumble through with some spirit. With the right person, even some very foolish things can work.

'That was amazing,' says Adrienne. 'When the show's over, I'd like to see more, do something different.'

The show will be over in a week and by then I will have been working for twenty-one days. 'I'll tell you,' I say, 'why don't you go see these friends of mine. I'll give you their address. They live in the Outer Hebrides.'

I did not know much about anyone's relationships except my own. We had a rule of confidentiality, and an ethic of success as well. 'How is Joyce? It's going well, then?' you would ask, and someone would reply, 'Not too badly.' As long as it was going well, you would hear very little;

but if it was going badly, one or the other partner would break the rule of confidentiality, and the truth would come out. Most people, I think, would not break the rule until they felt that everything was over; it was important to us to be loyal. But the result was that there were few stories about the good times, and there was no wisdom about good relationships, no tradition, no way to learn much from other women's experience.

Even novels gave very little away. The most successful, apart from the ones we called 'lesbian trash', were the comic novels like *Rubyfruit Jungle* and *Oranges Are Not the Only Fruit*, whose heroines were alone in the world. Their relationships were colourful and dangerous and over very quickly. 'Serious' novels and memoirs were qualified and cautious and some, like Kate Millett's *Sita*, were painful to read; it seemed that the only alternative to reticence was merciless self-exposure.

Few of the novels touched on anything like my experience of relationships. It was the same in talking with most people: we always took on the point of view of the group; we rarely mentioned what we had found relationships to be like from the inside. From outside they looked narrow; from inside they were vast. The novels and the gossip said everything about possessiveness and need; they never talked about the curious shifts in reality which happen when you are close to someone, the sense of unlimited potential which rarely finds its way into the outer world, the tenderness and protection which somehow give rise to the strength – and the wish – to survive.

I was glad of all my relationships, short and long. They were the core of the strange days and I came to feel they were the reason I had taken on all the hard work and risk and misunderstanding (though, at the time, I denied it). I was seeing things which were very real. I thought about the story of the daughter whose stepmother throws her down a well, where she finds a secret land full of gold and jewels. The truths I sometimes learnt had exactly that sort of value: they had cost the tellers a great deal. In the end, however, the good daughter refuses to do more than look at the gold and jewels; she opts for hard work instead.

Sometimes it was like that. But there were always exceptions.

It is Friday night. Festival is almost over. I can't take it in. I am too tired to go to bed, so I sit in the living room, blinking and taking a minute to answer every question.

The phone rings. It is Adrienne. Her show ended earlier than I thought and she is back from the Outer Hebrides. I think she is asking me out for a drink. Outside it is pouring with rain.

'Sure, that sounds fine,' I hear myself saying. I wonder what I can possibly mean by that. I do things one at a time: get my raincoat, say goodbye, walk down the hall, open the door, climb the steps out onto the street.

The pub isn't far away. We sit down. At the sound of Adrienne's voice, something inside me snaps on. All of a sudden the person who tells stories, thinks, laughs, listens, is there. I ask her about the Hebrides and about her life in New York and about being a musician. I can come out of any stage of tiredness for this sort of talk. She tells me about her life on the continent, her determination to get work in music and do it well, her relationships during the confused stage of coming out, her flat. The person inside me carries on as if with an old friend. The other person, outside, sits thinking *It won't be long before I can sleep*.

The pub closes. Adrienne is dithering. Last week I told her she could stay with me rather than in her company's deserted flat half a mile away. I realise I want her to do that. You can ignore the fact that you are exhausted as long as you do everything slowly. 'But I'll need help carrying my things,' she says. The rain roars down. We set off down the hill. I step very carefully. As long as I don't think about how far we have to go, I will forget, because I am too tired to remember. I laugh out loud to myself under the sound of the rain; I can't believe this.

It's past midnight when we get back to my flat, put on the fire, take off our wet clothes, and have hot baths. 'That's the hard side of the bed, and that's the soft side', I say.

We get into bed, and she puts her arms around me. 'It's nice to have someone to hug at the end of the day', she says. And just when I thought I had nothing left, everything is left.

## 5.

In 1968, at roughly the same time as I first saw the album cover of *Strange Days*, Joan Didion was interviewing Black urban guerrillas, striking students, a Black militant writer and others, whom she later described in her essay, 'The White Album': a piece about the atmosphere, and the subtle undoing, which surrounds revolutionary change. She tried to interview The Doors, but she did not succeed. On records, the Doors gave an impression of dangerous but friendly vitality. In person, they were tired. At the rehearsal Joan Didion attended, they seldom spoke; one of the group was hours late, but no one remarked on the fact; and the rest of the evening was a series of vague and banal arrangements about rehearsal times and places, which were never agreed. The Doors seemed to have lost the power to listen to other people, and though they could still talk, the effort was so great that they lost their grasp on the details of what they were saying.

Didion does not say whether the Doors were using drugs at the time. Her other interviewees probably were not, but they all shared the same magically meaningless style of conversation. Didion's subjects always seemed to be under pressure of time. If they were not busy, they had nothing to say. Their conversation revolved around everyday arrangements in a lifeless but frenetic way. No one ever seemed to have much definite information; the little rush which came from speaking jargon phrases and slogans was all that held things together.

These were people who had drained themselves. Most of them must have poured all their energy into their work or a new life, hoping to create enormous changes. Now they had very little left. It was as if the Doors, and others like them, were an exploding star whose light was just reaching me at that moment in 1968; but inside the shell of light, they had nothing left for growth, only for survival.

None of us ever considered that changing the world might work in a similar way for us. We were, after all, not celebrities. It never occurred to us that radical change might work the same way for anyone who pursued it. We were trying to live an ideal future into the present, and we had cut ourselves off, at least in our dealings with each other, from the past and from people outside.

We were making our lives into a kind of everyday street theatre: we tried to *create* the confident stance of lesbians of the future, lesbians who had never had our experiences, as actresses *create* a role. We lived collectively and worked collectively; we always had an audience. But we were not used to living so close to other people, and so we overworked, and put everything important into the work, in order to keep ourselves private.

We tried to become a close community through meetings and discussions, but we came to the meetings tired; and when you are tired, your best energy, the energy to connect, is gone. We found it hard to respond to each other and easy to compete in subtle ways. The vagueness of our relations undermined our self-assurance; and we used anger and quarrelling as an occasional cheap high, a way to spend energy on ourselves. The quarrels seemed especially bitter because we had no source of support, or way to act in a group, except each other.

Sooner or later it was impossible to avoid realising that the work was not connecting us with other women; it was cutting us off. I grabbed hard onto everyday facts and jobs in order to avoid facing the truth. If I lost sight of the work, of its importance, I might have to doubt the stories which had made life livable for me for a very long time.

Realisation turned out to be the last part of the process. The first part was a state of mind and later, a state of health. I lost friends over ideological quarrels, and I missed them badly, but I could not tell anyone about my feelings without casting blame: on the women who were gone, or the ones who were still my friends but seemed to think I was taking it all too hard. I began to understand some of the things the disillusioned had been saying to me. There was a dimension of the community, it seemed, which was about not taking the community very seriously. These things happened. They were life. They were not supposed to count.

I began to lose interest in seeing people. I came down with glandular fever. I felt angry and grotesque, and cut off all my hair in order to look grotesque; but everyone complimented my trendy new hairstyle. Little by little, all the meaning seemed to go out of the phrases and the air of serious effort we were constantly exchanging; even words like 'lesbian' and 'woman' no longer sounded quite the same to me. I would talk, but though I said the same things, something was missing from inside them; *I* was missing. Meanwhile, the situation in my flat was collapsing and I decided I wanted to live alone.

Part of me did not like feeling these things and kept insisting it was not happening. The other person wanted to be alone, and did not much care about anything else. When I moved into a bedsit near a large park, she got what she wanted. Just as the disillusioned had predicted, I was living alone.

My mind seemed at times to be crashing down around me like a block of flats under demolition, but I had no interest in telling anyone about it, and the few people who knew were bewildered. No one was supposed to care *this* much about politics. I did not know how to explain it myself. Later I wrote:

Perhaps you can fall in love with a whole group of people, with the atmosphere they generate between them, in the same way you can fall in love with one person, and spend energy just as recklessly and thoughtlessly, in the same way. I suppose lesbians are especially vulnerable to that sort of thing. We don't grow up in groups and gangs. We don't know how to deal with them. We're no more wise to them than a sixteen-year-old is to romance.

Eventually I saw a therapist. I had assumed, as a feminist, that I would never need therapy again. My therapist was neither a feminist nor a lesbian; she gave me a kind of advice I found it almost impossible to accept. 'Find things you enjoy doing,' she said, 'and do them. If other people won't take care of you, do it yourself.' Since then I have wondered if many of her patients were divorcees; my position was similar. Over the last few years, I had taken on an identity which suddenly was not 'me' any longer. I knew my friends almost entirely through feminism and work, but those things now seemed like barriers, not points of connection. But my earlier interests no longer seemed to have much to do with me either. They belonged to a younger, unformed self. I could not just take them up again, like a piece of knitting. I wanted to keep developing as a lesbian and a feminist, but I could no longer see how it was possible.

The strangest part of the strange days was the last part, and I am not sure how they ended, or if they ever did. I found new work and new friends, but I also kept working as an open lesbian. I became a person with 'interests' again, rather than a person with one overriding mission. I revived old interests (classical music) and discovered new ones (cycling). I kept reading lesbian books and eventually discovered that my experience with the community was not unique.

Some of the stories I read were more harrowing than mine. Rita Mae Brown, author of *Rubyfruit Jungle*, had been expelled from one of her early women's groups, the Furies collective. Sandy Kovahey published her journal of the 'great lesbian wars' around class in her community, and the isolation that followed, in *Sinister Wisdom 16*. Suicidal, unable to eat or sleep properly, she listed the things she needed to survive and still included 'dreams/hope/visions of change'. Michelle Belling, an American writer, told the story of a young and idealistic woman, fresh from a small town and a lifetime of secret lesbian reading, who barely survived her encounter with an unwelcoming big-city community. In an article for the mixed gay *Body Politic*, Belling described her friend's brush with drugs and a near-breakdown, and how she went on to rebuild her life around a musical career and heterosexual friends. Janice Raymond, author of *A Passion for Friends*, wrote her book, as she said, 'to put away grief'. Radical feminist friends, she explained, were hard to find. Some feminists told her they had had closer friendships in the convent or the army.

These women had written down their experience, briefly and without generalising. Few other writers seemed to doubt that lesbians were, could be, or should be, a group of people with unity of purpose bordering on the transcendental. The idea that women might dislike each other, disagree, compromise, and still belong to the same community in the same way, never seemed to occur. Within one community, there had to be perfect harmony of purpose; otherwise a new community had to hive itself off. One recent issue of a certain lesbian magazine was a battle between' glossy covers. Thin women, said one writer, were making the community impossible for fat women; fat women were spoiling it for thin women; non-separatists were ruining things for separatists; and everyone was threatened by those who did not PUT WOMEN FIRST.

Perhaps all this is not really so surprising. It was a long time before I was able to see beyond the view of the lesbian community I had held and desperately needed. Instead of the close and intense group of activists I had imagined, playing like a rock band on the stage of the possible future, sacrificing their lives for one blinding flash of change, the real community seems to be emerging. Large, diverse and scattered, going through an incredibly slow process of formation, with a good deal of mistrust and bad feeling and a gradual growth of confidence, it is developing toward a kind of change which none of us, no matter how hard she works, can foresee.

In the end, there was more to the story after all.

6.

I now know much more than I knew in 1980 about communities: what they offer, and what they demand. But I do not know, any more than I knew then, how to think or write about a lesbian community in clear and yet realistic terms; not when our need for it is so fierce, our vision of it so sharp, our experience of it so limited and our feeling for it so vague.

The use of the word 'community' in our writing creates paradoxes bordering on the mystical. The community can be specific, limited to women in one town; it can be general, taking in the women of several nations. We write as if it already existed; as if it were being created; as if it will never be realised. We write of more than one community, of communities within communities: we endow feminists, leftists, even heterosexuals with their own communities. We see community everywhere, in everything, but we rarely see it in detail. Like a mountain range on the horizon, it is most arresting at a distance.

Community is an old word. Its first usage in modern English is noted in 1561. The people of a community share ownership, or character, or identity. Later that identity becomes specifically religious or ethnic: 'the Jewish community' first appears in print in 1888. These definitions appear to have applied to groups whose existence and membership were well known. The sort of baggage I brought from my isolation, the dream of an all-accepting circle I could somehow come to deserve, is not part of this picture of community. Instead, being part of the group is simple: not everyone is liked or known or understood, but a place is always made for them. A friend of mine explained, 'Whatever I do, I will always be Jewish. No one can take that away.'

A community can never be created: not through hard work or in any other way. It must simply be recognised and respected. It cannot be exclusive, like a club or a class. It is an opportunity, a place to make things happen, not a favoured state or a promised land. If its promises are to be trusted, they should be few and very down to earth.

# PART FOUR
## Speaking Actions, Living Words

---

## How to Tame a Wild Tongue

Gloria Anzaldúa

'We're going to have to control your tongue,' the dentist says, pulling out all the metal from my mouth. Silver bits plop and tinkle into the basin. My mouth is a motherlode.

The dentist is cleaning out my roots. I get a whiff of the stench when I gasp. 'I can't cap that tooth yet, you're still draining,' he says.

'We're going to have to do something about your tongue,' I hear the anger rising in his voice. My tongue keeps pushing out the wads of cotton, pushing back the drills, the long thin needles. 'I've never seen anything as strong or stubborn,' he says. And I think, how do you tame a wild tongue, train it to be quiet, how do you bridle and saddle it? How do you make it lie down?

'Who is to say that robbing a people of its language is less violent than war?' *Ray Gwyn Smith*[1]

I remember being caught speaking Spanish at recess – that was good for three licks on the knuckles with a sharp ruler. I remember being sent to the corner of the classroom for 'talking back' to the Anglo teacher when all I was trying to do was tell her how to pronounce my name. 'If you want to be American, speak "American". If you don't like it, go back to Mexico where you belong.'

'I want you to speak English. *Pa' hallar buen trabajo tienes que saber hablar el inglés bien. Qué vale toda tu educación si todavia hablas inglés con un "accent"*,'[2] my mother would say, mortified that I spoke English like a Mexican. At Pan American University, I, and all Chicano students were required to take two speech classes. Their purpose: to get rid of our accents.

Attacks on one's form of expression with the intent to censor are a violation of the First Amendment. *El Anglo con cara se*

107

*inocente nos arrancó la lengua.*[3] Wild tongues cannot be tamed, they can only be cut out.

## Overcoming the Tradition of Silence

*Abogados, escupimos el oscuro.*
*Peleando con nuestra propia sombra*
*el silencio nos sepulta.*[4]

*En boca cerrado no entran moscas.* 'Flies don't enter a closed mouth' is a saying I kept hearing when I was a child. *Ser habladora* was to be a gossip and a liar, to talk too much. *Muchachitas bien criadas*, well-bred girls don't answer back. *Es una falta de respeto*[5] to talk back to one's mother or father. I remember one of the sins I'd recite to the priest in the confession box the few times I went to confession: talking back to my mother, *hablar pa' 'tras, repelar. Hociona, repelona, chismosa*, having a big mouth, questioning, carrying tales are all signs of being *mal criada.*[6] In my culture they are all words that are derogatory if applied to women – I've never heard them applied to men.

The first time I heard two women, a Puerto Rican and a Cuban, say the word '*nosotras*', I was shocked. I had not known the word existed. Chicanas use *nosotros* whether we're male or female. We are robbed of our female being by the masculine plural. Language is a male discourse.

And our tongues have become
dry     the wilderness has
dried out our tongues     and
we have forgotten speech.
                    *Irena Klepfisz*[7]

Even our own people, other Spanish speakers *nos quieren poner candados en la boca.*[8] They would hold us back with their bag of *reglas de academia.*[9]

*Oye come ladra: el lenguaje de la frontera*: Listen to its Howl: the Language of the Border

*Quien tiene se equivoca.*[10]
                    *Mexican saying*

'*Pocho*, cultural traitor, you're speaking the oppressor's language by speaking English, you're ruining the Spanish language,' I have been accused by various Latinos and Latinas. Chicano Spanish is considered by the purist and by most Latinos deficient, a mutilation of Spanish.

But Chicano Spanish is a border tongue which developed naturally. Change, *evolución, enriquecimiento de palabras nuevas por invencion o adopcion*[11] have created variants of Chicano Spanish, *un nuevo lenguaje. Un lenguaje que corresponde a un modo de vivir.* Chicano Spanish is not incorrect, it is a living language.

For a people who are neither Spanish nor live in a country in which Spanish is the first language, for a people who live in a country in which English is the reigning tongue but who are not Anglo, for a people who cannot entirely identify with either standard (formal, Castillian) Spanish nor standard English, what recourse is left to them but to create their own language? A language which they can connect their identity to, one capable of communicating the realities and values true to themselves – a language with terms that are neither *español ni inglés*, but both. We speak a patois, a forked tongue, a variation of two languages.

Chicano Spanish sprang out of the Chicanos' need to identify ourselves as a distinct people. We needed a language with which we could communicate with ourselves, a secret language. For some of us, language is a homeland closer than the Southwest – for many Chicanos today live in the Midwest and the East. And because we are a complex, heterogenous people, we speak many languages. Some of the languages we speak are:

1. Standard English
2. Working-class and slang English
3. Standard Spanish
4. Standard Mexican Spanish
5. North Mexican Spanish dialect
6. Chicano Spanish (Texas, New Mexico, Arizona and California have regional variations)
7. Tex-Mex
8. *Pachuco* (called *calo*)

My 'home' tongues are the languages I speak with my sister and brothers, with my friends. They are the last five listed, with 6 and 7 being closest to my heart. From school, the media and job situations, I've picked up standard and working class English. From Mamagrande Locha and from reading Spanish and Mexican literature, I've picked up Standard Spanish and Standard Mexican Spanish. From *los recién llegados*, Mexican immigrants, and *braceros*,[12] I learned the North Mexican dialect. With Mexicans I'll try to speak either Standard Mexican Spanish or the North Mexican dialect. From my parents and Chicanos living in the Valley, I picked up Chicano Texas Spanish, and I speak it with my mom, younger brother (who married a Mexican and who rarely mixes Spanish with English), aunts and older relatives.

With Chicanas from *Nuevo Mexico* or *Arizona* I will speak Chicano Spanish a little, but more often they don't understand what I'm saying. With most California Chicanas I speak entirely in English (unless I forget). When I first moved to San Francisco, I'd rattle off something in Spanish, unintentionally embarrassing them. Often it is only with another Chicana *tejana* that I can talk freely.

Words distorted by English are known as anglicisms or *pochismos*. The *pocho* is an anglicized Mexican or American of Mexican origin who speaks

Spanish with an accent characteristic of North Americans and who distorts and reconstructs the language according to the influence of English.[13] Tex-Mex or Spanglish, comes most naturally to me. I may switch back and forth from English to Spanish in the same sentence or in the same word. With my sister and my brother Nune and with Chicano *tejano* contemporaries I speak in Tex-Mex.

From kids and people my own age I picked up *Pachuco*. *Pachuco* (the language of the zoot suiters)[14] is a language of rebellion, both against Standard Spanish and Standard English. It is a secret language. Adults of the culture and outsiders cannot understand it. It is made up of slang words from both English and Spanish. *Ruca* means girl or woman, *vato* means guy or dude, *chale* means no, *simón* means yes, *churro* is sure, talk is *periquiar*, *pigionear* means petting, *que gacho* means how nerdy, *ponte águila* means watch out, death is called *la pelona*. Through lack of practice and not having others who can speak it, I've lost most of the *Pachuco* tongue.

## Chicano Spanish

Chicanos, after 250 years of Spanish/Anglo colonization have developed significant differences in the Spanish we speak. We collapse two adjacent vowels into a single syllable and sometimes shift the stress in certain words such as *maíz/maiz*, *cohete/cuete*. We leave out certain consonants when they appear between vowels: *lado/lao*, *mojado/mojao*. Chicanos from South Texas pronounce *f* as *j* in *jue* (*fue*). Chicanos use 'archaisms', words that are no longer in the Spanish language, words that have been evolved out. We say *semos*, *truje*, *haiga*, *ansina*, and *naiden*. We retain the 'archaic' *j*, as in *jalar*, that derives from an earlier *h* (the French *halar* or the Germanic *halon* which was lost to Standard Spanish in the sixteenth century), but which is still found in several regional dialects such as the one spoken in South Texas. (Due to geography, Chicanos from the Valley of South Texas were cut off linguistically from other Spanish speakers.) We tend to use words that the Spaniards brought over from Medieval Spain. The majority of the Spanish colonizers in Mexico and the Southwest came from Extramadura – Hernán Cortés was one of them – and Andalucia. Andalucians pronounce *ll* like a *y*, and their *d*'s tend to be absorbed by adjacent vowels: *tirado* becomes *tirao*. They brought *el lenguaje popular, dialectos y regionalismos*.[15]

Chicanos and other Spanish speakers also shift *ll* to *y* and *z* to *s*.[16] We leave out initial syllables, saying *tar* for *estar*, *toy* for *estoy*, *hora* for *ahora* (*cubanos* and *puertorriquenos*[17] also leave out initial letters of some words). We also leave out the final syllable such as *pa* for *para*. The intervocalic *y*, the *ll* as in *tortilla*, *ella*, *botella*, gets replaced by *tortiya*, *ea*, *botea*. We add an additional syllable at the beginning of certain words: *atocar* for *tocar*, *agastar* for *gastar*. Sometimes we'll say *lavaste las vacijas*, other times *lavates* (substituting the *ates* verb endings for the *aste*).

We use anglicisms, words borrowed from English: *bola* from ball, *carpeta* from carpet, *machina de lavar* (instead of *lavadora*) from washing machine. Tex-Mex argot, created by adding a Spanish sound at the beginning or end of an English word such as *cookiar* for cook, *watchar* for watch, *parkiar* for park, and *rapiar* for rape, is the result of pressures on Spanish speakers to adapt to English.

We don't use the word *vosotros/as* or its accompanying verb form. We don't say *claro* (to mean yes), *imaginate*, or *me emociona*,[18] unless we picked up Spanish from Latinas, out of a book, or in a classroom. Other Spanish-speaking groups are going through the same, or similar, development in their Spanish.

## Linguistic Terrorism

*Deslenguadas. Somos los del español deficiente.*[19] We are your linguistic nightmare, your linguistic aberration, your linguistic *mestisaje*,[20] the subject of your *burla*.[21] Because we speak with tongues of fire we are culturally crucified. Racially, culturally and linguistically *somos huerfanos* – we speak an orphan tongue.

Chicanas who grew up speaking Chicano Spanish have internalized the belief that we speak poor Spanish. It is illegitimate, a bastard language. And because we internalize how our language has been used against us by the dominant culture, we use our language differences against each other.

Chicana feminists often skirt around each other with suspicion and hesitation. For the longest time I couldn't figure it out. Then it dawned on me. To be close to another Chicana is like looking in the mirror. We are afraid of what we'll see there. *Pena*. Shame. Low estimation of self. In childhood we are told that our language is wrong. Repeated attacks on our native tongue diminish our sense of self. The attacks continue throughout our lives.

Chicanas feel uncomfortable talking in Spanish to Latinas, afraid of their censure. Their language was not outlawed in their countries. They had a whole lifetime of being immersed in their native tongue: generations, centuries in which Spanish was a first language, heard on radio and TV, and read in the newspaper.

If a person, Chicana or Latina, has a low estimation of my native tongue, she also has a low estimation of me. Often with *mexicas y latinas* we'll speak English as a neutral language. Even among Chicanas we tend to speak English at parties or conferences. Yet, at the same time, we're afraid the other will think we're *agringadas*[22] because we don't speak Chicano Spanish. We oppress each other trying to out-Chicano each other, vying to be the 'real' Chicanas, to speak like Chicanos. There is no one Chicano language just as there is no one Chicano experience. A mono-lingual Chicana whose first language is English or Spanish is just as much a Chicana as one who speaks several variants of Spanish. A Chicana from Michigan or Chicago or Detroit is just as much a Chicana as one from the Southwest. Chicano Spanish is as diverse linguistically as it is regionally.

By the end of this century, Spanish speakers will comprise the biggest minority group in the U.S., a country where students in high schools and colleges are encouraged to take French classes because French is considered more 'cultured'. But for a language to remain alive it must be used.[23] By the end of this century English, not Spanish, will be the mother tongue of most Chicanos and Latinos.

So, if you want to really hurt me, talk badly about my language. Ethnic identity is twin skin to linguistic identity – I am my language. Until I can take pride in my language, I cannot take pride in myself. Until I can accept as legitimate Chicano Texas Spanish, Tex-Mex and all the other languages I speak, I cannot accept the legitimacy of myself. Until I am free to write bilingually and to switch codes without having always to translate, while I still have to speak English or Spanish when I would rather speak Spanglish, and as long as I have to accommodate the English speakers rather than having them accommodate me, my tongue will be illegitimate.

I will no longer be made to feel ashamed of existing. I will have my voice: Indian, Spanish, white. I will have my serpent's tongue – my woman's voice, my sexual voice, my poet's voice. I will overcome the tradition of silence.

> My fingers
> move sly against your palm
> Like women everywhere, we speak in code . . .
> *Melanie Kaye/Kantrowitz*[24]

## 'Vistas', corridos, y comida: My Native Tongue

In the 1960s, I read my first Chicano novel. It was *City of Night* by John Rechy, a gay Texan, son of a Scottish father and a Mexican mother. For days I walked around in stunned amazement that a Chicano could write and could get published. When I read *I Am Joaquin*[25] I was surprised to see a bilingual book by a Chicano in print. When I saw poetry written in Tex-Mex for the first time, a feeling of pure joy flashed through me. I felt like we really existed as people. In 1971, when I started teaching High School English to Chicano students, I tried to supplement the required texts with works by Chicanos, only to be reprimanded and forbidden to do so by the principal. He claimed that I was supposed to teach 'American' and English literature. At the risk of being fired, I swore my students to secrecy and slipped in Chicano short stories, poems, a play. In graduate school, while working toward a Ph.D, I had to 'argue' with one advisor after the other, semester after semester, before I ws allowed to make Chicano literature an area of focus.

Even before I read books by Chicanos or Mexicans, it was the Mexican movies I saw at the drive-in – the Thursday night special of $1.00 a carload – that gave me a sense of belonging. '*Vamonos a las vistas*' ('Let's go to the movies'), my mother would call out and we'd all – grandmother, brothers, sister and cousins – squeeze into the car. We'd wolf down cheese and bologna white bread sandwiches while watching Pedro Infante in melodramatic tear-jerkers like *Nosotros los pobres* (*We the Poor*), the first 'real' Mexican movie that was not an imitation of European movies. I remember seeing *Cuando los hijos se van* (*When Our Children Leave*), and surmising that all Mexican movies played up the love a mother has for her children and what ungrateful sons and daughters suffer when they are not devoted to their mothers. I remember the singing-type 'westerns' of Jorge Negrete and Miguel Aceves Mejia. When watching Mexican movies, I felt a sense of homecoming as well as alienation. People who were to amount to something didn't go to Mexican movies, or *bailes*[26] or tune their radios to *bolero, rancherita,*[27] and *corrido* music.

The whole time I was growing up, there was *norténo* music sometimes called North Mexican border music, or Tex-Mex music, or Chicano music, or *cantina* (bar) music. I grew up listening to *conjuntos*, three- or four-piece bands made up of folk musicians playing guitar, *bajo sexto,*[28] drums and button accordion, which Chicanos had borrowed from the German immigrants who had come from Central Texas and Mexico to farm and build breweries. In the Rio Grande Valley, Steve Jordan and Little Joe Hernandez were popular, and Flaco Jiménez was the accordion king. The rhythms of Tex-Mex music are those of the polka, also adapted from the Germans, who in turn had borrowed the polka from the Czechs and Bohemians.

I remember the hot, sultry evenings, when *corridos* – songs of love and death on the Texas-Mexican borderlands – reverberated out of cheap amplifiers from the local cantinas and wafted in through my bedroom window.

*Corridos* first became widely used along the South Texas/Mexican border during the early conflict between Chicanos and Anglos. The *corridos* are usually about Mexican heroes who do valiant deeds against the Anglo oppressors. '*La cucaracha*' is the most famous one. *Corridos* of John F. Kennedy and his death are still very popular in the Valley. Older Chicanos remember Lydia Mendoza, one of the great border *corrido* singers who was called *la Gloria de Tejas*. Her '*El tango negro*,' sung during the Great Depression, made her a singer of the people. The everpresent *corridos* narrated one hundred years of border history, bringing news of events as well as entertaining. These folk musicians and folk songs are our chief cultural myth-makers, and they made our hard lives seem bearable.

I grew up feeling ambivalent about our music. Country-western and rock-and-roll had more status. In the fifties and sixties, for the slightly educated and agringado Chicanos, there existed a sense of shame at being caught listening to our music. Yet I couldn't stop my feet from thumping to the music, could not stop humming the words, nor hide from myself the exhilaration I felt when I heard it.

There are more subtle ways that we internalize identification, especially in the forms of images and emotions. For me food and certain smells are tied to my identity, to my homeland. Woodsmoke curling up in an immense blue sky; woodsmoke perfuming my grandmother's clothes, her skin. The stench of cow manure and the yellow patches on the ground; the crack of a .22 rifle and the reek of cordite. Homemade white cheese sizzling in a pan, melting inside a folded *tortilla*. My sister Hilda's hot spicy *menudo*, *chile colorado* making it deep red, pieces of *panza*[29] and hominy floating on top. My brother Carito barbecuing *fajitas* in the backyard. Even now and 3,000 miles away, I can see my mother spicing the ground beef, pork and venison with chile. My mouth salivates at the thought of the hot steaming *tamales*[30] I would be eating if I were home.

## *Si le preguntas a mi mama, '¿Que eres?'* If You Ask My Mother, 'What Are You?'

Identity is the essential core of who
we are as individuals, the conscious
experience of the self inside.

*Kaufman*[31]

*Nosotros los Chicanos* straddle the borderlands. On one side of us, we are constantly exposed to the Spanish of the Mexicans, on the other side we hear the Anglos' incessant clamoring so that we forget our language. Among ourselves we don't say *nosotros los americans*, *o nosotros los españoles*, *o nosotros los hispanos*. We say *nosotros los mexicanos* (by Mexicans we do not mean citizens of Mexico; we do not mean a national identity, but a racial one). We distinguish between *mexicanos del otro lado* and *mexicanos de este lado* (Mexicans from the other side and Mexicans from this side). Deep in our hearts we believe that being Mexican has nothing to do with which country one lives in. Being Mexican is a state of soul – not one of mind, not one of citizenship. Neither eagle nor serpent, but both. And like the ocean, neither animal respects borders.

*Dime con quien andas y te diré quien eres.*
(Tell me who your friends are and I'll tell you
who you are.)

*Mexican saying*

If you ask my mother, 'What are you?' she'll say, 'I'm Mexican.' My brothers and sisters say the same. I sometimes will answer '*soy mexicana*' and at others will say '*soy chicana*' or '*soy tejana*'. But I identified as '*Raza*' before I ever identified as '*mexicana*' or 'Chicana'.

114

As a culture, we call ourselves Spanish when referring to ourselves as a linguistic group and when copping out. It is then that we forget our predominant Indian genes. We are 70–80 per cent Indian.[32] We call ourselves Hispanic[33] or Spanish-American or Latin American or Latin when linking ourselves to other Spanish-speaking peoples of the Western hemisphere and when copping out. We call ourselves Mexican-American[34] to signify we are neither Mexican nor American, but more the noun 'American' than adjective 'Mexican' (and when copping out).

Chicanos and other people of color suffer economically for not acculturating. This voluntary (yet forced) alienation makes for psychological conflict, a kind of dual identity – we don't identify with the Anglo-American cultural values and we don't totally identify with the Mexican cultural values. We are a synergy of two cultures with various degrees of Mexicanness or Angloness. I have so internalized the borderland conflict that sometimes I feel like one cancels out the other and we are zero, nothing, no one. *A veces no soy nada ni nadie. Pero hasta cuando no lo soy, lo soy.*[35]

When not copping out, when we know we are more than nothing, we call ourselves Mexican, referring to race and ancestry; *mestizo* when affirming both our Indian and Spanish (but we hardly ever own our Black ancestry); Chicano when referring to a politically aware people born and/or raised in the U.S.; *Raza* when referring to Chicanos; *tejanos* when we are Chicanos from Texas.

Chicanos did not know we were a people until 1965 when Ceasar Chavez and the farmworkers united and *I Am Joaquin* was published and *la Raza Unida* party was formed in Texas. With that recognition, we became a distinct people. Something momentous happened to the Chicano soul – we became aware of our reality and acquired a name and a language (Chicano Spanish) that reflected that reality. Now that we had a name, some of the fragmented pieces began to fall together – who we were, what we were, how we had evolved. We began to get glimpses of what we might eventually become.

Yet the struggle of identities continues, the struggle of borders is our reality still. One day the inner struggle will cease, and a true integration take place. In the meantime, *tenémos que hacer la lucha, ¿Quien esta protegiendo los ranchos de mi gente? ¿Quién esta tratando de cerrar la fisura entre la india y el blanco en nuestra sangre? El Chicano, si, el Chicano que anda como un ladrón en su propia casa.*[36]

*Los Chicanos*, how patient we seem, how very patient. There is the quiet of the Indian about us.[37] We know how to survive. When other races have given up their tongue, we've kept ours. We know what it is to live under the hammer blow of the dominant *norteamericano culture*. But more than we count the blows, we count the days the weeks the years the centuries the eons until the oppressive laws and commerce and customs of the whites, and the oppressive elements of our own culture too, lie bleached and dead in the deserts they have created. *Humildes*, yet proud, *quietos* yet wild, *nosotros los mexicanos-Chicanos* will walk by the crumbling ashes as

115

we go about our business. Stubborn, persevering, impenetrable as stone, yet possessing a malleability that renders us unbreakable, we the *mestizas* and *mestizos*, will remain.

# Notes

1. Ray Gwyn Smith, *Moorland is Cold Country*, unpublished book.
2. To get a good job you've got to know how to speak English. Of what use is all your education if you still speak English with an accent?
3. The Anglo with the innocent face pulled our tongues.
4. *Choking we spit out the darkness*
   *Fighting with our own shadows*
   *the silence buries us.*
5. It shows a lack of respect.
6. Badly raised or bred.
7. Irena Klepfisz, 'Di rayze aheym/The Journey Home,' in *The Tribe of Dina: A Jewish Women's Anthology*, Melanie Kaye/Kantrowitz and Irena Klepfisz, eds. (Montpelier, VT: Sinister Wisdom Books, 1986), p. 49.
8. Want to put locks on our mouths.
9. Academic rules.
10. Who has a mouth makes mistakes.
11. Evolution, the enrichment of new words, invented or adopted.
12. Mexican laborers conscripted by the U.S. government to work on this side.
13. R.C. Ortega, *Dialectologia Del Barrio*, trans. Hortencia S. Alwan (Los Angeles, CA: R.C. Ortega Publisher and Bookseller, 1977), p. 132.
14. Zoot suiters are pachuco, Chicanos rebelling against linguistic and behavioral constraints of both the Mexican and the dominant cultures.
15. Eduardo Hernandez-Chavez, Andrew D. Cohen, and Anthony F. Beltramo, *El Lenguaje de los Chicanos: Regional and Social Characteristics of Language Used By Mexican Americans* (Arlington, VA: Center for Applied Linguistics, 1975), p. 39.
16. Hernandez-Chavez, xvii.
17. Cubans and Puerto Ricans.
18. 'imagine; it moves me (emotionally)'.
19. Tongueless, we are those of the deficient Spanish.
20. Mixture.
21. Jeers.
22. 'assimilated into Gringo (Anglo) culture'.
23. Irena Klepfisz, 'Secular Jewish Identity: Yiddishkayt in America', in *The Tribe of Dina*, Kaye/Kantrowitz and Klepfisz, eds., p. 43.
24. Melanie/Kaye/Kantrowitz, 'Sign', in *We Speak In Codes: Poems and Other Writings* (Pittsburgh, PA: Motheroot Publications, Inc., 1980), p. 85.
25. Rodolfo Gonzales, *I Am Joaquin/Yo Soy Joaquin* (New York, NY: Bantam books, 1972; first published, 1967).
26. Dances.
27. Ranchera music is a kind of Mexican Country and Western music.
28. Cello.
29. Stomach.

30. Meat in corn dough or wrapped in dry corn husks.
31. Kaufman, p. 68.
32. Chavez, pp. 88–90.
33. 'Hispanic' is derived from Hispanis (Espana, a name given to the Iberian Peninsula in ancient times when it was a part of the Roman Empire) and is a term designated by the U.S. government to make it easier to handle us on paper.
34. The Treaty of Guadalupe Hidalgo created the Mexican-American in 1848.
35. At times I am nothing and no-one. But even when I am not, I am.
36. We have to keep struggling. Who is looking after my people's land? Who is trying to close the fissure between the Indian and the white in our blood? The Chicano, yes, the Chicano that walks like a thief in his own home.
37. Anglos, in order to alleviate their guilt for dispossessing the Chicano, stressed the Spanish part of us and perpetrated the myth of the Spanish Southwest. We have accepted the fiction that we are Hispanic, that is Spanish, in order to accommodate ourselves to the dominant culture and its abhorrence of Indians. Chavez, pp. 88–91.

# Philosophy & the Big Exception – Why I Write Fiction

Ellen Shapiro

I was once a student of philosophy: my memories include long hours at my library desk hidden in the periodicals, where I'd wrestle with ontological questions, checking my thesis for internal consistencies, buttressing the conclusions with what I hoped was sufficient proof. Whenever I felt frustrated or chaotic, I'd turn to a magazine; one of my favorites, believe it or not, was a special-interest monthly called *Ducks Unlimited*, and as I flipped the pages I'd be soothed by pictures of flying mallards and antique decoys, or I'd wonder why the 'Waterfowl Artist of the Year' posed with an odd, defiant grin. Refreshed, I'd turn to some new formulation, but eventually that familiar anxiety would return: a shadow crept across the notebook and I'd begin to imagine that my argument contained holes so glaring that anyone (except myself, of course) would be able to see straight through them. Only one 'logical' counterargument need be uttered and my work would topple like a house of cards, rendering me lost and speechless.

I once even nicknamed that fantasy 'The Terror of the Big Exception'(making it sound like a B-movie calmed my nerves), and I felt its presence no matter how unchallenged or successful my work turned out to be. Now I'm not talking about doubt or skepticism or even the despair that the words won't flow; all these feelings are common and often necessary for the creative process. No. 'The Big Exception' is a pointing finger, a patriarchal voice that says: 'Your work is rifled with inconsistencies. I

117

can't deduce your conclusions from the premises, which are themselves parochial and subjective. Even a child could see the emotional biases which cloud your argument.'

Of course, many of these fears are symptoms of male-dominated, western philosophy: the positing of life as a problem to be solved, the inferiority of 'subjective' writing, the defining of emotions as unreliable, false, and detached from the intellect, and most fundamentally, the existence of universal truths about human nature.

I always knew that what I wrote could be but a sliver of reality; the world contained more voices than I could even dream of hearing, let alone categorize. There were kind fathers who designed neutron bombs, women painting beautiful images they say came directly from God, a grandfather who died in his sleep, leaving every present his family gave him stashed in a closet – neatly stacked and unopened. People twisted and bent and defied my every generalization, not, as that somber voice would have it, because I failed to appropriate enough of the world, but simply because human diversity was not to be contained.

The source of individual uniqueness is the body. By the body I mean not only physical and biological characteristics and the brain with its faculties for reason and memory, but also those qualities which traditional philosophy has usually discounted: emotions, dreams, unconscious messages, 'irrationalities,' sense impressions (not sense data: I'm not concerned with what the traditionalists think they can measure). At the same time, the body is the personal manifestation of social experiences – whether they be of a racial, sexual, familial, religious or class nature. In other words, what an individual feels is subjective, but that subjectivity has also passed through and been influenced by a variety of social filters. So, for example, a lesbian sensibility would not be found floating in some universal realm, though an individual's perceptions might certainly be influenced by her lesbianism.

Even when I was emphathizing with the subject matter, I still found the language of philosophy difficult. For example, Simone de Beauvoir writes this passage about lesbianism in *The Second Sex*:

Never in the presence of husband or lover can she (the lesbian) feel wholly herself; but with her woman friend she need not be on parade, need not pretend: they are too much of a kind not to show themselves frankly as they are. This similarity engenders complete intimacy. Frequently eroticism has but a small part in these unions; here sex pleasure is of a nature less violent and vertiginous than between man and woman, it does not bring about such overwhelming transformations . . .[1]

de Beauvoir is describing the idealized characteristics of the lesbian. There are few, if any qualifications in the passage; the tone is transcendental, as if she had distilled some essence from every lesbian in the world. But of course I know of lesbians who do not feel completely genuine with their lovers, just as I know that some lesbians engage in highly vertiginous lovemaking. Now I don't mean to sound petty. Obviously de Beauvoir isn't claiming to describe each and every lesbian, yet there is nothing intrinsic in

118

her language to allow for a diversity of life choices. And by not exploring her own subjectivity, de Beauvoir's writing takes on an assumption of universality; a prescription for 'the way lesbians are.'

And in my own work, I often found myself considering arguments because they fit within a particular jigsaw I'd created and not because they truly reflected what I saw in the world. For every assertion, I could think of many more exceptions: life was much more ubiquitous than my philosophy led me to believe. And so I finally had to ask myself a very difficult question: 'Did my philosophical conclusions exist in the world as I really saw it?'

That thought made my head spin so furiously that I picked up a *National Geographic* and stared at the intricate shadings of a canyon at twilight.

Finally, I had to admit a few things. My writing had begun as an intuition from my experiences, but only in relation to specific times, places, and individuals. I knew I was talking about a few molecules of reality, but they were surrounded by innumerous contrasting interpretations. And I found myself just as interested in what lay beyond the boundaries as I was in my preconceived definitions. Why, I questioned, had my thinking taken on this inside/outside dualism at all?

I thought of a possible resolution. After all, generalized speech certainly allows particular reactions and they are themselves a part and parcel of a diversified reality. However, as many people have experienced in conferences, for example, this kind of discourse can go on *ad infinitum* without the slightest reference to emotions, sense perceptions or any other information gleaned from the body. An argument can evoke many particular reactions, but as often as not they will come from detached, talking heads. Texts referring to texts, quotation upon quotation, and rarely is it remembered that the subject is living, fully-dimensional human beings.

The language of the powerful, whether they control a country or a particular academic discipline, reflects and maintains their dominance. Their power is a result of stripping-down a diverse and multi-faceted reality into a vision of the world as they would like it to be: provable, consistent, conquerable. Their dilutions are cast as universal standards by which all else is to be measured. It is this appropriation of complexity, this presumption of universality that enables the powerful to define, for example, the nature of a 'valid' philosophical argument or the dictates of political policy.

Thus, dissidents in Latin America are labelled 'terrorist,' a pseudo-term which not only denies a wide range of opposition but also justifies their brutal suppression. The words 'lesbian mother' are almost unrecognized in the ruling ideology; lesbianism is defined as a perversion and is not at all compatible with their idea of motherhood. By narrowing the meaning of these words, they have 'proof' that lesbians are unfit mothers.

Similarly, traditional western philosophy tries to dilute complexity by positing the existence of universal laws of human nature and by defining only certain ways of thinking as valid. This hierarchical set-up allows a select few to be closer to 'the truth' and thereby attain the system's validation. If philosophy were really interested in human diversity, it might well lose its distinct boundaries as a discipline, much as politicians would lose their power to appropriate the world.

And now for the really big question: Why did I stare at magazines during times of philosophical crisis? Simply because I needed to be grounded in the particular. To look at a facial expression or the colors of a landscape is to experience unique and tangible emotions. Those bodily feelings are the source and confirmation of a kaleidoscopic reality. The body grounds us; it affirms our differences and makes us splendid exceptions to attempts at creating static, predictable laws of human nature.

And so I stopped flipping through magazines and began teaching myself to write fiction. Fiction afforded me the opportunity to find out why, for example, a grandfather never opened his family's presents. I could imagine him not speaking to his daughter for the ten years since his wife's death, dying in bed with the TV on, looking annoyed rather than at peace, his white hair combed perfectly in place. The night table would hold a novel by Turgenev, a bowl of hard candy, and neatly lined photographs of his entire family.

Now by most philosophical standards, I've been quite audacious by taking this information and, without a speck of proof, creating fanciful elaborations. With fiction, however, the authenticity comes with the telling.[2] That's why most writers find it difficult to talk about their work; the final standard for their writing is not a justification, which is considered essential for philosophical writing, but the individual integrity of the artist's vision.

Most importantly, fiction is the medium whereby 'subjective' worlds can be explored with assurance. These visions are rooted in the individual characters and in what they say and do. Of course, there may be a character who pronounces on the ways of the world, but the words could never pass as universals, simply because the reader knows whose mouth they're coming from. To my mind, the most invigorating fiction dives to the center of its characters, gathering meaning from their ordinary gestures and words and then magnifying it all until the reader knows their world for all its complexity.

Consider a passage from Virginia Woolf's *Mrs. Dalloway*. Mrs. Dalloway has just learned that her husband, but not herself, has been invited to lunch with a prominent London hostess:

She began to go slowly upstairs, with her hand on the bannisters, as if she had left a party, where now this friend now that had flashed back her face, her voice; had shut the door and gone out and stood alone, a single figure against the appalling night, or rather, to be accurate, against the stare of this matter-of-fact June morning; soft with the glow of rose petals for some, she knew, and felt it, as she paused by the open staircase window which let in blinds flapping, dogs barking, let in, she thought, feeling herself suddenly shrivelled, aged, breastless, the grinding, blowing, flowering of the day, out of doors, out of the window, out of her body and brain which now failed, since Lady Bruton, whose lunch parties were said to be extraordinarily amusing, had not asked her.[3]

The physical action of the passage has Mrs. Dalloway grasping the bannisters, going up the stairs and pausing by the window. In addition, she has been snubbed by Lady Bruton and has imagined herself leaving a bustling party to stand solitary in the night. She feels apart from society, drifting away, her body and brain failing. Yet even as she talks of this physical deadening, every reference and perception is an enlargement of her sensibility. Mrs. Dalloway feels herself a failure, but the reader can see that it is her nature, with its feelings that roam and privately rebel, that causes her social discomfort. Virginia Woolf has created a character who has been left out of the rule-makers' parties.[4] Though she tries to fulfill her obligations, by listening to her body, Mrs. Dalloway has become a quiet outcast from the rigid expectations of her society.

Bodily information is not only a foundation for a work of fiction, it is very much involved with the process of writing. Many authors have said that a novel begins with a particularly vibrant image. The story I'm currently writing began with a scene of two women talking at a crowded party in Berlin. One is a Jewish American whose father landed in the second wave at Normandy. The other woman is German; her father was a Nazi assigned to the Warsaw Ghetto. The two women like each other. The American says, 'My father fought against your father. From the time I was a little girl I was taught to hate you. And now we're at a party, laughing and looking at each other's eyes.'

This story is being written because I want to know more about these women. Why is the Jewish woman in Berlin? What does the German woman feel about her father's deeds? What happens if one falls in love with the other? Even if I thought I knew the answers, they would further evolve in the writing. As with most authors, I have found my ideas changing shape as I move along.

Many writers talk about their writing with a seemingly peculiar passivity. They say that the 'story told itself to me'[5] or that they were 'following language.' And indeed, the process of writing involves a great deal of silence, waiting and faith. My own experience is that I hit my emotional extremes. For several days, my body feels incredibly scattered, as if my insides were flying off on their own. This feeling is interspersed with periods of darkness and gloom. This tension seems to be between what I think I ought to be saying versus what my body already knows. My body rebels at the faintest suggestion of 'reasonable' pressure: I simply will not do as I'm told. During this period I may read around the topic, or clean my apartment several times, but basically my stance is one of waiting and of faith. The faith, which must be maintained through terrible bouts of despair, is the belief that my body will find its gravity, the voice that says: 'Trust me. I know the things you've forgotten.' And when I can finally listen to my body, which of course means listening to myself as a fully-dimensional person, the words begin to flow. And it always seems a miracle.

# Notes

1. Simone de Beauvoir, *The Second Sex* (New York: Alfred A. Knopf, 1953), p. 420.
2. Susan Griffin, 'Thought on Writing: A Diary,' in Janet Sternberg (ed.), *The Writer on Her Work* (New York: W.W. Norton & Co. 1980), p. 110.
3. Virginia Woolf, *Mrs. Dalloway* (New York: The Modern Library, 1925), p. 45. Harcourt, Brace Jovanovich, Inc.
4. Thanks to Eleanor H. Kuykendall for suggesting this idea.
5. Joan Didion, 'Why I Write', in *The Writer on Her Work*, p. 22.

# Upsetting an Applecart: Difference, Desire and Lesbian Sadomasochism

Susan Ardill and Sue O'Sullivan

This article is about an ideological and political set-to over defining, discussing and organizing around sexuality as lesbians in the mid-eighties in Britain.

We were both involved in the battle at the London Lesbian and Gay Centre (LLGC) over whether SM (sadomasochism) groups should be able to meet there. This battle went on for almost six months in 1985 – explosively, at times viciously. It was not just confined to the centre. Battlelines were drawn in many lesbian groups, women's centres, even bars and discos. The consequences linger today.

We want to talk about the different feminist politics which informed the groups engaged in the tactics and open fights which went on over the months. We want critically to examine SM and its lesbian feminist manifestations. We want to discuss politics which arise out of and around our sexual practices.

Although this was ostensibly a political struggle over a sexual practice, sex remained the silent item on the agenda.

It seems to us that in the London Women's Liberation Movement (WLM) there is often a chasm between discussions about the 'politics of sexuality' and discussions about what our actual different sexual practices are. Over and over, workshops at conferences, even whole conferences, bill themselves as being about sexuality, only to turn into talk shops about the things which *determine* sexuality, or how frightening it is actually to talk about sex. Evocative words are thrown around, like 'pleasure', 'danger', 'lust', 'romance', but as often as not, on the day, it's other words which apply, like distance, analysis, evasion – and above all, frustration, confusion and boredom.

122

Sexuality is for both of us a political and a personal concept and fact. Intriguing, jagged, hurting, sunlight and shadows, movement and moment. Recalled alone and recalling together. But the divide remains as we attempt to bridge it. That's the skirmish which we, two socialist-feminist lesbian friends, are having to go through to get this article out.

We approach our sexuality to capture it. But is it ever steady enough to capture? To haul into the political arena? Can we break through the reactions of our feminist sisters, lovers and friends? Their disapproval or feigned boredom makes us falter, blush and backtrack. Is talking about sex political? Can politics encompass sex? Is feminism a dour tendency? Do feminists do peculiar things in secret? Do we tend to come unstuck in sex? Do we get stuck up about sex? Is secret sexy? Does any of it matter in cold, cruel light?

Here *we* are, with daring words to start yet knowing another page will be quite ordinary. But that's it: how to talk about sex – boring, passionate, regular, surprising, absent – and how it intersects with different women's daily lives as Black or white women, as workers, as people in relationships, with or without children, as feminists meeting all the oppressions and hierarchies of this society. Because it *does* matter – though it matters differently in different historical moments, in different geographical areas. The literature of oppressed people so often contains the dreams which sexuality seems to offer, intertwined with the struggles to do with class, with race and imperialism, and with gender roles.

The movements for gay, lesbian and women's liberation have offered a way to understand, change or enhance those dreams. Or, rather, they have increasingly offered many *different ways*.

## Shattering reality

This article is being written at a time of depression and lack of confidence in feminist and left-wing politics. The reality of fragmentation and the development of a politics around the autonomy of 'new' political constituencies – women, Black people, gay men, lesbians, old people, disabled people – has thrown up its own theoretical discussion around 'difference'.

From the beginning of the women's liberation movement in the west, when differences were sheltered (and hidden) under the benign umbrella of sisterhood, we moved to the situation of the early 1980s when 'differences' pulled down the umbrella and claimed sisterhood as an autonomous state for their own group. A multitude of identities defined lives, loyalties and political correctness, as the totalizing world view feminism offered to some, mainly white, women cracked open. Conflict became the keynote.

This article is about one such conflict – one which was crucially concerned with differences *between* lesbians. It struck both of us that while recognition for the oppression of different 'other' groups of people constantly came up during this struggle, in fact our political opponents had a basic difficulty in acknowledging that within our own shared identity of lesbianism, other women could drastically differ from them in attitude or practice. We wanted to take apart this apparent contradiction, wondering if it could offer us any insights into the roots of the bitterness of the conflict, or give us any help in creating the alliances or coalitions we must make to affect radical change.

## Hello. What's your name?

What we felt happened with the increasing dominance of 'identity' as the organizing factor of so many feminist activities and discussions is that 'naming' and 'claiming' came to be invested with a peculiar moral authority. Just to *name* yourself as part of a given group is to *claim* a moral backing for your words and actions.

Where does this sort of 'naming' get its power? Why have certain words become icons? In the LLGC battle, for example, speeches by women who were opposing SM often began with a declaration of identity: for example, 'I am a lesbian mother and I think . . .' In this context the words 'lesbian mother' are meant to convey a specific moral weight, not just that of personal experience. What was being invoked was a particular feminist ideology. We cannot *name* this ideology. It's not a simple political tendency, but an amalgam of various strands of feminist politics. As we see it, there are two key ingredients: an analysis of the world as made up of a fixed hierarchy of oppressions (or a select collection of oppressions) around gender, sexuality, race and ethnicity, age and ability; and notions of the 'authenticity' of subjective experience – experience which can be understood only with reference to the hierarchy. So, to say, 'I am a lesbian mother' within this mode of politics during the LLGC struggle was to allude to a whole set of oppressions as a way of validating the speaker's current political position. (A number of other things were going on too, but here we want to get to the root of the tone of self-righteousness we often heard.) Within these politics, there's little room for distinguishing between politics and those who speak them, little space for such things as evaluation of strategies or criticism, or making mistakes.

Somehow, the radical power of uncovering by describing, creating language for experiences that have previously gone unarticulated, just becomes labelling, slotting things neatly into place. In this value system 'naming' and 'experience' are privileged – but there is little room for movement once the words are out. To speak experiences, to claim identities, is to be tied into positions, and everything is assumed to follow on from them. A lesbian mother, then, will automatically have certain positions on men, women, money . . . sex.

The inherent problem with taking subjective experience as the main key to political action is that people have differing experiences. Not only that, they may also interpret the same experience in differing ways. The solution of some feminists, be they revolutionary feminists, cultural feminists or socialist-feminists, is to fall back on their own particular hierarchy model; those more towards the bottom bear more of the weight so our/their experiences must speak more 'truthfully' of oppression. In this context, any clash, whether between groups or individuals, becomes a matter of rank determining righteousness. While this hierarchy model has developed partly as a response to difference, and conflict, it doesn't do particularly well with diversity or contradiction. It too easily lends itself to a politics of 'truth'. Taken to extremes, if there are divisions within the same 'rank' or group, suppression becomes necessary, so as to protect the 'official' version's claim to define and describe the oppression.

These basic premises, with their reliance on the truth of the hierarchy or the sacrosanct nature of a collection of oppressions, and the claiming of identities, have increasingly become an implicit part of much feminist politics. They act as the framework, the supports, for political positions around the different issues.

Feminists' ideas about lesbianism have formed and changed over time. In the last few years one ideology of lesbian feminism became dominant and claimed feminism for itself. This ideology operates within the framework we have just outlined. 'Anger', 'identity', 'experience' have become the hallowed passwords among large numbers of lesbian feminists.

Imagine their consternation, then, if another group of lesbians pops up – who are *angry* and who want to *identify* around a different *experience* and *interpretation* of it. But this interpretation, in the realm of sexuality (that most subjectively experienced area), upsets the whole previous applecart of lesbian feminist assumptions about who lesbians are. It is this fundamental clash which forms the basis of the entanglements over SM, and because it's a struggle over definitions and the power to define, now at the crux of some political positions, emotions ran high. Unravelling the tangles at the roots of the bitterness that fuelled the LLGC SM debate has been emotionally fraught for us as participants, and difficult to do. But ultimately that unravelling exposes many of the underpinnings of the various politics involved. It presents possibilities for stating differences and divisions while working to change and challenge exploiting power. And, in the course of the struggle at the LLGC, it's just possible there started a fracture which could impede the ascendancy of a brand of lesbian feminist politics which has been prevalent in this country for long enough.

# The premise of the premises

The London Lesbian and Gay Centre is the result of certain possibilities meeting certain perceived needs. It would not exist in the form it does today without the politics which the radical Labour GLC embraced and propagated. It wouldn't exist as it does now if a particular cross-section

125

of gay men and lesbians hadn't come together with an understanding of all this and with a vision of a centre.

The centre, an old four-storey building, almost across from London's Farringdon tube, opened unofficially and unfinished in late December 1984. The plans were for stylish and well-appointed premises which would meet the needs of a wide variety of London's gay and lesbian population. Included were the inevitable disco/bar/theatre space, a café and kitchen, another bar, a bookshop run by Gay's the Word, a creche, a large lounge and meeting room for lesbians, a media resource floor, various centre offices and a number of spaces for rent to gay and lesbian projects and enterprises.

By the time of the 'official' opening in March 1985 the centre was being booked for meeting space by a number of different groups. The co-opted management committee (MC) had already discussed the issues which would soon break out into bitter fighting between users or potential users of the centre. Wendy Clark, one of the co-opted MC members, told us, 'We knew from the women's movement what some of the issues would be and that sometimes clashed with some of the views that the men held.'[1]

Bisexuality, paedophilia, sadomasochism, transsexuality, dress codes – all came up in the MC discussions about who could or should be welcomed into the centre. At the same time the MC, an all-white group of men and women, discussed making the centre accessible to more Black and working-class gay men and lesbians.

Wendy Clark maintains that the majority of the women on the MC were antagonistic to the SM groups who wanted to hold meetings in the centre, and in particular they were not keen about the men. Yet the centre's ideological underpinning was a liberal tolerance which incorporated the 'wide diversity of the gay community'. This contradiction was not fully faced, until it hit them in the face.

## Zoning in on the centre

It was in this context that the first stirrings of a more public debate about SM and the centre occurred. Different eddies and currents, already swirling elsewhere in the WLM, settled on the centre with histories already in the process of gelling, with scuffles recorded and bad guys and good guys named. A coalition of lesbian feminists saw that the centre was (unenthusiastically) giving a place for SM groups to meet. Already they had managed to trounce the possibility of any of this ugly business happening at A Woman's Place (the central London women's centre) or of SM being discussed in the central London women's newsletter. Letters arrived at the centre from these women demanding that SM groups be forthwith excluded. They declared with their usual confidence that they represented *the* lesbian feminist position on the subject.

By the time the centre opened officially, the 'debate' was underway, particularly within the weekly meetings of lesbians who were trying to co-ordinate events in the lesbian-only lounge and work out the relationship that space had to the rest of the centre.

It was not a new debate – only the instance and place made a difference. Political positions over the SM issue by no means followed a clear-cut path. But certain trends could be discerned.

## Sexuality and feminism

In the mid-seventies lesbianism and/or separatism were first presented within the women's liberation movement as possibilities for all women to take up as part of their political struggle. For many feminists the printing of the CLIT statement from the USA in issue after issue of the London Women's Liberation Workshop newsletter was shocking, frightening and led to the first significant withdrawal of women from under the umbrella of sisterhood. (We're aware that many, particularly Black and working-class women never got under it in the first place.) In the CLIT statement all heterosexual women were named as untrustworthy dupes at best, or, at worst, as active collaborators with the enemy. Given that, the only feminist choice was withdrawal from men and bonding with women.

In London there was no sustained political rebuttal of CLIT – only the outraged cries of wounded and angry heterosexual feminists. In this instance, heterosexuality was attacked on moral/political grounds and the response was moral/personal outrage. No one spoke directly about sex; there was no ongoing discussion about desire or sexuality. But, after this, the earlier possibilities for heterosexual feminists to explore their relations with men didn't exist in the same way. Being a heterosexual feminist, even an angry-with-men one, was not enough any more.

However, from then until the emergence of revolutionary feminism, and in particular the Leeds revolutionary feminist writing on political lesbianism in 1979, heterosexuality was still the assumed sexual identity of most, if not all, women in most feminist circles. Lesbians had certainly made their presence known inside the WLM, but often they still had to assert their presence in order to avoid being incorporated back into the assumed heterosexuality of all women. This was true even on *Spare Rib*, a magazine of women's liberation. Continued sorties against that assumption were made by lesbians and/or separatists. Often the basis of the criticism was confused. In some cases it veered towards biological determinism, as in the then-infamous 'boy children' debate in London, where the presence of the boys of feminists at women's centres created a furore. In other instances the argument tended to be couched in terms of lesbianism's 'natural' subversive and revolutionary character in relation to the patriarchy.

Revolutionary feminism, as distinct from radical feminism or socialist-feminism, is the forerunner of a particular English feminist politics which six years later ended up fighting SM at the LLGC in the garb of Lesbians Against Sadomasochism (LASM). LASM had links, through particular women and, more importantly, through its political opposition to SM, with the early political lesbianism of the Leeds revolutionary feminists, and with the anti-porn politics of Women Against Violence Against Women (WAVAW): 'Porn's the Theory, Rape's the Practice.' But other lesbian feminist political positions were also present in the anti-SM grouping.

Radical feminists, even if in relationships with men, tended to say that they rejected male sexuality as it is now, totally. But on *Spare Rib* magazine, the early years produced confident articles on sexuality; articles which were going to teach women how to have orgasms, how to demand what they wanted from men. By the late '70s that confidence had gone.

*Spare Rib* spent much of 1980 tearing itself apart over the issue of sexuality. The collective was split over whether a submitted article claiming that lesbians had silenced heterosexuals in the women's movement was anti-lesbian and, secondly, whether *Spare Rib* should print it. The lesbians and heterosexuals on *Spare Rib* (all white women at that time) differed over the article and the lesbians differed among themselves. However, the 'naming' and 'claiming' tone was set by those lesbians on the collective who felt that the article was anti-lesbian and that they suffered as a result of it. Because they suffered, their position had to hold sway. The other lesbians, who either did not think the article was anti-lesbian or who felt that the best way to deal with anti-lesbianism among feminists was to bring it out in the open, air it, confront it and struggle with it, did not count. They didn't display the requisite pain. The *expression* of anti-lesbianism in whatever form, from whoever, became the *oppression* of lesbians, full stop. The article was not printed and the collective went on in a confused, moralistic and contradictory way to confront and be confronted by racism, Zionism, and anti-semitism.

## What's that you're grappling with?

The rise of revolutionary feminism in the late 1970s claimed a certain place for sexuality on the feminist agenda – firmly in the centre. Men's sexuality was the key problem, but in a different way from the view of many radical feminists. In revolutionary feminism, male sexuality was, for the foreseeable future, irredeemable. Feminists' struggle was *against* male sexuality, not *with* it; they mobilized against it in WAVAW and anti-pornography groups. Woman's sexuality was the key to both her oppression and liberation.

Suddenly everyone was grappling with compulsory heterosexuality and political lesbianism, separatism, non-monogamy, lesbian lifestyle, lesbianism as the practice of feminism. Where was socialist-feminism in all this? Despite the brief existence of Lesbian Left, the terrain around lesbianism seems to have been left wide open for revolutionary and radical feminism to claim as their own. In the late '70s and early '80s, heterosexual socialist-feminists, confronted with the growing divisions in the autonomous women's movement, not the least of which were accusations of consorting with the enemy, dropped out in droves. And they made a beeline for the mixed organizations of the left – trade unions, the Labour Party, campaigning groups – leaving those socialist-feminist lesbians who remained socially and/or politically active in the grassroots of the WLM not a little isolated in the face of the now dominant assumptions about lesbianism and feminism.

It is ironic that while many of the best-known socialist-feminist intellectuals are lesbians, over the years socialist-feminism has come to be associated with heterosexuality. It has concentrated on analysing desire in the abstract and has had virtually nothing to say about lesbianism. It has made no significant political intervention in the ongoing messy debates about sexuality, heterosexuality and lesbianism. This is a schematic view, of course, but one which we think accurately describes the relative power (or lack thereof) of socialist-feminism *vis-à-vis* radical/revolutionary feminism in speaking to lesbians about the experience and politics of sexuality.

## Tipping the cart

So, 'woman-identified' ruled OK. Then *Sex Heresies* came along, published in the spring of 1981. This issue of an American feminist periodical was an attempt to combat the latent feminist assumptions about how we, hets or dykes, 'should' express sexuality. With a paucity of feminist writings around on sex, and after a few years of *The Joy of Lesbian Sex* and others of that ilk, it was definitely exciting. And shocking to some – with articles on butch-femme relationships, sadomasochism, masturbation and celibacy, prostitution, fag hags and feminist erotica. Whatever else, *Sex Heresies* signalled a move to put the erotic back into sex. Whereas the British revolutionary feminists appeared to see sex as a pleasant possibility between women who had withdrawn from men, *Sex Heresies* underlined the deep and confusing currents of desire between women.

In the USA *Sex Heresies* seems to have been the first salvo in a battle over sexuality which has been intense, overt and wide-ranging. A loose coalition of sexual radicals (who include lesbians, heterosexual feminists and gay men) has sprung up, stringing together the unrespectable issues, like paedophilia, SM, promiscuity, willing to dissect, bring into the open and mostly defend all the variations of sexual pleasure and desire. All of these overlapping issues have had specific ramifications amongst lesbians – but, in the lesbian feminist subculture, SM has become the peg from which all the others have been hung. And it was the SM debate which turned up among lesbians in Britain.

# SM's shifty meanings

Why do we keep naming it 'the SM debate'? One of the most difficult aspects of this ideological struggle around sexuality has been sifting through a quagmire of shifting definitions. A simple description of SM might be the sexual dramatization or acting-out of power relations, with its own history of codes and meanings, of ritual and paraphernalia. But is SM a clearly delineated physical practice which only a certain percentage of lesbians will ever be into? Is it therefore of limited relevance to most lesbians? Or is SM the crystallization of the most vital components of *all* erotic tension: teasing, titillation, compulsion and denial, control and struggle, pleasure and pain. Alternatively it could just be that, in the vacuum of lesbians speaking and writing about sex, the language of sexual excitement used in, for example, *Coming to Power: Writings and Graphics on Lesbian SM*, resonates with a great many women who are not, technically speaking, into SM (SAMOIS, 1981).

Debates specifically around lesbian SM *have* taken place in the context of a general challenge to feminist sexual orthodoxy. SMers indeed have aligned themselves with other self-defined 'sexual outlaws' – prostitutes, butch and femme lesbians, bisexuals. Several things seem to have been happening at once, and at times it's hard to keep a grasp on exactly what it is at any given moment.

SM lesbians have been engaged in a struggle to 'come out SM', to be open and proud of their sexual practices. Because of the negative connotations of sadism and masochism (linked to actual torture, cruelty and emotional suffering), and the hegemony of political lesbianism, they have been come down on – hard – by large sections of lesbian feminists. Other lesbians, including many socialist lesbians like ourselves, have acted in defence of SM dykes around issues of censorship and exclusion. This defence has necessarily broadened into an intense struggle over definitions of feminism and lesbianism, the rights and wrongs of lesbian sexual practice, desires and fantasies in general.

In participating in these struggles, we've become aware of the absence of language that can deal with different lesbian sexualities. To some extent, SMers have captured the market of sexual description. But it's plainly no use dividing all lesbians (as some SMers do) into SM and vanilla dykes. During the last year we've been dismissed as liberals (from both sides) because we've appeared to be just tolerantly defending the rights of others. However, we don't disavow our own interest or involvement in some aspects of SM. We do think, though, that a socialist-feminist critique of SM as a political theory and pleasure as a supposedly neutral playground is needed.

In Britain, the struggle around lesbian sexuality has been muted and spasmodic, though accompanied by often violently intense reactions. This struggle to retrieve eroticism in the face of, among other things, the political desexualization of lesbianism, has been characterized here by an almost complete absence of talking or writing about sex. A magazine like the explicit Californian *On Our Backs* seems unthinkable in London. Even the sexual liberationists, in discussions about 'Pleasure and Danger' in the avant-garde *Square Peg* (No. 10, 1985), resort to allusions to 'tops' and 'bottoms' and various interpersonal dynamics. Having bought their under-the-counter (yes – from Sisterwrite in London) copies of *Coming to Power*, lesbians might make either covert references to their 'favourite article', or disdainful jokes. The possibility of having, for example, a frank and public discussion on the lesbian gang 'rape' fantasy ('Girl Gang' by Crystal Bailey) seems out of the question in London – and yet one of us has been in on a discussion on that, and many others like it, in Australia. We're forced to fall back on the suspicion that sex itself *is* relatively more hidden in British society, and that goes for the women's movement too.

## Reactions

The reaction against *Sex Heresies* and all it stood for was well under way by late 1981. Articles in the internally published *Revolutionary and Radical Feminist Newsletter* posed a dichotomy between sexual liberation and women's liberation reminiscent of the early 1970s – only this time it was some forms of lesbianism, not just heterosexuality, that were under attack. Revolutionary feminists and some radical feminists sought to set the terms of the discussion: political lesbianism (lesbianism as a political strategy for fighting male power) was such a central tenet of their politics that any challenge to the orthodoxy of lesbian sex was a challenge to the entirety of their feminism. Anyone mounting such a challenge was not a 'true' feminist.

But the sexual pleasure brigade continued to make inroads, in books, conferences, discussions. By late 1982 articles in the *Revolutionary and Radical Feminist Newsletter* had to take some of the issues on board, though still with a completely hardline rejection of SM. They were obviously worried that talk of sexual fantasy, masochistic feelings and erotic pleasure was ringing a few bells among lesbians. They felt the 'SM lobby' was capitalizing on the silence of its opponents, so their strategy became one of talking about sexuality. They wanted to demonstrate that most lesbian feminists had perfectly reasonable non-oppressive sex lives (and thus didn't need SM). They acknowledged that many women had masochistic (even sadistic) fantasies. However, if feminists were 'afflicted' with the 'internalization of the male (hetero) sexual model', change was possible and *necessary* for feminism.

With this strategy in mind, revolutionary feminists organized the Lesbian Sex Conference in London in April 1983. However, although they planned it and wrote all the pre-distributed papers, the conference ended up having a non-specific atmosphere. Attended by hundreds of women, with workshop titles ranging from 'Lesbians and Fashion' to 'Monogamy' to 'Heterosexism', there was a general air of waiting to see what would happen. With no organized speakers in workshops, and no plenary session, complete pot luck determined any individual's experience of the weekend (see Egerton, 1983). There was the odd rumour of disagreement from the SM workshops, and there were conflicts involving the felt exclusion of some working-class women and the physical exclusion of women with disabilities. But in general nothing much seemed to happen. If there were few open discussions about sex, neither was revolutionary feminism much in evidence. It was a diffuse and defused occasion.

In the following two years, questions of sex and sexuality went slightly out of focus, as struggles and eruptions, especially around racism and anti-semitism, took centre stage in the WLM. The 'sex' debate had been, in Britain, primarily conducted between two (or more) camps of white women, with individual contributions by some Black lesbian feminists (Bellos, 1984). This, we think, is unlike in the USA where the concerns and theories around sex of Black women and women of colour had a strong voice among the pro-pleasure groupings, though not without hard criticism of the racist elements of much white theory. Here, the increasingly organized and powerful presence of Black lesbians has had a gradual impact on the terms of reference of the SM debate. Some Black lesbians have made it clear they don't want anti-racist rhetoric used in an opportunistic way to bolster up *either* side of the debate, particularly as it has remained a white-dominated discussion. Racism in sexuality remains largely unacknowledged on the white lesbian political agenda.

## It's getting closer

On to the next round of skirmishes. During the winter of 1983-84, the *London Women's Liberation Newsletter* refused to carry a notice about a meeting called by SM Dykes to discuss sadomasochism. The few individuals (including members of a lesbian sexuality discussion group we were in) who raised voices in protest at the censorship were shot down in a barrage of abuse and condemnation.

At the 1984 Lesbian Strength March the storm in a teacup blew up again when SM Dykes appeared with a provocative banner (lesbian symbol intertwined in chains). Newsletter writers raged at the shame and horror of it all. SM Dykes, having been silenced, kept silent in feminist circles.

Less than a year later, the LLGC opened its doors and the anti-SM lesbians were busily writing letters to the MC protesting about any SM presence there. A few of these women started to attend the weekly meetings of the Lesbian Co-ordinating Committee, set up as an open voluntary group to plan and organize the lesbian-only space. Instead the meetings (in which we took part) spent a lot of time skirmishing, fighting, going over and over the subjects of SM, lesbian identity, political acceptability and the role of the centre. No one talked about SM *sex* or whether anyone should do it. We were talking about the presence of small groups of women and men who might use the centre for meetings on the same basis as many other lesbian or gay groups. No one defended the 'right' of any fascist or racist group to meet at the centre, no matter how 'well' they might behave. In fact the centre's constitution clearly excluded any such groups from meeting in it. The argument remained one about definitions of SM, and the supposed behaviour of SMers.

Because no one really believed SMers were going to do 'it' in the centre, the focus was on their presence – how they looked became all-important. The practice of lesbian SM was, on both sides of the debate, described with dualistic pairings of words: power and submission; pleasure and pain; dominance and subordination; passive and active; top and bottom. Alongside these went the apparel and (optional!) accessories: whips, chains, dog collars, caps, leather, studs, handcuffs. The 'look' (often indistinguishable from punk) became overloaded with meaning, and as threatening as the acts themselves. The question of women who might take part in SM sex without dressing the part was never dealt with. An extreme image was set up to be knocked down.

SM acts were, in the eyes of LASM women, irredeemably connected to heterosexuality. As most heterosexuality was considered violence to women, the added ritualization in SM sex made it more horrific and dangerous. In lesbian SM the fact that the oppressor (man) wasn't actually doing it made it even more reprehensible.

The Leeds Revolutionary Feminist Group had written their paper 'Political Lesbianism: The Case Against Heterosexuality' in 1979. In it they said '. . . it is specifically through sexuality that the fundamental oppression, that of men over women, is maintained' (Leeds Revolutionary Feminist Group, 1981). The Leeds group stated it very directly. In 1979 they wrote as if class, race and disability didn't exist, even if they were heavily criticized for this at the time. Now the same revolutionary feminist analysis came shored up with the opportunistic use of race, class, anti-semitism and disability. In a sense these become the stage props of the central drama which, for them, is still the determining division between men and women. But this is our interpretation and lies beneath the surface of the politics we are describing. The debate over lesbian SM was carried out by using their hierarchies of oppression, their collections of 'most oppressed', and attaching them to the practice of SM sex – thereby 'proving' how dangerous, disgusting and politically incorrect SM is. SM Dykes became the walking repositories of racism, fascism and male violence.

## Mixing it up

It seems in retrospect, no coincidence that this long-running drama in lesbian feminist circles finally came to a head in a mixed centre, though at first glance it might seem strange that women whose political position tends towards separatism even bothered to care about what would go on there. After years of separation, the LLGC marked an auspicious attempt for lesbians and gays to bridge the gap. A whole generation of lesbian feminists had gained their political experience in women-only centres and groups. It may have been a shock, even an affront to some that an attractive, well-equipped centre was opening outside of their assumed sole claim to lesbian politics.

Lesbian SM, and SM Dykes themselves, had been fairly easily squeezed out of the increasingly prescriptive feminist channels of organization and communication. (Long gone are the days when a feminist cabaret act could call itself the Sadista Sisters and get away with it!) But owing to the different historical development of gay liberation politics, a mixed gay centre potentially offered them a home. Confirmation to its opponents, perhaps, that SM *is* an essentially 'male' practice, and that the struggle against it is part and parcel of the larger feminist struggle.

At most points during this struggle, LASM's main argument was against the contamination of lesbianism *and* the centre with a violent 'male' ideology. At other times it seemed that some anti-SM women were in complete opposition to any alliances or solidarity with (gay) men at all, and that was really the basis for their involvement at the LLGC. It was when this fundamentally destruction-minded position seemed to be gaining the upper hand that some of the group of women we were working with gave ourselves the somewhat dull title of Lesbian Feminists for the Centre.

Not that our support for the centre, or for working with men, was unproblematic, but then, we had entered into it anticipating that. When the SM debate came along, the primary aspect for us two was the struggle over ideologies of sexuality and lesbianism. The playing out of antagonisms between lesbians in front of men obviously posed difficulties. We had to be very wary of colluding with the view of feminists as spoilsport puritans perpetrated by some gay men (and women). One of us was disturbed by the anti-feminist tone of some statements at the first meeting of the Sexual Fringe (a coalition of women and men who defined themselves as sexual radicals). On the other hand, we would have liked to know how to protest openly at some lesbian behaviour towards men at the mass meetings, without swelling male egos. Too often we found ourselves silent, loyalties and politics pulling us all ways at once. Our main concern was to focus on the other lesbians involved, and to mobilize more lesbians to get involved. So, throughout the struggle we organized in an autonomous group of women. We wanted to keep distinct from the centre, and from men, in order to engage fully with LASM women within a feminist framework. But at no time did we consider the presence of men as incidental, or something we'd rather have done without. When it became apparent that we'd struck, and were up against, a deep anti-coalition vein within feminism, our commitment to this mixed centre clarified. It became, then, partly also a struggle to maintain the right to political optimism; to retain a sense of the possibilities for new things which the centre stood for.

# Putting the extraordinary into EGM

In April 1985, the first extraordinary general meeting (EGM) was held at the newly opened LLGC. Most women and men came thinking that they were there to discuss and resolve the issue of SM at the centre. The management committee, after its initial acceptance of SM groups meeting at the centre, had reversed that decision. After receiving letters and protests from LASM women and their supporters, they changed their minds. Wendy Clark says, 'So we took an interim decision that as a group they couldn't meet until there had been an open meeting or the first general meeting of the centre members and ask them to decide.' In fact SM groups took legal advice, consulted the constitution and called the first EGM.

It was a packed, tense meeting. Nothing was resolved. For constitutional reasons we were unable to take a vote on the proposed ban. For us the tension arose from our own silence and inability to support SM groups meeting in the centre in the face of the emotive presence of LASM women and their supporters, some of whom had never set foot in the centre before. Immediately after some angry scenes, *lesbians* were invited upstairs to a meeting in the lesbian meeting room. When some of us went our presence was challenged because we were 'pro-SM'. By this point feminism and lesbianism were claimed as LASM's own.

LASM's reports of the meeting were outraged. In newsletters and on the grapevine came news of a meeting packed out by SM men and women dressed in fascist gear who, by displaying continuous misogyny and hatred of children, oppressed the LASM women. The act of opposing their demand for exclusion of SM groups was, they claimed, an SM act in itself. (As far as dress goes, some strange outfits were worn, some leather and a few studded collars and leather caps. We saw no fascist gear.) The North London Lesbian Mothers Group, supporters of LASM, produced a leaflet for the EGM which illustrates some of their politics. 'For those of you who claim to oppose censorship of any kind, ask yourselves if you would allow a group calling itself "Gay Fascists" to organize in the Centre. There have to be *limits* in order to *prevent oppression* of all kinds' (our emphasis).

Here is the usual equation of SM with fascism. But we are interested in other aspects of the quote. So – oppression of all kinds can be prevented by imposing limits! Well, unfortunately oppression is not the product of 'no limits'. It comes, in however devious a route, from particular social systems and from particular sets of relationships which are part and parcel of those social, economic and cultural systems. To propose setting 'limits' as if that could take care of oppression and exploitation in our society is a travesty of the sort of changes we need to go through in order to transform anything. Our criticism of the lesbian mothers' leaflet is on this basis, not about whether or not 'limits' are sometimes necessary or a good thing.

The static moralism of this political position is ripe for reformism too. It's been noted often enough how many socialist-feminists have been drawn into municipal socialism and the Labour Party. What has not been noticed

135

at all is the number of revolutionary feminists and those influenced by them now working in the same institutions, usually around women's issues. It would be interesting to trace out the reception their politics are getting in the Labour Party, and the influence they are having.

## An extraordinary repeat

After the April EGM many centre users became more organized. Spurred on by LASM's tactics at the first EGM and ashamed of our inertia around that event, Lesbians for the Centre began to meet independently to formulate a proposal for the next EGM (on 9 June at Conway Hall) and to discuss how we should go about trying to engage with LASM in order to defeat it. Our politics were diverse; we were not a group of SMers, nor were we all socialist-feminists. We lacked a common theoretical base, but shared general agreement in practice about the centre. We knew that LASM would propose an outright ban on SM groups, and that the Sexual Fringe wanted a completely 'anything goes' situation. We wanted to defend strongly the rights of the SM groups, while raising questions about what *could* be problems in such a centre in terms of dress and behaviour.

## Stuck in dilemmas

This led us into hours of debate over a dress code. Our proposal reflected the compromises we all made. Tagged on to the end is the one dress ban we all agreed on (the swastika, in the west a symbol of fascism past *and* present) and the one we compromised on: that no one should be led around the centre on a leash or chain. (Yes, we know it sounds ridiculous.)

No one in our group questioned that certain clothing or equipment evoked images of reaction and oppression. What we divided over was whether some styles or equipment – handcuffs, for instance – were in themselves symbols of oppression and therefore in themselves racist, fascist or anti-semitic. The two of us agreed that meanings of objects are socially and culturally constructed. That did not mean that certain dress or behaviour could not be contested or even banned, but it should be on the basis of political discussion about the relationships between people in the centre and between the centre and the outside. Our motion said:

The LLGC is a centre for a wide variety of lesbians and gay men who have different political perspectives. We are committed to an outreach programme to actively encourage the participation of black and ethnic minority lesbians and gay men, disabled lesbians and gay men, and younger gay people. In order to ensure participation, the centre holds a firm policy of anti-fascism, anti-racism,

136

anti-sexism, and an opposition to anti-semitism and aggressive behaviour. The centre is closed to any group that advocates fascism, racism, anti-semitism, or sexism as any part of their stated aims or philosophy.

Lesbians and gay men have a diverse range of 'sexualities'. We advocate no *one* sexuality for lesbians and gay men, understanding that sexuality is very complex, but we do recognize that the centre should be a place for constructive discussion around all aspects of our sexuality.

Certain symbols and actions will not be permitted in the centre, namely the wearing and displaying of swastikas, and the leading around of individuals by means of chains or leads.

Of course this was seen as the very life blood of liberalism by LASM. Our aim neither to identify with a simplistic pro-SM stance which absolved anyone of critically looking at *that* sexual practice nor to dismiss the fears of LASM was not particularly appreciated by anyone.

In any case the second EGM was beset by similar constitutional problems to the first, and the few motions or proposals discussed could be voted on only in order to ascertain the sense of the meeting. A large group of LASM women and their supporters demanded and got separate votes for men and women, obviously in order to *prove* the connexion between 'male values' and pro-SM politics. Finally, at the end of the day, about one-third of the women present and three-fifths of the men voted to allow SM groups to meet in the centre.

The meeting was as acrimonious as the first, at times disintegrating into shouting matches. When a small group of women (about twelve of us) who sat together on one side of the hall raised our hands to oppose a ban, women on the other side of the room, LASM supporters stood up to stare at us. The divide by the aisle was as literal as the divide between our politics.

# Gathering forces

All during the spring other groups had been meeting and politicking around the centre. The Sexual Fringe included SM lesbians and men as well as bisexuals, transsexuals and celibates. They saw themselves romantically as sexual outlaws, wherein the very fact of 'difference' put them in the same political position. They produced several leaflets which took on what they called prescriptive feminism.

When LASM put out a leaflet headed 'What Is This Big Fuss About Sado-Masochism?' it sparked off a number of responses. The LASM leaflet itself is interesting. Its pompous question-and-answer format compares very closely with the Leeds Revolutionary Feminist paper of 1979 on political lesbianism. There, the same irritating, moralist question-and-answer format places the authors in the superior, vanguardist position of explaining it all to backward children: For instance:

Q: But we don't do penetration, my boyfriend and me.

A: If you engage in any form of sexual activity with a man you are reinforcing his class power.

Q: But I like fucking.

A: Giving up fucking for a feminist is about taking your politics seriously.

Q: Are all lesbian feminists political lesbians?

A: No. Some women who are lesbians and feminists work closely with men in the male left (either in their groups or in women's caucuses within them), or provide mouthpieces within the women's liberation movement for men's ideas even when non-aligned.

The 1986 LASM leaflet, 'What Is This Big Fuss ...' includes 'answers' too:

S/Ms often wear clothes expressing real power, pain and humiliation, eg Nazi style caps, dog collars, chains. This is racist, anti-semitic, and offensive to all oppressed people.

A pathetic questioner goes on to ask:

Q: But isn't Lesbian and Gay Liberation about freedom, not more limitations?

A: Total freedom is the freedom of the powerful to oppress – do you condone racism, anti-semitism, heterosexism?

Q: But I like wearing long spiked belts and dog collars – and I'm not into S/M.

A: So what. If you don't care that others see them as racist, anti-semitic etc then you are being racist, anti-semitic, fascist.

In that leaflet and in another called 'Sado-Masochism – the Reality', which was produced after the second EGM in June, SM takes on vast meaning: 'Remember that SM was a significant part of the "decadent" social scene in 1930s Berlin – part of the political climate of the day. People acclimatized to SM brutality would have failed to notice the threat of the "real Nazis" approaching.' Not only is SM equated with racism, fascism and anti-semitism, but it also appears now to have allowed the rise of fascism in Germany! A view of 'decadent homosexuality' which is uncomfortably similar to the Moral Right's. The leaflet goes on to say: 'Similarly, we are all brought up to have racist feelings, otherwise the institution of racism could not survive.' These are the sentiments which fuel much of the racism and heterosexism awareness training industry: it is feelings which allow the institutions to survive.

The Sexual Fringe members responded to these lectures with some wit and precision, though their libertarian outlook sometimes weakened their insights. However, one of their leaflets which appeared before the second EGM was more sophisticated and responded to LASM's equation of SM and fascism. In 'Who Are the Real Fascists?' they say:

To label SM fascist is to trivialize the real fight against fascism. To throw the word fascism about with no reference to what it means is to make the real fight more difficult. To use people's sexual revulsion as a scare tactic against sexual freedom is a real insult to fascism's victims.

In an unpublished letter to *Feminist Review* last summer, four women members of the Sexual Fringe wrote:

We feel that the women's movement has become more concerned with constructing and policing its own categories of sexual identity than with attempting to understand the complex and often contradictory construction of women's sexuality in a male-dominated, capitalist society.

All of these positions and arguments circulated in the weeks leading up to the second EGM and afterwards before the Lesbian Strength March and the July AGM. The LASM women were furious and disgusted when they lost. The fallout was heavy. Various lesbian groups had to decide what to do after the defeat. Some decided not to hold any meetings at the centre – fair enough. But at least two or three groups wrote letters to the GLC claiming that the centre was racist, fascist and excluded lesbians. They wanted the GLC to chop its financial support. A few LASM supporters inside the GLC even attempted to represent LASM's position on SM and the centre as the one and only true feminist one. It's quite a turn-up when lesbian feminists, some of whom advocate withdrawal from men on an individual sexual basis as a political stance, run to a male-dominated bureaucracy to denounce other lesbians and gay men. All that was quite shocking and indicative of the bankruptcy of their politics.

In the weeks leading up to the Lesbian Strength and Gay Pride March in June and before the AGM at the end of July, leaflets attacking the centre were distributed at women's venues, clubs and discos. Immediately before Lesbian Strength March, when the centre served as a meeting point and the evening celebrations were in the lesbian lounge, a warning was handed out to women in London: 'Warning. Do not go to the London Lesbian and Gay Centre unless you are prepared to be in an environment that is rife with fascists, racists, misogynists and sadomasochists.' It offered an alternative social event after the march at Tindlemanor, a women's centre. Hundreds of women ignored this, and a fantastic evening followed. The centre was claimed as a place for many of London's lesbians.

## Opening up the space to explore

So what were the consequences of all this fighting? The centre doesn't appear to have been overrun with whips and chains – at times it's a positively tame place to be. A large number of lesbian feminists undoubtedly stay away. But many others do come. Most significantly, for us, a politics founded on an apocalyptic vision of what would happen if SM groups merely met at the LLGC has been publicly defeated and proven wrong. We definitely get a sense that LASM's ideology has suffered quite a big dent, and that some space has opened up for more discussion about lesbian sexuality. For, if anything, this debate showed that we are hardly at the beginning of being able to talk about it.

SM literature has said much about sexual daring, openness and excitement. It has said a lot to verify our own experiences, to incite us to further fantasies and possibilities. It has brought into the open naked desires. But it hasn't said much about situations where desire is absent or fantasies won't come; much less about, for example, the mundanities of a fetish-less long-term relationship.

We don't want to fall into the trap of posing these as opposites of each other (cruising *v* monogamy!). We're not saying that SM Dykes are responsible for articulating all sexual possibilities. The struggle around the rights of SMers has made space for more writing about sex – some great, some awful – though there's still far too little of the good stuff about. However, we do think that the Sexual Fringe (not an SM group, but from within the same political stream), during the LLGC struggle, *failed to acknowledge* that 'vanilla' sex can be exciting or that sexuality can be problematic (and not just because of 'repression'). By default, their position seemed to amount to one of 'uninhibited pursuit of the sexual high' – which leaves a lot to be desired!

Ultimately the Sexual Fringe's libertarianism ended up glorifying a kind of individualism. They romanticized categories of 'deviant' sexual practice – if you can't claim one of their identities, well, frankly, you're boring.

Boring equals vanilla sex, which is what? For lesbian SMers and for us, the ritual of the sexual interchange is very important. But for us an SM interchange can be as much about finding pleasure in the unplanned holding down of one lover by the other. 'The way we think about sex fashions the way we live it' (Weeks, 1985). Our own political position on SM is that we are all on a continuum. (We refuse the label liberal over this – stuff it.) Is the thrill of deliberate touch on muscle, a pressure on shoulders, done with a sense of dominance, accepted with a sense of submission, any less exciting than tying someone up? We suspect most of our sex lives and sexual histories are very uneven: cuddly sex, bondage, kisses and affection, one-night stands, dressing-up – any of these can be what we crave or pursue at any given time.

We should make it clear that, issue by issue, we would line up with the Sexual Fringe in defence and support of a radical sexual politics and practice. The question of desire is crucial to our understanding of sexuality. Where we disagree is over the context for those politics.

The centre's 'Fringe' and the SM groups saw their rebellion against society's 'norms' and, further, against the 'norms' of what constitutes 'acceptable' sexual practice according to certain groups of lesbians, as a radical act with political significance. In denying that playing out society's power roles in bed had any causal connexion to the continuance or development of such relationships in the big wide world, they tended to exclude any discussion about the ways in which sexual relations *are* related to the rest of our lives. For instance, around housing, work, family – as well as state institutions. Lesbian SM literature suggests that organizing around oppositional sexual difference constitutes not just a political practice but a whole political perspective. It's here that SMers come unstuck. By failing to situate themselves as within particular subcultures, linked to certain lifestyle requirements, they inflate their sexual politics with a universality it almost certainly does not have.

The most absurd extension of the SM political position is the implication that if we all played out our SM fantasies in bed, the world would be a better place. The connecting line between this mode of thinking and the LASM one is striking, even if they draw the opposite conclusions.

LASM women claim that they have no real interest in the acts of SM sex except as they represent and become all of the pain, horror and degradation of women, Black people, Jewish people, mothers, disabled people, and so on. Unlike the SMers who deny any harmful reality of sexism, fascism and racism in SM sex roles or rituals, LASM goes to the opposite extreme and claims that things like tying up, spanking, whipping, and wearing collars or belts with studs are in themselves violence against all the oppressed peoples of the world. LASM say they 'do not consent to being terrorized by the presence of the symbols of brutality, which are *just* as threatening as the presence of the real thing' (our emphasis). They deny any possibility of consensual agreement or equality in SM sex, just as the political lesbians do to women in 'ordinary' heterosexual sex. In an unquestioning SM view, we can choose our stage and role. In LASM's view we are acted *upon*; we are permanent victims (or bearers of oppression) except when we refuse the acts, deny the feelings which make us victims. We are implicated in our own victim status if we refuse to do that. This is where morality makes its entrance. (It's a remarkably religious scenario.)

Neither of these views sees the world in movement, in tension, dialectically. Still, is any of this SM debate/struggle really important enough to go on about? Why do we care so much?


# Taking a stand

Sexuality in Britain in the 1980s sits uneasily in the political domain, with other matters such as class despair, racist attacks and economic depression demanding feminist attention. They demand our attention too, but we don't want to loosen our claim to the sexual as political and as important to our everyday lives. The thoroughgoing heterosexism of this society makes the struggle around sexuality an especially crucial one for us as lesbians.

Both of us live out our lives at least partially within the lesbian subcultures – socially and politically. We have no intention of quitting that world, and every intention of standing our ground there as lesbian feminists. As lesbians we have chosen to criticize the words and actions of other lesbians, we hope in a way consistent with our politics. A LASM leaflet said about *us*:

SM Dykes have in fact never spoken up at any of these meetings, leaving the shouting to SM Gays and a group of 'liberal' women – none of whom are interested in defending any 'minority groups' other than the so-called 'sexual fringe' groups. The 'rights' of SMs, paedophiles and transsexuals are given priority over the right of women who are Black/Jewish/Irish/of Colour/disabled – and all other women who are threatened by male violence and are therefore excluded from the centre.

That leaflet exemplifies the sort of intimidatory tactic which has fuelled our anger during this struggle. We think this sort of tactic has serious implications for lesbians and for feminism. We know of many individual lesbians who have taken up the LASM position on the centre because it was presented so heavily as the 'correct line'. This represents a wider trend. Doubts, ambiguities, confusions are shoved under the carpet under this sort of pressure. The mere expression of dissenting ideas has become synonymous with endorsing oppression. There is no room in the LASM view for struggle, for admitting that we all can harbour reactionary ideas at the same time that we hold on to progressive ones.

Exploring complexities within the framework of the need for socialist-feminist change is a way of understanding where we are now – alone, together, in different groups. As lesbians, we do not want to be restrictively told what we are, or should be. As women, we do not want to be presented with a feminism predicated on a false portrayal of ourselves. That will not take us anywhere.

## To sum up, then

The fight between feminists about SM groups meeting at the LLGC represented a lot more than that. It was the location, for a brief and tumultuous time, of a battle around particular feminist politics. It was ostensibly about sexuality and yet sexuality was hardly mentioned in detail. For us it was largely a political struggle between different groups of lesbians. We don't believe for a moment that many of the LASM women gave two hoots about the centre. In that way it was a symbolic occasion for the anti-SM women and, even though we were very involved in the centre, for us too.

History, in the short and long term, while open to analysis, has a messy daily life. It's a sad if not unsurprising irony that a socialist understanding, one which could help explain at least some of the reasons behind the exploiting divisions between particular groups of people, has not 'fitted' in a lasting way with the development of the women's liberation movement here. All through the 1970s the voices of excluded, ignored or patronized women sang angrily, accusingly about class, about race, about sexuality. Yet the practice of the white-dominated women's movement, with a large and vital socialist-feminist presence in it, was unable to answer those voices.

Whether this says more about British socialist history, contesting Marxist analyses of the 1970s, or about women's attempts to merge socialism and feminism, is open to debate. In any case, by the late '70s and early '80s those different voices finally resonated in many of the organizations, structures and publications of feminism. 'Difference', so long acknowledged but not dealt with, came home to roost, at the same time that socialist confidence in affecting social change was waning. It was then that the whole reality of unequal power relations between feminists and in the world was taken on board by an increasingly dispersed WLM. In some instances, the resulting lessons and achievements offer exciting possibilities for really radical change. But, for some, 'difference' became *in itself* an explanation, an organizing method, a static and moralistic world view. The anxieties about differences between women provided fertile ground for the rise of a simplistic politics within lesbian feminism which grasped for the seemingly easy answer of 'authentic experience'.

The possibility socialist-feminism had of pushing forward a historical and dialectical analysis of difference between feminists and women in general which could produce a politics that could move, embrace, challenge yet forgive, had been overtaken by a rigid feminist politics which elevated some differences to the basic underpinning of political organization. What any one individual 'makes' of what she undeniably feels is open to many possibilities. The 'truthfulness' of the experience of the individual is not what we would question. Nor the reality of conditions which give rise to the experience. But the fact that there is no one unifying response to sexism, to racism, to class exploitation, to heterosexism, forces us to examine the *place* that individual experience should hold in the development of theory and practice.

The contradictory responses of people to their particular oppression and/or situations alerts us to the often contradictory and complicated intertwining of the forces which course through the body politic. Far from making us throw up our hands in despair, we believe feminists can use that reality to develop an analysis and practice which takes into account the messiness of real life, the hopes, fears, angers and acquiescences.

The 'things which divide us' are as hard to discern as a sliver of glass and as huge as a boulder. The individual experience, however subjective, is an engagement with a force with a half life of its own and another half owned by other social forces. Racism exists. Sexism exists. Class exploitation exists. Imperialism exists. But each tangles with the other, feeds from or subtracts, adds to or bloats up another.

The way we 'feel' or experience any of these forces, either directly or indirectly, either one or the other or all, cannot be claimed as the only authentic one. In the first place that totally individualizes the effects of social forces. The social construction of an individual neither means 'free will' nor victim status. And secondly it removes individual constructions of feeling or experience from the impact of historical, economic and cultural forces. Thirdly, it proposes that there is a straight, short line from experience, to consciousness, to understanding and, finally, to political action.

What we feel as women from a thousand different realities, as oppressed and oppressor, actor and object, is a vital *part* of what goes into our political analysis as feminists. Often it is the key to our political awareness, or our awakening. But we don't base our understanding of women's continuing oppression and exploitation on it. No white person can claim to define a Black person's experience, nor a man a woman's, nor a heterosexual a homosexual's. Any of us must be able to develop politics which make us sensitive and open to learning from the experience of others *and* provide us with the tools and a framework for critically assessing theoretical analyses and daily political life.

It is the absence of discerning, exciting and accessible feminist and left political theory and practice at this particular point which makes it so difficult to stand up against the politics of experience or 'identity' politics. It's one of the elements which has swept through so many of the bitter eruptions in British feminist politics during the past five years in particular. It's what we falteringly and finally tried to come to grips with at the London Lesbian and Gay Centre.

## Notes

Thanks to *Feminist Review* members for helpful notes and reactions. We would both like to thank the women with whom we worked politically during this debate. As well, Susan would like to thank Penny, Gerri, Anne and Paula for comments on the article, and Norie and Kim for thought-provoking discussions about sexual politics while writing it. Sue would like to thank Ruthie, Jill and Diane for long discussions on sexual politics over the years.

1.    From a very helpful interview we did with Wendy Clark in September 1985.

# Excerpts from Letters
## Brant and Raven

December 10, 1982

Dear Ms. Brant,

Greetings of peace. I hope my words finds you happy and content upon all your paths of living.

As you can see from the above address, I am incarcerated, as a matter of fact I have been sentenced to die. I stand innocent, but there's no justice in white man's courts. I have much knowledge of the law. But I cannot have faith in any courts, that sentenced me to death, for a crime I never had any part in.

I'm of Cherokee blood, from North Carolina. I also have a little white in me. I've been raised in white man's world and was forbade more or less to converse with Indian people. As my mother wanted me to be educated and live a good life, free from poverty. I lived a life of loneliness. Today I am desperate to know my people.

Ms. Brant, I would appreciate any thing you can or will do, that will aid me in my need of my people.

Thank you for any and all concern to my words.
    I, remain
    Raven


December 14, 1982

Dear Raven,
    I was so happy to get your letter. It made my day very beautiful.
    Please tell me more about yourself. I was very moved by your letter. It seems that so many of us have missed out on our own heritage. My family is Mohawk but education was the highest goal, and it was hard to not assimilate. I am not educated. I got married when I was 17. My three daughters are grown up now. I am 41, no longer married, am a feminist and a lesbian. I began writing two years ago, and now feel like I can do my political work in this way. I am poor, but live in relative freedom. I have received many letters from my sisters in prison, and I am struck by the mobility and freedoms that I have. I admire your courage and you are all an inspiration to me. I am honored and blessed that you will be contributing to the issue. Thanks for writing. Nah weh.
    Beth


December 19, 1982

Dearest Beth,
    Greetings sister; peace and love.
    Thanks for the letter, cards and stamps. I really appreciate you taking time and concern for me.
    I admire you greatly. You are of freedom. I seek friendship of those who know and accept themselves, and stand in truth, without plastic covers. I salute you!
    I've been in this tiny cell for 11 months. I do not have visits. My 'white' family ignore me. I do not call them or bother to write. Each of them live in the world of booze & drugs, my half-sisters and half-brothers have very little going for them. I do not hate them. I understand them. They are not my people, 'they are white.'

I was hurt at first, but I've worked myself up from this emotional level. I do not want more hurt. I find it hard to believe that all people are mean and cruel.

Beth, I value your opinion greatly. I think white people are lying evil monsters. They have no truth, love or honor. My Grandfather taught me the red man is wisdom and loyal. Is this correct? I am as my Grandfather taught me, that I should be and I do get hurt often, but my dealings with Indians is rare, as my mother wanted it.

Beth, I am giving serious thought to asking the state to drop my appeals and set a date for the gas chamber for me. I do not want a life sentence or to fight years of appeals. The state says I killed a elderly lady. I won't even kill a dog. I am so ashamed by this. I'm in this cell 23½ hours a day. I have my radio to keep me comfort. I read a lot and exercise. I'm into keeping my body agile and firm. As my mind I will not allow to stagnate, I work both body and mind. I thirst for knowledge. I've read all the books here on Indian people. I sketch a lot. I am a loner.

You are in control of your life and self. I'm so thrilled to meet someone who is there own person. Its important to me, how people are. I do not bend in my values to please others who disrespect me.

Thanks for the ear. I guess I needed to rap. I guess I consider you a-ok. The best to you sister.

May all your dreams come true, and peace be ever constant with you.

Thanks for listening to me.

Walk freely sister.

peace and love

Raven

December 28, 1982

Dear Raven,

Thanks for your wonderful letter. There are so many things to write to you, so many words to share.

Yes, I do know myself, but often hate that woman. I am proud to be an Indian, proud to be a lesbian, but have to constantly fight the hatred, the desperation. My people hate me because I'm a lesbian. Whites hate me because I choose to identify with being Indian. It is a vicious circle, one that never stops.

I would like to know more about your life. Do you remember much from when you were a kid? I lived with my Grandma & Grandpa until I was 12. They wanted so much for all of us kids to be successful and educated. I never finished high school. I got married when I was 17. It was 1959 and I was pregnant. There wasn't much of a choice. Abortions were dangerous and illegal and besides that, much too expensive for the likes of us. So I married, had three daughters, finally threw my husband out. He abused all of us.

Sometimes I *do* think that all white people are evil. But my mother is white and some of my blood is hers. I have spent too long hating

146

myself, and I don't want to anymore. My lover is white. She comes from a poor Polish family. She understands so well. Probably because she was raised so poor. She knows what it is like to be despised and to be ashamed. I have several women friends who are white. I love them. The difference is that they work very hard to understand, to speak out against the racism and classism that exists. We are not supposed to talk with each other about important things. We are supposed to assume and to hate. I want to stop that in myself. I used to think that only Indians were good. But that is not true. None of us has escaped the hatred and racism heaped on us by the elite few. I believe that we will act out the negative things expected of us. My uncle was a drunk. He didn't start out that way. He certainly didn't want to be one, but he became the stereotype expected of him by whites. I loved him very much, although he hurt many people, my Grandma especially. I truly believe that white man hates and craves what is inside those of us who are colored. They envy our connections to the spirit, to the earth, to a community, to a people. Because they envy that; they hate us, and will do anything to get rid of us. So all the things ... slavery, genocide of Indians on this continent, as well as in Latin America; the Holocaust, missionaries in China, the Vietnam War ... all of these a calculated program of extermination. And I add to that, the millions of women burned at the stake centuries ago, because we were women, because we were lesbians. As long as we don't make the connections between us, we are lost and will be played by white man. I am sending you a book called *This Bridge Called My Back*. I think you will understand everything. It was written by women like you and me. Indian, Black, Latina, Asian. It is a book that made a great change in my life.

What I want to say is that I'm frightened much of the time. I may never know what it is like to be in prison. But I have been in a mental institution, unable to get out, unable to go to the bathroom without asking. Unable to stop the harassment by the nurses, by the orderlies. Unable to stop the drugs they shoved down my throat. When I refused to eat, they stuck needles in me to feed me. They threatened me with shock treatments, with insulin therapy. There was a point where I had to decide to live or to die. I chose life for myself. At that point I didn't know why I did. But now I know I am needed for something. I would never have known you. And I am blessed by knowing you. So perhaps there is a reason for choosing life over death. I am your sister. I will listen to you. I will be on your side.

Stay in peace, little one. I am thinking of you. Nah weh.

Beth


January 6, 1983

Dearest Beth,

Greetings: my sister and peace be with you. Thank you for your very beautiful letter, and the stamps.

Enclosed please find a article done on me. The photo sucks, but then they always show the worse ones. Very little of what I said was printed.

I asked them to state why my lack of faith in the maryland court system was so bad, but as you can see they didn't. I say I am innocent, and if the courts can convict a innocent person, how can I have any faith in the same court system.

I only wish to be free of this place. I'm dieing slowly. I need to feel the earth under my feet. This place resembles a tomb. I'm sealed away from the things that make living, living. I need fresh air and space to move.

I often ask the guards to bring me a cup of fresh air, in a joking manner. Some of the guards here are real people. Thats not a odd statement even though it may be hard to understand.

Beth, thank you for entrusting me enough to speak to me of your pain. I surely agree, white men both hate and envy us. How can they not. We are strong, we can relate to the earth, while they cannot relate to themselves! I should think, rather than be envious, those ones should seek knowledge and learn our ways. But to do this, they would have to accept Indians as wise. Our bonds are different.

I do not think much about this up-coming event [the execution]. I simply await it. My dream would be to have a medicine man with me and a couple of my own people.

I just had a hour with a female reporter for the paper. I'm drained, but I believe she was sincere. She says she will print the true me. I hope she does.

Well, my sister, as you can see many changes have taken place in my life. I do not know how I feel. I'm only confused and tired.

I think of you often and how well balanced you appear to be. But as you spoke to me, you are fearful also. I surely understand you are as me. I do not let my fear to show and rarely admit I have any fear. With you I feel comfortable. I do not fear your rejection of me in my true form. I've grown more since I wrote you last. I've accepted myself more and I've looked at myself from all angles. For the most part, I like what I see.

I feel like a child who is undressed in public. Many people asking questions, but printing falseness.

Dear sister I will conclude here and get some rest of body and soul. Stay in peace.

Love, Raven


January 26, 1983

Beth,

Greetings may your peace be great and your paths smooth. Beth, the article you have and all the others have not printed my words.

*All* these articles that I've seen say that I want to die because I can't stand this place. But the articles don't say that I say I'm innocent and do not have faith in the same court system to free me, that gave me death, when I'm not guilty. Its not so important that people know I wish to die, but it is important that the reasons be brought to life. I can die

148

easier for a cause, when I walked into that courtroom, I was as naive as the rest, but my sister I'm proof of the corruption. The next time you or one of yours could be here. We need to kick these people back. I do not trust anyone. I talk to you. My lawyers do not contact me at all. They are poor excuses for lawyers.

I know how reporters like to write about our pain, but they print lies. For example the Jan. 24 *Time* article.

Many christians write, but I do not believe the way they do. They are really weird sometimes. I usually ignore them. They only want to save my soul. I need to save my life.

These church people speak on many things that I do not believe is any of there business. I got into an argument with the chaplain here. He says I shouldn't smoke and he talked of homos (his word). We got into a heated rap. I'm not into women, or at least, I haven't been, but if I am or if I'm not, I do not feel he should judge. What difference does it make whom we love??

I hope you are ok my sister. Let me say if I should have to die, I shall be as brave as anyone can be. But somehow the country just should be aware of this lousy justice system.

I shall keep you in my thoughts. Take good care of yourself special one.
　　Love,
　　Raven

# Lesbians of (Writing) Lore

## Nicole Brossard

*Translated by Marlène Wildeman*

In the first place, not everyone is a writer and not all women are lesbians. We have here then two modes of existence which inscribe themselves in the margins of the normal-normative course of the language and the realm of the imagination and, consequently, in the margins of reality and fiction.

Before going any further, I would like to begin by asking this clarifying question: what is necessary in order to write? I *could* ask: what does it mean, to write? But it seems to me more pertinent – given our subject – to try to answer the first question, which to a certain extent concerns the identity of lesbian writers.

Generally speaking, I would say that in order to write one must a) know that one exists, b) have a captivating and positive self-image, c) respond to an inner necessity – if only in self-defence – to inscribe in language one's perception and vision of the world; in other words, one has to want, consciously or otherwise, to make one's presence known,

149

to declare one's existence, and finally, d) feel a profound dissatisfaction with the prevailing or mainstream discourse, which denies differences and congeals thought.

In sum, then, to write is to be a subject in process, constantly calling into question the existing order. To write, one must first belong to oneself.

We can say, therefore, that with respect to the actual practice of it, writing is a subject which concerns, first and foremost, the individual. But as Jean Piaget so aptly remarks, 'One who has not had a sense of the potential collectivity has absolutely no awareness of (his or) her own individuality.'[1] What this means is that to be conscious of oneself as an individual, that is, conscious of one's uniqueness, one must first acknowledge one's belonging to a group or the larger community. Whatever our ethnic or religious origins, we belong quite visibly to the category 'women' – what characterizes women as a group is that we are colonized. To be colonized is not to think for oneself, to think in terms of 'the other', to put one's emotions to work in the service of 'the other' – in short – not to exist and, above all, to be unable to find in one's own group, the sources of inspiration and motivation essential to artistic production. It is crucial to find in the group to which one belongs captivating images which nourish us spiritually, intellectually and emotionally. Who and what then inspire women? Who and what inspire lesbians? and this in an integral and non-fragmented manner. In fact, one ought perhaps to distinguish between what motivates us and what inspires us. Thus, I could say that women motivate me because as a woman and a feminist among women, I have a profound motivation to change the world, to change language and to change society, but I could also say that lesbians inspire me in the sense that we are a challenge for the imagination and, in a certain way, a challenge for ourselves, to the extent that we give birth to ourselves in the world. Only through literally creating ourselves in the world do we declare our existence and from there, make our presence known in the order of the real and the symbolic.

When I say literally give birth to ourselves in the world, I really do mean that literally. *Literal* means 'that which is represented by letters'. This is what is meant by being taken to the letter. For we do take to the letter our bodies, our skin, our sweat, pleasure, sensuality, sexual bliss. From the letters forming these words emerge the beginnings of our texts. We also take to the letter our energy and our knowing skill, thus rendering of our desire a spiral which delivers us, one and all, into movement toward sense. Sense in which we are at its origin and not moving counter to the established order like so many tiny stars trailed in tow through the great patriarchal cosmos. Symbolically, and realistically, I think only women and lesbians will be able to legitimate an orbit toward the origin and the future of sense, sense that we ourselves are bringing about in language.

To be at the origin of sense means that we project to the world something resembling what we are and what we discover about ourselves, not the patented version of women which patriarchal marketing has made of us, in person and in giant posters.

To write, for a lesbian, is to learn how to take down the patriarchal posters from her room. It is to learn to live for a time with bare walls. It is to learn how not to be afraid of the ghosts which take on the colour of the bare wall. In more literary terms, it is to draw fresh comparisons, establish new analogies, attempt certain tautologies, dare to brave certain paradoxes; it is to start over a thousand times one's first sentence, 'a rose is a rose'[2] or to think as did Djuna Barnes, that 'an image is a stop the mind makes between uncertainties'.[3] It is to take the risk to have too much to say and not enough. It is to take the chance of not finding the right words to say with precision that which only we can imagine. It is to risk everything for the universe that takes form between the words, a universe which would, without this passion we have for the other woman, remain lifeless letters.

I think that wild love between two women is so totally, in a sense, inconceivable that to talk or write *that* in all its dimensions, one must almost rethink the entire world in order to understand what it is that happens to us. And it is only through words we can rethink the world. Lesbian love therefore seems to me intrinsically a love that largely goes beyond what is generally called love. Something that is at the same time part of us yet goes beyond us – now there's an enigma for writing and fiction but, especially, for poetry.

Having said this, it seems to me that for lesbians who write to step out like this, essentially in front of what they are, what they need is a bed, a worktable to write on, and a book. A book we must read and write at the same time. This book is unpublished but we are already quite familiar with its substantial preface, in which one finds the names Sappho, Gertrude Stein, Djuna Barnes, Adrienne Rich, Mary Daly, Monique Wittig, etc. This preface contains, as well, a certain number of biographical annotations recounting guilt, humiliation, contempt, despair, joy, courage, revolt, and the eroticism of lesbians throughout time.

The book is blank; the preface sets us dreaming.

I know that lesbians don't look up at the ceiling when they're making love but one day I looked up and I saw the most beautiful fresco it ever was given me to see as far back as women can remember – on my lesbian word of honour. This fresco was perfectly real, and at the bottom of it was written: a lesbian who does not reinvent the world is a lesbian in the process of disappearing.

## Notes

1. Quoted by Edgar Morin in *L'Homme et la mort*, Paris, Seuil, Collection Point, no. 77, 1976, p. 112.
2. Gertrude Stein, in *Sacred Emily*, 1913 (listed in *Bartlett's Quotations*, 15th Edition, p. 752:8.)
3. Djuna Barnes, *Nightwood*, 1937, New Directions Paperbook No. 98, New York, 1961, p. 111.

# Notes on Racism Among the Women

Donna Allegra

In some circuits, Black women have become valuable commodities on the social scale. As feminism has become respectable and Black women criticize white women on their racism, a lot of whites want to prove it's just not so. They invite us to submit articles, perform, read, or speak on panels. This has brought about a relatively new situation in my life – whites coming to me, asking for input.

Once I welcomed being in this position; often I went for it. I consciously figured on getting across as a token. That position would be my point of entry to places where white racism would ordinarily have left me out of the program. Now, with a Black women's community to live and work in, white structures are not so appealing. I look back with bitterness at whites whose dealings with me were not based on who I am, but on what I look like: a Black woman to fit into their program.

It was a real disservice when white women looked at me, saw the Black, and greeted me with eagerness because of a hidden agenda. It took a while before I realized it wasn't my charm and personal magnetism that was operating – I've got a big ego and I'm a slow learner. How bitterly I remember the white women who took me in as a token and how bitterly I remember myself going for the bait – hook, line, and sinker. I want to be treated as an individual, not seen with awe and fear as someone's dream nightmare. I want to be seen as a person who wants to do a job for reasons not unlike their own: a person subject to pride, fear, greed, anger, ambition, high ideals, willingness, trust, and love, like themselves. Instead, many see me as a 'Third World' woman to be used to make a project look good if I act right.

I feel a personal shame for having been willing to be that statistic or chocolate chip in the sea of white cookie. From that token's position, I tried to take myself somewhere, but doubted underneath that I could have gotten in on my own merit, not being sure of my place in the structure. That's the legacy I inherited from the perverted relationship where some whites looked good practicing tokenism and I was willing to let them get over through me. I was left not knowing where I really stood with them, trying to figure out what they thought I was, and then trying to be that so I could do what I wanted to do in service of who I really was.

Once I looked with trust to the feminist option. It was the minority viewpoint I would read and hunger after and identify with. I appreciate that there is a women's community with networks and publications, and that we do share a general point of view. With feminism established as a part of the current order, some things are easier for me, but elements of the old ways do continue to take on new forms. Now that a feminist angle is being targeted into cigarette commercials, I feel ripped off all over again. In a like manner, Black is 'hip' – well, not so hip anymore. More accurately, now white women are supremely sensitive to being accused of racism and try to avoid the word like the plague; it makes their shit turn to water if anyone even thinks the word in their direction. Now that they are conscious of Black women who come out with such very hip analysis and delivery, many of them want to hold onto us.

I resent feeling that they want us around for the power of our image: picture a handsome, angry Black woman on the cover of many a magazine that ever so rarely deals with a Black viewpoint. So many women who are talking about racism are more concerned about public relations than they are with gut-level sisterhood. They want us so that they don't have to feel uncomfortable should any Blacks call them on the question, or should any other whites get into the game of reminding their sisters that there are no women of color in evidence. Real reconstruction is bypassed. It's easier to opt for the cosmetic treatment. This is like being a nice girl. You smile at anyone who smiles at you and you don't dislike anyone because that's the way you've been brought up. But the truth of it all is that only by trading honest viewpoints can people negotiate and work out frank differences.

White women deny that they seek out women of color because pressure has been put on them. These white women are almost trained to respond with a politically correct manner when they're questioned. If some of them would acknowledge resentment or that they are bewildered that they can't seem to do anything right by Black women anymore, some truth could emerge that'd free us on all sides. But so many are afraid to come from anything other than masks of good behaviour.

Yet I know now when whites are running from me, trying to deflect any confrontations they fear I will want to bring into play. I can tell by their aggression on the subjects of race and racism – as though it were outside of them somehow, or as if by giving an appropriate nod to guilt, blame, and responsibility in a politically correct stance, they'll be safe from the anger they seem to expect from me. They are ill at ease and run from a feeling of discomfort that they project onto me. When whites beat their breasts and talk about what's being done to the poor darkies, they are still taking the missionary position and fucking Black people.

I have yet to hear white women talk about Black women as people, as individuals they like or dislike. In the conversations I have heard, we are either 'heroic,' 'surviving,' or 'triply oppressed.' They'll urge sympathy on us for Black men's purported sexism or condemn white men as a class group, but never voice a criticism of Black women. It makes me wonder. When a white woman assumes I'd be interested in something just because I'm a Black person, I withdraw one giant step inside. I'm dismayed when I see women at concerts or poetry readings knowing how to clap in all the right places and saying a nervous 'yeah' – as if by verbal affirmation of Black women's performance their guilt can be discharged and penance done so blame is deflected from them.

Today, white women see a lot of Black women who want to give their energy solely to Black women rather than deal with whites. I imagine white women often don't know what to do and feel perplexed.

A good number of Black women don't want to be bothered teaching or working with them because whites aren't as innocent in their racism as they put out. Others get mad at whites for trying to include Black people. It seems like you're damned if you do and damned if you don't – so what's a poor little white girl to do?

This thinking is, of course, not leading to the real truth. I think the answer to the seeming paradox is for the white women to do their own consciousness-raising and examine what they come up with among themselves. The working out of racist attitudes is process work for white women to do for themselves, with one another. Once they can see themselves through the rough stuff, they will actually be freer and truer to themselves. I appreciate that kind of honesty in an individual more than a correct line. Honesty is something I sense, can open up to and trust. Race differences are real, but they're not everything. We work out our real differences from honesty.

But after they've done their own CR, I hope these whites don't come to me for a stamp of approval. I'm having a hard enough time dealing with my own stuff and hoping my women will given me the pats on the back I crave. I don't think many Black women are going to credit whites for doing their own homework. Whites seem to want this at some level and when it doesn't come, they feel pissed and neglected. Well, that's not enough for Black women who have other concerns and don't want to play nanny in any mode. I've been brought up to feel I should be grateful for every little bit of progress, but I frankly do get angry at white women who are actively trying to deal with their racism and the new trips they lay on me in their growth process. Those white women who aren't so anxious and eager to clean up their acts and attitudes around race are the ones I can have friendships with. It's a tricky balance to find, but I think the important personal quality I respond to is honesty.

What is going on with all our concerns about racism is, indeed, change. There is a willingness among some white women to do some work, but the transformation isn't complete yet. Racist attitudes linger because the job isn't all the way done. People who haven't seen that change is possible can't wholeheartedly believe in it. If they haven't lived it in their personal lives, it's hard to see change in political terms. It won't all come together in one fell swoop. After the major reconstruction, there will be corners to straighten out and the maintenance work will be a day-to-day job. But this is Life Work. Any attempt to make it better can only work to good.

# PART FIVE
## Recovery

---

## The Colour of the Water, The Yellow of the Field

Christian McEwen

*For Aurora and Janice and Janey*

> *There is the story of a Zen monk mourning beside the grave of his recently dead teacher. One of the other monks comes up to him and says, 'You are supposed to be a monk, why are you crying?' The grieving monk turns and says sternly, 'I am crying because I am sad.'*
>
> Stephen Levine, Who Dies?

I was the eldest of six children. Me and Katie, James and Helena, John and Isabella. I am still the eldest, but there are only four of us now. In June of 1983 James shot himself, and the following September Kate was drowned. I try to talk about it, and my tongue goes round and round inside my mouth. One tooth missing, two.

Absence, almost by definition, cannot be faced head on. When James and Katie died, I wanted furiously to act, to march straight up to them and know their vanishing, thoroughly, once and for all. I thought I could do my mourning fast and get it over with: choke down the hard fact of the deaths and push on with the business of my own life. Not surprisingly, this turned out to be impossible. 'Life must go on,' people tell each other. But death must go on too. Mourning has a pace and rhythm of its own. It cannot be rushed.

This month it is four years since Katie died. I have worked, made love and travelled in that time, but most of my mind and heart (and even body) has been taken up elsewhere. It is a strange sensation, like being underwater, sodden with old memories and questions, while the bright surface of the present glitters up above. I haven't always welcomed being

155

so totally immersed. But if nothing else, I do understand a little better now what mourning is about. It is information I am very glad to have.

For several months after the deaths, I used to wake up crying, my throat choked with unshed tears. My dreams were ugly and frightening. There were many images of sexual assault. I remember the exhaustion, and the sense that I had become utterly unpredictable to myself. My stomach ached. My back hurt me. My whole body was trapped in a state of extreme disorder.

Along with this physical upheaval went a mental and emotional and spiritual one. To mourn is to be extraordinarily vulnerable. It is to be at the mercy of inside feelings and outside events in a way most of us have not been since early childhood. Grief and desperation, angry tears, what Eliot called 'undisciplined squads of emotion' – these things do not simply have their locus in our being. They take us over. And however much we may try to protect ourselves, to name what is happening, to talk, perhaps to scream, our solutions are themselves skewed by the shaky people we've become. I remember both craving and resenting touch, both wanting people to talk about the dead and hating it when they did.

Given such violent and contradictory needs (and such underlying rage), it is not perhaps surprising that friends and well-wishers should withdraw a little. The culture I grew up in (British, Catholic, upper to upper-middle class) has anyway small language for such things. If someone in a family dies, people do what is expected of them. They call, they order flowers, they send their cards and letters of condolence. There is a certain understanding that 'recovery will have to take its time', some lip-service paid to the importance of 'expressing feelings'. But beyond such well-meaning commonsensical behaviour stretches a vast domain of ignorance and fear.

Six weeks after Katie died, an old friend gave me a ride in his car. He was an artist and sculptor, a man of nearly seventy, someone I'd known for most of my life. 'Of course you're getting over it by now,' he said. I was so taken aback I could hardly find the words to answer him. *Getting over it*? At that point I was barely getting by. I didn't expect to 'get over it' for some time yet. Nor would I have wanted to. Mourning had become my task, my responsibility. Asked if, in effect, I would be so kind as to 'tidy up my feelings', most of what I felt was rage. James was dead and Kate was dead. Those were the facts. Only in the blazing light of absolute truthfulness was I large enough to face them. To pretend at such a time, so that other people should not be met by the reflected dazzle of my pain – that seemed not only difficult, but deeply, deeply wrong.

And yet, again and again, that tidying up did seem to be what people wanted. They saw the tragedies hung like a pair of billboards round my neck, and it embarrassed them.[1] They had no idea what to do. They would have liked to help somehow, to act, to solve the problem, but clearly they could not bring the loved ones back from the dead. Awkwardly they reached for other, more familiar tactics: cups of tea and glasses of whiskey, tired words of religious consolation, none of them quite right or good enough, and all of them weighted, finally, with that same uneasy fear. *Don't break down in front of me. Don't tell me you can't cope. Don't cry, oh please don't cry –*

Even now I remember the pressure of those unspoken words, and the strange mixture of contempt and panic they induced in me. *God damn the British for their emotional timidity. How stiff it was, that famous upper lip.* In the States, I told myself, I could have found the help I needed.

The States, the States: that, I thought, was where I really lived. And the truth was, that by the time I came back to Britain for my brother's funeral, I was a foreigner. I had been away (in Berkeley and New York) for the best part of four years. I had come out as a lesbian, I had begun to write. Catapulted back into my mother's house, and deprived of most of the trappings of adulthood, I felt perhaps an extra urgency to name what I was and what was happening to me (and an extra desperation when that was refused). But I think such *wanting to tell* is very common. A mourner is, perforce, a person with a story. The pity is, how very rarely it gets told.

If I now choose to tell the story of my mourning, it is because it was through telling (even more than crying or screaming), that I was able to survive. Keeping track of daily changes in my journal, what I called 'drawing the line around the bruise' was something that I utterly relied on. When I look back now through the pages, I keep finding lists. *Write*, they say. *Cry. Trust your friends. Be kind and helpful to people you can help. Do other things you like doing – walking, singing, picking mushrooms.* It is as if I knew I would forget. *Grace, grace, grace. Remember that. The flowers on the riverbank today. The small dots around L's nipples. The colour of the water, the yellow of the field with the wind blowing the barley apart –* And indeed my world was so unsettled then that I did need to tell it over to myself, holding tightly to each tussock of grass, each separate numbered joy.

Nonetheless, journal-keeping was not my only telling. For all my grumbles about British ignorance, I did have friends that I could turn to. It is true that to begin with I was up in Scotland, whereas they were down in London, or far away in the United States. But even so, their presence made an immense difference to me. I was able to do what had to be done, to cope with each tumultuous day, by building that day towards them, and rewarding myself with a brief telephone call, or a letter. Oddly enough it was as useful to write letters as to receive them. What really mattered was that people would bear with me as I was, that however hard things might be they were not afraid to listen.

In the years since the deaths, I have had friends in a number of anonymous fellowships, and have myself been part of the world-wide Re-evaluation Co-counselling network. I know that it is not a dream to have 'enough help', 'enough support', that trouble can indeed be cried out, talked out, aired, shared, not just with beloved close friends but with a far wider community. But in the autumn of 1983, when I first moved back to London, I had no idea that such a thing was possible. I traipsed around (with minimal success) from feminist therapy to bereavement counselling to lesbian this-and-that, hoping always for that 'permission to cry' which never came. For real support, I turned as usual to my friends.

There were not many of them, and, appalled by my own neediness, I rationed myself carefully, trying to gauge what could be fairly asked from each. Some had busy lives and family commitments; seeing them meant spending time with their lovers and children, visiting a museum perhaps, or planning a doll's tea-party. Others lived alone, and could afford to be more generous. With them I talked and talked, asked questions, listened, cried.

I particularly remember one visit to my friend Leonie, not long after James' funeral. She made me welcome, gave me tea and so on, but she did not use her kindness as a way to keep me quiet. When I began to talk about James, she encouraged me and asked me questions. For a long time I walked up and down her kitchen, talking and crying, crying and talking. If the stories and the tears grew too much, or the death itself became too sharply focussed, I would go to her and she would hold me for a while. She knew, as I did not just then, that the desperation and the chaos wouldn't last forever. One day I would be well again, coherent, sane. In the meantime, those hugs, that trust, were of immense importance. They allowed me to go down deep into the grief, into the murky hopeless places where only sobbing lived. And in doing that they gave me clarity and strength, allowed me what I needed to move on.

That 'moving on' had many different forms, but of them all my old desire to tell remained the most important. Flayed and graceless as I often felt, unbuttressed, unprotected in the world, I wanted at very least to say what it was like, and I tried again and again, in poems, letters, journal entries, even a small article. It wasn't easy. Mourners are always praised for their forbearance ('She's so brave'), and to speak out was, by implication, to be something of a coward. I remember feeling odd and awkward about it, as if I were slighting the dead in some way, taking advantage of them for my own aggrandisement. The social rules sprang up under my feet, bristling and denunciatory. Then too, my head itself was in such turmoil. Guilt and rage and competition, angry pride, an unusually strong sense of greed, of need, of lust: the violence and illogic of these feelings frightened me. There was information there for me, that I did know, and ultimately, I hoped, for other people too. But I remember feeling as though I were inhabited by demons.[2]

The first of these demons was guilt, an on-going chorus of 'shoulds', 'coulds', 'oughts' and 'if onlys' which from time to time solidified into intense reproach. *It's your fault James is dead. If you'd got the early plane home, like you said you were going to, then he wouldn't have done it. Katie too. They asked you to go to Africa with her. Why didn't you go to Africa?* There was no cure for those voices except to hear them out. I listened by the hour, both to my own and other people's. I often felt that it was only by the slimmest chance the deaths had taken place at all.

Guilt is not a comfortable feeling, but at least, with friends and family, it can be given room to speak. Rage, and its malevolent derivatives, resentment, self-hate, glowering mistrust, are harder to admit to. Staying with my mother for Christmas, the first Christmas without James and Katie, I spent most of my time hiding upstairs in the bedroom. I was terrified of the rage I felt inside me, and of its possible consequences. I felt both corrupt and corrupting.

Looking back on it, I see that I felt rage in every possible direction, with the living for continuing to live (*Why are you still alive, goddammit?*) and with the dead for being dead. With James especially I was furious: he had chosen to die, chosen to take himself away, and I wanted him back, *mine, mine*, like some possession of my own. That was the rage at the suicide. But I was also angry, both with him and Katie, in the most ordinary brother/sister way. It was time to do the washing-up and I was alone again. *Where were they?*

Along with the rage at the dead went a strange sort of competition. Apart from the usual labelling that goes on in families, 'Katie is the artistic one, Mary Christian is the academic –' we had all been treated more or less equally throughout our growing up. Now everything had changed, and the dead were being singled out for special praise. *Katie has meant more to each of my children than any of their contemporaries –* The postman brought more letters every morning. They described people whose lives had come to an end, and whose characters, because of that, suddenly took on a sleekness and a finish (the word is almost cruelly exact), very far from our everyday raggedness.[3]

James' popularity, Katie's talent and beauty: I kept tabs on what was valued, envied it. I'd never get so many people to come to *my* funeral. But why I should I expect to? James was nicer than me, funnier, better company. Kate had lots more lovers. Following my thoughts along such tracks, there was barely time to register that they were dead.

With another part of my mind, however, I did know very well that they were dead – and at that point half craved such a solution. It was all too easy to move from rabid praise of the dead to vicious hatred of whatever had survived – which inevitably centred on myself. For months I floundered in self-hatred, seeing again and again a rope which dangled from a beam. *Pain is everywhere*, I wrote. *There is nowhere to sit down.* When I travelled on the underground I used to stand well back from the edges of the platform. Suicide seemed perilously close.

In reaction, perhaps, to that emptiness and terror, I grabbed out at anything which came my way, scared myself almost, at the extravagance of the greed. I had always preached the worthlessness of possessions, and suddenly there I was, demanding, pleading. I wanted James' journal, Katie's books and pictures. I wanted their jerseys and their T-shirts, their jackets and their books. All summer I talked about my 'beggar's hands'.

I liked the phrase, and it seemed accurate. *I want, I want* – I could see the hands spread out in front of me: thin and grimey and muscleless. But even as I accumulated things, I knew I didn't really give a damn for them. It was Kate I wanted, not her Stevie Smith or her complete Brecht poems, James' looming presence, not his navy jersey. And yet the hungry beggar in me wouldn't quiet down. It was as if my interest in life had come back oddly and erratically: obsessive want and then complete indifference, a kind of psychic pins and needles.

To some extent the same was true of immaterial things: attention, comfort, sexual reassurance. I didn't always want sex. But the truth was that during that desperate first year I mostly did, one of the hardest things to admit to, then or ever, and surely one of the least mentioned. I remember noticing the night I heard about James how 'very cold' the dark had become, and begging my ex-lover to share the bed with me. I wanted, if not sex, then human warmth and consolation, and for two nights she was there, and I could have it. But once back in Scotland, there was nobody to ask. I did try once or twice (an old close friend), but even he refused. Such requests were clearly against the rules.

They were curious things, those rules, rarely spelled out, and yet enormously powerful, in some ways heartless, and in others oddly fortifying. As a kind of cultural espalier, a sense of tradition and proportion, they provided me, I think, with some of my more dubious consolations. The previous year my uncle had committed suicide. To have an uncle and a brother kill themselves, and then a sister drown, made for a ghoulish kind of melodrama. There was an excitement in the very extremity of the thing, a sort of self-importance, almost pride. *Oh yes,* I wrote wryly in my journal. *Some exhilaration at the tragic story which allows me to exhibit my amazing qualities of stoicism, clarity, honesty, persistence* – I would have been glad to have avoided this display of virtues. But given the dogged business of real loss, perhaps after all I was right to look for comfort where I could. And it was a genuine satisfaction, that self-conscious courage. *Look how brave I'm being! See, no hands!*

Where the courage and the clarity failed me was, predictably, in my dealings with my family, most especially my mother, brother and sisters. Each of us had a different kind of mourning, and often these would grate against each other. I wanted to talk things out, my mother wanted to hand them over to God. The younger ones wished everybody would find something else to discuss. They had had enough of priests and doctors and Catholicism – and of my endless search for explanations too. In turn I found myself impatient with their music and their television, and the perpetual mess they left behind them, which I always seemed to be tidying up.

We were only together in Scotland for two or three weeks, around the time of the funerals, but the intensity was none the less for that. There was love and conversation, but there were fights as well. I remember Mama and me in the kitchen exchanging desperate words, and another argument, not long after, over whether or not I could carry a cord on Katie's coffin, since I was 'only a girl'.

*Only a girl, only a sister after all.* Christ, those old assumptions. I knew, I knew, by then I knew it in my bones, that although the entire family could be said to be in an unusually pitiable and tragic position, this was particularly true of our mother. 'How is she?' people asked, implying by their tone of voice that the death of a child was the hardest thing imaginable, infinitely more difficult to bear than the death of a brother or a sister. *How is she?* I always wanted to mock, infuriated beyond manners by my role of social interpreter. *What do you think? Why don't you ask her yourself?*

Looking back at it now, I think the questions about my mother were probably extremely well-intentioned. People wanted to help, they just were not sure how. It was natural to use an intermediary. But at the time, caught up in my own competitiveness (*Why should it be presumed that Mama suffered most?*), and raw with juggling real pain and social niceties, I saw their tentative enquiries as cowardice. Instead of having to meet my grief head-on (or Mama's, for that matter), they could listen to it packaged, second-hand, solved in advance to some extent, with all the ugly worries taken out. Most of the time I gave them what they wanted, 'Mama's managing just wonderfully; all the rest are fine –' But once or twice I dug my heels in and made trouble, punishing those who asked purely social questions by providing more information than they really wanted, telling proprietary stories about James and Katie which left my listeners awkward and uncomfortable. Not good manners, not at all. But it did give me great manipulative glee.

There were other consolations too, less lean and mean and personal, more abstract and large-spirited. I remember, for example, wandering into John's room, and coming across a tape he'd put together. *Rumours, Hard News, Never Going Back Again, Don't Stop, Go Your Own Way, The Chair, I Don't Want to Know* – in relation to what we were going through almost every title had tremendous resonance. I felt no surprise. By then the deaths had a force of their own, drawing everything they touched into their own magnetic field.

The same thing had happened after Papa died. I was walking in the field behind the house, and stumbled on a pheasant's nest with seven eggs in it. About a foot and a half away there was another egg, all on its own in the long grass. That egg, I knew, was Papa. The nest was all the rest of us: my mother and the six children. This was simply so. In each case I read the facts immediately, like a parable, obscurely soothed by the number of ways they could present themselves.[4]

It was perhaps for this reason most of all: to see, to hear, to make the connections, that I took no drugs or medication after the deaths, did not smoke, and very rarely drank. I wanted to look straight in the eye of what had happened, without stimulants or panaceas. And I was right, I think, it did help make a difference.

There was comfort to be found in natural parables, comfort in dreams and memories and other people's stories, but I found comfort too in far more humdrum things. My mother was responsible for most of the household arrangements, but even she could not do everything. There were beds to be made, there were dishes to be washed, there were calls to be answered, there was shopping to be done. And then of course, on each separate occasion, there was the funeral.

It seems right to keep 'funeral' in the singular, even though I know of course that there were more. Papa's funeral, James', Katie's, for me they overlap and merge, blurred grey photographs, oddly superimposed. It was at Papa's funeral that Helena and I had our fight over who got to wear Grandmama's tartan skirt (she won). It was at James' funeral that Binning's dope disappeared, and the two dogs fucked each other endlessly on the turned earth of the grave. It was at Katie's funeral that Helena read from *The Color Purple*, and I screamed when flowers landed on the coffin. Separated out, these things are sharp and painful. And yet the funeral itself, with Mass at Marchmont where we'd all grown up, and the burial at the little church just down the road, was always reassuringly familiar. I remember how glad I was, each time, to help in choosing hymns and bagpipe music, and to be one of the three or four who read aloud. Making wreaths helped too. For Papa I used forget-me-nots, which shrivelled in the night, and had to be replaced at the last moment. For James I picked copper beech and honey-suckle, with strawberry leaves and rosemary for remembrance. For Katie I chose brambles (for our old antagonisms), but set about with rosehips and field-daisies, an apple and a rose. Everything came wild from the garden. These things felt right and accurate, and there was tremendous consolation in the doing of them.

Running parallel to this more obvious and immediate doing was something else: a kind of investigative detective work, an asking of questions and a joining-up-of-dots which I particularly felt compelled to undertake. *What had James been doing the day before he died? Who were Katie's friends? What did they think of her?* 'Absent, absent –' my brother John had scrawled across his blotter. Before I could learn to 'integrate with the absence' (something the text-books, anyway, seemed to think was possible), I had to understand what I had lost, and so I followed James through the pages of his journal, Katie through her pictures and her letters. In my dreams I told them that I loved them both, shaped a peace between us that we hadn't had.

I had an image of myself about that time, standing at the side of a twelve-lane freeway while everyone I knew rushed past me at top speed. Noise flew from them, rising and falling like the sound of static on the radio. *My piece just got accepted. We are buying a new house. My baby's due in March* – They went so fast that I could barely hear them.

Who was I then? I hardly think I knew. To be 'inhabited by nothing', that was how I described it to myself, to have no room for anything else, because the dead were in me, like threads which had seized my veins. It made me numb and frightened listening to them. I used to think I might go mad, as each one did battle with the others for my energy and affection. But at the same time I didn't want them to go away. I was all too aware that that might happen. *But when I look for Papa, all I find is a pair of broken spectacles* –

Perhaps to live in ordinary life again, to get beyond the identity of mourner, you have to believe your dead are in you, irrevocably, or that they are somehow *placed*, whether in heaven or the grave. I know that in my own case this took a very long time. *Oh this busy fury to recover and recover.* But at the same time I understood what I must do. *Trust the mountain, the lake, the tears, the intermittences.* I tried, I did keep trying. But it wasn't simple. Time bucked and dipped. The mountain changed its shape. Intermittence stretched out into blinding absence and covered the horizon for as far as I could see.

I moved to London in October 1983. The months went by, and very gradually I began to reattach myself to the world. 'You're a survivor,' a friend said to me about this time. I did not believe her. But the word was important. It gave me courage in my dealings with new people, patience with my oh-so-slow recovery. It also gave me, what I hardly knew I needed, a way of separating from the dead.

On the day of Katie's funeral, one of my mother's friends came up to me with condolences. 'I'm so sorry you have lost your sister,' she said. *Lost*, I seethed. *What did she mean by 'lost'?* Katie was no comb or pencil-case that I could stupidly mislay. On the contrary. She might be dead (that was the word, *dead*), but I have every intention of holding on to her.

To learn not to hold on was a hard, hard lesson. But with that word 'survivor', I began to learn it. I remember the odd creaky sensation as I started to expand into the gaps that James and Katie had left, the exhaustion and bad temper (and the fear too), as I learned to acknowledge my anger and impatience with the other mourners, and the even more difficult rage with both of them. *I love you, of course I love you. But damn you both for giving me such a hard time. Where have I vanished in all this? I want my own head back.*

There was, on some level, just too much to accommodate, from the loss of land and house and furniture to more transient personal things, how, for example, the deaths had rearranged family relationships, cutting me off from my younger brother and sisters, and leaving me off on the edge of things, odd and isolated and much less powerful, the dyke outsider. I was hampered in my writing by the sheer weight of what had happened, forced to be literal, to concentrate on things as they were (*drawing the line around the bruise*), rather than things as they might be (the old pleasures of the imagination). And yet, and yet – that literal-mindedness helped me too. Grounded by sheer need, I learned to recognise the strengths in other writers: Alice Bloch's *Lifetime Guarantee*, for example, or the chapter in *The Well of Loneliness* where Radclyffe Hall describes Stephen's feelings after her father's death.[5] There was room there for both accuracy and imagination. If Radclyffe Hall could do it, then maybe I could too. *I hold to the writing, a great sullen fish, which I hope one day will jump and pull again –*

I stayed in London through the winter of 1983, and into the spring and summer of the following year. By December I had a job, working as a freelance reader for the feminist press, Virago. I had a cheap place to live, and plenty of free time. But for all that it took a long while for me to locate my own 'ordinary' again, to set up a life and believe it would continue, and, beyond that, to make order and thought-space for myself, to read and write, to manage to be 'selfish'.

It was in pursuit of the writing that I went back to California, to the Women's Voices Conference in Santa Cruz. There, under the redwood trees, in the class of my old teacher Gloria, I was finally able to scream the tall screams which for so long had been rocketing inside. Screams gave way to tears, and tears to sexual healing, in a concentration of love and touch which still amazes me. 'Love medicine', someone called it. I was given love medicine by four women that summer. Warmed and held by them, soothed and exhilarated, for the first time I felt no urgency to talk (or even write) about the deaths. Death was being thrust out of me by love, and love meant being alive again. It was enough just to lie back and give thanks.

I include this sequel to my desperate yearning time because, again, I don't believe it's so unusual. If mourning is so very much a physical thing, then it makes sense that it should sometimes have a physical solution. *Can't live this sexless life much longer*, says the journal. *Will wants body-comfort, spirit doesn't trust –* My summer love-affairs gave me that body-comfort, and the very beginnings of that trust. Perhaps having been taken from so enormously, I simply needed to be given to again. Certainly that uncalculated love-making seemed to unlock some paralysis inside, to realign my body and my mind (so separate for so long), and to remind me, in a language I could not mistake or argue with, that there were things worth living for.

I have always hated those people who look with conscientious fervour on the 'bright side of things', who remind you sanctimoniously that 'all is for the best'. James was twenty-two the year he killed himself. Kate was twenty-five. They had not finished living. They left books unwritten, pictures unpainted, friendships in disarray. Of course I wish that they were still alive. Nonetheless, their deaths have (fiercely) schooled me,

164

and for that, I suppose, I am not sorry. Trying to patch together the ordinary fabric of my daily life, and somehow to incorporate the odd, stiff, awkwardly shaped piece that is their vanishing – so that it makes a pattern, so that it belongs – that is a task worth doing. In the four years since, it has put me in touch with many people: teachers, students, friends and strangers, all of us brought together by a common 'death apprenticeship'.[6] There have been differences between us, differences of race and class and age and sexual preference, but in the larger scheme of things these do not matter. What is important is the unembarrassment, the lack of fear or hesitance among us. That is the basis for all the other things: the ability to ask for consolation and to give it (hugs and an open-ended 'How are you?' not a sermon), the welcoming of tears, and, most of all perhaps, some common acknowledgement of the fact that we ourselves are not immune: death is ours too.

Stephen Levine has a story about a Thai meditation master who was given a very beautiful drinking glass. He took great pleasure in it, even though for him it was 'already broken'.[7] Because my brother and my sister died, I know, in my gut, that all of us must too, and I try to reckon in that frailty in my dealings with the world. It is a paradox, but when I see or smell or touch or taste or listen most completely, I often find that I have access to another world as well. I see Katie in a grey-white London sky, hear James in a burst of sudden laughter. It is as if there is another world running parallel to this, in which they both live on. Increasingly, I believe this, and am glad.

# Notes

1. 'I sometimes think that shame, mere awkward senseless shame, does as much towards preventing good acts and straightforward kindness as any of our vices do.' C.S. Lewis, *A Grief Observed*, p. 12.
2. 'That is one of the aspects of grief which is left out when people talk about the message of sorrow: they never mention its unbecoming side: the legacy of bitterness, bad-temper, ill-adjustment.' Virginia Woolf, *Moments of Being: Unpublished Autobiographical Writing*, p. 123.
3. One of the side-effects of this was a strange numbness in relation to them both. I'm sure that it was partly physical (sheer exhaustion), but there was a strand too of absolute terror that I might end up hating them: James and Katie, whom I loved. *Why can I not teach myself I do care?* I wrote hopelessly in my journal.
4. I remember too, the year my father died, driving home with Mama from the local town, and coming across a pair of hares on the tarred road. One hare had been run over and its guts were spilling out of it, red strings shiny as we slowed the car. The other hare was sniffing anxiously by its side. 'Just like Papa and me,' said Mama. There was no self-pity in her voice.
5. Radclyffe Hall, *The Well of Loneliness*, Chapter 15, Section 1.

6. Many thanks here to Gloria Anzaldúa, Mary Allgier, Katya Benjamin, Laetitia Bermejo, Beth Brant, Lis Cox, Susan Davis, Rich Fournier, Sharon Franklet, Janice Gould, Katinka Haycraft, Annie Hole, Rhashama Khalethia, Simon Korner, Joan Larkin, Andrea Freud Loewenstein, Isobel MacGilvray, Sally Malin, Maria Margaronis, Jane Miller, Kate Millett, Ricky Sherover-Marcuse, Aurora Levins-Morales, Nina Newington, Cathy Ramey, Alison Read, Leonie Rushforth, Kateri Sardella, Julia Sovrin, Christopher Spence, Mary Taubman, Anne Twitty, Janey Winter, Anne Witten and Lynne Zeavin.

7. Once someone asked a well-known Thai meditation master, 'In this world where everything changes, where nothing remains the same, where loss and grief are inherent in our very coming into existence, how can there be any happiness? How can we find security when we see we can't count on anything being the way we want it to be?' The teacher, looking compassionately at this fellow, held up a drinking glass that had been given to him earlier in the morning and said, 'You see this goblet? For me, this glass is already broken. I enjoy it, I drink out of it. It holds my water admirably, sometimes even reflecting the sun in beautiful patterns. If I should tap it, it has a lovely ring to it. But when I put this glass on a shelf and the wind knocks it over or my elbow brushes it off the table and it falls to the ground and shatters, I say "Of course". Since I understand that this glass is already broken, every moment with it is precious. Every moment is just as it is and nothing need be otherwise.' Stephen Levine, *Who Dies?: An Investigation into Conscious Living and Dying*, pp. 98–99.

# Bibliography

Alice Bloch, *Lifetime Guarantee* (Persephone Press, 1981)

Simone de Beauvoir, *A Very Easy Death* (Penguin, 1969)

T.S. Eliot, *The Four Quartets* (Faber and Faber, 1944)

Tess Gallagher, 'The Poem as a Reservoir for Grief' in *A Concert of Tenses* (The University of Michigan Press, 1986)

Radclyffe Hall, *The Well of Loneliness* (1928, Virago Press, 1982)

Lewis Hyde, *The Gift: Imagination and the Erotic Life of Property* (Vintage Books, 1979)

Dr Tony Lake, *Living with Grief* (Sheldon Press, 1984)

Stephen Levine, *Who Dies?: An Investigation into Conscious Living and Dying* (Doubleday, 1982)

Deidre Levinson, *Modus Vivendi* (Penguin, 1984)

C.S. Lewis, *A Grief Observed* (Faber and Faber, 1966)

Christian McEwen, 'The Business of Mourning' in *Feminary* (Fall 1984) and *Granta* (Winter 1984, Penguin, 1985)

Alice Walker, *The Color Purple* (The Women's Press, 1983)

Virginia Woolf, *Moments of Being: Unpublished Autobiographical Writings* (Harcourt, Brace, Jovanovich, 1978)

# Transformations

## Sunna 🖋

The landscape of my life is difficult to write or talk about. I look back across its terrain with eyes wide open trying to soak in, explore and chart my progress in order to understand and not pass through that way again. Too often I mark time by skirting the edges in the hope of finding a diversion, any diversion that will draw me away from looking at myself.

Why am I scared?

Is it the fear of not being able to stop, fear of what I might reveal to myself, fear of failing or just fear itself?

Four and a half years ago I was an isolated Black woman suffering from a physical breakdown and working towards reaching emotional breaking point. My survival and growth since that period are inextricably linked to meeting other Black women and, in particular, the Black woman who now shares my life. She especially has played a significant part through her constant challenging, determination and faith in me. When I would have given up she spurred and rekindled the desire in me to understand and love myself.

It was also through discussions with other Black women, also incest survivors, that I began to find a vocabulary, an expression of something that previously went unnamed and unheard. I began to familiarize and associate the words with me. Until then, for the biggest chunk of my life, incest was my secret . . . mine and my uncle's.

Wanting to be as open as possible, I had spoken to my lover about my early 'experiences' with my uncle. Although she tried to reassure me that it wasn't my fault, that it was nothing to be ashamed of, and that I wasn't the only one, I found it difficult to talk about. I could do nothing to challenge my uncle's insistence on keeping it 'a secret' but simply perpetuated my guilt by burying 'it' into recesses of my memory.

Through listening to similar stories by other women, I re-awakened the experiences I had between my tenth and eighteenth years. Only recently have I begun to realize that I'd shut away and forgotten this very significant part of my life, partly because I couldn't deal with the guilt of such a 'secret', and partly as a means of survival.

Coming into contact with Black women who were beginning to vocalize their experiences of incest, I was, by association, being forced to examine my own. And yet I could not discuss my experience in a group as I did not feel ready or secure enough. Slowly gaining in strength, reassurance and confirmation of myself in learning that I was not alone, I began to take the first tentative steps towards examining the issues I had so carefully locked away. At first this meant retrieving, mulling over and understanding my life experiences with the expectation of eventually coming to terms with and loving the person I was. Many women around me were doing this by visiting a therapist and also by talking with other women.

Initially I found it strange that women I knew went to therapy rather than utilizing the friendship networks they had created. But I soon realized that it was also difficult to speak in depth to women who were my friends, and recognized the need to speak to someone who could be objective, someone who didn't know the first thing about me and who wouldn't judge me, yet would act as a guide to assist me in my journey of self-discovery.

The therapist I decided to go to was one that many other Black women were visiting; a white, lesbian feminist therapist. I knew that Black women friends had searched for a Black woman therapist but at the time none was available and there was not much choice. Hearing that Black women felt trust for this particular woman, I decided to see her myself.

Before reaching the decision, I had gone through six months of resisting therapy. Frequently I felt the panic and wanted to stand back avoiding confrontation with the issues that were coming up. But I knew if I persisted in this way I would risk the growth in myself that was necessary, as well as possibly suffocating the relationship I was in. Often I would make excuses by conveniently misplacing the telephone number or being too busy during the day to phone. I couldn't accept the idea of therapy. My knowledge was based on what I had seen on North American television programmes where white middle-class people indulged themselves and paid for the privilege of having someone listen to them. In contrast, another strong image I had was of working-class people who didn't conform to the stereotypes that society had of them and who were as a result, locked away in hard, cold institutions in order to 'get better'.

I felt that therapy was a luxury and not something for the likes of me: an Asian woman born in the East End of London. Even after I began, particularly during the initial stages, many issues were extremely difficult to deal with and in some situations I'd catch myself making excuses for why I shouldn't continue. It was simply too painful to admit that there was such a large chunk of my life so totally unresolved. At other times I had genuine misgivings about the situation, around the power differences that do exist between Black and white women anyway, let alone those that exist between therapist and 'client'.

I felt that a white woman could not possibly understand the struggles that Black women have faced and continue to face because of racism. It was and still is crucial for me that my therapist should have an anti-racist perspective. Fortunately she and I were able to talk about the power differences that can and do occur. A basis of trust was established because she was committed to trying to break down these structures by being more accessible and in some situations, as vulnerable as me the 'client'. But, despite these difficulties, the overriding factor was my urgent need to examine my childhood experiences and to begin to take control of my life.

I have been going to therapy for a year now and it has helped untangle the patterns that have formed the framework of my life, even though the process is slow and often painful. In the early sessions I realized that I had compartmentalized my life by having held onto a belief that incest was the only issue for me, and that if I came to terms with the fact that 'it' existed in my life, then that understanding and acceptance would explain me and the way I have grown. I have learnt, however, that my life hasn't been dictated by that experience alone, but by other factors such as racism, religion and the upbringing I had in a traditional Muslim household. All are meticulously interwoven and responsible for the woman I am today.

I dream and remember the time when I couldn't bring myself to believe that I am an incest survivor. It was something that happened to other Black women, to the women around me, and no way could it possibly have happened to me. It had always been a secret kept between my uncle and myself. I thought that no one should know because if they did they wouldn't like me, would think it was dirty, that it was my fault. For so long I kept it a secret even from myself.

I had my first experience of incest around the age of eleven and the last around the age of sixteen. It was in my eleventh year that I began to experience the bottomless pit of fear and it was then that I established feeling powerless. FEAR: fear of being found out, fear of being pregnant, fear of myself and my sexuality. My uncle didn't live with us or even near us. He'd come unannounced, stay a few days and then disappear. None of us knew exactly how he earned his living or where he really lived. What we were sure of was that he would come to visit at least once every three months. My mother was always pleased to see him. He'd tell her news of India and they would often gossip about it as they cooked. My father, however, was jealous of the attention my uncle received and well after he'd gone my parents would still be arguing about him. My father always lost.

Between these visits I would survive by totalling dismissing the experiences and changes that were occurring within me. It was only at intervals, when he would reappear in our home, that I was forced to address myself to what was happening to me. I strongly believe that this was the starting point of dissociating myself from my body in order to survive.

My uncle always said it was a secret, that no one should know, and if they did then they would think it was my fault. From the very beginning I experienced an overwhelming sense of guilt about taking part in something that was not only a secret from the two people I cared for most, my parents, but also against my strict Muslim upbringing. To my parents I represented a worry: I was a girl, albeit in their eyes 'a good girl', and as a girl in a traditional Muslim family not much was expected of me except that my virginity be kept intact at all costs prior to marriage. In my teenage ignorance I reasoned that I had not managed to do even that. How could I tell my parents, my mother? She would never have understood, she would have blamed me and I would have run the risk of being ostracized from my family. I could not bear the thought of being isolated so completely.

By the time I was sixteen I had slowly developed the courage to say 'No'. At first my uncle couldn't believe it and would try exerting his power and strength over me in an effort to force me to participate. I continued to say 'No'. There was little he could do to break down my determination and newly-found strength. Subsequently, my uncle's visits became less frequent and eventually we heard that he had got married. When I was about twenty-two I went with my family to visit him and his wife. He already had two girl children and wore the mask of respectability. At one point I was alone with him and he tried it on again. I remember getting really angry and threatening to expose him. That was the last time I ever spoke to my uncle.

My mother became concerned with my physical appearance the year I was eleven. She wanted me to lose weight so I would be seen not only as a 'good' girl but as an attractive one as well. The more she wanted me to be attractive the more I wanted to hide and be unattractive and insignificant. I blamed myself for my uncle's behaviour and wanted to avoid 'it' happening again. I thought that it was me, my physical appearance that had caused 'it', and reasoned that if I could destroy that veneer then 'it' wouldn't happen again. Despite my mother's efforts I longed to be left alone, to have no sexuality and to be invisible. From eleven to twenty-two my weight fluctuated from high to low, never remaining stable. I compensated my mother in other ways by being the epitome of a 'good girl'. I cooked, cleaned, looked after my brother and excelled in domestic chores because to do so meant that I would be seen as 'good'. Glancing back, I can see that I hibernated. I never left home except to go to school, the library or the bookshop. I continued my domestic chores with real fervour and read *Woman* and *Woman's Own*. I suppressed my anger and lived through books. There was also my own writing through which I could escape from the confines of my life. Often when I could no longer go on I would contemplate suicide or fantasize that I was someone else.

My mother had a nervous breakdown when I was fifteen. All those years of isolation as an Asian woman in this country, trying to cope with bringing up four children with little support from my father, plus the accumulation of frustration, anger and loneliness, had all taken their toll on her. She was not hospitalized but kept under heavy sedation at home. This meant she would either be continually asleep or walking around as though half-asleep. Her periods of wakefulness were often filled with anger. I spent my time, as was expected of me, looking after her, my father, my brothers and taking on all the domestic chores. I had nothing else to do.

I found my preservation in books, writing and painting. Writing gave me a sense of self, a feeling that I existed and that I was real. I would often write poems or prose about how I felt, about being alone. I also hungrily scanned the libraries and bookshops for books that would reflect my life experience and help me to understand myself. I found nothing that would help lessen the isolation of growing up as a Black child in a hostile white environment. Nor did I fine anything that reflected my experiences with my uncle. The books that I found and read, which were helpful at the time, were by Herman Hesse and Sylvia Plath. Hesse spoke to me of spirituality, endurance and escape. With Plath I lived through and exorcised my need to commit suicide. I discovered in some way I wanted to live. Her book, *The Bell Jar*, helped me to understand that I wasn't alone or alien in feeling the way I did.

I began to look at all possibilities and recognized the need to escape. I felt the only way I could break free from my parents and still be acceptable to them was through education. To my parents, who had no formal education, going to college was a legitimate way of spending my time prior to marriage and would increase my chances of getting a good husband. After a struggle I left home at twenty-one and continued with my college course.

College was not easy. From the first day I could see I was different. Still literally in pigtails. I was fat, shy, passive and wore clothes that hid my body. I had no friends. The women who were popular, or who could boast friends were white women trading on their sexuality. To be liked equalled being white and stereotypically attractive. Although I did want to be liked, my isolation continued up until my second year at college. At some point I decided that I didn't want to be different. With the secret that existed between my uncle and me consigned to the remotest point in my mind, I felt free to concentrate on being attractive. I became obsessed with losing weight, and after a year of struggle with my parents I had my hair cut. In those years very few Asian women had really short hair. It was seen as a symbol of losing one's cultural and emotional roots, and of losing one's beauty. I didn't care, I just wanted to be like everyone else and that meant not dealing with being Black.

In physical terms I was now acceptable but with the attraction came the need to make a decision about sex. Many of the women students at college were expected to have sexual relationships with men but I never had the desire for sex with any man. At school I had found myself attracted to girls and women, always wanting to have close relationships with them rather than with boys or men. This is still the case. Being brought up as a strict Muslim meant that ingrained in me was the value that sex before marriage was wrong and also prohibited. I couldn't cope with the guilt of going against this value as well as the guilt of incest.

I never had any boyfriends. When men asked me out it was on the understanding that the relationship was platonic. If they tried it on then I said I wasn't using any contraceptives, when in fact I should have said 'no'. But how could I have said 'no'? Saying 'no' meant taking control of my sexuality, something I wasn't used to. If I took control then it would have meant I was responsible for my actions. How could I possibly do that then when I hadn't done so before?

I felt my life had no meaning or direction and began to drown myself in alcohol and drugs. If I hadn't, the people around were sure to think I was a good, meek, mild and passive Asian girl, a common stereotype of Asian women. Eventually the drink and the drugs made me feel good, allowing me to forget myself and comfort my loneliness. I used these props to help me through my day-to-day life, my confusion and despair. But it was when I was pissed or 'out of it' with drugs that I was at my most vulnerable. Out of loneliness I would then go home with men for comfort. I tried various tactics to avoid sleeping with these men but ultimately none of them made any difference. I gave in because I didn't make these excuses strongly enough and because I didn't know I had the power to say 'no'. Eventually, when I did have a full sexual experience with a man, I realized after he had gone that despite my experiences with my uncle, I had been a virgin. Slowly I began to realize that in a few meaningless moments I had lost a part of me that I truly thought I had lost sixteen years before.

I felt angry; angry because I knew nothing about my own body, angry at my mother for not telling me about my body and for making me ashamed that I was a woman; angry at all the years of guilt and despair that I had carried around with me. I felt cheated of knowledge and robbed of life and choices. Until therapy I had a lot of uncontrollable anger towards my parents, especially towards my mother. I think I projected a lot of the anger I had towards my uncle on to my parents. I held them responsible for forcing religion down our throats for so many years. I felt anger that I'd not been told about sex, anger at being Black and born in England and having to cope. Anger, Anger, Anger.

I blamed my parents for everything wrong in my life. I felt ashamed of myself, insignificant and lonely. I drank more and took more drugs. The drugs I took elicited a paranoid response and exaggerated my perceptions and hold on reality. I was not able to talk to my parents without wanting to scream at them or tell them how much they had hurt me. I wanted them to let go of me, to let me develop as an independent woman.

At this time I began wanting to take control over my life. I wanted a meaningful relationship; a relationship with another woman. I knew no white women who were lesbians let alone any Black women. I had no network to pursue. However I did know that there were clubs where women went to meet other women. I decided to go. I went near closing time, pissed so that I could avoid responsibility for myself. Seeing other women, who were also pissed, meant that I would not stand out and wouldn't have to deal with their stares. I was often the only Black woman there. I slept with the first woman who asked me. I continued my patterns of taking no responsibility. This nihilistic attitude continued until I met and had a long relationship with a white woman. But at the end of that relationship I lost all remaining sense of self and I felt rejected and inadequate. I was devastated. I was sure that I had absolutely nothing to offer anyone.

But then I came in contact with a network of Black lesbians and met the woman with whom I now share my life. Yet at the time everything was happening too fast for me, and I decided I needed to go away; to recover and to think. Whilst away I was involved in a serious car accident which left me with a broken back. From being a strong and active woman I had literally overnight, become helpless and inactive. I was on painkillers and almost immediately began drinking to try and alleviate the pain. I was hurting both physically and mentally. My body, having suffered years of maltreatment, was now given a legitimate excuse to collapse. I mourned and gained weight which helped to cushion me from everything I had felt and was feeling. The only reason I survived was because I had someone who had faith in me, who forced me to look at myself, to believe in myself and to take control over my life. Rather than continue the nihilistic pattern I had established and had no control over, I decided that I wanted to grow, to be calm and to have control.

The first one and a half years after my accident were extremely difficult, it took time to learn to come to terms with my disabilities. By the end of the second year I was determined to heal my body and began swimming. By swimming regularly not only did my body begin to heal but I was gaining a sense of inner strength and confidence. I stopped smoking and taking drugs, and with great effort and recurring difficulties weaned myself off junk food.

Then came the decision to begin therapy. It is from here that I have begun to examine the complex relationship between my parents and myself. Although there were strong bonds, I am working to establish an equally strong identity away from them. In therapy I have begun to look at my first sexual experiences and examine how these have formed the pattern and framework of my adult life. In understanding these, I am beginning to take control of my life.

The creative part of my life dried up several years ago and it is only recently that I have reawakened and integrated this aspect of me. I have begun writing and painting again and feel that my life is at a turning point. Even though it is still difficult to assume control over my actions, the struggle is most definitely worthwhile. The most important thing I have learnt is to take responsibility, to recognize my own needs and the importance and confidence to be able to say NO.

# Recovery: The Story of an ACA

## Jean Swallow

San Francisco: January . . . February . . . March. It is the winter of 1983. Rain sweeps in from the ocean. Every day, the rain sweeps in slashing from the ocean. Roads wash away; houses slide off hills. The pain in my legs shudders through me in the rain. I am drenched in the three blocks I walk to the subway and work all day in clothes that stay wet.

We try to get to the farm in Albion on the weekends, even though the road washes out about once a week. We are planning to go tonight and I am afraid the road will be washed away just before we get to the stretch that threads through the redwoods. Highway 1 is out ten miles above Fort Bragg and somewhere below; I'm not sure where. The highway conditions tape drones on and I have a hard time remembering which roads we can take to get there. Finally I remember I can ask Sher to help. I'm not going alone. Sher. The farm. Roses.

## You sound like you're a long ways off. Can you hear me?

March. Saturday. San Francisco. Usually the rain stops for a few hours a day, but not in any pattern. We want to make a plan to go to the beach with our friends Sim and Jay for a picnic. We ask them. Sim laughs and says . . . in the rain? It has been raining for six weeks up at the farm. Pammie who lives there and ought to know, says 60 inches in that time, some every day.

Not so bad in the city. Not 60 inches here. But still it rains. Every day. Today the clouds streak gray and white and in between, the sky shows blue. The rain hovers over the ocean. We are trying to get to the farm tonight because the new roses come from the nursery this week. We need to get them into healthy soil with good air around them; we need to plant them soon or they will die.

I look out the car window to the ocean and feel the wind through the seams. The air turns cold again and within a half-hour, the sky is a solid gray. The lighthouse blinks on and off. And I am crying. I am still here, crying again. My legs hurt in the rain. My knees buckle and swell and give out. Each time, when I can barely walk, I go to Misha. Misha says the evil chi is trapped, stuck in my knees. She pushes needles into my skin and tells me to relax. She massages my head. Before she leaves, I have shut my eyes and the tears begin to seep out from under my eyelids and roll down into my hair. The tears are not from pain from the needles. The pain is not from the needles.

## Outside the rain begins, and it may never end

When I was a child, we lived in the city during the winter and in the country during the summer. This went on until my father 'decided to change jobs' or 'went bankrupt' depending on who you talk to. This went on until I was nine. This went on all my life. Listen to me, can you hear me? Things are not as they seem. We stuff the truth behind our eyes and then see as we are told. My father drinks. My father has been worried about his drinking for the last thirty years. My father has been worried about his drinking since before I was born. Things are not as they seem.

I was raised upper middle-class by decorum and expectation. But only sometimes did my family have the requisite amount of money. Sometimes we just didn't have the money. But always, my father made money magic. He could find it when he needed it. He could spend it how he wanted. He could make it do as he wished. Like the rain.

He could make the rain stop. He would snap his fingers and the wipers would scrape noisily against the windshield as we sped through the tunnel. He would snap his fingers again and the rain would splatter on the windshield and smear into the glass and then the wipers would work and we would be able to see the trees on the side of the road outside the tunnel again.

I would tug on his sleeve and jump up and down on the seat. Do it again, Daddy, make it stop again, I would scream. And he would just smile and say he could only make it happen if I would be a good little girl and sit down on the seat and be quiet. Then he would make magic again. And I would try, I would try so hard to be quiet. I hardly ever knew when it would happen again, or what exactly I had done right, but when it happened, it was like the illegal fireworks he shot off over the lake on summer nights; it was like a floating shower of stars.

For a long time, he was able to make magic. I adored him. When there was trouble, he would ask what did money mean? What good is it? It's only money. He would snap his fingers, take his cigarette out of his mouth and pick up his drink, his eyes bright and loving on me. It's only money, not love. And it is love that matters, he would say as he gathered me into him. He is small for a man and handsome and heavy. He would hold me in his arms, gathered up over his belly and kiss me on the forehead with his whiskery heavy cheeks.

Now he lies in his bed for weeks at a time, exhaustion or stress. He lies in his bed in Carolina where he lives and he watches the rain just like me. March in Carolina: the rain pours from the sky in sheets and the soil slides off into the sides of the road and runs in ditches the color of blood. I know March in Carolina. It was my home too. The wind and rain come up from further south and bend the trees backward, pounding in the air like the hands of God. After the storm, the redbud covers the road like a woman's shorn hair on a cold floor.

My father travels all through Carolina, through those storms on his trips to the mills, and he's gone there more than he is home. Except when he can't get up. Sometimes he just can't get out of bed anymore and the sadness washes over him as though it were the ocean and he could not pull himself up any higher on the beach. He is still handsome but his eyes are not bright. He still is there, drinking. They say I am the only alcoholic in the family. And I cannot make the rain stop.

I haven't seen him or my mother in three years. I haven't talked to them for a year. I haven't talked to them over the telephone for a year. What would I say? What would I say to them? It rains here too. The rain turns the air cold and moist and I learn to wear my boots from the farm here in the city.

But the roses came this week. One night last fall, after a hard weekend, Sher and I sat in bed and picked the roses. We picked out rose bushes from a special catalogue and took the whites and lavenders and blues. Eight of them. We sat in bed that night and held each other. And though we were terrified, we decided to put a little something down on the future. We waited for them all winter and this week they arrived: small spindly little things. We need to plant them within a day or two, or they will die in their plastic sacks. We are trying to get to the farm tonight. I hope the roads to the coast stay open.

## Things are not as they seem

When I was a child, I lived in an old hunting lodge during the summer. I lived there with my sister and my brother and my mother and when he was home, with my father. The lodge had been turned into a house and sat on a hill just above the lake. A path led through lilies of the valley and pine trees to a steep drop-off and then the lake. The lake spread out in front of me as though it were the ocean. I would sit on the porch of that old house in the middle of the northern Rhode Island woods, in my little white cane rocker and read my books from the library. It would be warm and sunny and a breeze would blow and pretty soon my mother would come by and say it was time to start walking down the long dirt road to meet my father coming home from work in the city.

We waited for him all day. And when he got home, his tie off and collar thrown open, they would have drinks on the porch. After a while, we would eat dinner, though often they didn't eat with us. And it wasn't like I got more attention when he was there, except right at first when he saw us standing by the road, waiting for him. He would stop the big Oldsmobile and haul us all in and there were kisses and questions and he would run his big hands through my hair. He would be sweating, his white starched shirt wilted in the heat. He and my mother would exchange glances, they thought over my head, and then they would kiss. No, it wasn't that he or my mother would pay attention to me when he got home. It was more that they were together there and I knew everyone was where they were supposed to be.

And though I was frightened when I heard them arguing and crying on the porch after I had gone to bed, and though I sometimes got up and watched them laugh as they drank from beautiful glasses in the moonlight, it didn't so much matter what they did; it mattered that they were there. It always seemed to me they might not be there. And even that seemed normal to me. I reckon it seemed normal to them. It was the way it was supposed to be.

176

And sometimes it was wonderful, like being on the porch in the middle of the afternoon with a warm breeze and my books and a profound sense of peace. Why as a child I was able to appreciate that sense of peace and rest and order, strikes me as odd now. Why I forgot how my legs hurt all those years strikes me as odd too. But now, the feelings return. The ache returns and I wonder if I've moved at all.

In the night, when I was a child, my legs hurt when I lay still in bed. They would throb with the hurting and I would cry out and after a long while, my father or mother would come in from the porch and rub my calves with horse linament and try to get me to lie still. It hurt worse when I lay still. I couldn't sleep. I couldn't sleep. They would be out on the porch drinking, talking and I would hear their voices rise in anger and know that I shouldn't say anything, shouldn't call to them. And my legs hurt and I would look into the darkness in the bedroom and see faces, always the faces of the devil and the sounds of evil and I would twist into a clenched knot and finally, after a while and maybe from exhaustion, I would sleep.

## Outside the rain begins

In the fall, my mother and I would go for one last weekend to pack the house up for the winter. The air would turn cold. My mother would wear her red wool cardigan and I would wear something cast off from my brother and we would clean up the house. At lunch, we would sit in the sun and my mother would take her cardigan off and run her long fingers through her hair and shield her eyes to squint at the sun. Then sometimes she would stretch her legs out a little longer in her slacks, warming herself just a little longer as though ten more minutes would carry her through the rest of her work, as though she could memorize the warmth, as though for one minute she could just rest.

My mother doesn't rest. My mother lies awake at nights, has lain awake nights for years. I don't know what she does in the night. I know she has wanted to die; I've known it since I was a child and watched her try to drown herself in the lake one night at twilight. I wished then I knew how to save her. I wish now she would want to save herself. I wish that my loving her made a difference.

When I was a child, I knew my mother was the most beautiful woman in the world. Nothing was ever out of place. Like her rose garden in the city, carefully tended, each bush a beauty and all the flowers growing beneath the tall climbing roses, each in a special place. And then she had to move and leave them. My father went bankrupt or changed jobs, depending on who you talk to. This changing jobs and moving went on five more times up and down the Eastern Seacoast. She never grew another rose. She never works in the yard now. They don't have a yard now to keep anything in place. She just holds herself.

She holds herself like a metal spring welded in a tight coil. New Englanders only look cold from the outside. She loves me. I know she loves me though it is hard to believe from here. And she loves him. (Who she doesn't love is herself.) For a generation, the manifestation was psychic, not physical. It wasn't her parents who drank. It was their parents. They just passed it along. And the death is coming, the death has been lingering there since before I was born. They've both been trying it, ever since I can remember.

I remember the lake. I remember autumn days when the wind picked up over the lake and the sky turned gray and the smell of wetness seeped up from under the leaves and we shut the house up and went away. One fall we went away for good. And then we just kept going away from places. Now it is a Saturday in March. I am in San Francisco. It is raining as usual.

We are trying to get to the farm. Sher and I go to the farm on the weekends, to what is left of the farm she spent ten years building, to a small cabin set in a circle of redwoods, where we sit by the wood stove in the rain. We talk. We talk and hold each other and remember things. We walk through the fields and the wildness that has grown in the five years since she's been gone. In the cabin, it is warm with the fire. We go there whenever we can.

And though the perennials were killed and the garden is overrun with thistle and blackberry vine, we can fix it. We are going to plant the roses this weekend. By the end of the summer, we will live there. Sher is going home too, but that is her story and you will have to ask her for it. She will tell you, if you ask, but her voice will scream and whisper and you must listen to the night if you mean to hear the whole of it.

## You sound like you are a long way off. Can you hear me?

About two weeks before my legs started to give out this winter, we were at the farm and the devil came back. We were at the farm, come to cut fallen hardwood for the fire, but just at that moment, it was stormy and night, a full moon. We were outside, and Sher said, I just love this weather, don't you and I said No. Actually. Not at night. Not on the full moon. And we went back inside and the devil face swam up in the window before me and I saw how the light could fall just right on her face so that it might become his and I tried to hold on. I have been sober two and a half years, but I have always seen him.

178

That night he was six feet tall and thin as a wisp and in his full regalia. I could smell him, the burning smell of sulphur and rancid meat. He was there, in the room, almost next to me. He was waiting. Been waiting.

She stared at me, her eyes held steady with effort. I watched her. She watched me and measured her voice. I was gone too far; she said she didn't know if she could help me. Try to hold on, she said. Try to talk to me, she said. She sat on the chair, her arms on her knees, inched forward. I tried. I wanted to trust her. I love her more than I have ever loved anyone and I trust her more than that. She does her work. She does her work, but that night, in a room where we had made promises, there was almost nothing to hold on to. The room was warm. The light glowed in a small circle around the stove and outside the wind tore at the underside of the roof.

I tried. I began. I could feel the muscles in my leg start to spasm. I looked at her and held on to the stool and said he would catch me if I was outside and draw me up by the side of my wrist and make me lie. I could feel the claw of his hand on the soft side of my arm and I lowered my eyes, away from her.

I could not look at her then, and I began to shake and I could not stop. If he got me, he would make me tell people things that were not true. And it would hurt them and confuse them. Nothing would be real, except him, but most people would not know that. They would spend their lives as I had, one foot nailed to the floor. And they would be lost and hurt and confused. And I would have to spend the rest of my life doing that, in league with him, smelling like him, with him.

Maybe I had already done that. Maybe he already had me, had a right to me, had bought me somehow and what had I done, what had I done? The pain in my knees began to throb and I could feel it rise up in a panic into my face and my voice died in my throat. And I knew if for one moment I showed that I was afraid he would have me completely.

I could feel my face grow wild. I am twenty-nine. I am the same age as my mother when I first saw her trying to die. I sat on a small stool in front of the wood stove and held on tight to the sides of it and I could not let Sher touch me. I could not cry for fear of letting my eyes close. I could not, would not look in the window. But I forced myself to see her. I forced myself to see how the light might play on her face and how it was only the light and my fear, my awful fear. She was not afraid. But she was not sucked in either, and I was stuck, far, far away.

We talked late into the night. He was still all around, had spread his evil stickiness on all the trees, dripping down from leaf to leaf like the rain. I finally fell asleep, rigid on the bed, with my clothes on. The next morning, it was not better. In the morning, the rain dripped from the trees. Sher talked a little about how much she loved the land and I wanted it too and knew finally, I would have to see Tasha when I got home because I could not, would not be robbed of one more home.

179

Tasha is small and wiry-energied. She is not calm but she is generous and strong. She helps women with spirit things. I was raised in the Congregational Church in New England, but I refused their Christian communion and prayer and I would refuse them to this day. Since I came to California though, I found I could grow a tail into the center of the earth and once, as a present, Diane showed me how to put my small white-weak little roots down through the pavement into the earth, so I guess my washing in the blood of the lamb came in a yoga studio above an automobile showroom and the backyard of a women's bar in San Francisco.

Still, the spiritual makes me nervous and I don't like the words of it. But at some point in recovery you just have to start trusting somebody and use whatever you can. I think you have to breathe deep; you have to keep breathing and then, jump.

Tasha lives on the second floor of a Victorian in the Mission and her work room is scattered with things on the floor as if life on the material plane is not of interest to her, though what is scattered is often beautiful. There is no furniture in her room, just pillows and pallets on the floor and candles and an old record-player. Outside that day, the kids on the street shouted and shrieked in play. Tasha looked at me and held me steady and gentle and asked me did I have anyone to help us with this. I did, though who, I was reluctant to say.

When I was living with Marie and Cindy in Carolina, my angel came to me in a dream. I have never forgotten her, though for a very long time I didn't tell people because they thought it was too strange and I am not into being strange. It is hard enough as it is. But when I got back to town from that devil weekend, Sim called to fill me in on city news and I found myself forcing my mouth to make words against the air, trying to tell her about the devil. In her slow, careful way, Sim's love slipped over the line to me in a hush and she asked me did I have anyone to help. And then I remembered my angel. After a long pause, I told her. She said she didn't think it was strange at all. So at Tasha's, it felt a little easier to talk about her aloud, but not much, Still, I told her.

My angel lives off-world and is about six feet tall and wears a long robe with a hood; under the robe are britches with huge pouches. She has no hair and is quite beautiful. I cannot now see what her face looks like but she smiles at me a lot and leans laconically against walls, waiting for me to ask for help. She won't help without being asked. She just waits. And she helps.

That day, when I went to Tasha and laid down on a pallet in her room, feeling raw and alone, I tried to let Tasha near me and tried to listen to her voice warm and steady in my ear. She began to breathe with me, giving me psychic directions, and I slipped behind my ears, holding her hand and weeping. And then, shortly, the angel was with me and I asked her and she came back with me to that hunting lodge house back at the lake. There was so much sadness and fear stuck there, lingering in cold corners, that we burned the house to the ground. The angel firebombed it with a torch that sprang from her hand and the house exploded and the meadow and the lake all burned, flaming and wild in the night. After a while, we took the stones from the foundation and the porch and scattered them into the woods and replanted the meadow that had burned. And I could see the grass beginning to grow there, wild and green in the rainy Rhode Island winter.

I buried my face in the angel's breast and she wrapped her cloak around me. I breathed into her, felt her around me and then, when Tasha called us and I was ready, we flew to the winter city house. Someone else lived there now – but still my parents' things were in the house. The angel and I brought them out of the house and piled them in the front yard and burnt them, a big bonfire in between the house and the two maple trees at the edge of the street. In the back, the roses were still alive but they were different somehow; someone else was tending them and they looked like strangers to me. The angel held my hand as I stared.

And then I heard Tasha's voice again and she asked me what about my parents? Where were they? And as I looked around, I saw them standing in the street, bewildered and forlorn. Like a child who runs terrified to an adult in the face of fear, I turned to the angel and held my hand out. And the angel shook her head and I knew we could not help them and I buried my face into her again, so afraid I would run to them, so ashamed and devastated because at last I understood that the love I had for them burning like a hole in my chest would not make any difference, would not even be a soothing drop in the bonfire of their sadness. And the angel held me while I sobbed and then Tasha asked again what would I do with them.

I knew I couldn't leave them there alone, but I knew too I couldn't help, so I called Aunt Ida who has been dead for more than ten years to come with the car and drive them away; I didn't know to where. And she did and I sobbed and tried to wave good-bye to them as they drove off, but they never looked out the window, never looked back into the night filled with flames.

Then I heard Tasha again, and she took us to the Albion farm. It was still night but the angel could see and she extended her fingers and wiped off each leaf in the forest and took the sticky-messy evil and wrapped it around the devil and burned them both in the small clearing in front of the cabin. He burnt like a flame of molten lead in the night and I watched as he turned into nothing but ash. I sat in the cabin and I watched and then sat still with the angel, holding her hand.

And then Tasha brought us back. The angel stayed with me, even walked home with me that day. The devil burnt and was gone then. Of course he was back the next week, but the angel kept him away from me until he changed one night at Misha's.

# I hear an old voice. Can you hear me?

My legs ache now. My legs ache as I wrap them around each other and try to keep my back straight as I type for eight to ten hours a day. The ache is in my knees and in my thighs and in my calves. I wake up in the night and find my legs clenched around each other. I am frightened by something in a dream from the day and the clenching pain of my legs wakes me. I find it hard to sleep. The next morning, I can barely walk. When it rains, my knees echo. I limp. First the right knee, then the left; at night it is both.

Misha says the wind of my body, the chi, moves from one leg to the next. We work with the needles. She says my liver is working overtime, that I have stored my fear and changed it to anger in my liver for years. She is not surprised to hear I am in recovery and she begins to rub the upper part of my ears. She says my chi is blocked. Tears are the sweat of the liver, she says. I scowl and tell her I don't cry much. She puts a needle in each of my palms and then one on the bottom of each foot, one on each wrist, one on each ankle, moving back and forth on my body just like a mobius strip, opening the energy. She rubs my head. Just relax now, she says and she leaves the room.

As soon as she leaves, the devil comes in and makes the lamp over my head swing as though it would drop on me and finally I say, alright, goddamn it, you want to be in here so much, come in and sit in the chair and shut up. I have work to do. The angel, who has been watching all of this from the wall next to my right side, claps her hands and smiles at me. The devil sits down and rocks.

Next week, another opening. Misha inserts the needles, softly padding around the table and my body. The devil rocks in his chair and I begin to weep and the tears run off my face, out from under my eyes and the sadness fills the room. What sadness? I don't know from where, but the room is filled with it. I sob, quietly, like I've been taught. Never making a sound except when I try to breathe. I try not to call attention to myself. The sadness in the room is as heavy as fog after rain all day, hugging the ground, filling the air. The devil rocks. Through my tears, I watch him. He becomes younger and younger in age until he is very small, just a baby. I get up and hold him and he becomes a real baby and after a while the baby jumps down and grows until he looks like he is about four or five years old and wanders off.

I find myself rocking myself as a baby. This baby is very sad. She is crying too, and quietly. The room is filled with sadness and it is too much. I cannot bear it. I want to let it go, I want to just let go of all of it. I cannot bear it anymore, I can not bear to have so much sadness near me in the world anymore and I sob. Then I remember the angel. I ask her and she nods and I hand the sadness to her. It takes a long time, but I gather it from the room and I hand it over to her. She fills the pouches in her britches with it and then covers it all with her robe and promises to take it off-world.

The next week it rains. And this week, my legs hurt less. This week at Misha's, she works on my elbows and my left knee and then my right knee heats up like it has a radiator in it. The evil chi is being released, she says. We know now how to get to it. When she leaves the room this time, I do not feel the sadness so much. I hear a very old voice, can you hear me? I am moving far away. The devil has not come back, and the angel is still here.

## Outside the rain begins

This afternoon Susan and I meet at the gym. I am late, of course. Susan asks about my knees. One of hers is covered with two long serpent scars. We do quat sets, her with weights, me without. We talk when our machines are next to each other. She is learning aikido. She is learning not to panic when someone grabs her, not to panic but to take the energy and turn it around, to throw, using the other person's energy. Her eyes open from their sleepiness. We talk. It's not about how to prevent panic, but about how to use it. Her incest survivor crystal dangles from her neck as she works her weights.

I look at her and watch her. Usually we meet three times a week at the crack of dawn before I have to go to the office and we talk and work out together, reporting on the survivor work from outside. Today, we meet in the afternoon, waiting on the rain. It's getting better, she says. Don't you think? I nod, wondering does she mean the rain or our work. Both are true, I think. It's getting better, I say. It's only when the old feelings come back and I recognize them again that I think I am stuck. It's like lifting weights. Inch by inch. She nods. She laughs, her long hair tossing in the shower.

We walk out into the rain. She won't cross Market Street like I do, in the middle of the road, so we walk to the intersection. She asks are you going to the country? If the roads hold out, I say. Sher will know. We need to take the roses. Susan nods. We kiss good-bye under her umbrella. She asks what we do up there in the country when it rains. We just watch and sit inside and be warm and dry, I say. It only rains in clumps, you know. We talk. We remember. We do our work. Susan smiles and kisses me. Have a good weekend, she says. See you Tuesday. She walks off in the other direction.

I walk towards my '63 Falcon. It is cold and gray. It is like Rhode Island in November. I get into the car and lean back on the seat, waiting before I push in the clutch, before I pull out the choke. I just sit there, my head tilted back on the top of the seat and I feel the sadness washing through me again, as though it were pressing out from the inside of all of my skin. The car is cold and damp. My tears slip down into my hair and then I remember to breathe. Breathe steady, feeling the sadness through me, then out through my feet. Breathe deeply, filling myself steady.

The air comes in through the old seams of the vent window and the car is silent with my tears. Then I realize I don't hear the rain on the roof. The rain has been stopped for a little while now. Well, maybe we will get there tonight. I keep my eyes closed and keep breathing my slow rhythm. Take in, let go, take in, let go. Well, if we can't, we'll figure something else out. We'll get the roses planted this weekend, even if we have to plant them in pots here in the city and take them up later.

Between me and Sher and the rest of us, we can probably figure this out. I begin to feel a little more soothed. I turn around and peek at the angel who is sitting in the back seat. She is smiling at me, softly, patiently. It will be okay. And soon, we'll be able to stay at the farm for good. Pretty soon. It's not so far away as it seems.

I look at the angel and she motions to me to dry my eyes off with my sleeve. This makes me smile and I turn back to the window and I wipe my eyes with my sleeve. The wind still comes cold and the sky is not clear, but the rain is holding off. Breathe. And then finally the sigh, which means my own rain is holding off. Just to be able to sit in the warm with Sher and be dry and talk seems like a home to me now. And this weekend, we will go to this home. When the rain stops, we will walk; Misha said I could walk if I use a strong stick. I know I can; it doesn't hurt so much as before, even in the rain.

*AUTHOR'S NOTE:* Women have asked me if this story is true; if it really happened. The answer is that this story is as true as I know how to make it; yes, everything I wrote here actually happened.

# PART SIX
## Power and Coalition

---

## The Distances Between Us: Feminism, Consciousness and the Girls at the Office – An Essay in Fragments

Irena Klepfisz

*For Melanie Kaye/Kantrowitz who insisted I write it.*

I am indebted to a number of people who helped me think through many of the issues raised in this piece: Gloria Anzaldúa, for her sympathy, feedback and dialogue; Esther Hyneman, for dialogue, feedback, and editing; Melanie Kaye/Kantrowitz for dialogue, editing, and above all, editorial patience; Bernice Mennis for consciousness-raising around the issue of shame and for helping me get past the block; Judy Waterman for ongoing dialogue over the past two years, criticism, feedback, and willingness to read it 'just one more time.'

My acknowledgement of these women's support in no way indicates their endorsement of positions that I take.

*This essay is based on my experiences doing office work, something I have done on and off for the past 25 years, supporting myself through college and graduate school as a typist, receptionist, medical transcriber, and librarian's assistant (file clerk). This was not unusual. In the late '50s and through the '60s most students at my college, CCNY,[1] and most graduate students at the University of Chicago worked (stipends and government loans never sufficed; men usually got added income from wives). During this period, office work seemed to me necessary and tolerable because I assumed it was temporary. While I was sensitive to many of the inequities, I did not really focus on them. I assumed they*

185

*would not be* my *problems. I was looking forward to a teaching career. I received my Ph.D in 1970.*

*Between 1969 and 1973, I had a full-time teaching job as an assistant professor of English in New York City. When enrollment dropped, the teaching market was already glutted and I, along with non-tenured faculty across the country, was laid off. While I have done some adjunct teaching since then, I have never held another full-time teaching position.*

*After a year collecting unemployment, I fell back on my office skills. For the past 10 years, with breaks for adjunct teaching and editorial work, I have held what seems an infinite number of jobs — frequently 2 or 3 part-time jobs at once. These were usually higher level office positions such as legal secretary, proofreader, copyeditor. In addition, I taught Yiddish for a while, tried my hand at Yiddish translation, and taught creative writing workshops at home. But always sandwiched in was simple office work; typing, answering the phone, xeroxing, filing, and more recently word processing. My income has never been steady, always uncertain. I remain constantly worried about where the next job will materialize.*

*In the mid-'70s it was still possible to survive by working part-time, but by the end of the decade, I had to return to full-time secretarial work — first in a law office, later in a school for disturbed boys, finally and more recently, in a posh psychiatric hospital. During this four-year period which ended in November, 1983, I managed to carve out one block of uninterrupted time — eight months unencumbered by a job — that allowed me to write. I had saved some money and received support from my mother and then from a grant. One thread: my livelihood.*

*The second thread: my writing. Since I began to publish in the early '70s, my writing itself has brought me virtually no income. I have self-published or been published, have accumulated a substantial number of credits, but as for money, in 11 years, I have earned a total of $695 from contributions to anthologies.[2] As an editor of* Conditions, *I received $1,200 for 4 years of work.[3]*

*Where the threads converge.* Keeper of the Accounts *was the collection I worked on during my eight month 'break' in 1981–82. Though I have so far made no money from it, it has been the positive response to that collection that has freed me, at least for now, from office work.* Keeper *has made me better known as a writer, therby qualifying me for a number of creative writing jobs and for a writer-in-residence grant.[4] Since November, 1983, I have lived on income from these as well as from adjunct teaching in two different colleges. It has been a relief.*

*I offer these details about my work history, my career as a writer and a teacher, and my economic situation because I want to be clear that I am* not *writing from the perspective of an office worker who has only done office work and has never had other kinds of opportunities. Clearly, for a long time my life had all the markings of upward mobility, and the Ph.D was intended to place me solidly in the middle class. It was a course I had chosen and which I was not ashamed of. It was only the economic situation that checked these plans.*

*My history is not unique in this sense; I believe there is a far greater mixture and mix-up of education, class, and economic insecurity among women than feminists recognize. Some of the reasons for this I discuss in this essay. Melanie Kaye/Kantrowitz, in one of our numerous dialogues, pointed out that on the whole our movement has too often equated the issues of class and race, thereby obscuring the need for a separate analysis of each. One result has been an erasure of the white working-class experience. A white woman – and especially a Jew like myself – is usually assumed to be middle class, while a woman of color – especially Black, Hispanic, or Native American – is usually assumed to be working class, or poor, which is often but not inevitably, true.*

*My own experience in the movement substantiates Melanie's analysis. Much of the impetus for this article has stemmed from my frustration and anger at what I have observed: distortion and erasure of the lives of women I have worked with at various jobs; ignoring, misunderstanding, and romanticization of my own experience. The resistance to clarity has, predictably, been greatest from middle class and downwardly mobile women who have never felt and thus simply do not understand economic traps and limitations.*

*Because the office experience is not my life's work either, because I expect that the next 10 years will be like the last, with office work comprising only part of my working life, because I expect to continue benefiting from my writing and my training as a teacher, I too cannot completely convey what it means to remain 25 or 35 years typing at a desk and never to have any other options. And while I have frequently been broke, have been and am constantly in debt, I have never been the poorest of the poor. But I have experienced the sense of entrapment and futility that office work can bring for periods long enough to enable me to glimpse their meaning. For this glimpse I feel peculiarly indebted, knowing that had my life gone according to my class, I would have known no work but office work; and had my life gone according to my plans, my knowledge of this kind of working life would have been almost non-existent. In fact, this knowledge and my friendship with other office workers have been the only benefits of the experience.*

I keep asking myself why I need to write this – what it is that I need to say. As often happens with my writing, the title comes first: 'The Distances Between Us.' The 'us' – my sisters in the women's movement (however one defines it) *and* the women in the offices I work in – who talk disparagingly about that movement, about 'libbers,' about how they like to have doors opened for them, about the poor 'spinster' living down the road.

I did not say my 'sisters in the offices I work in' because I'm not used to writing or reading that phrase. My failure. Our failure. But sisters they are with a connection I feel strongly despite our different lives, our different levels of consciousness, despite the fact that most of the time I cannot be open about myself as a dyke, a Jew, a writer. But then, am I fully myself in the women's movement when the life I lead – the experience of office work and economic pressure – is not part of the feminist consciousness? So there is distance there too.

This essay represents my attempt to balance a perspective in a movement I am deeply committed to – the feminist movement. I want to view the world, or at least the immediate society in which I function, not only from the vantage point of a deliberate, conscious lesbian/feminist, but also from the vantage of those women who seem to reject feminism theoretically, but obviously need a feminist movement because they are affected by women's issues – including class, work and economics about which *they* are the experts and can teach us. Too often these women are excluded because they do not have the correct political language or consciousness. Ironically, much of our political rhetoric includes their condition and living circumstances. And yet how often do we dismiss them or put down their perspectives as uninformed and unenlightened because *they* do not talk like *we* talk, do not operate from the same framework.

*March 11, 1983*: The deadline for this essay is almost past and nothing that looks like an essay has yet emerged.[5] I have a pile of separate sheets of paper with first-draft notes: memories, observations, half-formulated ideas and theories, questions, suggestions for answers, reminders to look up certain passages. Most of these have been jotted down at high speed on my office IBM selectric, usually when I should have been doing something else and was tense that I might be caught.

These separate sheets physically embody part of what it is I want to write about. What it is like to be an alert, thinking human being absorbed, assaulted by mindless unintelligent work. The fragmentation. The sense of being scattered. What it is like not to have time to think, to consider an idea and follow it through to its logical conclusion. This condition – devoid of logic because it is irrational, devoid of structure because it is aimless, devoid of theme or thesis because it is pointless – is not unique to me just because I happen to want to write. Rather it is the common experience of many working people, an experience that I have observed and shared primarily with those who do office work.[6] Most of the office workers I have met are not writers and do not want to be; nor are they lesbians or conscious feminists. Yet how often between transcription tapes, during extended coffee or smoke breaks, on those Friday afternoons that seem endless – how often have I heard them speak of the sense of deprivation, of being robbed, the sense of loss that I happen to experience in relation to my writing. Eight hours a day, five days a week, we all lose possibilities, lose self.

I am stuck with this paradox. Those who do not share this life of aimless, meaningless work, those who do not sit and feel day after day go to waste, simply do not know, cannot, I believe, fathom the depth of its destructiveness. They do not know, and yet they think they know, frequently creating theories about it, stating how work and economic issues are important, yet how we must move past them towards 'deeper' or 'higher' ones. Poor and working-class women know that a lot of the time these are the *only* issues; no wonder, therefore, they find such theoretical writing – not too difficult as some would have us believe – but too abstract, too divorced from their own daily struggles.

My own experience has taught me that work and economic issues are essential starting points for feminist discussions, ones which cannot be quickly skipped over. They affect us psychologically, affect our personalities, our creativity, our ways of thinking, affect our relations with each other. Unfortunately those of us who understand this through direct experience – well, the experience itself frequently blocks us from communicating what we know. After all, how many of us have the time or space to pull together our knowledge and observations? How many of us have the energy, in fact, both to absorb the experience and to convey it to others in whatever form? And this is precisely the trap in which I now find myself. Knowing. Yet not being able to speak.

*Fact 1*: My life at this time does not allow me to write the traditional essay: beginning, middle, end – state your thesis clearly; develop the argument; illustrate appropriately; smooth out transitions; refine the logic, conclude. And I really do not want to produce such an essay, but rather something that is closer in form to my way of life and, equally, important, closer to the process of my writing.

The fragmentation of this piece, therefore, is not unlike the fragmentation of the lives of those of us who have no time, to ourselves. The leaps, ellipses, zigzags are the result of a specially developed thought process, one that is not linear because it is always interrupted, frequently free-associative and haphazard, rarely schematized. We think. But we think differently. Sudden realizations, half-finished paragraphs, an outline, a sketch. But not smooth development, ordered philosophy.

*Fact 2*: If those of us stuck in these situations are going to say anything at all, then we must say it in non-traditional ways. We must speak in leaps, in zigzags, in incomplete parts. To wait until we can speak smoothly and completely is to doom ourselves to silence.

## Inside and Outside

I frequently talk about being in the 'real' world as opposed to the feminist or lesbian circle. What is the opposition I set up?

Everything outside the feminist movement is the 'real' world. This consists of the institutions, the office and office workers at my current job, my family and friends 'from before.' When I think this way, do I mean the feminist world is 'unreal?'

Not so much unreal as sifted. To some degree. To a great degree. The 'movement' world – the inside – is created through choices. We choose the people we want to work with, we choose the causes we want to work on, we choose the feminist institutions we want to create. None of this is absolute, but certainly it seems true to a greater degree than in the 'real' world – the outside. Because we are so used to these choices, coalitions are frequently difficult to make. We think we have a choice about whom we work with. And there are people we choose *not* to work with.

## Outside

I have no control over the circumstances in the office I work in. I look for a job and usually take what I can get, hoping for a decent salary or benefits or a manageable travelling time – all the considerations surrounding work. But I do not choose the other people in the office, just as I do not choose other members of my family, just as I do not select who can be a Jew or woman. These all come with birth. And working circumstances come with the job.

What always astonishes me is how quickly people whom I have never seen before begin to exert enormous power and influence over my life. My boss could be constantly proving his authority by demanding I let him know when I need to leave my desk and go to the bathroom. My supervisor might hate her job, be frustrated with the administration and take it out on me by constantly dropping in to see 'exactly what you are doing.' The supply person might take a disliking to me and not give me a good transcribing machine. When you consider that you must spend 8 hours a day, 5 days a week dealing with any or all of this, life can become a complete nightmare. It it not easy just to say: I guess I'll leave and find something else. Not in these times when jobs are scarce, when you're middle-aged and no longer can 'pretty up' some man's office, when you've been conditioned by poverty not to leave any job.

Given these circumstances, most women in offices know it's to our advantage to pull together. There are always exceptions, the ones sucking up to the supervisor or boss; but these individuals are easy to spot because of their isolation. There is no faking around this issue. Most of us know who the enemy is, even if we are very different from each other. In the office, we rarely mistake what side of the line we are all on.

## Inside

We act as if we always have a choice. We are insulted when asked to associate or join with someone we disagree with or dislike. We try as much as possible to pick and screen those around us.

This is probably an exaggeration.

This is probably not an exaggeration. Look at the in-fighting, the pulling apart, the trashing and back-stabbing. We confuse who the real enemy is, frequently fingering each other. We act as if we can afford to pick and choose. And we can't.

# Two Episodes

*Outside*: I am being interviewed for a secretarial job. I have made a mistake in this application by admitting, not that I have a Ph.D (which I know never to admit to in these situations), but that I have an M.A. The job as advertised seemed to require some research and editing experience. I misread. My prospective boss, a psychiatrist, worries that I'm overqualified. Would I be bored? he asks. I've been asked this question before whenever the issue of my education has come up. The implication is, of course, that the more educated you are, the more tedious the work will seem.

Does he think women with a high school degree find transcription and typing interesting and stimulating? What kind of hierarchical conception of human beings does this psychiatrist have? How is it that a well-educated man, supposedly trained in sensitivity, does not have any idea that every single secretary around him sees through his arrogance and condescension and is repeatedly outraged by them? And to what degree does he – and those like him – have to dehumanize office workers in order to maintain this limited view of them?

Let me put it another way: what deliberate ignorance and callousness to people – high school drop-out and Ph.D, secretary, housewife, athlete, construction worker, farm worker – would allow for the conclusion that anyone would find this work anything but boring?

*Inside*: Another writer has just finished reading my short story 'The Journal of Rachel Robotnik.' The story is about a woman office worker – and a writer – trying to find time to write, trying to cope with the tensions between other transcribers in her steno pool and their boss, trying to find some balance in her chaotic life. My friend, a political writer, proud of her political awareness and commitments, likes the story very much, but confesses: 'I've always wanted to write about office work. But it's so boring. I've never been able to do it.' At first I am stunned. Then I feel rage at the ignorance, insult of the remark. *Office work*, I know *is very boring*, very boring indeed. But *the people* who do office work *are not*. Certainly not any more than any other people. My friend knows she must be aware of the 'working class,' must 'reach out' to *them*, but in her own life, what she does is distance. For her the work and the people are one and the same: only boring people would spend a lifetime doing boring work. No wonder she – and others like her – can't build personal or political bonds with working-class women.

*Inside and Outside*: One night when I had a bad case of insomnia, I remembered these two episodes and suddenly realized that in *both* the word 'boring' loomed large – though the judgment came from two people seemingly opposed politically and ethically. Neither my boss (and he finally hired me) nor my politically correct friend with her guilt toward the working class sees the woman office worker for what she is: as complex a human being as the political writer wanting to make an impact on the world through her radical political analysis; as complex a human being as the head of a research department of a modern psychiatric hospital, claiming to have insight into the psyches of others. As complex and as simple. But only those who have allowed themselves to look beyond the occupation label and made personal contact and shared experiences will know that.

I have encountered extraordinary arrogance and ignorance concerning working-class people, often from feminists who are well educated, of middle-class backgrounds, and who pride themselves on their political analyses, their raised consciousness and awareness, and their critical appraisal of privileges. Some examples:
– I review a novel about a waitress and ask for some feedback. On one note I receive the following question: Given that this novel is written in different voices and from different perspectives, should you not deal with the fact that a working-class woman will not understand it?
*Why should she not understand it?*
– I present a poem to a workshop that I am leading. It describes a working-class woman who – among other things – mentions that she believes in seeing things 'aesthetical.' Members of the workshop object. How could such a woman know such a concept, much less the word itself?
*Why should she not know it?*
– A woman tells me about a political group in which members decided to use the word 'ain't' in their flyers so that the group would seem like 'one of the people.'
*No comment.*
– Another woman tells me of rewriting leaflets primarily in monosyllables so the 'masses' could understand them better.
*No comment.*
– A 'downwardly mobile' dyke tells me she's going to get unemployment. It's not very much, but she's decided to collect anyway even though it seems a lot of trouble and somehow, she implies, is demeaning to fill out all those forms and stand on line once a week.
*What must she think of the rest of us who line up obediently and to whom it never occurs that we should do otherwise because we have no choice?*
Arrogance. Contempt. But above all – incredible ignorance. The 'masses' out there are stupid, uneducated, unreachable unless you speak to them in kindergarten English. They are not people with a different way of living, surviving, with their own perspective. They are inferiors. To most middle-class feminists, as to most middle-class non-feminists, working-class women remain mysterious creatures to be 'reached out to' in some abstract way. No connection. No solidarity.

# A Feminist Consciousness

*A memory from the late '70s*: I am teaching a course: Introduction to Women's Studies. It is summer and we meet four times a week in the evenings. The class is a typical New York City mixture of Third World and white women, middle-class and working-class, gay and straight, Jew and Christian, old and young.

Before I started teaching, I had been warned that women registering for it would probably have a low level of consciousness on feminist issues in general. This turns out to be too true. Though they live in New York City, not one has ever stepped inside a women's bookstore (at the time there were three) or attended a women's event (and there were dozens). Most are here out of a conscious curiosity as well as an unconscious pull towards feminism. And so we spend a great deal of time on what is basically consciousness-raising. After about three weeks they are much more sensitive, more aware of sexism, of feminist perspectives and analyses. Initially very skeptical, they are now frequently angry.

At the midpoint in the course, I assign a story from the violence issue of *Heresies*, a story about a family outing at a lake.[7] As I remember it, no overt violence takes place; but throughout the outing the father bullies the wife and children incessantly. The class discusses domestic violence, the different degrees, levels, types. Without thinking very much about it, I ask casually: 'Well, what about the mother? What do you think of her? After all, she's fairly passive. Do you think she can be reached?'

The answers come quickly. No. Absolutely not. She's beyond help. Maybe this is naive of me, but I am genuinely shocked. Most of the women in the class seemed in her condition only three weeks before. And now – they deem her a hopeless case: *She's the type that never changes.* Why, I wonder, do they give up on her so quickly? Why do they distance themselves from her?

Suddenly I am angry. Everything we've been doing for the past three weeks seems worthless. What's the point if there is no identification, no empathy? So I return the next day and make a very clear statement: I refuse to let them give up on this character. I tell them I am willing to sit in silence for the remainder of the course until they come up with some kind of satisfactory answer in relationship to the woman in the story.

And so we sit. And I wait. No one is particularly comfortable. The silence goes on for a long, long time. And then finally one woman blurts out: 'What the hell is she supposed to do? Just pick up the kids and go? Where? And do what?'

And with that question, with what is clearly an identification with the woman's perspective and options, the class is off. They begin a serious discussion of choices. Of helplessness. Of indoctrination. Of breaking through the indoctrination – what makes it possible, what blocks it. Of available support systems. Of support systems that should exist but

193

do not. Of the feelings that led them to register for the class. The fact that the class existed. The fact that they knew someone who encouraged them. And on and on.

What they bridged at this point was the distance their consciousness created between themselves and other women who had not reached the same point. They *remembered* and *integrated* their past experiences with their new perceptions. They realized that a young mother with two children, with no independent income or social support will tolerate a great deal from a cruel husband. Her remaining with him might not be just stubborn resistance to feminist ideas of women's strength and independence, nor her 'ineducability,' but rather a realistic acceptance of the circumstances which allow her and her children to survive, even if painfully.

*A Recent Interpretation*: When I described this episode to Melanie Kaye/Kantrowitz, she remarked that when people first discover new parts of their identity, their tendency is to strengthen their self-perception by separating themselves from those who do not share it. This solidifies one's new position. We see this frequently with just-out lesbians who can't bear heterosexual women, or newly born radicals who scorn all who are not politicized like them.

Still, if this type of separating is a necessary stage of the process, it should be only temporary. For when consciousness does nothing except separate us from each other, it is useless. Maybe worse than useless. It is divisive.

I have watched feminists with such 'raised consciousness' be contemptuous of the office worker who wears make-up and worries about her weight (never mind if these might be legitimate concerns in relation to her job). Such a judgment reveals: one, that the working-class woman is seen as completely passive, having to be changed by others and having nothing to offer; and, two, that her experience as well as her being are deemed too lowly. This analysis frequently passes for 'consciousness' or 'being political,' again separating those who are from those who aren't. In this context, being political means being morally superior.

I am reminded of Anzia Yezierska who, in her story 'Brothers,' wrote: 'Education without a heart is a curse.' And a raised consciousness without a heart is not only a curse, but a fraud.

*February 22, 1983*: Why do we always assume that having a 'raised consciousness' or 'political awareness' is desirable? I remember my initial exhilaration after finishing Tillie Olsen's *Silences*. Though much of the content was not 'new' – my background had already clued me in to many of the limitations that this book describes – I had never really thought about silencing in such a systematic way, nor had I thought about how it applied to myself as a writer.

For example, I had always characterized myself as 'not very prolific.' This was not said defensively, just descriptively. I did not produce much.

194

It hadn't occurred to me that the circumstances of my life did not lend themselves to my being prolific because most of my energy was expended on trying to support myself. Writing was, of course, important, but not *most* important. It was not anything I cried about. Who cries about such things? Certainly no one I knew while growing up. I was taught that everyone works. And no one expects any pleasure from it. You just do it. And writers are no exceptions.

I read *Silences* at a time when I was taking my writing more and more seriously. As I said, the initial realization of the various barriers – sexist, social, economic, racial – that silence us, that prevent us from externalizing our vision and experiences of the world was exhilarating: certain discrete perceptions suddenly fell into place and created a pattern in the midst of complete chaos.

But as the recognition took hold, as it sank deeper into my consciousness, as the true implications of that pattern became clearer, as I realized the full force of the 'givens' of my life in relation to my writing, I began to experience a tremendous upheaval – a period of intense rage and pain. I became acutely aware, in a way I had not been before, of all my limitations.

I read *Silences* in 1979 during a short three-month 'break' from work. Afterwards, I began working full-time in a law office. I had begun to write the story 'The Journal of Rachel Robotnik.' Every day during that period, while typing, while transcribing, while xeroxing, while filing, I would think: I could be writing. I could be writing my story. I could be working on many stories, on many poems. I went through a period of intense self-observation, of focusing on the exact meaning of what I was living through. Day after day completely wasted in meaningless work. Getting up every morning. Crowding into the dilapidated subway. Other people crowding around me. Empty, bleak days. All I could think was: I am wasting, wasting everything in me. For almost a full year I counted and measured every minute, every second in my life that was being wasted. The constant calculating was excruciating.

The rage was soon accompanied by an envy that worked like a high-powered microscope, making visible and enlarging differences, magnifying what others had and what I did not have. A writer I knew who didn't need to work was looking for a room so she could write in seclusion and peace; her home, she said, was chaotic. I envied her, could barely look directly at her when she explained 'her problem.' Another woman was taking time off because she was feeling scattered and just couldn't focus (she had income from sources outside of her job). Someone else went away on vacation to unwind. Someone else was just staying home. I envied them and sometimes hated them. I could not forgive them for not being in my position.

These were the kinds of emotions that erupted in me as I awakened to the limitations of my growth as a writer. Envy is a horrible thing, especially when directed at what is not within our control. It is like raging at a thunderstorm. It is stupid. It eats you up.

But I felt it. And it came with the perception that consciousness brought. At the time, there was nothing I could do about my condition. And so I yearned for the time when I was oblivious to it.

I remember another feeling I experienced during this period. Every morning I would take the train from Brooklyn and get off at 42nd Street and Grand Central Station in Manhattan. I would hurry through the station surrounded by hundreds and hundreds of other people, all also rushing to get to work on time. Thousands of us would bunch up near the escalators that took us up into the Pan Am Building, a short cut to the Helmsley-Spear Building where I worked. As I waited, completely surrounded by masses of people, completely lost among them, and then as I began to move upward on the escalator and saw those above me getting off and those below me still crowded and waiting patiently, I would be overcome with a feeling I can only imagine close to mystical. I, raised an atheist and completely non-spiritual in my approach to life, would be overcome with such a sense of oneness with the people around me, such a sense of being with them – a feeling I had never before nor since felt. I knew we were all lost together, that we were all being eaten up, swallowed up as if we were on a large conveyor belt feeding us to oblivion.

At those moments, I neither envied nor raged. I felt enormous peace with everyone. I knew I was sharing a basic experience with thousands of people. I did not feel alone.

## Wasting a Life

*A memory*: I am meeting a friend who is working for the 'Fair Hearings Court' of the State of New York. She transcribes the court proceedings of welfare recipients who challenge decisions on a local level.

The transcribing pool is in the midst of a vast floor space – on the edges are crates filled with files, desks piled on top of each other. Smack in the center of this upheaval – there's no way to tell if they're moving in or moving out – there are 10 transcribers sitting in two rows facing each other. At the head of the two columns sits the supervisor, a woman who used to be one of the girls. She has risen through the ranks and along the fringes. Behind each row of transcribers are a few other desks with extra space around them – state bureaucrats. And then the cartons, crates and stacked office furniture. Large windows look out on the State Capital. Outside, I can see the enormous towers built by Rockefeller in honor of himself. His labyrinthian highways run under this plaza, unnecessary highways which required the demolition of century-old bridges.

The transcriber who is my friend is also a sculptor of massive structures that seem to push themselves out of the studio, that always seem to demand more space than she can provide. Karen is sitting, one of the girls, dressed in typical 'bohemian' fashion – bright green Indian pants, a burning pink blouse, her long black hair defiantly loose and the grey streaks quite unashamedly visible.

She sits the third one down. She is facing a young woman who has her hair cut punk, defiantly green. Karen sits and transcribes. She is wearing boots, her foot is on the pedal, the headset over her ears. I stand for a moment and watch her silently. She cannot see me.

Later she will tell me how not a single case that she has transcribed during the past three months, not a single welfare recipient who has come for a hearing in order to increase payments or be reimbursed for a refrigerator, for an electric bill, for nursing care, for food – *not a single one* has won a case in the state's 'Fair Hearings Court.' And how can they? she asks. The state picks the judge, the prosecutor and the defending lawyer. So why should anyone win?

I look at Karen and watch her foot press the pedal.

Stupid is not the word for it. Criminal.

And I know that I could walk along these two rows of women and stand and watch each one and say the same thing:

Stupid is not the word for it. Criminal.

I am attending a feminist brunch. An intense discussion develops around the issue of women's lives and the lack of opportunity, the repression, oppression, the exploitation. One woman becomes extremely upset, indignant because she cannot bear to think that her mother's life has been a waste. Some women try to comfort her. I do not say anything. I know, of course, that no person who has exhibited kindness, caring and support can be said to have wasted her life entirely. But I also know the bitter fact that most lives are incredibly wasted, that the opportunities for developing identity, for receiving pleasure, for achieving a sense of self-worth are limited and, not only underdeveloped, but in most cases not developed at all – because no one thinks that a housewife, or a mother, a typist has anything to develop. It simply has never occurred to most people. And that judgment is passed on through the silence surrounding them.

I do not say anything. But I know that this woman's mother has probably wasted a lot of her life, just as I have wasted periods of my life. And there is no getting away from that knowledge.

## Art and Other Callings

I have been asking myself why I always focus on the artist. I focus on her because art – in my case writing – is the most obvious yardstick I have to measure the waste in my own life. I do not know what yardsticks to use for others, for most people have not been allowed to see their own possibilities. Art, after all, is not the only means to self-expression and though some of my co-workers might – given the chance – want to be artists, others might want to be organizers, engineers, philosophers, full-time housewives and mothers, physicists, athletes, greenhouse keepers, animal doctors, furniture strippers.

How easily do I and many of the feminists I know accept the fact that some of us are born with 'talent' that should be nurtured and supported, without considering the implications of labelling and naming *only* talents associated with art or professions. In doing that, aren't we implying that those born without a specific, *visible* talent are automatically meant to be transcribers or xerox machine operators or factory workers?

Sometimes I wonder if, in fact, most formally educated people do believe just that. Just as an artist or doctor must have the proper, conducive working atmosphere to flourish, so the secretary or office worker must have the proper, conducive working atmosphere for her calling. So how can we help her? How can we nurture and support her? Musak perhaps? Good lighting? A self-erasing selectric typewriter? A word processor?

When people think in these structures, when they separate the artist, intellectual, or professional and think of her as a person apart, as special, as disconnected from the 'masses,' from the assembly line, from the stenographic pool, they reveal their basic distance from working people. When feminists think in these structures, our commitment to helping the 'non-artist,' the 'ordinary' woman becomes nothing more than a desire to make her *more comfortable in the current social order*, a failure to see the separate value of her life. Such distancing denies our connection to her. For while we place ourselves outside that order by virtue of our 'unique talent,' we doom her to remain forever inside the xerox room or steno pool. That is not radical thinking. That is plain elitism.

*November 30, 1982*: Talked to Nina this morning. She is the cook for the staff – psychiatrists, administrators, office workers. She makes our lunch. She works fast. Uses all her free time to read. I wonder about her. She's tough. Used to work in a gas station. Raised dogs. Yes, I wonder about her.

Said to me she didn't like working. Said she's wishing her whole life away. (She's only 22). Isn't it terrible, she asked, to live just for 2 days out of 7, and to wish the other 5 away?

# Bonding

Given external facts, friendship between Elizabeth and me would seem impossible. Born a Catholic in a small Massachusetts town where she lived all her life, she was the oldest of four children. Went to work immediately after high school at the same psychiatric hospital where I met her more than 20 years later. Learned about sex by typing charts. Married at 20. Did not say much about Kenneth except that he never complained and was a good father. Had three children. The oldest boy had visual problems, hated school, was denied graduation until he passed a certain reading test. Elizabeth had worked with him almost every day since he entered second grade. The second boy just began college, the first one to do so in his family. The 'baby,' a girl, is still in high school. All worked. Elizabeth was exactly my age when we met: 41. She returned to work in this hospital about a year before I arrived.

I am a Jew, a survivor of the Holocaust, a lesbian, an author of two books of poetry, a Ph.D, a teacher, an activist, I have never married and have no children. I knew a great deal about Elizabeth within a couple of months. Until I left, almost a year later, Elizabeth only knew that I was a Jew, a survivor, that I aspired to write, and that I had a roommate.

Yet Elizabeth and I did become close friends. I admired her and listened as she analyzed and reflected on her life at home and at the office. She taught me about the hospital and kept rejecting my suggestions for greater efficiency and accountability with: 'Haven't you learned they're not interested in your opinion? That they don't care what we do or how often? That they simply don't care?'

She hated her job with a passion, but saw no way out. She was in constant crisis. Five adults, all needed transportation to jobs and schools, and cars and motorcycles were forever breaking down, kids getting into accidents, bills constantly popping up and out of control. She said she felt cheated because she could never enjoy the house whose mortgage she and Kenneth were killing themselves to pay off – she was either in the hospital typing or at home cooking and cleaning. Once, I came into her room when she was collating a long monograph and was moving from desk to table. She said: 'Irena, I feel like a corkscrew, just driving myself deeper and deeper into the grave.' And then she began to turn in place and say: 'Work. Grocery. Home. Work. Grocery. Home.'

She understood basic feminist principles, though she openly rejected any feminist labels. She analyzed the structure of male thinking in relation to organizations and stated that men simply could not diversify and do more than one thing at a time while women had learned to play multiple roles in the home. She was sure if the women took over the hospital, it would make more sense.

Yet she was devoted to family and the job. I would try to convince her, for example, to take a day off because she was totally depleted and exhausted – that 'sick' did not mean exclusively 'physically ill.' It was hard for her to accept this; she thought it a form of lying. She felt responsible to the doctors. They relied on her. She refused to fudge or short change anyone, even though they constantly short changed her.

I understood her attitude. She wanted to salvage some sense of integrity. It was through her job and her family that she saw any possibility for achieving self-esteem. And so typing a report, quickly and flawlessly, was important. Meeting all deadlines was important. Never lying was important. Though I had things outside of the office that gave me a sense of worth – my writing, my political work – I too would often set goals for myself so I could have some sense of achievement during the day.

Still, I lied all the time, determined to use every sick day I could. I had no shame about it and Elizabeth and the others knew what I was doing. Yet no one blamed me or guilt-tripped me. They simply accepted me and my behavior. Elizabeth was particularly giving, enjoying our differences. She liked hearing about my outings to New York City, about my mother, about the woman I lived with – though that relationship was never clarified. She sympathized when I was really bored or disgusted. She sympathized when I was broke. And I was always eager to hear about her life, about how she had grown up in this town, her pre-marriage innocence, the progress of her kids in school, and to give any kind of advice based on my own experience outside the office. She in turn advised me patience, showed me short-cuts and pitfalls of the institution, and became a model of how to live without envy and constant rage. I tried to help her make more room for herself, pointing out the kids were old enough to take over more responsibility. I also felt helpless and stymied, as with other friends, because I could not get her to break a lifelong pattern of self-sacrifice. At times I would feel angry and frustrated, especially when I found her asleep, her head resting on her typewriter. She countered: 'It's not so much that we're not as good as we were. We're just not as good for as long.'

Elizabeth made me feel privileged because I had reasonable hope that eventually – in a year or so – I could leave. I would get a break, if only temporary. I knew what one free week would have meant to her. Talking to her month after month, I realized over and over again, no matter how deeply unhappy I was, how depressed, that it was not the same as her unhappiness, as her depression. She made me feel the great difference between us and our lives.

And yet this difference did not separate us. It was possible for us to share equally – to share the particular strengths we had developed from our different lives. We formed a close bond based on a common experience of trying to cope with nonsensical regulations and the callous behavior of our bosses. Elizabeth made me more conscious than ever that her life was like so many others – devoured by meaningless work. She made me conscious of the kinds of lives so many women lead and the waste of it. As she put it: 'You know, Irena, when I got out of high school in '58, no one thought I should do anything but type.'

# 1982: A Photograph

*Source*: A local upstate New York paper.
*Content*: Two people shaking hands.

He is older. The president of a college. It is obviously graduation. He is dressed in an elaborate cap and gown – inverted collar, tassles, colored stripes, a multitude of folds evoking complexity, emeritus, honorary, distinguished, doctor.

She is young, very young. She is wearing the plainer costume: black cap and gown. No frills.

It is graduation.

They are shaking hands.

She has just received an award from the Secretarial Arts Department for 'outstanding achievement in typewriting.'

## A Soap Opera

She was not glamorous. That is important. Because receptionists are always supposed to be glamorous. But Sandy was 35, wore casual make-up, clothes that were clearly frayed at the edges.

It took me a while to piece together the full portrait. Initially, Sandy struck me as happy-go-lucky. She was always laughing and joking whenever I came into the main office to pick up mail or do my xeroxing. She talked a lot about her kids, about her baby, twelve-year-old daughter, who was now wearing her 'training' bra; about her fourteen-year-old son who had decided he was a 'breast man' and not a 'leg man.' She was divorced and talked a lot about crushes she had and dreamed out loud about meeting someone, about trying to show interest without overstepping the limits of ladyhood, about the middle-aged man at the post office who was interested in her but who she couldn't abide because, after all, he was balding.

She talked endlessly about all this. It all seemed fairly usual, simple.

But Sandy's life and history were complicated, so complicated that some people – mainly the administrators of this special school for boys – laughed behind her back and called her life a soap opera.

Her health, it turned out, was poor. She had kidney problems and she was taking special medication for arthritis. One day I noticed a black and blue mark on her arm and, without thinking, asked about it. She blushed, and then confessed that her brother had beaten her. Many family members were alcoholic, she herself was one, though she was sober now. The night before one of her brothers had arrived drunk. She shrugged and blushed again.

She also had custody problems. The arrangement was not permanent. Custody was reassigned on a monthly basis. And it was partly contingent on her ability to support the kids, pay her mortgage, her fuel bills, etc. She kept reassuring me that her husband was really a nice guy and loved the kids.

Since she had been hired to replace someone who had gone on maternity leave, Sandy had no job security, or benefits. She was earning $3.25 an hour working a 40-hour week (not including lunch).

Her 'responsibilities' included switchboard, typing, xeroxing, collating, and filing. She worked in the main office of the school. I was a

201

secretary, but in a different building. Compared to other secretaries – there were six of us in all – Sandy was not very good. Her work at the switchboard and xeroxing was fine. But her typing was filled with errors and misspellings, her filing sloppy and confused. Most of us would help her out whenever we were in the main office; but we could never give her all the help she really needed.

One day towards the end of the summer, she got sick – sunstroke complicated by the arthritis medication she was taking. She collapsed and was rushed to a hospital. She remained critical for a few days and then finally stabilized. After two weeks, she was back home.

The day after she got home, the supervisor called and gave her two weeks' notice. Another secretary came to stay with her. She could not get out of bed yet. She had absolutely no money. She was worried about custody.

Another woman had been interviewed for the position. But when it came time to negotiate the salary, she refused the $3.75 (50¢ more than Sandy was getting). Not anticipating any problems, the supervisor had fired Sandy before the other woman had actually accepted. Now the school was stuck.

Shameless, as always, the supervisor called Sandy. Forget what we said.

And, of course, she did. What else was she supposed to do?

The other secretaries tried to make her deal with the situation, emphasizing that the administrators had no scruples, that this could happen again, that Sandy needed to get a firm commitment. It was obvious the woman she had replaced was not returning and that the administration was not going to offer the job to Sandy. She had to clarify the situation. If they refused to make a commitment, she had to start looking for something else – *now*.

Sandy listened, but was afraid to move. And then things changed. The supervisor gave notice and was replaced by a Mrs. Conroy. Everything got very quiet. We all sat tight and watched. It could get better. It could get worse.

We told Sandy that there might be some hope since Conroy was new. We urged her to talk to her and finally she did. Though it was now the end of October and though Sandy had been working for the school since April (eight months!), Conroy told her she would be put on 3-months probation. If she did well, the job was hers.

We were appalled. We knew it was a set-up. Clearly they intended to let her go. We told Sandy she *had* to start looking for another job, *had* to start *now*. But she just smiled. She felt hopeful. She was going to work hard, get her typing speed up, and then she'd become a permanent employee.

A couple of weeks later, her car broke down. She had no money to fix it. She lived about 25 miles from the school. During the next week, she hitched, once walked 12 miles, a couple of times got rides from people who deposited her at the office at 7 a.m. and picked her up at 8 p.m. She was keeping up, but barely. She was beginning to apply for jobs.

And then one day, they fired her. It was November, the week before Thanksgiving.


## Oppression

*Inside*: There's a romance about it, a romance by middle-class women who feel guilty about their privileged backgrounds. Downwardly mobile, guilt-ridden, they embrace the status of the oppressed and wear it like a badge. They point with pride to how little they have, able to measure it by what they've given up. They are, they claim, clerical workers, office workers, struggling with the injustices of the capitalist system.

*Outside*: I do not believe anyone really chooses to be a clerical worker, though I know many women might say they do. I believe that most people have never had the opportunity to examine what their true potential is and so the selection of clerical work is not done in a framework of complete freedom. Most women are told they are without potential – intellectual, athletic, artistic – are raised to fear responsibilities outside of the home and to question their ability to deal with non-domestic issues.

My experience in offices is that clerical workers, who are the lowest in status and pay in the hierarchy of office workers, despite all conditioning, dream privately and sometimes quite openly about doing something else. Most never do and instead spend endless years doing the worst office shit work, 8 hours a day, 5 days a week. They spend this time in dead-end rooms, usually the useless corners or walk-in closets of large suites, rooms blocked off for files that don't need air or light. These women work for years, stooped over folders or climb ladders to reach drawers close to the ceiling. Dusty, dirty, boring, unhealthy work, endless index cards, endless folders, staples, paper clips, punched holes, reorganizing, pulling, shuffling, filing.

They do this when they are nine months pregnant, when they can barely bend, when they are too exhausted to move, do it till the day before the baby is born. And then, two weeks later, after the delivery, they are back while a sister or a grandmother takes care of the newborn. Whenever you walk into their workspace, that dark area that nobody else wants, they greet you eagerly, chat, show photographs of the baby, try to delay your departure.

There are some who hold two or three part-time jobs in different offices. Some sneak in books, take correspondence courses so they can develop new skills and perhaps one day become a secretary.

These are the clerical workers I have known. They do not think about their status with pride or with shame. It is simply where they are in this society. The work they do is not a ticket to anything. And the only thing they get for it is a very, very small paycheck.

In the hospital where I worked, *each* doctor received an $11,000/year *raise* between October, 1982 and January, 1983. In January, 1983, each secretary received a $10/week raise. Out of thirteen women, not one had been earning more than $10,400 a year ($200/week before deductions) and, because health insurance went up that year, a number of secretaries took home less in '83 than they had in '82.

## Victim

A woman was once describing a friend of hers to me – someone who was always hurrying from one part-time job to another, trying to piece together a living, always in a kind of frenzy and chaos that I know well. Perpetual deadlines. Different focuses. Irregular schedules. The woman concluded her long detailed description by commenting: 'I don't think she'll ever get it together.'

I swallowed hard. I had completely identified with the woman in the story. Get it together? I thought. With what assumptions does this woman operate? Who gets it together? How many people in this society ever get it together?

Most of us fail miserably at it. And we're meant to. Yet, we cannot accept the concept of ourselves as totally victimized, totally done in. We must feel some measure of possibility in our lives, for how else could we ever hope to gain any degree of control?

So victim? Yes and no, I suppose. I know a lot of people – skilled and hard working – who cannot get it together the way society wants them to. They do not meet current needs – whether that be typing skills or computer knowledge. They have many other skills – skills to care for the old, skills associated with compassion and patience, skills to build and construct, skills to teach and awaken. Are we to say they are playing victim, that they're not taking responsibility for their lives because they cannot, however hard they try, get their typing speed up or learn to use a word processor?

How glib. Would we ever say to anyone outraged at sexism, you've got to accept the givens of this society? But how quickly we say – accept your lot because you've chosen it or otherwise you would have gotten out long ago and 'gotten it together.'

## Money

Feminists have barely learned to say the word to each other. How afraid we are to talk about it. Whenever the subject is broached, we run as if on hot coals and don't stop until we reach a cool spot. Talk about anything but that.

A woman I know has so much more than me. She has a good job - good pay, benefits. She is secure, takes vacations. Another woman doesn't have to work at all. Both leave, take long, what seem to me luxurious periods of time off. I say good-bye to them. Wish them well. And I mean it. But I also think, why them, not me?

Another woman I know has so much less than me. In her eyes I am rich. She works as a chamber maid, is dependent on tips, is never quite sure how much she'll take home. She can never save, thinks it's a real luxury that I can take a day off with pay because I have sick leave. She thinks it's good that I have a day to write. And she means it. But she also thinks. Why her, not me?

Women sit around a table. Perhaps they're planning a benefit. Perhaps they're writing a statement. Perhaps they're organizing to participate in a conference in another city. One glances impatiently at her watch and calculates the cost of the babysitter. Another is thinking of the cost of a round trip ticket out of town and if she can afford to go. Still another feels depressed because she has to work that day and can't afford to take off. But they do not mention it. Some don't even think about the differences between them. Some do and feel guilty. Others want them to feel guilty. Others don't give a shit. *But no one talks about it.*


## Shame and Humiliation
## When Need Becomes Shame and Asking is Begging

*November 10, 1984*: I have postponed and postponed finishing this piece. I must finish it, I tell myself. But I am blocked, have been blocked for over a year now on an issue that sticks in my throat. It is the issue of shame and humiliation.

How can I write about this without exposing my own sense of shame? How can I write about this without confessing that just publishing this article about economics and money is intertwined with shame and humiliation? A shame that stems from early poverty. A shame that stems from my having internalized the worst of Jewish stereotypes. That because I'm a Jew, I must be rich. And if I say, no, I am not rich, then I am hiding my wealth, trying to get out of something.

I remember the first time I heard that some people would rather die in a burning building than run out and be seen naked. At the time, I could not quite grasp the depth of shame that could force someone to accept death rather than be exposed.

For the past year or so I have been thinking about this phenomenon, *the power of shame* over our lives, over my life – its power in stopping me from completing this essay, for example. I have been trying to sort out the times when I have felt ashamed as if I had done something wrong when, in fact, I had done nothing; to sort out the circumstances in which I have felt humiliated.

*Need.* I feel shame in feeling need, a shame that I associate with my early childhood of not having, of always wanting, of feeling that not to have a dress, a game, a toy made me somehow deficient, beneath, below, less than – *apart.*

That is, if those I am with have more. For if others share my circumstances, there is no shame. What occurs is complete understanding, camaraderie: a comparing of notes, of swapping suggestions, of exchanging strategies – how to write a check and not have it bounce if the account is empty; which gas station gives credit; how to get an advance; etc.

But when the need is visible and public in the presence of those who are above it, or who have power to choose to help or not, who could bestow their resources, use their privileges, call it what you will – then *need becomes shame and asking feels like begging.*

Why?

I think back to group situations where assumptions are made, assumptions I do not share. It might be a question of which restaurant to go to. Or whether we should go to an event I want to attend but can't afford. Or even a discussion of whether the price of a certain book is reasonable. And what is reasonable? *How can something be reasonable if I can't afford it?*

I think about these situations and my own sense of exclusion – of wanting to be a part of a group and feeling I can't, of having to draw attention to it, knowing I will embarrass everyone, knowing I will be the wet blanket and burst the happy bubble of togetherness.

And what is it I really want of them? To carry me? Do I have any right to ask anything, I who have not gotten it together?

Sometimes, I think, all I want is the issue acknowledged. That in itself. But above all, I want someone else to raise this issue, someone for whom money is not a problem, but who recognizes that her framework, her 'reasonable cost' is not necessarily everyone's.

As feminists, we pride ourselves on our 'awareness' of class. Our events invariably have the 'more if you can/less if you can't' tag attached to the entrance fee, hardship rate for journals, sliding scales. And yet, I know that many women who cannot afford the standard price will not admit it because to admit it is to admit to failure, to inadequacy – to admit to something shameful – the fact of not having gotten it together. Often, it is the feminist with the middle-class background, downwardly mobile, who pridefully puts down her dollar at a five-dollar event. Many women I've known who stem from poor backgrounds, from a life of welfare and unemployment, a life of piecing it together, barely, week by week, day by day, would rather die than admit to their present poverty. Everything in their upbringing, everything in this society says that 'failure' (and that is equated with economic dependence) is their own fault, a deficiency in them. They have not worked hard enough to 'succeed' in the climb – it is all their fault, they should have tried harder.

## TRAIL OF 2 LIVES THAT DISINTEGRATED LED TO LONELY DEATHS ON AN ICY DAY – by Nathaniel Sheppard, Jr. (*The New York Times*, February 3, 1983)

This article has been hanging over my desk now for a year and a half. The first few paragraphs read as follows:

Chicago, Feb. 2 – The lifeless bodies of Norman and Anna Peters were found, wrapped in tattered blankets against the January cold, on the icy seats of the dilapidated 1971 station wagon that had become their home. With no resources and no place to go, they had died of carbon monoxide poisoning, presumably while running the car's engine in an effort to keep warm.

It was the sad final chapter to the tale of the disintegrating lives of two ordinary people, a struggling blue-collar couple who exemplified the lives of a sizable part of America. Theirs had always been a difficult existence, a constant struggle to make ends meet for a family of seven with an income from Mr. Peters' periodic employment as an equipment mover. . . .

The Peterses had been a proud and private couple who had maintained a code of silence about their personal problems. It was a silence that often extended to their children.

The Peterses had lost their home – unable to keep up mortgage payments. Financially depleted by hospital costs to correct the birth defects of a child who had died 15 years ago, plagued by alcoholism and unemployment, Norman and Anna saw no way out. Their life had been an endless series of crises – member of the Riggers Local 136, the machinery movers' union to which Norman belonged, commented:

'There was no reason for them to sleep in a car. We would have figured out some way to help. If Norm had just come in, you can always get the guys to give, five, ten dollars, fifteen dollars each. If only we had known.'

But they didn't know. Norman did not say anything. Anna did not say anything.

When I decided to lead my first writing workshop in Brooklyn around the winter of 1976-77, I began to experience enormous anxiety when it came time to advertise. I needed to put up posters locally as well as in gay bars and women's bookstores in Manhattan. I felt enormous resistance to doing this and I kept procrastinating. Finally, a friend walked with me up 7th Avenue in Brooklyn and the signs went up.

**POETRY WORKSHOP**
led by
**IRENA KLEPFISZ**
author of *Periods of Stress*
an editor of *Conditions* magazine

My paralysis went beyond any insecurity over my ability to lead such a workshop. Like everyone else, I have self-doubt, but never to the degree of near incapacity. It was only after trying to sort it out and understand it, that I realized that for me the placing of such an advertisement was a public admission that I needed money, that I was doing this *only* because I needed money.

And I really did need the money. It didn't seem to matter that I was providing a service. My name was appearing in huge shameless letters and announcing, just as shamelessly, that I was broke. Of course, no one necessarily knew; after all there are many writers who lead workshops for the pleasure of teaching or for even the prestige. And no one looking at my advertisement could distinguish me from them. Still, I knew of my need. *I knew* I was dependent on people signing up. And it was that sense of need, of dependence that paralyzed me.

When my mother and I came to the United States in 1949, we lived on charity from Jewish organizations. We occupied one room – the living room of a one bedroom apartment – and shared the kitchen with an older Jewish woman who did piecework in the garment district. We lived in this room for four years and much of this time my mother earned some money as a seamstress – doing alterations (taking up hems, taking in waists, puckering shoulders, and tightening darts) and sometimes creating originals of her own design. It was a difficult existence – uneven in income, very crowded and depressed, completely suffused by what we had just managed to survive in Europe.

The charity we were living on was never clearly defined for me. My mother wanted to protect me and tried to hide it. But it could not be completely blocked from my consciousness and instead what was strongly communicated was that we were not to refer to it. When pressed, we were, in fact, to lie about it. It was a source of shame.

Once someone she knew offered to print advertising cards for her. Since she wanted to build her list of customers, my mother accepted and soon there were hundreds of cards to be distributed.

**ROSE KLEPFISZ**
Seamstress
**Originals and Alterations**
**Building –1, Apt. H-22**

We took the cards and went out to the newer buildings of the cooperative complex we were living in. I was about 10 at this time and I found it all very exciting. We rode in the elevator to the 14th floor and then began slipping the cards under each door. For reasons I could not understand, if someone stepped out of an apartment, my mother would immediately slip into the stairwell. She did not want to be seen.

Everything about this endeavor seemed magical. The modern building, the elevators, the cards with my mother's name, the feel of the cold metal bannister as I ran down the stairs, skipping, jumping, leaping off the last four steps on to the next landing, rushing out into the hall ready to push more cards under the doors. But if someone stepped out of an apartment, my mother would immediately slip into the stairwell. She did not want to be seen.

She did not want to be seen.

You must ask, a friend once advised.

Yes, I thought, she is right. By my tongue could not form the words and at different moments I have been like the person in a burning building *willing to die rather than stand bare with my need.* I know that I could pass up the opportunity of a lifetime because of this deep-rooted shame. Some, I know, would categorize such behavior as 'playing the victim.' I don't agree. The person overwhelmed by shame, unable to move while the flames inch closer and closer and the heat becomes more and more intense – that person is not playing victim. Rather she is paralyzed by a socially learned lesson so deeply absorbed it has become almost an instinct life itself cannot counter.

The opportunity of a lifetime. Let it pass rather than ask or inquire. It is too humiliating to acknowledge the power of others over you, your dependence on them. It is too humiliating to think that you might risk asking and they will turn you down. It is too shameful to wonder why you must go through this, why you do not have such power. Why it is that you have failed and have so little control over your own life.

You must ask, a friend once said.

## Inside and Outside

What is real? What is feminist?

What is inside? What is outside?

All false distinctions, something I've known all along. There is no inside or outside. I do not live in two worlds. I live in one. The economics of the 'real' world are not separate from the 'feminist' world, even though the attitudes are often different. And this fact is one we ought to begin paying more attention to. For example:

—Women working in a battered women's shelter decided to unionize because they feel 'their labor was exploited.' The workers in Women Against Abuse (Philadelphia) stated that they did not view their problems as 'isolated' and that 'they have talked with staffs in other programs who have similar problems and concerns.'[8]

—A feminist editor rejects a reconsideration of distribution of profits in an author's contract on the basis that such notions are 'child-like' and inappropriate for the 'real' world. The same editor sympathizes with protests of clerical workers over conditions and salaries, prints pamphlets about these injustices. Still she tells an author to 'grow up' and face 'real' facts when it comes time to sign a contract.

—A political organization becomes financially stable enough to hire women to do the paper work. Immediately a hierarchy is established. Political activists – feminists – have become employers and now must relate to employees, in this case also feminists, whose work is inevitably more mechanical and less prestigious.

209

–A number of writers protest treatment by *The New York Native* and publish their statement in other gay papers. They maintain that gay institutions must have economic responsibility to their workers and are not exempt from the standards that would be applied to mainstream institutions.

–A Woman's Studies Department has its 'own' secretary or 'shares' one with another department. She is, of course, an employee of the school. But how do members of the department deal with her and *use* her?

–A writer complains she received only a token honorarium for her contribution to a feminist anthology, and that out of 25 contributors, only the editor made any money. Why, she asks, is this woman not sharing some of the profits? Isn't she living off the work of others? Isn't that what we fight against in all other places? Why should this be the exception?

–A collective gets a grant and is able to pay one of its members for some of the shit work all have shared so far. On what basis is the person chosen? The neediest? Or the one with skills because she already has the experience? And when she messes up, another member, without thinking, says angrily: 'But you're being paid!' And suddenly behavior that was tolerable as a volunteer is totally unacceptable. What happens when our commitment turns into a job?

–A three-day feminist conference is scheduled for Thursday, Friday, and Saturday. All working women are automatically excluded from participating in two-thirds of the activities. The feminist organizers have forgotten that we live in one world and that some of us do not have the luxury of stepping out of it even for a minute.

But if society has taught us to be ashamed over *not having* money and privilege, some feminists' romance with oppression has also made them ashamed over *having* money and privileges. The result has been a kind of dishonesty, a fudging around economic issues, of falsifying backgrounds and current possibilities, of blurring distinctions, of ignoring or denying power and achievements. With all our emphasis on truth, on breaking taboos – why is it that so much lying occurs around economic issues?

I remember that among the first feminists I met some were downwardly mobile and considered oppression a status symbol. Some had higher degrees. Some were college drop-outs. A predominant criticism was directed at anyone who had any education beyond high school. Because I was new to feminism and still naive, because I wanted to be accepted, I did not challenge attitudes which even then, in my heart of hearts, I knew to be wrong. Instead, I went along to such a degree that in my first book of poetry I was too embarrassed to list the Ph.D. in my biographical note. I – an immigrant, a Holocaust survivor, despite economic obstacles, having worked 20 hours a week through most of graduate school and full time during the summers, having managed to overcome psychological odds and traumas – I, Irena Klepfisz received a Ph.D. Truly something to be ashamed of.

How utterly crazy, when I think about it now. How utterly crazy.

*The aspirations of most people – security, pleasure, leisure, meaningful work, creative and intellectual pursuits – are to be supported. These desires and dreams are not shameful. In supporting them, we are showing solidarity with working people, for whom these are luxuries and not givens.*

Feminism cannot be separated from the economic realities of our society, and, as feminists, we need to face the economic unity of our lives; we must also learn to identify those of our actions that fall short of our best hopes. There is no such thing as purity. We must be willing to recognize and name powers and privileges that we do have and assess their significance and usefulness. And we must all recognize that these are not constant, but sometimes change in different contexts.

Sitting at various conferences, workshops, collective meetings, I have often marvelled at our ability to articulate perfect political theory while remaining insensitive and stubbornly ignorant to the life of the feminist sitting right next to us. At those moments, I have understood why so many women – deeply oppressed by sexism and economic necessity – find feminism and feminist theory abstract and irrelevant. At these feminist events, I too have sometimes felt alienated from discussions of sexism, homophobia, racism, or anti-Semitism, though all these touch me personally. But the fact that there is no allusion to the working day from which I've just emerged or to the economic pressures which I carry with me has frequently made these discussions seem highly theoretical and left me estranged and angry.

It has occurred to me that it would be a good idea every once in a while to begin meetings with a 10-minute round robin so that each woman could say how she had spent the day and thereby ground the group. The differences between us, not only in terms of work, would then be clarified as each woman's assumptions, framework, and mental state on that particular evening become evident. The political discussion, no matter what its focus, would, I believe, be ultimately enriched and informed by the immediacy and concreteness of this information. We would then be not simply feminists speaking about feminist issues, but feminists rooted and bound in different ways in the same society – stating our frustrations *as well as* our pleasures and achievements. At the end of the meeting, members might want to do another round robin, this time focused on what each woman was going to be doing the next day. Thus, the political discussion would in some way be framed by and connected to our daily lives.

I offer this suggestion even though I know it is fraught with obvious dangers: self-hate, breast-beating, envy, anger, guilt-tripping, and lying. But I think, also, this kind of process contains the possibility of a much deeper view of our differences at any given moment and their relationship to our politics.

Above all, such a process might actually help all of us articulate the words we most fear and face the discomfort of our economic and class differences. For we need to put an end to the shame and guilt surrounding both power and powerlessness. We can begin with direct questions, of ourselves and each other:

—What should I do with what I have? Share it? Keep it? Give it all away? Will you talk to me about your life? Will you help me understand? Can I learn from your strength? Will you tell me how I can be most useful to you? *Can you trust me?*

Difficult questions. As difficult as:

—Can I ask without shame? Can I show my strength? Can I stop equating all power with money? Will you listen to me? Will you give up some control? Will you see my need and not blame me – or fear me? *Can you trust me?*

And always the underlying question: *How do we work together?* For if we want liberation for women, then we're committed to building a society in which these distances – of class and economics – dissolve, and all our authentic differences – cultures, personalities, sexualities, talents, and aspirations – emerge and are equally nourished.[9]

# Notes

1. City College of New York was free at the time, yet there was hardly any student I knew who did not work at least one part-time job.
2. My first collection of poetry, *Periods of stress*, was self-published through Out & Out Books and later distributed by me directly. I borrowed money for this venture and never broke even. My contributions to *Lesbian Poetry, Lesbian Fiction,* and *Nice Jewish Girls: A Lesbian Anthology* have netted a total of $145 and a complimentary copy of each anthology. When Persephone Press went bankrupt, it had already distributed almost 2,500 copies of my second collection, *Keeper of Accounts*, but I had received no royalty payments. Ultimately I borrowed $1,500 to buy the remaining 2,400 from Alyson Press to whom the books had been sold. *Sinister Wisdom* is currently distributing *Keeper* and I am expecting royalty payments. The biggest royalties I have ever collected were for an essay anthologized in *Why Children?* (The Women's Press, London: 1980). Editors Stephanie Dowrick and Sibyl Grundberg shared profits equally with contributors; so far I have received approximately $550.
3. This was not from a salary, but from a $5,000 editorial grant which the collective received from the Coordinating Council of Literary Magazines and split four ways.
4. This was awarded by the New York State Council on the Arts, 1984.
5. As this indicates, I have been trying to finish this essay for the past year and a half.
6. Gloria Anzaldúa pointed out that this is true of those who also do physical work or for that matter any kind of work not involving the self.
7. Anita Page, 'The Pleasure Outing,' *Heresies* 6 (1978), pp. 27–33.
8. *Womannews*, July/August 1984, p. 8.

9.  I'm indebted to Melanie Kaye/Kantrowitz for her discussion of the feminist movement's failure to address class issues in her unpublished essay, 'Is There Post-Feminism Before Women's Liberation?'

# Power and Helplessness in the Women's Movement

Joanna Russ

> A strong woman is a woman in whose head
> a voice is repeating, I told you so,
> ugly, bad girl, bitch, nag, shrill, witch,
> ballbuster, nobody will ever love you back,
> why aren't you feminine, why aren't
> you soft, why aren't you quiet, why
> aren't you dead?
>
> *Marge Piercy, 'For Strong Women',*
> *from* The Moon Is Always Female[1]

Really good women, really 'nice' women, really sisterly women, are dead women.

Well, no. Nobody literally expects millions of us to drop down *ker-flop* clutching flowers to our bosoms like Elaine the Lily Maid of Astolat, and yet I wonder. Women are supposed to make other people feel good, to fill others' needs without having any of our own – this is the great Feminine Imperative. Such self-suppression amounts to the death of the self. Why demand such an impossibility?

All oppressed people must be controlled. Since open force and economic coercion are practical only part of the time, ideology – that is, internalized oppression, the voice in the head – is brought in to fill the gap. When people discover their own power, governments tremble. Therefore, in addition to all the other things that are done to control people, their own strength must be made taboo to them. Vast numbers of men can be allowed to experience some power as long as they expend their power against other men and against women – a desirable state of affairs since it keeps men (and men and women) from cooperating, which would be a grave menace to the powers that be. Therefore the Masculine Imperative is less severe than the Feminine one.

The Masculine Imperative means that men avoid the threat of failure, inadequacy, and powerlessness – omnipresent in a society built on competition and private property – by existing *against* others.

But the Feminine Imperative allows of no self-help at all. We exist *for* others.

213

But *women* are also terrified by female strength, *women* judge success in women to be the worst sin, *women* force women to be 'unselfish,' *women* would rather be dead than strong, rather helpless than happy.

Feminist women, too.

If you've been forbidden the use of your own power for your own self, you can give up your power or you can give up your self. If you're effective, you must be so for others but never for yourself (that would be 'selfish'). If you're allowed to feel and express needs, you must be powerless to do anything about them and can only wait for someone else – a man, an institution, a strong woman – to do it for you.

That is, you can be either a Magic Momma or a Trembling Sister.

Magic Mommas are rare and Trembling Sisters are common; the taboo is so strong that it's safer to be totally ineffective, or as near to it as is humanly possible. Moreover, election to the status of Magic Momma requires some real, visible achievement, which, in a male-dominated society, is rare. Nonetheless, every feminist group contains at least one Magic Momma; success being entirely relative, *somebody* can always be elevated to MM status. (If canny group members, aware of this possibility, refuse to do, say, or achieve anything, they can be chosen for past achievement, or smaller and smaller differences in behavior can be seized on as evidence of Magic Momma-hood.) Since we are all struggling with the Feminine Imperative, one of the ways achieving women combat the guilt of success is by agreeing to be Magic Mommas.

MMs give to others – eternally.

MMs are totally unselfish.

MMs have infinite time and energy.

MMs love all other women, always.

MMs never get angry at other women.

MMs don't sleep.

MMs never get sick.

If MMs don't fulfill the above conditions, they feel horribly, horribly guilty.

MMs know that they can never do *enough*.

Like the Victorian mother, the Magic Momma pays for her effectiveness by renouncing her own needs. But these don't go away. The MM feels guilt over her achievements, guilt over not doing more (in fact, this is the common female guilt over not doing everything for everyone), and the steadily mounting rage of deprivation, as well as the added rage caused by having to feel guilty all the time.

Meanwhile the Trembling Sister has plenty to be enraged about too. Having avoided the guilt of being effective, she's allowed to feel and express her own needs, but she pays for these 'advantages' by an enforced helplessness which requires that somebody fill her needs for her, since she's not allowed to do so for herself.

The trouble is that nobody can.

No matter how much *being taken care of* the TS manages to wangle out of others, it is never enough. For being taken care of is exactly what she does not need. It reinforces her helplessness, while what she really needs is access to her own effectiveness – and that is something no one can give to another person.

The Trembling Sister, insisting on being given what she doesn't need and can't use, becomes more and more deprived, and more and more enraged. The Magic Momma, enraged at her enforced guilt and similar enforced deprivation, sooner or later fails to meet the Trembling Sister's needs. She may become ill or reveal some human flaw. She may withdraw, or criticize, or get angry. If MM-hood has been bestowed on her without her knowledge and consent, she may not know what's expected of her and may 'sin' in ignorance.

The Trembling Sister can tolerate achievement in women only when such achievement is 'unselfish' – *i.e.*, accompanied by visible giving to everyone else and divested of visible satisfaction – and remember, it's precisely her own effectiveness that she's suppressing. She now has the unbearably enraging experience of being (apparently) abandoned by someone who is (apparently) enjoying the very sort of effectiveness she has made inaccessible to herself. The Magic Momma, already angry from years of self-deprivation which have turned out to be useless (since nothing she does ever satisfies either the TS or her own conscience) has the unbearably enraging experience of ingratitude and complaint from someone for whom she has worked hard and 'sacrificed everything.'

Worse, neither can justify her rage, since our (usually false) social assumption that people cause their own failures happens, in both their cases, to be perfectly true. At the same time both feel their rage to *be* justified, since – according to the Feminine Imperative – the MM is right to deprive herself and the TS right to be helpless.

Put the MM and the TS together and you get the conventional female role.

You also get trashing.

Trashing in the feminist movement has always proceeded from 'below' 'upwards,' directed by the Trembling Sister (that is, those who've adopted the TS position) at the self-elected (or merely supposed) MM. The hidden agenda of trashing is to *remain helpless and to fail*, whatever the ostensible motivation. The payoff is to Be Good (though miserable). The TS/MM scenario is predicated on the unrealistic ascription of enormous amounts of power to one side and the even more unrealistic ascription of none at all to the other. It assumes that hurting another woman's feelings is the worst thing – the very worst thing – the most unutterably awful thing – that a woman can do. In a world where women and men are starved, shot, beaten, bombed, and raped, the above assumption takes some doing, but since the MM/TS script requires it, it gets made. (The script also assumes that the MM has no feelings, or if she does, hurting *them* is a meritorious act.)

MMs do less harm; they can work themselves to death or – paralyzed with guilt – do nothing. Or they can encourage other MMs' guilt or fail

215

to discourage TS's expectations of MMs. But discouraging a TS's expectations of an MM is an enterprise fraught with risk, as many feminists know to their cost.

What to do?

Both parties need the confidence that self-love and self-assertiveness are not evil. The MM needs to learn that feelings of guilt are not objective political obligations; the TS needs to learn that feeling intensely conflicted about power has nothing to do with objective helplessness. The MM needs to be helped. The TS needs not to be helped.

No one originally takes either position of her own free will. The Feminine Imperative is forced on all of us. But in adulthood, and certainly within a feminist community, a woman who remains in either position is her own prisoner. The women's community as a mystically loving band of emotional weaklings who make up to each other by our kindness and sweetness for the harshness we have to endure in the outside world is a description that exactly characterizes the female middle-class sub-culture as it's existed in patriarchy for centuries – without changing a thing. This is not a revolutionary movement but a ghetto in which anyone seen as having achievement, money, or power is cast as a Magic Momma, whose function is to make up to everyone else for the world's deprivation and their terror of effectiveness. This is impossible. So the requirement becomes *to make others feel good* all the time, an especially seductive goal in times of political reaction when activity directed outward at the (seemingly) monolithic social structure is not only frustrating but frighteningly dangerous. So honesty goes by the board, hurt feelings are put at a premium, general fear and paralysis set in, and one by one any woman who oversteps the increasingly circumscribed area of what's permissible is trashed. Eventually, after the demons of success and effectiveness have been banished, and all the female villains who made everyone else feel miserable have left or been silenced, what happens?

*The group disintegrates.*

The Feminine Imperative has been faithfully served. The enemy has been driven from the ranks. Feminism has been destroyed.

Some revolutionary proposals:

Self-sacrifice is vile.

Martyrdom cults (like that surrounding Sylvia Plath), which link failure, death, and female approval, are abominable.

Anyone who ascribes enormous success, money, or power to any woman – certainly any feminist – is daydreaming.

'Uncritical support' is a contradiction in terms.

There is a crucial distinction between the personal and the political. The former leads to the latter but not automatically or without hard work.

Women are not beginners at art or politics; we need to recover our forerunners, not remain in a socially and self-imposed infancy.

Public, political activity is crucial for a political movement.

Demands for the right 'tone' in women's interactions are like those statements made to us by men about *our* tone, *i.e.*, 'I would've listened to you women if only you'd been ladylike.'

Political theory is crucial for a political movement. I favor the incorporation of class analysis into feminism (*not* vice-versa) but any way of dealing with political relations between male groups will do. Unless (like J. Edgar Hoover about Communism) you think all we need to know about contemporary patriarchy is that we're agin it.

What makes the MM/TS scenario so stubborn is the hidden insistence that a woman cannot, must not, be allowed to use her power on her own behalf. Our society runs on self-aggrandizement for men and self-abasement for women; talk of self-love terrifies men (for whom it means admitting interdependence and emotionality) while women can only expect that I'm recommending brutality and callousness.

One remedy would be to remember Cicely Tyson's TV portrayal of Harriet Tubman.[2] Biographers are always surprised when women like Tubman 'sacrifice' their personal lives (or so the biographers assume) for a 'cause.' That is, they interpret such women's actions in terms of the Feminine Imperative. But to be General Moses was no Victorian self-sacrifice, any more than Cicely Tyson (in my opinion, the best living performer in the theatre, uncontainable in a conventionally superficial role) sacrificed something she really wanted to do in order to do her duty by playing Harriet Tubman. When Harriet Tubman said that God wanted her to lead her people to freedom, she was not submitting her will to another's but arrogating to herself the authenticity and truth of her God, not losing herself but uniting herself with her own transpersonal dimension. Viewers who saw Tyson tuck her chin down in maidenly shyness and whisper, 'Momma and Daddy, the last thing I want to do is cause you to worry,' – and then burst forth in fire, 'But GOD –' knows that they have not seen anything remotely like self-sacrifice, either on the character's part or the actress's. An action may be hard, unpleasant, dangerous, the salvation of others – and heroically self-creating.

Nor is there anything wrong with that unless you believe that human selves – especially female selves – are intrinsically bad, or that we are a lousy species.

To insist that women challenge their own fear of effectiveness and their own guilt for behaving effectively, to insist that we both behave honestly and responsibly *and* risk hurting others' feelings (which is hardly the worst thing in the world) is emphatically to disobey the Feminine Imperative. It's selfish. It isn't sisterly. It isn't 'nice.'

But it is, I'm beginning to suspect, *the* feminist act.

I haven't, needless to say, written the above out of pure, altruistic concern for the women's community. And I can't envision any of it affecting those women so alienated from their own power that they feel desperately that they must have a Magic Momma (somewhere, somehow) at all costs, even the cost of being miserably helpless. But there are many women who don't feel helpless themselves, yet feel

217

guiltily (a) that everyone else must be, and (b) they don't want to risk the possibility that these totally helpless and vulnerable people may create a very nasty scene. (Quite a contradiction, that!) I also violently resent being first elevated to mythological status and then slammed for it. And the insistence on this person's hurt feelings and that one's tremendous vulnerability and the exquisite fragility of everyone (which doesn't prevent some of them kicking up a very nasty fuss when they don't get what they want). People dealing with external oppression don't act this way. (For one thing, they don't have time.) The MM/TS syndrome is a sign of *internalized* oppression and a form of addiction; that is, since it reinforces the Feminine Imperative, the more you get, the less you have and the more you need. The scenario strikes me as class-linked; I suspect that those oppressed in a directly economic way or by open force don't do this nearly as much — or at least that it doesn't reach the same pitch of feverishness. However, it may be that the kind of services women *qua* women provide (affection, admiration, R&R, personal service) require that women be controlled by ideology, since these services must be provided voluntarily at least to some degree.

I think that the unexpressed, unformulated, and very bitter belief *that sexism is true* is also at work here, that is, the idea that women can't do this or that. It's this belief that causes the MM's passionately angry disappointment when Unknown Woman A's work proves to be terrible, and the TS's conviction that the only way most women can ever have the pleasures of public success is for the few of us who have (in some magically mysterious way) gained access to the public world of culture and action to tell lies about the achievements of the others. Such a conviction adds to the pain of dispraise (which everybody of course feels) and rage at its seeming arbitrariness. *Why* is Famous Woman B saying such things about Unknown Woman A's work when A's only hope is for B to be nice to her? Explanations like 'elitism,' 'male identification,' selling out, or intoxication with fame, explain nothing; you might as well say Original Sin and be done with it. B is simply being *mean*, a dreadful act when all access to success is (supposedly) in her all-powerful hands.

There is also the problem of ignorance. Those without much access to the public world are unlikely to have had contact with the real hatchet-women of the patriarchy, or real Queen Bees, or know the conditions under which Famous Woman B actually has to work.

For example, feminists have no control over the covers trade publishers put on their books. Sometimes even the editors don't. *Authorial control over the very text* of a science fiction novel is not standard in the trade and must be negotiated. It is often resented; I once lost a magazine sale by insisting that a story of mine stay as written. (How many book sales I or others may have lost by getting a reputation for being 'difficult' I don't know.) Even when negotiated, an author's control over the text amounts only to veto power over the editor's or publisher's changes, 'not to be unreasonably refused' (you figure that one out). Good editors don't change good authors' mss. – but 'good editors' means a minority of those in the field.

Did you know that the hardcover publisher of a book gets half of all the author's paperback income for ever and ever?

That one of the most famous American feminists has been on welfare and had to have money raised by others to pay her hospital bill when she fell ill?

That another, internationally known, lives on less than $9,000 a year, out of necessity? By *farming*?

That you can publish six books in twelve years, sell 100,000 of some of them, and make less than $2,500 a year, including money from book reviews, other non-fiction, short-story sales, and foreign sales?

I'm not complaining, but trying to demolish the illusion of the MM's enormous power and success.

There is simply no such thing. What does exist is the American – or simply modern – illusion that 'celebrities' (in however tiny a community) have real, pleasure-filled lives, and the rest of us have – what, unreal ones? – and the insistence on failure and dependency that underlies such attributions of power.

To understand that no one has or can have your power, that it remains in you no matter how forbidden you feel it to be, means defying the patriarchal taboo and that's very hard. It means claiming one's own limited but real power and abandoning one's inflated notion of other women's power. It means engaging in a direct public confrontation with the patriarchy as embodied in men and men's institutions, not concentrating on its symbolic presence in other members of the women's community.

To risk failure is bad enough. To risk success is even worse. After all, women have been burnt alive for claiming a power which was, paradoxically, not enough to save them. It's safer to be weak, safer to have someone else be strong for you and be punished for it in your place.

I believe that trashing, far from being the result of simple envy, arises from a profound ambivalence towards power. The intensity of feeling, the violent inculcation of guilt, the extreme contrast of omnipotence and powerlessness, the lack of substantive complaint,[3] the anger, the absolute lack of impersonality or a sense of public activity, the utter demandingness – all these echo a mother-daughter relationship in which the terrible, hidden truth is not that our mothers are strong, but that they are very weak. The complaint, 'You are so strong and I am so helpless' hides the far worse one, 'I am strong enough that my strength will get me into terrible trouble, and you are too weak to protect me if that happens.'

For all oppressed people strength and success are double-edged: heartbreakingly desirable and very dangerous. But to 'risk winning' (Phyllis Chesler's phrase from *Women and Madness*, a book to which I owe many of the ideas in this piece) is the only way out of oppression.

'Successful' feminists aren't immune to this terror of power; all the women I know feel it. We take the risk anyway. That's the only secret, not some fantastic, illusory power-fame-and-glory that some women have and others don't. I recently heard a conversation between two Lesbians, one of whom was living openly as such and one of whom was afraid to leave her marriage. The married one said, 'I can't leave my husband because I'm not brave, like you.' To which the other (who had left *her* husband only two years before) said, 'Don't give me that. I was just as scared as you when I left my marriage, but I did it anyway. *That's what made me brave.*'

The MM/TS polarity is illusory. Both are positions in the same belief system. Both are engaged in ritually sacrificing the possibility of a woman's being effective on her own behalf, not needy and ineffective, not effective and altruistic, but *effective for herself.*

It's selfish, vicious, and nasty, and will cause everyone within a thousand miles to faint flat.

But it beats being dead.

## Notes

1. Alfred A. Knopf, New York, © 1980 by Marge Piercy.
2. A Woman Called Moses.
3. 'Cruel,' 'unfair,' 'unkind,' 'After I worked so hard,' not 'gentle' or 'positive,' are typical phrases (I'm skimming back issues of feminist periodicals). The claim that someone has stopped writing or publishing as a catastrophic result also crops up. Years ago a very young (junior-high-school age) woman asked me to send her copies of all my work and the answers to three pages of questions about it for a paper her teacher had suggested; I wrote her, explaining that writers hadn't the time to fulfill such requests and referred her to her teacher, who ought to be teaching her how to do research. Her older sister then wrote me, stating that she was going to expose me in *Ms.*, that because of my bad behavior her sister, who had hoped to be a writer, had given up all such ambitions.

# Dyke-tactics for Difficult Times

Sarah Franklin and Jackie Stacey

Recently, one of us was invited to attend a local television programme about the decision of the Synod to prevent 'practising homosexuals' from holding office within the Church of England. This programme was meant to be structured around the question of 'whether or not homosexuals are born that way'. The question one of us was supposed to answer was whether or not homosexuality is 'natural'. The answer, of course, was to be that it is not natural but socially constructed, varying cross-culturally and historically in its forms. However, as soon as the debate began, it quickly became apparent that members of the audience, the good burghers of Branston invited to represent the general public, did not care at all whether homosexuals were born that way or not. In fact, pre-empting the intended debate, one avid christian geneticist expostulated at length about the scientific evidence available disproving the inborn hypothesis. This, he implied, was all the more reason why homosexuals should be banned from positions of authority within the church, since, if homosexuality is a 'choice' rather than a condition, it can more easily be resisted. Many more among the faithful agreed: it made little difference whether it was the sinner or the sin, it was still wrong.

Experiences such as this may lead us to despair about the relevance of academic distinctions between social constructionism and essentialism. To the bigoted zealots in the audience, this fine point was obviously of little consequence. Yet it is precisely the extent to which sexuality, especially homosexuality, is being publicly debated in Britain at present which increases the imperative for lesbians and gay men to think about these issues seriously. Dominant discourses about sexuality are rapidly being reformulated in Thatcherite Britain in such a way that heterosexuality and the family are being reaffirmed as the only acceptable contexts for the expression of sexuality. At the same time, there is a growing movement of resistance amongst lesbians and gay men against these attempts at repression. January 1988 saw the largest lesbian and gay rights march in British history when over 12,000 demonstrators marched through London in protest against Clause 28. Such powerful expressions of resistance demonstrate the impossibility of forcing lesbians and gays back into the closet. In continuing this resistance, it is vital for us to have clear arguments and theories about our sexuality with which to enter these public debates and participate within the current struggle over the regulation of lesbianism and homosexuality.

An opportunity to develop these theories and arguments was recently provided at the much-publicized 'Homosexuality, Which Homosexuality' conference, held at the Free University of Amsterdam in December, 1987. This conference was intended to be a continuation of earlier debates begun at the 'Among Women, Among Men' conference (Amsterdam, 1983) and the 'Sex and the State' conference (Toronto, 1985). Funded by various government bodies, and intended not only to promote but indeed to celebrate lesbian and gay culture, this conference coincided quite ironically with the successful first reading of the Local Government Bill in the House of Commons, containing the anti-gay Clause 28 which is specifically designed to discourage the 'promotion of homosexuality' in Britain.

The conference was impressively organised by the Research Group on Gay and Lesbian Studies of the Free University of Amsterdam in

221

collaboration with the Schorer Foundation, a public lesbian and gay counselling centre. Both the Chancellor of the Free University and the Mayor's office of the city of Amsterdam publicly welcomed participants to the conference, demonstrating the quite remarkable and encouraging degree of formal public respect shown to Lesbian and Gay studies in The Netherlands.

## Essentialism and Social Constructionism Revisited

The focus of the conference was the relationship between essentialist and social constructionist theories in debates about lesbianism and homosexuality. In particular, the aim was 'to question the way in which constructivism and essentialism are viewed in scholarly debate on homosexuality as mutually exclusive approaches' and to consider '. . . whether historical and cultural continuities exist alongside discontinuities (or vice-versa)'. The conference's success can in part be attributed to the fact that papers on subjects as diverse as history, theology, visual representation and science all addressed these common themes. This resulted in considerable overlap between workshops at a conceptual level, which in turn facilitated a sustained dialogue among participants on the themes of the conference.

For most people familiar with recent debates in the study of gender and sexuality, the terms 'social constructionist' and 'essentialist' are a well-known shorthand for important political and epistemological differences within the field. 'Essentialism' generally refers to arguments about either gender or sexuality which appeal to biological or genetic determinism, universalism or explanations based on the idea of 'nature' or 'human nature', such as those of the early sexologists who believed homosexuality to be pathological in origin. Essentialist explanations are often characterised by a fixity which may be extremely difficult to challenge, and an 'it just is that way' connotation which has made them both appealing and enduring belief systems in the past.

Social constructionism, on the other hand, is the argument that sexuality and gender are not natural, fixed or universal, but specific to their social, cultural and historical context. The argument that sexuality and gender are socially constructed in accordance with different sets of conditions in different contexts thus emphasizes change, discontinuity and contradiction.

Within various feminist debates over the last decade, the need to see both sexuality and gender as socially constructed has been largely taken for granted. The emergence of this position as dominant represents an important political and intellectual triumph over various forms of determinism which previously naturalized both heterosexuality and male dominance, placing them in the realm of the inevitable and unchangeable. In particular, certain privileged institutions, such as the patriarchal nuclear family and compulsory heterosexuality, enjoyed substantial legitimation and reinforcement through the ideologies of biological and genetic essentialism, which were in turn legitimated by the authoritative discourses of science. Both the feminist and the gay liberation movements prioritized the need to challenge the operations of these essentialist ideologies of sexuality within scientific discourses and at the level of commonsense beliefs.

What emerged at the conference was that the taken-for-grantedness of this rejection of essentialism and the emergence of social constructionism as the 'correct discourse' of gender and sexuality have led to certain confusions. Beneath the superficial obviousness of the differences between social constructionism and essentialism remain certain unresolved tensions which threaten the distinction between the two. Once we actually began to discuss the precise relationship between social constructionism and essentialism, the boundary between them became increasingly blurred. Contrary to the received wisdoms within studies of sexuality about the significant analytical differences between these two approaches, and the historical formations which produced them, many discussions demonstrated that social constructionism and essentialism are not necessarily the unified, coherent and distinct discourses many assume them to be. Neither are the differences between them as definitive as the supposed opposition between them would suggest. Deconstructing these discursive differences proved to be enlightening.

## Essentialism, Which Essentialism?

One source of confusion was that there are many different kinds of essentialism, and the profusion of these discourses on sexuality led to the greatest difficulties in defining what exactly we mean by essentialism, and whether we need to be equally critical of all its forms. Under the general heading of biological essentialism, for example, we could include explanations of lesbianism and homosexuality which are based on the 'born that way' argument, genetic determinism, discourses of pathology, and various ideologies of the natural. Another form of essentialism can be identified in beliefs or arguments about historical and cross-cultural continuities in lesbian and homosexual experience (the 'we have always existed everywhere' argument). Within psychoanalytic theory there are also various assertions about sexuality which are keenly debated in terms of their essentialism. For example, the idea of a human libidinal drive or an innate bisexuality, are seen by some as fundamentally essentialist. Equally contested within post-structuralist debates is the question of the essential self in which any notion of a unified identity (sexual or otherwise) is seen as complicit with essentialism. Such a diversity in forms of essentialism obviously raises questions about its definition. One further problem is that there are clearly different degrees of essentialism, resulting in the need to be more critical of some than others. Finally, such a broad diversity of definitions of essentialism not only produces confusion but also active, and often quite intense, disagreement about what should be subject to the pejorative and dismissive label of 'essentialism'.

What also emerged when we began to consider the variety of essentialisms was the question of whether essentialisms are themselves socially constructed and socially deconstructed. The fact that essentialist beliefs vary in different social and historical contexts, and that they are constantly shifting and changing, would seem to support this claim. Another characteristic of essentialist beliefs is that they are often contradictory, reproducing the contradictions of their time and place. Ideas about 'the natural' are a particularly good example of both of these features of essentialism. The belief that heterosexual intercourse is a totally natural form of sexual practice, for example, directly contradicts the fact that it is a socially constructed ritual which may only be conducted under certain very specific conditions which change over time.

It also became apparent that new forms of essentialism, socially constructed in relation to specific historical shifts, are continually emerging. Essentialist definitions of parenthood, specifically designed to exclude lesbians and gay men, are currently being formulated through legislation of the new reproductive technologies, for example.[1] As well as challenging older, more obvious, discourses of essentialism, such as the pathological constructions of homosexuality by sexologists, it was felt that lesbian and gay studies need to challenge new emergent essentialist discourses about sexuality.

Thus, in answering the question 'essentialism, which essentialism?', several considerations emerged from this conference which are central to debates about sexuality. Firstly, there is the need to take into account the diversity of beliefs, arguments and explanations related to sexuality which could be labelled essentialist. This raises the question of how to define essentialism, and whether or not critics of essentialism should be equally suspect of all its manifestations. A more challenging approach to essentialism derives from the question of whether or not it is itself socially constructed. Indeed, this claim would undermine the basic premise of essentialism.

# The Limits of Social Constructionism

Confusions about social constructionism raise a different set of problems from those discussed in relation to essentialism. If we as feminists want to be critical of essentialism, and argue that sexuality and gender are socially constructed, then we have to be able to explain *how* it is socially constructed, and to account for changes in sexual identities and desires. If sexuality is socially constructed, then we need to identify *where* in the social it is constructed. Feminists have offered different accounts of where these processes take place. Some have emphasized the family, others have emphasized education, the media, or economic factors, in their accounts of the social construction of sexuality.

224

One of the main problems of social construction theory which emerged, however, was the limitation of these accounts in providing a satisfactory explanation particularly of lesbian sexuality. This appeared to be especially true in terms of individual accounts of sexual identity, the need to explain why particular women became lesbians and others did not. Given the tremendous amount of social pressure to conform to heterosexual femininity, it is very difficult to account for some women's resistance to it, and even more difficult to explain why other women never participated in it in the first place. Despite its understandable unpopularity amongst lesbians and gay men, psychoanalysis is one of the only discourses of sexuality which attempts to explain differences in the individual acquisition of particular sexual identities. There were a few sessions, however, which engaged with the possibilities, and the difficulties, of constructing a more psychoanalytically informed methodology in the study of lesbian or gay identity.[2]

In her opening lecture, Carole Vance provided a helpful overview for assessing some of the limits of social construction theory.[3] One of the most striking aspects of her talk was the extent to which the features of social constructionism, originally seen to be its greatest strength, have since come to be seen as amongst its greatest weaknesses. She argued, for example, that in its emphasis on deconstruction and discontinuity, social constructionism threatened to make sexuality disappear altogether. 'Is there an "it" to study?', she asked. Similarly, in its emphasis on denaturalizing sexuality, she argued, social constructionism has excluded the body from its considerations, thus denying the materiality of its subject of study. Since sexed subjects also have bodies, how might we incorporate the body into our analysis without becoming essentialist or determinist? Finally, in its emphasis on dismantling existing systems of difference, such as those which maintain the sex/gender system, she argued, social constructionism threatens the very identities lesbians and gay men want to preserve. This results in a paradox: on the one hand, politically, we may want to insist on the unity and coherence of lesbian or gay identity in order to defend our interests as a group, whilst, on the other hand, this may simultaneously reify and fix the sexual identities we are intellectually seeking to deconstruct.

## The Workshops – the Social Constructionist Debate in Action

In addition to the limits of social construction theory outlined by Carole Vance, several of the papers in workshops analysed its limits with specific reference to lesbianism. Celia Kitzinger's paper, drawn from her recently published book *The Social Construction of Lesbianism* (Sage, 1987), called particular attention to the liberalism of social constructionist approaches to lesbianism within mainstream psychology.[4] Whereas psychology twenty years ago depicted lesbianism as pathological,

225

'enlightened' psychologists of today, she argued, see lesbians as normal and natural, with the potential to be 'well-adjusted human beings just like everyone else'. In emphasizing the privacy of sexual preference, the fundamental similarities between lesbian and heterosexual women, and the compatibility of lesbianism with the family and 'society as we know it', liberal humanistic psychology, or 'gay-affirmative' psychology, as she calls it, depoliticizes lesbianism. In this case, social constructionism is no more politically progressive an approach to lesbianism than its Victorian antecedent.

Yet another set of questions about social construction theory emerged out of the lesbian motherhood workshop. Although Carole Vance argued that sexuality and gender are 'the last domains to have their naturalness thrown into question' by social constructionism, this workshop demonstrated the importance of including reproduction within this list of supposedly 'natural' domains. Many of the issues engaged with were examples of the social construction debate in action. Also demonstrated was how the struggle against forms of essentialism and the need to take account of the bodily dimension of women's experience (such as pregnancy) were clearly being waged in very intimate contexts. Indeed, it indicated the very good reasons lesbians continue to debate the questions social constructionism first posed.

The motherhood workshop began with a discussion of the contradiction between the category 'lesbian' and the category 'mother', the one representing the supposed antithesis of 'womanhood' and the other representing its supposed fulfilment. What was highlighted was both the inadequacy of existing kinship terms to describe lesbian parenthood and the threat posed by lesbianism to dominant definitions of the family. There followed from this a debate about lesbian co-parenting and the category 'mother': many lesbians seeking to co-parent wanted to be equal mothers; however, they disagreed about whether the biological mother and the social mother could necessarily be 'equal'. This point proved highly contentious: as feminists, some lesbians wanted to challenge the supposed 'naturalness' of the mother-child bond, but they also felt, as lesbian co-parents, the difficulties of overcoming their feelings of exclusion. Some lesbians said they felt the term 'father' better described their feelings as the co-parent-to-be and sexual partner of the expectant-mother. Other lesbians who had children felt the social mother might not have the same intimacy with the infant at first, but that things could even out or be reversed as the child grew older. Still other lesbians took a more radical view, asking whether having a sexual relationship with the person you are co-parenting with is 'putting all your eggs in one basket', and suggesting that co-parenting relationships between lesbians should not necessarily be sexual relationships as well.[5]

This discussion demonstrated the inadequacy of existing kinship definitions, roles and terminology for lesbian mothers, and the extent to which lesbians are forced to become social constructionists in order to build alternatives for ourselves.

Another subject which raised questions about social construction theory and lesbian identity was 'the butch-femme debate'. At the morning session of a day-long workshop, a paper by Saskia Wieringa and Noor van Crevel entitled 'Beyond Feminism: the Butch-Femme Debate', highlighted both the cross-cultural and historical 'continuities' of butch-femme experience which were seen as evidence of the shortcomings of social constructionist accounts of lesbian identity. Why, it was asked, does this particular version of lesbian sub-culture re-emerge, time and again, both historically and cross-culturally, and how do we explain why some women take up the position of 'butch' and others of 'femme'? Perhaps, it was suggested, we should not be frightened of moving 'beyond social constructionism' to answer these questions, towards a framework which could take the biological and ethological dimensions of sexuality into account.[6]

Interestingly, there appeared to be two versions of butch-femme, one 'essentialist' and one 'social constructionist': according to the essentialist version, espoused by some, some women were butch and others femme by temperament, or even, it was suggested, constitution. Others argued for a model of butch-femme as roles, a more 'playful' 1980s version of butch-femme as interchangeable identities. This latter position was the subject of a paper delivered by Anja van Kooten Niekerk and Sacha Wijmer entitled 'The Comeback of Butch-Femme Roles in the 1980s', which presented the results of a recent interview project with lesbians in Amsterdam.[7]

This and other events concerning butch-femme roles proved to be some of the most popular sessions at the conference, and many were 'sold out' before the conference even began. Perhaps this popularity was due to the 'comeback' of butch-femme roles in the eighties, or perhaps these workshops were seen to promise a more personal discussion of lesbian sexuality and desire than was on offer elsewhere. Joan Nestle, founder of the Lesbian Archives in New York and self-described 'passionate advocate of butch-femme lifestyles', used her role as chairperson to urge participants away from dry academicisms and into the pleasures of confession and self-disclosure. However, some lesbians found this invitation more appealing than others, and, as in many other workshops, the opportunity to speak more personally about sexuality was resisted. This lack of personal discussion also characterized the very well-attended international panel on Lesbian Identity, although the setting of this event, the chapel on the sixteenth floor, was not particularly conducive to intimate disclosures![8]

Precisely because they were so popular and well attended, we found quite disturbing the frequent characterization of feminism in the butch-femme workshops as 'prescriptive', 'oppressive', and 'moralistic'. Although we found these attitudes echoed elsewhere at the conference, they seemed to be particularly virulent here, where we heard feminism described as 'a rigid strategy for regulating sexuality', and feminists described as 'self-righteous vegetarians'. There is an understandable antagonism between feminism and butch-femme, an aspect of lesbian subculture to which feminism has never shown a particular affinity: from the point of view of butch-femme subculture, feminism has been seen as imposing only one version of politically correct lesbianism on a subculture it has failed to understand. However, the stereotyping of feminism as a prescriptive 'killjoy' perpetrates a dangerous rewriting of history which obscures the ways in which feminism opened up new possibilities of sexuality for women, particularly the possibility for many women to become lesbians and to come out as lesbians. The casting of feminism as 'right but repulsive' and butch-femme as 'wrong but wromantic' only serves to reproduce clichés, and does little to facilitate an understanding of the more complex relationship between the two. Moreover, it seemed to us that feminism was being scapegoated as 'big bad sister' at a time when it is a particularly easy target. In an increasingly conservative, reactionary and anti-feminist climate, it is important not to blame feminism's 'failures' entirely upon feminism itself. Likewise, it is misleading to construct feminism as a monolithic discourse, thus attributing to it a prescriptive power it has never come close to achieving.

Stereotyping and caricaturing certain kinds of feminism seems to be particularly in vogue at the moment. In his report of the conference in *The Pink Paper* (1987:5), Simon Watney seems to delight in joining in this popular pastime. In his opening paragraph, in enlarged print, he boldly states:

It proved an immensely productive conference for almost everyone involved, save perhaps for a small group of die-hard lesbian separatists whose political posturing seemed remarkably like that of the last dinosaurs. It was sadly indicative of British insularity that the separatist tendency hailed largely from England. For everyone else, the conference provided an all too rare opportunity to compare international situations . . .

This is not only a totally inaccurate but also a rather baffling representation, since lesbian separatism was certainly the most glaring, although hardly surprising, absence at this conference. The fact that statements such as these appear to be coming from many different sources at the moment, from both lesbians and gay men, as well as from more familiar opponents, is deeply disturbing. We question the need for this kind of unwarranted antagonism against 'unfashionable' politics in the current political climate.

## Constructing Lesbian Identities: The Appeal of Essentialism

The frustrations with social constructionism demonstrated within some of the workshops were accompanied by evidence of the enduring – if not increasing – appeal of certain forms of essentialism, particularly in personal accounts of lesbian identities. The appeal of essentialism was strongest in relation to the need to construct personal narratives in order to make sense of our 'deviant' sexual histories. Not only were social constructionist accounts perceived as somehow invalidating the intensity of deep feelings about their lesbianism (what Carole Vance called 'the implication of disingenuousness'), but it also became evident that these accounts failed to fulfil emotional needs met by various forms of essentialism.

The appeal of various forms of essentialism has long been a part of lesbian sub-culture, and many of these forms were in evidence at the conference. Essentialism appeared more frequently in the workshop discussions than in the papers themselves, indicating, perhaps, that although many lesbians may agree with the intellectual criticisms of essentialism, they nevertheless continue to use essentialist discourses when representing themselves more personally. Examples of discourses of essentialism which continue to be popular among lesbians include: the 'I was born that way' argument (or the 'I might as well have been born this way' argument), the 'we've always been here' claim, the naming-famous-lesbians pastime, the 'lesbians exist in many different cultures' argument, and, finally, the 'same-sex acts exist in the natural world' claim, sometimes referred to as the 'gay seagulls argument'. Despite the fact that these examples draw on different forms of essentialism, and differ in their degree, all of them appeal to lesbians, we would argue, for similar reasons.

First, they provide a strong validation of lesbian existence, and they satisfy a need to assert the imperviousness of lesbian identity to the constant attempts to deny, silence and repress it. Second, they offer a more fixed and permanent identity to lesbians, who are so frequently told that their sexual identity is 'only a phase', that it 'can be cured' or that they will 'grow out of it'. Third, they may offer the only option available for lesbians who are isolated and are searching for confirmation of their identity. Finally, pastimes such as naming-and-claiming-famous-lesbians offers lesbians a rare opportunity to see themselves legitimated in mainstream culture, and to experience a sense of triumph that, despite their low sexual status, some lesbians have nevertheless achieved high social status.

So, whilst the insistence upon historical and cross-cultural continuities of lesbian identities can be seen as complicit with essentialist definitions of sexuality, a belief in these continuities is often an important touchstone in many lesbians' personal development. Despite the political limits of these forms of essentialism, it is nevertheless important both to recognize the context of lesbian oppression in which these discourses function, and to highlight the fact that social constructionism has not been able to offer satisfactory alternatives.

In sum, there are several central points the conference raised about the relationship between essentialist and social constructionist approaches to the understanding of lesbianism and homosexuality. Most importantly, the discussions demonstrated the inadequacies of representing these two approaches as antithetical. Struggles over definitions of sexuality, such as in the butch-femme debate which draw on the discourse of social constructionism and essentialism, do indeed place them in apparent opposition to one another. However, the superficial obviousness of this opposition often obscures more than it reveals. The idea of antithesis, of irreducible opposition, cannot be said to describe the relationship between social constructionism and essentialism for the following reasons: there are many versions of essentialism, demonstrating that it cannot be seen as a unified or coherent discourse, and the many criticisms of the limits of social construction theory suggest the need to rework it in order to develop a more thorough account of lesbianism and homosexuality. Furthermore, essentialist and social constructionist discourses cannot be seen as entirely separate, for, as we have shown, there are considerable areas of overlap between them, resulting in disagreement about where the boundary should be drawn. Finally, definitions of social constructionism and essentialism are constantly shifting and changing, and mean different things in different contexts, making it difficult to make definitive assessments of them either intellectually or politically.

We suspect that many conference participants, like ourselves, initially responded to the theme of the conference with little enthusiasm, anticipating few new insights from this well-rehearsed debate. However, as the conference organizers no doubt suspected, this topic is far from exhausted and generated many productive discussions amongst us.


## The Broader Social and Political Context

According to social constructionist theory, the formation of ideas and identities occurs in accordance with specific social and historical conditions. It should, therefore, be possible to speculate upon the relationship between recent shifts in the debates about sexuality and sexual identity, as evidenced at the conference, and broader changes in the social and political climate for lesbian and gay people in the late 1980s. There are many possible interpretations to explain these shifts.

For those of us living in either Britain or America, in an atmosphere of tangibly increasing anti-lesbian and gay prejudice, one explanation of the increasing appeal of essentialism might be its strategic uses in times of need. In response to the threat posed by Clause 28 of the Local Government Bill, which is so broadly worded as to make the basic civil rights of lesbians and gay men extremely vulnerable, essentialism may be increasingly appealing as a means to protect and legitimate our right to exist, both as a group and as individuals.

A related, but in some ways opposite, explanation might be that essentialist beliefs are themselves the product of increasingly conservative eras, and that what we are witnessing in the return of essentialism within

230

the lesbian and gay community is symptomatic, rather than strategic. Different political conclusions will be drawn from different assessments of the kind and degree of essentialisms in operation within the lesbian and gay community. If they are symptomatic of reactionary social climates, then they must be resisted even more in times of threat to the lesbian and gay community. Conversely, if the uses of essentialism are strategic, then their use as a defence is fully warranted.

The trend away from a consensus about the adequacy of social constructionist explanations of sexuality also invites several possible interpretations. On the one hand, the emphasis on change and discontinuity may feel increasingly vulnerable when there is increasing pressure on lesbians and gay men to go back into the closet or to go straight. Reading the *Sun*'s recent invitation to readers to send in stories about 'gay conversions' to heterosexuality they have witnessed and/or helped to bring about might make an emphasis on the shifting nature of sexual identity look less attractive. It may be that social constructionist arguments make more sense in eras of progressive social change, in which change has a slightly more hopeful connotation. On the other hand, it is for the same reason that social constructionism may be most important in times of reactionary, anti-gay sentiment, for it is precisely its emphasis on change and contradiction which may offer the only way forward.

## Notes

1. Workshop S08, *New Reproductive Technologies*, 'Implications of Reproductive and Genetic Techno-Science', Sarah Franklin.
2. Workshop S21, *Psychoanalysis*, 'Freud and Homosexuality', John Fletcher; 'The Construction of Heterosexuality or Homosexuality', Eric de Kuyper. Workshop L18, *Problems of Lesbian and Gay Art*, 'Lesbianism and Sexual Difference Theory', Jackie Stacey.
3. Opening Lecture, 'Social Construction Theory: Problems in the History of Sexuality', Carole Vance.
4. Workshop S15, *Changing Conceptions 1*, 'The Scientific Construction of Lesbianism: the Liberal Humanistic Trap', Celia Kitzinger.
5. Workshop C02, *Lesbian Motherhood*, 'My Aunt Became a Father', Ruth de Kanter; 'Lesbian Motherhood', by Maaike de Klerck; 'The Lesbian Teenage Mother', Sharon Thompson (absent from conference). See also, Workshop S08, *New Reproductive Technologies*, 'Reproductive Technologies and Motherhood', Juliet Zipper.
6. Workshop H14, *Butch-Femme 1*, 'Beyond Feminism: the b/f debate', Saskia Wieringa & Noor van Crevel.
7. Workshop H14, *Butch-Femme 1*, 'Gender Stereotypes and Lesbian Lifestyles', Noretta Koertge; Workshop 18, *Butch-Femme 2*, 'The Reproduction of b/f roles', Madeline Davis & Liz Kennedy; 'The Comeback of b/f Roles in the '80s', Anja van Kooten Niekirk & Sacha Wijmer.
8. The members of the Lesbian Identity Panel were: Saskia Grotenhuis, chair (NL); Claudia Card (USA); Noor van Crevel (NL); Elizabeth Kennedy (USA); Brigitte Lhomand (FR); Jackie Stacey (UK); Martha Vicinus (USA).

## Further Reading

Birke, Lynda, (1982), 'From Sin to Sickness: Hormonal Theories of Lesbianism', in *Biological Woman – The Convenient Myth* ed. Ruth Hubbard, Mary Sue Henifin and Barbara Fried, Cambridge, MA: Schenkman Publishing Co.

Cruikshank, Margaret, (1982), *Lesbian Studies: Present and Future* New York: Feminist Press.

Faderman, Lillian, (1981), *Surpassing the Love of Men: Romantic Friendship and Love Between Women from the Renaissance to the Present* London: Junction Books.

Friedman, Estelle, Gelpi, Barbra, Johnson, Sue, and Weston, Kathleen (eds), (1985), *The Lesbian Issue: Collected Essays from Signs* Chicago: University of Chicago Press.

Rich, Adrienne, (1980), 'Compulsory Sexuality and Lesbian Existence' in *Blood, Bread and Poetry: Selected Prose 1979-1985* New York: W.W. Norton.

Snitow, Ann, Stansell, Christine, and Thompson, Sharon (eds), (1984), *Desire: The Politics of Sexuality* London: Virago Press.

Vance, Carole S. (ed.), (1984), *Pleasure and Danger: Exploring Female Sexuality* London: Routledge & Kegan Paul.

Weeks, Jeffrey, (1985), *Sexuality and its Discontents: Myths, Meanings and Modern Sexualities* London: Routledge & Kegan Paul.

## Acknowledgements

We are grateful to Hilary Hinds and Richard Dyer for their helpful and encouraging comments in the rather rapid production of this review. We would also like to thank Mieke Bernink and Klaartje Schweizer for their very generous hospitality in Amsterdam.

# A Fem's Own Story:
# An Interview with Joan Nestle

Margaret Hunt

*I first saw Joan Nestle in action at a conference on lesbian pornography held in Boston in May 1987. It was a small but up-beat affair where sex educators and publishers of tiny grassroots lesbian magazines mingled with readers, writers and would-be writers of lesbian erotica and old-time gay and feminist activists. Joan spoke about her own identification as a fem, the experience of writing pornography, and the need to nurture sexual diversity within the lesbian community. Not only was she one of the most effective advocates for the pro-pornography/anti-censorship position I had yet seen, but she spoke in an incredibly sexy black slip. She was smart, she had chutzpah, and she was passionately committed to the cause of women and lesbians. My lover and I were both enthralled.*

*Perhaps best known as one of the founders of the Lesbian Herstory Archives, now in its thirteenth year, Joan is among a small group of people who have worked tirelessly to uncover evidence of gay and lesbian lives in the past. Joan herself came out in the 1950s, and has written some compelling pieces about lesbian communities of those times. In recent years her insistence that butch/fem relationships – both in the past and in the present – are deserving of respect and acceptance has caused her to run afoul of the so-called radical feminist wing of the women's movement. A collection of Joan's writings entitled* A Restricted Country *has recently been published by Firebrand in USA and Sheba in Britain.*

*Prominently linked to the anti-censorship side of the sex debates, Joan was one of the signers of the FACT (Feminists Against Censorship Task-force) brief opposing the Dworkin-MacKinnon ordinance. However, when I talk to her she is most insistent that her personal views be disassociated from those of the Lesbian Herstory Archives. 'The Archives are available and open to every lesbian no matter what she is. She can be a devout member of Women Against Pornography, Andrea Dworkin's sister, or Andrea Dworkin herself.' She jokes, 'The Archives may be the only place in the world where a member of Women Against Pornography and a member of a lesbian s/m group can sit quietly at the same table.'*

*The Archives are actually housed in Joan Nestle's Upper West-Side apartment and it is there that we meet to conduct the interview. Joan is very hospitable, and far handier with the tape recorder than I. Packed to the ceilings with files and books (more than 20,000 of them) and hung with old photographs and other lesbian memorabilia, the Archives weaves a special spell. Joan admits that after living here for a while one begins to hear voices. I'm already starting to hear them and I've been here less than an hour. One of the two Archive cats dozes on the table as we talk . . .*

Margaret: *One of the things that draws me to your work is your focus on ordinary people, and the sense I have that the kind of history – and politics – you do argues against the view that people are just passive victims of their circumstances.*

Joan: I think everything I do is about that. For me that very much grows out of my personal history of coming out in the '50s, from experiencing the McCarthy era as a queer, and knowing that lies were being told about whole groups of people. I was a latch-key child; my mother worked and my father died before I was born, so I never knew him, and I had an elderly woman teacher who used literally to preach to us from a book called 'the isms' about what's wrong in America. This would have been around 1948, which was the hey-day of the House Un-American Activities Committee. I remember sitting in those little wooden chairs, and one afternoon she came out from behind her desk, which meant it was going to be a very important sermon. She started by saying, 'You know what's wrong with America today? It's those wild, dirty children running around the streets, whose parents don't care enough about them, and you can always tell them, because they wear a key around their neck.'

Now I was the only one in the room with a key around my neck, and I remember, as she was speaking, I took the key very slowly and hid it underneath my collar because I didn't want anyone to see it. But at the same time that I did that — it was my first act of 'passing' — a whole other consciousness was growing in me, which was that I knew my mother. And I knew how fucking hard she was working to keep me in school and to keep me alive. What was born in me was this sense of the total discrepancy of world views, and the knowledge that people in power, (and I saw that teacher as being in power), will tell total lies about other people, and will scapegoat people about whom they have absolutely no understanding. That was a profound insight, and it was based on a loyalty to my mother which I never lost.

But that's a beginning point, in some ways, for a real sense that people have wonders in them. So when I talk about a people's history, I mean a collectivity of individual resistance stories. Making people into victims doesn't tell their story, it just reinforces the power structure. Whether one is a role model as a victim or a role model as a good girl, it still impoverishes us.

Margaret: *Is your mother still alive?*

Joan: No, she died in 1978. She was living with me in this apartment, with the Archives all around her. We used to have these meetings every Thursday night and my mother would come out without her teeth and she'd say, 'Okay girls, you just keep doing your work girls . . .' and she'd go back inside. No, she's not alive anymore.

Margaret: *So she was very supportive of that aspect of your life?*

Joan: Well, we worked it out. My mother left school when she was in the sixth or seventh grade, and at fourteen she was gang-raped and became pregnant and had to have an abortion. But I didn't know any of this until she died. My mother was a bookkeeper and her only legacy to me was a kind of diary she wrote on the backs of ledger sheets . . . and it was there that I found the entries about the rape, and her own sense of sexuality, and other things. But over the years we had our battles. I left home when I was 17.

Margaret: *Yet she ended up living with you.*

Joan: Yeah, once she came to terms with it. I mean she used to flirt with my girlfriends. My mother was a free sexual spirit. There were times in her life when she worked as a hooker. When I think now of the support she did not have as a single mother and a sexually free woman, who was also sexually stigmatized, and wounded, with no sense of feminism as a collective movement, only her struggle . . . I think how much easier it would have been if she had been able to take advantage of the things we have now.

Margaret: *Let's talk about your view on sex and sexuality. You're associated closely with the anti-censorship side of the sex debates . . .*

Joan: You know, in the midst of all these battles, the sex wars, I and others have been driven to make very committed and angry speeches. Yet there is always an agonizing doubt in my mind about all the work I do. For instance, I'm terrified about my forthcoming book in some ways. Because I want to do good in the world, just the way Andrea Dworkin wants to do good in the world.

And yet I believe in what I do. I have a gut sense that writing about sex, and talking about it the way I do is life-affirming. But I'm frightened about it. I guess what I'm trying to say is, I always hear such certainty on the other side of the pornography debate. I am passionate about my work, but I'm not certain about it.

Margaret: *Can you articulate why you think writing explicitly about sex is life-affirming?*

Joan: Well, let me start with myself. It was life-affirming for me because it healed wounds. It gave and still gives me a sense of power, not power over anybody, but a sense of being visible in some way. I grew up as a fat woman, a big woman, and there was a whole period of my life in the '50s when my mother took me to doctors as a sexual freak. The first piece I wrote about sex was about butch/fem relationships, and that grew out of a particular personal history.

I think of my history in three stages: the queer '50s, the activist '60s — when I was active in the civil rights movement and the peace movement and the protests against the House Un-American Activities Committee — and then the feminist '70s. And I realized in the mid to late '70s that I was really passing in the lesbian feminist movement. That the part of me that I was not speaking about was my whole queer past up to that point. And I started to see things happening in the movement, in the rush for respectability, that I thought would lead us into big political trouble. And I saw whole communities of women disappear, accompanied by sighs of relief from feminists, because those were the women who looked like men. Or the women who looked like whores. And I kept silent for a long time and then I just couldn't anymore, because it was my own history that I was denying.

I guess it goes back to holding that key. So I wrote that first piece on butch/fem to affirm a part of my life that I had witnessed courage in. I couldn't understand why I should be ashamed of a history that put women I knew up against the state in such a direct way. I could not see why, in a time when there seemed, by comparison with the '50s, to be so much safety, that these things should be secret.

But it was somewhat self-serving. I wanted my own life to be able to surface again in this new world. This is almost a cliche in our community now, but what happened was that I was doing a theoretical piece and I found myself writing about wetness, and about the use of dildoes. And I just took a big breath, a big sigh, because although I myself may feel moments of shame for the things I do sexually, I will never feel shame for a community. I was really writing that first piece in honor of a community of which I was just one part. And I found that incredibly life-affirming because it showed me how I could be who I really was in this new movement. The problem was that as soon as I did it, (I say I; there are many women writing and doing this work) I ran up against a tremendous amount of anger and, I think, fear in the feminist movement – women saying, 'Don't say these things about us, they are just what they always say about lesbians.'

Writing about sex is life-affirming because it documents courage. And I think erotic self-definition by women and by lesbians is a courageous act. I guess one basic principle I've evolved is that if you live by the decrees or the world-definition of those who are in power, who created the narrowness of experience in the first place, you will starve to death. Because the complexities of our experience will never be clean enough to suit them.

Margaret: *I know that in recent years you've been quite ill. Could you talk about the effect that has had on your work?*

Joan: I got sick eight years ago having never been sick in my life. I had always been a really strong street kid and I used my body to do everything I had to do, to run from the police, to survive in the bars, on the march from Selma to Montgomery. I got sick when my mother died, and it took a long time to figure out what it was. It was a long, horrendous ordeal during which I changed from a totally independent woman to not being able to leave the house by myself. And I have to say that without Deborah Edel – we're no longer lovers, but perhaps we're something deeper than that – without her, I never would have survived.

Eventually, only a year-and-a-half ago, they defined what I had. Because of AIDS they've discovered new blood tests for something called chronic Epstein-Barr virus, which is a debilitating, though not terminal illness. I won't go into all the symptoms, except that, as someone said in a recent article, it just totally changes the experience of life.

Now, people who have been ill will know this, but before I got sick I always enjoyed sex. Even though I had to be seduced by lovers to like my own body, I was always lucky to have wonderful lovers who did that. The point is, I thought my body was sturdy, a real peasant's body, that it would never turn me in. And then all of a sudden I felt like I had this enemy from within, this fifth-column that was turning me into a freak again.

I hadn't really done any obvious sex writing up to that time, but one of the things I did when I was house-bound was that I joined a small lesbian writing group and I did write a piece in which sex played a part, though the point of the story wasn't sex. I think what writing erotica does for me is it makes me more than my illness. In the larger scale it's a resistance battle, something that gives me a chance to celebrate desire rather than grieve for it. In a really deep sense I see the flesh, the body, as a very frail thing in this world, where there are so many different kinds of deaths waiting for us, institutional, economic, and all the rest. But within the body's frailty is this incredible power of desire, which makes people survive concentration camps, wars . . .

I'll tell you a story. One of the visitors we had here at the Archives was a woman who was a survivor of a concentration camp, and she was saying to us that she had read *The Well of Loneliness* – such a small thing – but she had read it in a Polish translation, and she was taken into the camps when she was a teenager. And she said one of the things that gave her the will to survive was that she wanted to live long enough to kiss a woman.

How does one protect this frail thing called the body, that carries with it such a celebration of life and of possibilities in a time like this? I think erotic writing is one way. And for me it was a way to fight back against illness, and a refusal to let the body be defined, either by outsiders again, which were the doctors, or by an accident of nature.

But what is most important is when I write a story, like the butch/fem essay, and women write back to me and say, 'You gave us back a part of our own lives . . .' That's what's really important. We all have private ways of working out how to survive. Writing the way I do is exciting to me because it seems to break the private, and to give other women voices.

But I could be silenced very quickly. In my own community, every year, there's a battle about letting me read at the lesbian feminist poetry reading. And the woman who puts it together has told other women when my name came up, 'What Joan does is damaging to women,' which in my nightmares are the words that I wake up hearing. But my answer has always been, 'If that is true women will let me know. When I read to an empty room I'll know.' I have a basic sense of two things, one is that I'm not certain at all what the truth is, and if I had any evidence that my writing was truly adding to the oppression and suffering of women I would stop. The second is that I believe deeply that this work is worth a life-time to do.

Margaret: *You were telling me earlier that you'd recently seen the movie* Full Metal Jacket *and that you'd found it very disturbing. Does that tie into these issues?*

Joan: Yes, and what upset me was the incredible connection the movie made between male sexuality and killing. 'This is my gun, and this is my penis' and all that. One of the arguments I have with Andrea Dworkin and others is around the issue of penetration, and my sense has always been that they tend to see sexuality in a very one-dimensional way. But, it was very interesting. Here I was, watching this movie, and I'm someone who likes a woman to use a dildo, and I will call it a cock sometimes, and I will go down on her, and I've written stories about that, and I was sitting there the whole time, saying, 'Am I glorifying *their* image of a cock?' And I could barely watch the scenes with the Asian women prostitutes. I just wanted to kill, which upset me as well. I kept getting into traps.

I was with my present lover, a wonderful woman, who I'll talk about because she helped me with this. She's been a working class woman her whole life. And she enjoys the sexuality I enjoy, and feels no shame about it. So we were talking, and she was saying, 'How they see the world, and what they do with what's in the world is not how we see the world. To give it over to them is to let their ugliness and their corruption of flesh be the rule of flesh; to see the body the way they do is to be delivered into their nightmare.' And she told me to trust that what we do is done with love, and caring and in a different world.

A part of me really does believe this, but another part of me is frightened. I'll say this though, that if I had my choice between having doubts in this world and being completely certain, I would choose doubts.

Ultimately I have no war with the penis. Of course it's true that government institutions know how to link male sexuality with killing, but the penis is just a piece of flesh that can respond to desire. How a government or a culture orchestrates that into a weapon is what one must fight, not the flesh. And not a woman's desire.

I spent ten years of the women's movement hiding the fact that I liked to be penetrated by women. The anti-penetration position will just engender shame and fear and judgment and kill desire. That analysis leaves no room for autonomous desire because any women will be suspect. It reminds me very much of the McCarthy period. A woman says, 'This is what I desire and what I want to do' and an overruling voice says, 'The verdict is that that desire is guilty because it's an eroticizing of your own oppression.' When do we listen to someone other than them? When do we listen to ourselves? A woman's self-defined desire is never an accommodation. I don't know how else to say it.

And what I see is the reverse situation. I see that women die, are beaten in bedrooms, never get into bedrooms that they want, because the power structure is truly so terrified of female desire, and all the 'radical feminist' argument is doing is adding a new layer of terror. To focus on the alleged betrayal in a woman wanting penetration when the power of maleness is so huge in the world is a sad place to wage a political battle.

My personal belief is that it's crucial for women to have a nurturing place for their own sexuality, whether it be their own home, or sex clubs, which are harder to come by, or our journals. I think as long as sexuality is nurtured we will come to enlightened positions as a community. We will know what can be dictated sexually and what cannot as we discover our own desires. One of the reasons the AIDS crisis is so huge is that it stops that process. But if the voices of shame and of judgement and of disease and the fear of disease become stronger, if we close down personal sexual exploration, I think there will be real danger of lesbians becoming a sexually conservative community.

Then the politics of protectionism and of allowing leaders to define sexuality for us will become life-threatening, and we will become another kind of community. The word 'lesbian' will mean something totally different.

Margaret: *How can we avoid being 'protectionist,' seeing women only as victims, but at the same time fight to end the real wounds that are inflicted on women?*

Joan: I think one way to answer that question is by looking at prostitutes' lives. There is no question, especially if you're talking about a street hooker, of the huge dangers, of the crimes against her person that go on. And certainly if a woman had other ways to feed herself and her children she might choose not to be a prostitute. But what I am saying is that we need to listen, as I think this recent book *Sex Work: Writings by Women in the Sex Industry* (Cleis Press, 1987; Virago Press, 1988) does, for the stories of women who work as prostitutes. We need to listen *both* to what they say is being inflicted on them and can be changed socially, and what they say their personal choices are.

To do this you have to listen very carefully, without an agenda of your own. If a woman says, 'This is my life, and I'll tell you what you can do to help make it better, and I'll tell you what's my own autonomy and don't step on that,' then you need to listen, even if you have in your head a different view of how her world should be. But it's an agonizing sorting-out process.

One of my real problems with the position of – I don't like to call them radical feminists, because I don't believe they're radicals – is that from what I have seen, in discussions with Women Against Pornography, for instance, they have not suffered many moments of agonized doubt about 'am I really hearing this right?' 'What is the best thing I can do in this situation?' Because I think the only way we can sort out these questions is by listening closely to what women say. And I think there are authentic women's voices all the time. I don't think only women in the movement know how to talk about their lives.

But I think it may take a very long time to know clearly what is victimization and what is resistance. I think if you go out looking for victimization that's what you find. And if you go out looking for resistance that's what you'll find. The most important thing is to keep a flow of both discoveries, which is one of the reasons that censorship is deadly to us. In whatever form it comes, silencing any side of the debate is deadly.

Margaret: *Are coalitions important for us, and if so who should we be allying with?*

Joan: Coalitions are essential, because we are currently facing a very powerful coalition from the other side. As a lesbian, I think we should especially be making coalitions with gay men at this time. Perhaps for me this seems especially pressing, being chronically ill with a virus that shares some of the symptoms of AIDS, although it's certainly not anywhere near as devastating. But this is an important time to affirm our allegiance with anyone who is queer and who will bear the brunt of state repression or neglect because of that.

I also think it's time for coalitions with prostitutes' rights organizations around the world. And certainly, though it will not be easy, we should be working with civil rights groups, with labor. And with feminists, though there will be troubles with the more traditional feminists. I also consider myself a socialist, and listening to Oliver North this summer I was reminded again that we're fighting a fight that is much larger than just the future of the lesbian and the gay community. I think we're fighting for the future of a world of compassion for difference, and for a committed belief that people have a right not to go hungry and not to go homeless and not to be ill, and not to go uneducated. But I really believe that we must fight as sexual radicals, and that that should be our special message.

Margaret: *Could you talk a little bit more about your socialism?*

Joan: Well, I didn't become a socialist because of something I read. I became a socialist from watching my mother's life, and growing up as the daughter of a woman who worked her whole life for bosses. I got a real education in class, which in this country we're not supposed to have, though everybody breathes it in and you see it all around you.

Economics became one of the primary ways I understood things because my mother often couldn't hold our house together, and I would have to go live with an aunt or uncle. And I realized very young that there was nothing my mother could pay for outside of food and shelter and sometimes not even that. So that if I wanted to go to school, even to high school, I had to have a job. And that by going to school I was taking away a source of income. It was that kind of stuff.

Now I teach in the SEEK program at Queens College, which is basically a program that grew out of the street anger of the '60s. It was a response to very specific populations, Black and Puerto Rican young people who felt closed out of the university. I've been teaching there for 21 years and I've learned more from those 21 years in terms of how my own personal struggle fits into a world-wide struggle for economic justice than from any other experience I've had. I see my students struggling against such overwhelming odds and struggling to be 'good Americans' at the same time. . . .

It's just a basic thing: there is economic injustice in this country. I have been asked, how can you write about sex when people are dying for not having enough food to eat? Isn't it trivial? Isn't it privileged? And my response has been, I would have trouble with it if one *only* wrote about sex. But the other part of it is that every human life has a sexual dimension to it. In my own life my mother fought back through sexuality, and I don't think she was the only working-class woman who did that.

It's become almost a cliché but I think there has to be an economic revolution, and I think there has to be rage at inequality, not just by those who don't have, but by those who have also. We have to get tired of seeing the same faces in the same menial positions in this society year after year. It has to enrage us. It's hard to find words for this in Reagan America, but I once wrote a poem about the Reagan sneer. It's as if there's a sneer on the face of this land. And Black Americans, people of color, still bear the major brunt of it, and nothing has really changed. And until we are enraged by that sneer of indifference or even worse, by the calculated writing off of people and of countries, things will not change.

Margaret: *Let's talk about your work on butch/fem relationships. One of the problems that some feminists have had with butch/fem is that it seems to impose another set of normative roles on women. Was this true in your experience?*

Joan: It is true that butch/fem women formed a very unified communal bloc, and yes, in order to enter those communities you had to show your awareness of certain codes, and sometimes your acceptance of them. But it wasn't that we were being forced into a role. It was that the bar community was the only safe space that one had publicly, and you guarded it with every code of behavior that you could.

Something which is not discussed much in lesbian circles, but which I can testify to from personal experience, was police entrapment. Some recent evidence has come to us of a diary that was written about a lesbian bar in Columbus, Ohio, in the 1950s. This woman who was new came into the bar, nobody knew her, she didn't know the ropes. Well she walked in and no one spoke to her for two or three hours until this fem waitress came up to her and befriended her, and told her the reason no one spoke to her was that because of the way she was dressed no one could tell what her sexual identity was, and they were afraid she was a police-woman.

What I'm saying is that the community had to really struggle for a public space, and yes, there was definitely an initiation. That I don't find that surprising. It was a self-protective space. The same thing is true in lesbian-feminist circles. I mean there was a whole time when, if a woman walked into a typical lesbian feminist meeting and she was wearing makeup, long hair and heels, she was treated as an enemy infiltrator. And that was how the butch/fem bars were; we were very frightened of infiltrators of one kind or another.

I do think that every community when it is under pressure of some sort organizes itself. And it organizes itself culturally, erotically (because that was our battle line), and visually. I think the mistake was that the complexity of butch/fem as a cultural and personal expression was so totally denigrated in the '70s that those of us who came from it and crossed over into the feminist movement got frightened, and we remained silent too long. And in so doing we allowed a whole decade to become entrenched in a way of viewing that community. I think if the dialogue had opened up much sooner there would have been less of a sense that butch/fem involved a rigidly normative behavior.

One important point I want to make is that when I write or speak about butch/fem I am not putting any kind of pressure on anyone. You can't argue someone into being a butch or a fem. I'm excited that in our new world there is a mixture of sexual styles. To me a united nations, or interplanetary council of lesbians would have women in full leather, women in full flannel, women in fem to the highest order, in butch

241

three-piece suits and lesbians who look like anyone else. It would have the total array of self-definition.

Margaret: *That's a great fantasy. We're running out of time, but could you talk about your forthcoming book?*

Joan: Well, first I want to say that I'm very grateful to Nancy Bereano for having agreed to publish it and for having done so much along the way. The book is a collection of my erotic pieces along with some speeches. Now, I expected Nancy to say 'yes' to the speeches and 'no' to the erotic pieces, but she didn't. And she revealed it was her own personal struggle to be able to accept all of it. But she's been saying to me off and on, 'We're gonna get crap for this book, Joan, we're gonna get crap . . .' And I have been very divided over whether this little book has a right to be in the world.

But I want it to be read as history. And I think it is history in the sense that the documentation of erotic lives is as much a biographical statement as any other kind, even though the erotic element isn't usually accepted as history. But writing about sexuality, no matter how glibly I have come to speak about it, has made me face all the terror that I have about it. I teach in a radical program, and I'm out as a lesbian, but at school when my friends and colleagues say to me, 'Joan, we can't wait to see your book' and I know I'm speaking to, say, a wife and mother from Guyana, and I know in my book there's a story about my going down on a woman's dildo, I don't know how I'm going to give her that book.

By including explicitly sexual material I have learned how restricted the world is, the doors that might shut in one's face. And I've also faced, once again, my own potential for shame. So I have very mixed feelings. I think it's a sad and interesting comment that we never need a reason to justify an exploration of victimization and we always need a reason to justify celebration.

Margaret: *One last question: What are you planning for your next project?*

Joan: Well, it will be about Mabel Hampton who's an 85-year-old Black lesbian woman whom I've known since I was ten years old. I've made tapes with her over the years, and I got a grant from a feminist granting organization to start transcribing them, so that has to be the next project. There are not many spaces for an 85-year-old Black lesbian woman to tell her story. And also . . . Mabel is my friend, and I would like to do it while she's still alive.

She's quite a lady though. I'll tell you a story about her. She's having real trouble walking, and we got her a cart through the help of SAGE (Senior Action in a Gay Environment). She lives in the South Bronx, and she'll probably eventually be living here within the year. So she had this idea that she was going to get into her little electrical cart and come down from the South Bronx to here. And I said, 'Mabel, you know I don't think you realize that cart is not sturdy enough for that.' And my example to her was, 'Mabel, you're gonna have to cross bridges. . . .' And the minute

I said it I should have known, and there was a silence, and finally she said in her sharpest voice, 'Joan, no bridge is going to stop Mabel Hampton.' And it was a metaphor for her whole life.

# To Be a Radical Jew in the Late Twentieth Century

## Melanie Kaye/Kantrowitz

*For Irena Klepfisz who pushed me*

> To be a Jew in the twentieth century
> Is to be offered a gift . . .
> > *Muriel Rukeyser, 'Letter to the Front, VIII,' 1944*

*So, Melanie, what's with all the Jewish?* This was my father speaking, sometime in 1982, the year he died. I answered him clearly, carefully, the way I did that year because he often got confused, but the answer was not hard to find. I had been away from NY since I was 20 – I was then 37 – and I had noticed two things: my own hunger for Jewish culture, music, food, language, humor, perspective, Jewish *people*; and, the anti-Semitism palpable – and growing – around me.

Twenty years earlier I had marched on my first demonstration, against nuclear testing. My parents had not pushed me into activism, yet clearly they raised me to do these things. Their parents had come to this country from Eastern Europe, Poland and Russia. None had been political. Yet, as a teenager in the Depression, my father had belonged to the Young Communist League; and, even as an adult, his major hero remained his dead friend Aaron, a Communist who had spoken on street corners and fought in Spain. My mother had circulated petitions against the Korean War, walking up to people on the streets of Flatbush during peak McCarthy period, and she had been spat on. Later she became president of the PTA at Walt Whitman Jr. High, and fought to bring blacklisted performers to sing at the annual PTA meeting.

My mother often says, 'When Melanie was 3 years old, I knew it would be Melanie against the world, and I was betting on Melanie.' One of her favorite stories of me dates from 1950, when my class and my older sister's had been given dog tags – issued to NYC schoolchildren, as to soldiers – so that in the event of a bomb, our bodies could be identified. My sister, 7 years old, asked what the dog tag was for, and my mother told her. I listened. And had bombs ever been dropped? Roni asked. Imagine the discussion, my mother explaining to a 7-year-old about war, about Hiroshima and Nagasaki . . . And the next time the 5-bell signal rang for a shelter drill and my kindergarten teacher said, 'Now, children, it's only a game, remember, under your desk, head down,' I, 5 years old, stood up and said it was not a game, it was about dropping bombs on children and they our own government had dropped bombs on children and their eyes had melted and people were burned and killed. The other 5-year-olds began crying and screaming, and the principal summoned my mother to school. 'What are you, crazy, telling a kid things like that,' the principal is reputed to have said, and my mother to have answered: 'I will not lie to my children.'

My mother's version of this story emphasizes my role: as class conscience and rebel. But what delights me in the story is *her* courage: though a good student, she had dropped out of high school at 15 and was always convinced that educated people were smarter. Yet she had the political and intellectual backbone to defend me and defy authority.

This was my Jewish upbringing, as much as the candles we lit for Hanukkah, or the seders where bread and matzoh shared the table. My father had been raised observant, my mother, not. But to us breaking religious observance was progressive, the opposite of superstitious; when we ate on Yom Kippur, it never occurred to me that this was un-Jewish. I knew I was a Jew. I knew Hitler had been evil. I knew Negroes – we said then – had been slaves and that was evil too. I knew prejudice was wrong, stupid. I knew Jews believed in freedom and justice. When Eisenhower-Nixon ran in 1952, I noticed Nixon's dark wavy hair, like my father's, and said: 'He looks like Daddy.' My mother was furious: 'Nothing like him!' and went on and on explaining how Nixon had gotten elected to Congress only by smearing Helen Gahagan Douglas (the liberal Congresswoman). I was 7 years old.

Soon we would get our first TV, so my mother (and I) could watch the McCarthy hearings. I knew the whole fate of humanity hinged on these hearings, as surely as I knew the Rosenbergs had been good people, like my parents, with children the same age as my sister and me. I knew government people, like McCarthy, had killed the Rosenbergs, and I was terrified, but it literally did not occur to me that real people, people I might meet, people who had children and went to work, hated the Rosenbergs, thought they should die. Nor did it occur to me that there were people who thought unions were bad, people who did not know you never cross a picket line, did not know prejudice was wrong and stupid.

This is not to say I never heard alternate views, but my parents – though not formally educated or trained in political analysis – had very definite opinions about right and wrong which they passed on to me like the 10 Commandments, ideas I have yet to find wanting.

That this set of principles was Jewish never occurred to me. Around me was Flatbush, a swirling Jewish ghetto/community of first and second generation immigrants, including Holocaust survivors (though they were noted in my mind simply as the parents who brought umbrellas to school when it rained, spoke with my grandparents' accents); there were clerks, trade unionists, salespeople, plumbers; small business people, radio and TV repairmen, people like my parents and their friends; there were teachers and there were even doctors who lived in what we called 'private houses' in the outreaches of the neighborhood at the point where not everyone was Jewish.

But where I lived, everyone was, or almost. Jewish was the air I breathed, nothing I articulated, everything I took for granted.

1963. I was 17, working in the Harlem Education Project.[1] HEP had organized a tutoring project, several rent strikes, an anti-rat campaign;[2] had pressured schools for decent facilities and a Black history curriculum, and helped to create freedom schools for children to attend in protest. A block organization was gradually turning a lot filled with garbage (and once or twice dead bodies) into a park. It was my first experience with a mobilizing proud community and with the possibilities of collective action. I was hooked, though it took me years to recognize how my upbringing had brought me to 133rd St. and Lenox, and primed me for this commitment.

It was also my first experience in a non-Jewish environment. Harlem was the center of Northern Black culture; there were community people, students – some from other cities and communities – some from middle-class homes, some travelling back and forth from the South with stories of Fannie Lou Hamer, James Farmer or of the past: a grandfather lynched in Florida, a great-great-aunt who learned to read in slavery in Mississippi (and Mississippi is still the most frightening word I know). And there were white people, these almost all young, almost all students, some who were my first contact with WASPs; some Jews, though I barely registered that fact since they were not like the Jews I knew. All these students went to colleges like Columbia and Sarah Lawrence, while I went to no-tuition City College, riding the subway 3 hours a day to classes and to Harlem, and would the next year – at 18 – move into my own apartment and become financially self-supporting.

At the end of my first summer in Harlem, on the bus returning from the historic March on Washington, a Black man my age flirted with me and I flirted back, and he sang me this song:

> Jew girls from Brooklyn they go wild over me
> and they hold my hand where everyone can see
> O they paint their face like whores
> have me leave them at their doors
> They go wild, simply wild over me

Intensely focused on white racism, utterly unaware of racism against Jews, or of the possibility of Jewish danger (the Holocaust was eons ago, irrelevant), I felt only shame at the label – Jew girl from Brooklyn – and at the stereotype – hypocrite, liberal in public but won't bring him home to meet the family. I determined not to be like the others; not to be like myself. . . .

245

1966. I was 20, preparing to leave NY for graduate school at Berkeley. I wanted to get away from NY, from my family, my people, to be part of the radical politics developing on the West Coast. At a summer demonstration against the war in Viet Nam, I marched with a slim pale woman from California. She had long straight blond hair, wore some easy cotton shift and sandals; she seemed not to sweat and her voice lilted when she spoke. I had the same body I still have: sturdy, strong legs, heavy black eyebrows, dark hair which in NY's August frizzed and bushed; my skin glistened with oil. I could not imagine how I would fit into the West Coast.

I discovered in Berkeley that the Brooklyn Jewish accent which in NY had always marked me as lower class now marked me as one of those smart Jews from NY. Apart from this observation, passed on by an admiring gentile friend, I have few memories of being a Jew in Berkeley, little consciousness that people's reactions to or assumptions about me had something to do with my particular style of Jewish culture. Jewish political issues moved me not at all, including the 1967 war in the Middle East – I did not identify with Israel – and, when in 1968 I had a minor operation, like Tillie Olsen's Anna I wrote 'none' next to *religion* on the hospital registration form because 'I didn't want anyone mumbling religion at me if I died.'

1972. I had just moved to Portland, Oregon and was attending a feminist conference, talking with a woman while we waited for the elevator. I have forgotten the context for what she said: that she did not like Jews. They were loud and pushy and aggressive. This was the first time I had heard someone say this outright. I was stunned, didn't know what to say – 'no they're not'? – and I couldn't believe she didn't know I was Jewish. I said, loud, flat, 'I'm Jewish.' I can't remember what happened next or even her face, only the moment by the elevator.

1975. Yellow Springs, Ohio, at the Feminist Socialist Conference, on the lunch line, the woman in back of me was talking about a Jewish caucus. I didn't ask her anything, didn't even seriously eavesdrop. I couldn't relate to it. I went to a workshop on economics instead. Years later I wonder what they talked about.

1978. I was working at Rape Relief Hotline in downtown Portland doing counselling, advocacy, community education and organizing. I was talking with my best friend and sister organizer – a middle-class WASP woman – about my sense of awkwardness and ineffectiveness with 'straight' women – meaning some combination of middle-aged heterosexual non-movement women; that I seemed to have no social skills, everything I said had the wrong beat. A couple of days later a woman called the hotline to talk about her experience some years back of being battered. She wanted to get involved in hotline activities, and I invited her to stop by. She did. The woman was some 30 years older than

246

I, had raised 2 kids, worked in an office, had never considered herself political. I might have been the first lesbian she'd ever knowingly met. She was everything I was supposed to by my own analysis feel awkward around. We went out for coffee, talked for hours, easy. She was a Jew, an east coast Jew. I realized in some ways I was in the wrong city, the wrong part of the world; I was an alien.

By the time I left Oregon in 1979, I had developed an interest in Jewish immigrant history and an obsession with the Holocaust. I read avidly, vaguely aware that I needed Jews but feeling as out of place as ever with those who'd received religious education, as with those women in Portland who had started getting together on Friday nights to eat and *shmooz*, to 'socialize.' I was political. My rejection of these Jewish women's gatherings paralleled closely my pre-feminist contempt for women's consciousness-raising groups. My failure to register this similarity is a tribute to the mind's ability to resist information which threatens.

And then a time of moving, from one *goyish* environment to another. A summer in Maine, Down East, the easternmost point in the US, and if I thought I had seen a Jewish vacuum before, I hadn't. The house we moved into had a swastika smeared on the bedroom door in what looked like blood. A car parked down the road had swastikas and crosses painted on the doors (we spray-painted over them one night). I was becoming very very conscious. Driving out west, passing signs for Greensboro, Atlanta, Birmingham, Montgomery, Jackson, names I knew as sites of struggle and danger, listening to the radio's furious anti-Arab anti-Iranian aggressively fundamentalist christian tirades unleashed by the taking of hostages in the Tehran embassy complex; hearing christian hymn after christian hymn, seeing more crosses, more churches than I had ever imagined: I was afraid.

By the time I got to northern New Mexico – where I lived for the next two years – I knew I needed Jews, nothing vague about it. I sought out a Jewish women's group which met on and off. I was reading and writing about Jewishness. My political work was still not Jewish-related – I helped to organize a women's coffeehouse, and a demonstration against militarism at Los Alamos Science Museum, and at these and other women's events I read work with strong Jewish content. Some women hugged and thanked me, especially Jews and others strongly grounded in their own culture; responses which warmed, emboldened and confirmed me. And some looked blank, perhaps wondering why I was bothering, or why I was being divisive, identifying with a patriarchal religion, or ... responses which alienated me, pushed me deeper into my Jewishness, sharpened my awareness of difference so that I began to notice and respond to cultural stimuli or casual remarks or jokes or, even, political analysis differently.

1980. I recognized in Reagan's election that the liberalism I had for years seen as the real danger was being superceded, that the right was gaining power, with all its Jew-hating, racist, sexist, homophobic capitalist thrust. At the same time the anti-Semitism I was encountering in the women's movement and on the left hurt me more, not because it was more threatening but because the feminist left was where I needed to be: this added to my sense of isolation as a Jew.

I was also reading analyses of racism and discussions of identity, mostly by Black women, and my proximity to Chicana and Native American cultures allowed me tangible lessons in diversity and in non-mainstream survival. Cultures, people were being defined as Third World or white; where I lived it was Chicana, Indian or Anglo. But none of these categories, none of the descriptive analyses fit me or my culture. I was an English-speaker, my people came from Europe, but we were not Anglo and neither was our culture.

There are many more details, scenes, some I remember and some which still elude me. What is clear to me is this: the more outside of a Jewish ambiance I was, the more conscious I became of Jewishness. For me, it was like Marshall McLuhan's perhaps apocryphal remark: I don't know who discovered water, but I'm sure it wasn't a fish. Inside a Jewish environment, where I could take for granted a somewhat shared culture, an expectation about Jewish survival, where my body type and appearance were familiar, my voice ordinary, my laughter not too loud but hearty and normal, above all, normal . . . in this environment, I did not know what it meant to be a Jew, only what it meant to be a *mentsh*. I did not know that *mentsh* was a Jewish word in a Jewish language.

As I lived longer outside Jewish culture, as I became more fully aware of anti-Semitism, internal as well as external, as I understood my own hunger for home, kin, for *my people*, I was walking further and further along a mostly unconscious, gradual, zig-zag and retrospectively inevitable path.

## I. If I am not for myself . . .

There were many of us on distinct but similarly inevitable paths. What happened as Jewish women began raising Jewish issues inside the women's movement?

Even at the beginning, some of the issues we were raising seemed almost mundane, obvious: issues of direct insult, stereotypes, omission, exclusion, indifference, discrimination, assumptions of sameness, passing, invisibility, cultural difference, concern for cultural survival . . . I – and I think many of us – expected that the groundwork on these issues had been laid, that the heroic and tedious labor undertaken by women of color, with some white and Jewish support, to raise everyone's consciousness about racism would carry over somewhat to inform response to Jewish women.

Not that I thought white – or Jewish – women had always been adequate in their commitment to fight racism. Not that I assumed experience and issues for Jewish women and for gentile women of color were the same; nor did I expect identical experience and issues for all women of color, including Jewish women of color. But I did expect some analogy to be apprehended. I expected that the movement would continue building on general principles, as well as differentiate what was unique.

And this did not happen. I saw resistance, overt rejection, ridicule, a willful ignorance. Not from everyone. From some I saw respect, support and desire to extend themselves. From many I saw hypocritical silence masquerading as respect. From some, hostility. And – most often – I saw a bewilderment, an inability to grasp what was being said about anti-Semitism or Jewish identity, an incapacity to recognize why it mattered. And, of course, the too-polite silence, the bewilderment, the hostility intensified my self-consciousness as a Jew.

Examples are not hard to find. The policy statement that doesn't mention opposition to anti-Semitism.[3] The many courses that include readings by women from a variety of cultures but, somehow, no Jews. The decision that to have a Jew as keynote speaker is too particular, too specialized.[4] The 1984 Women & the Law conference, with its theme *Bread and Roses*, which offered, out of nearly 200 workshops, none on Jews or Jewish issues. (Let me honor those Jewish women who ensured that the 1985 conference would have several Jewish workshops and events.[5]) The flyer for an anti-militarist protest which voiced opposition to misogyny, racism, homophobia, ableism, a number of other -isms, but not anti-Semitism; named a string of identities including 'Black, Latina, Asian, Palestinian . . .' but not Jewish.[6] A flyer soliciting material for a feminist journal on issues such as:

Imperialist Intervention
Racism, Sexism, Heterosexism, Ageism . . .
Hunger Education Reproductive Rights
Disarmament Health Self-Determination Housing[7]

I guess the '. . .' after 'Ageism' is supposed to leave room for the inclusion of anti-Semitism, but the general effect is to make Jews feel invisible, unwelcome, or worse.

Why? Why have the basic points been so hard to get? Why have so many radicals been impermeable to a pro-Jewish analysis and activity? Why are we getting the message that many of our erstwhile political comrades and sisters – including some Jews – think it contradictory to be a radical Jew?

The explanation, as I have tried to track it down, is as tangled as the nature of anti-Semitism; as unconscious, as willfully ignorant as an ordinary American's relationship to the rest of the world; as inadequately grasped and developed as the women's movement understanding of race and class and why the movement should oppose racism and class hierarchy.

249

## Anti-Semitism, Race and Class

I am not one who believes anti-Semitism is inevitable, yet I confess my heart sinks when I consider how resilient this hatred is: Jew as anti-Christ, embodying materialism, money, Shylock's pound of flesh; Marx's analysis of the Jew as irrelevant parasite; shameful victims, who went like sheep to the slaughter; the UN General Assembly's proclamations on Zionism; killer Israelis.

Nor does Jewish oppression fit into previously established analyses. If capitalism is your primary contradiction, the Jewish people is not a class category. If racism, many Jews have light skin, pass as gentile if they wish. If sexism, why should Jewish women identify with Jewish men? If Jewish is an ethnicity, a peoplehood, why don't you live in Israel, or call yourself Israeli? If it's a religion, how are you Jewish if you don't observe?

But not only does Jewish oppression elude conventional categories, Jewish stereotypes prove that anti-Semitism does not exist. Jews are rich, powerful, privileged, control the media, the schools, the business world, international banking: the Zionist conspiracy rides again. How could such powerhouses ever be in trouble These stereotypes, I've realized, prevent recognition of how we are threatened or demeaned as Jews.

For example: in 1982 when WBAI, NYC progressive radio station, broadcast the disarmament march and interviewed – as the lone voice against the demonstration – an Orthodox Jew, I was one of several who phoned to complain. 'Why pick on an Orthodox Jew as the single representative of conservative politics?' I asked. 'Why not?' a man answered. 'I've always wanted to pick on an Orthodox Jew.' When I expressed shock/tried to explain (obviously I was in shock if I tried to explain), he immediately said, 'I'm so sick of hearing about the fucking Holocaust' (which I hadn't mentioned). So I called the station manager, who apologized and proceeded to explain how when someone was making $7000 a year and someone next door was making $15,000 a year (clearly this man knew a lot about neighborhoods) I could understand the resentment.

Sure I could understand. But I had been talking about Jewhatred, not class antagonism. The station manager of NYC's progressive station had leaped from one to the other instantly, automatically. As if all Jews were wealthy. As if all wealth were Jewish. As if anti-Semitism were indulged in only by the poor.

By speaking about anti-Semitism, Jewish women unsettle an unspoken equation in the radical women's movement: in a society like ours, deeply racist and absurdly pretending to classlessness, class comes to be seen as identical to race. People of color are considered the same as working and poor people. Other aspects of racism – cultural erasure, assimilation, self-hate, just to name a few – are simply not heeded, nor are – god forbid – strengths of ethnic or racial minorities acknowledged unless – in a wash of white self-hate – people of color are romanticized as stronger, more authentic, somehow better than whites; but better because they are seen as such victims that mere survival is a miracle.

Meanwhile, these same analyses which ignore class as an independent category, related to but separate from race, ignore the variety of class experience and location of Jews: Jews, you remember, are all rich or at least middle class. Why, then, are we complaining?

Such a non-analysis not only belies the experience of middle-class people of color – the upper middle-class Black families, for example, whose LA neighborhood was firebombed in June, 1985; the middle-class Japanese home-land-and-business-owners on the West Coast who had everything confiscated and were imprisoned in camps during the second World War. This perspective also erases the existence of Jews of color and working-class Jews, and the entire white poor and working class; a very substantial group of women.

Related to this unspoken equation: analyses of racism – both on the left and in the feminist movement – have been spearheaded by Black people, and to some extent the experience of Black people in the US provides the model by which we understand racism. And despite the existence and even growth of a Black middle class, the continued grinding poverty of most Black people in this country also suggests an equation of race and class.

And it's true: most immigrant groups have moved up the class ladder, at least to lower middle class or trade union status (which – for men – means pretty good pay), usually pushed up in what has been called 'the queuing effect' by a newer group of immigrants against whom prejudice is fresher and stronger.[8] But American Blacks, in their forced passage to this country, in the destruction of many elements of African culture by slavery, in their confrontation with classic American racism against the darkest skin, and in the exploitation of this racism by capitalists to 'explain' inequality, have been painfully excluded from the process of queuing. This is evident from the progress of Puerto Ricans and Koreans in NYC, for example, or Cubans in Miami; though more recently arrived than Blacks, these groups have, in effect, cut in ahead of Blacks economically.

But there's another kind of distortion. I have lived outside of NYC for half my 40 years now, and have come to think that the usual explanations of racism and anti-Semitism focus unduly on New York, a focus which has everything to do with location of media and ambitious intellectuals, not to mention a huge Jewish and a huge Black community, each deeply rooted in the city, each a cultural center for their people. And these two communities have often, in the past 20 years, been at odds, not utterly, but noticeably: on community control of schools, in the struggle for the city's limited resources, on affirmative action and quotas ... And the contrast – between a visible relatively secure Jewish community, mostly (except for the old) employed, and a continuing impoverished Black community with an unequal share of the city's resources, unequally protected and unequally harassed by the police, with an astronomical rate of unemployment among Black teenage males and not much prospect of improvement – the contrast has got to seem stark.

It is this sense of contrast that is drawn upon again and again in people's discussion of anti-Semitism as opposed to racism. But when I look more closely at places other than New York – at Boston, where working class Italians and Blacks have been at odds over school busing; at Detroit, where Iraqi small merchants and Blacks have had racial tension reminiscent of the 'Jewish shopkeeper in Harlem'; at northern New Mexico where Chicana/o and Native American communities may have differences, and where Anglos moving to the area are wresting political control from the Chicanas/os; at Miami, where non-Spanish speakers may resent the bilingualism requirement for civil service jobs dealing with the public – my grasp of the complexities of race, Jewishness, ethnicity, class, and culture is greatly enhanced. Instead of being characterized by polarization, in which anti-Semitism is treated as a phenomenon different *in nature* from racism, anti-Semitism can be clearly seen as a *a form of racism*.

## The World According to America

There are other factors blocking recognition of the weight of anti-Semitism on Jews. Jewish experience in the US, isolated from the experience of Jews around the world, seems fairly rosy. But Jews are an international people, and the nature of Jewish identity, oppression, fear and danger derive from and connect to experiences outside this country.

Wars between the US and other countries have always been fought *in* other countries; most people in the US live in an extraordinarily protected context. Not only is our country vast and populous and proud of an isolationist spirit (often masking an imperialist reality); but, in addition, the strictly limited immigration during the middle portion of this century has restricted most Americans' knowledge about war, persecution, torture, the experience of refugees. Most Americans seem to believe ourselves peculiarly unaffected by what goes on in the rest of the world. If it didn't happen here, if it isn't happening now, why worry? Nor does a nation busy constructing a California or Texas future over Native American and Chicana/o culture care much about history.

From this vantage point, Jews seem ridiculous when we talk about Jewish danger. We are up against a failure of Americans to take seriously the pitch Jewhating attained so quickly in Europe in the thirties, for example, because Americans think Europe and the thirties so far away. They know about evil Germans, sheeplike Jews, and heroic Americans, but are not taught to see the war against the Jews as a culmination to centuries of Jewhating. Americans are told lies about the base of Nazism, so that we imagine Jewhating goes with a lack of education: working-class people are – as with white racism in this country – blamed. We are not told of the doctors and doctorates trained in Europe's finest universities. For most Americans the Holocaust blurs safely, almost pleasantly, with other terrible events of the past, like Bubonic Plague in the Middle Ages.

Nor have most Americans paid much attention to the persecution of Jews in the Soviet Union, or Argentina, or Ethiopia, unless an ideological point is to be scored against these nations. As for the fact that Jews are *not* in danger in some communities around the world because Jews have been exiled or violently excised from those communities – this is not recognized as a legitimate source of grief and suspicion for Jews to reckon with, a loss – of our people, our culture. Women in the feminist movement, not necessarily educated on these issues, respond pretty much like other Americans.

## The Scarcity Assumption

Then, too, an assumption deeply integral to capitalism has been absorbed by all of us, since it is reflected in so much of what we see. I have called this the Scarcity Theory,[9] not enough to go around: not enough love, not enough time, not enough appointments at the foodstamps office, not enough food stamps, not enough money, not enough seats on the subway. It's pervasive. We learn mistrust of each other, bone deep: everything is skin off somebody's nose.

And in the short run, certain things *are* scarce. To what causes do I apply my limited 'free' time? Where do I donate 'extra' money? What books do I read, what issues do I follow and become knowledgeable about? Where will my passion be deep and informed, able to make connections and inspire others, and where will it be superficial, giving lip service only? The women's movement has only in the last few years and under considerable pressure begun to face its own racism; class is still addressed in the most minimal ways. Meanwhile, international crises – apartheid in South Africa, intervention in Nicaragua, torture and repression in Salvador and Guatemala – compel attention.

Few of us have learned to trust our own rhetoric, that people will fight harder as they also fight for themselves. So when Jews begin talking about anti-Semitism, it's only 'natural' that even the left, which should welcome a people's coming to consciousness, responds as if we're asking for handouts – and whose pocket will they come out of? Ignoring how much political energy can be generated as groups develop a cohesive identity and analysis, the left accuses Jews of draining the movement, of competing for status as victims, of ignoring advantages and options open to us.

Identity politics of all kinds do contain an inherent potential not only for victim-competition but for splintering movements into 1000 groups whose members at last feel sufficiently the same: comfy but not a powerful resource.[10] But while the focus of some Jewish women on identity as a source of personal discovery and support is hardly unique, criticism of identity politics has been aimed disproportionately at Jews, sometimes *by* Jews. I'll put this another way: anti-Semitism has sometimes masqueraded as a disdain for identity politics.[11]

**Hurry Hurry**

Some – including some Jews who identify, as I do, with the left – if not disdainful of our attention to Jewish identity, seem to be rushing us, implying that we are lingering over what Rosa Luxemburg – a Jewish leftist – called 'petty Jewish concerns'; that we are evading important struggles, being selfish or self-indulgent. Aren't we done already?

A Jewish lesbian/feminist who has written about racism publishes, as part of a long essay on anti-Semitism and racism, 5 pages of consciousness-raising questions directed at Jewish women, prefaced by:

Since many women have engaged in consciousness-raising about Jewish identity and anti-Semitism . . . I have skipped over a basic avenue of inquiry . . .[12]

New Jewish Agenda, a progressive Jewish organization founded six years ago – and to which I belong – holds its second national convention, Summer '85, inspired by Hillel's second question: *If we are only for ourselves, what are we?* The question has two possible takes: an ethical one (the answer is, 'less than human'); and a practical one (the answer is, 'a failure,' because we are a tiny minority who needs allies.) This is the question which prompts joining with others, the question of coalition.[13]

But before Hillel asked, 'If I am only for myself . . .' he asked, 'If I am not for myself, who will be?' This is the question of separatism, the question that prompts a gathering of one's people. Literally, who will stick up for me if I don't respect myself enough to stand up for myself, if I can't articulate my own concerns so that others understand and care about them? Here is our beginning. Have we been for ourselves sufficiently already? Do we even know who our selves are?

## II. Jewish Diversity, Assimilation and Identity

Who, what is the Jewish people? This question dazed me when I first voiced it. I had always known the Jewish people: we lived in Brooklyn, and those whose fathers made money moved to Long Island. It was simple.

And suddenly it was not simple at all. I began to discover the different experiences, cultures, languages of Jews. I was 34 when I learned about Ladino, a couple of years older when I learned of Arab Jews, Kurds, the Beta Israel of Ethiopia, the Colchins of India. The diversity of the Jewish people shocked me.

Even in this country, I realized, there are vast differences: place of origin, part of the country, class background, religious or secular upbringing and practice, knowledge of and attachment to Jewish culture (which one?!), degree of assimilation.

For some Jews, 'passing' seems a choice; for others, passing means total denial and pain; for still others, passing is something they do without even thinking, and for still others, passing – as white/American/normal –

is impossible. Some Jews have never felt a moment of Jewish fear; others smell it daily. Some were raised in comfortable suburbs, sheltered from knowledge of anti-Semitism; others came from Europe or the Middle East and relive their own nightmares or those of their families; others grew up in mixed neighborhoods where they were beat up every day after school for being the Jew, and especially on Easter.

To observant Jews, a persistent reluctance by others to take Jewish holidays, *shabes*, dietary customs into account means that they – observant Jews – are not welcome;[14] to others, ignoring these traditions embodies anti-patriarchal struggle. Some Jews are passionately attached to Yiddish culture and want to preserve this; others feel alienated by a Yiddish emphasis: they grew up with Ladino or Arabic, and resent the assumption that Jewish means Ashkenazi roots; some share the rejection of much of the New Left for European anything, and, seeing the future in the Third World and only a moribund or embarrassing past in the remnants of European Jewry, feel no desire to preserve Ashkenazi culture. (Though one might question this last position as self-hating, the people who feel this way do not perceive what they hate as their *selves*.)

Some Jews identify deeply with other Jews; others identify only with white middle-class privilege; some consider themselves people of color. Some invalidate, trivialize or otherwise deny Jewish experience, oppression, and values, say 'I'm a Jew' only as a label or a credential, not a perspective. With the diversity of our experience unarticulated in a way that supports all of it, even Jews tend to perceive the needs, complaints, experience of other Jews as extreme, atypical, threatening, not really or not necessarily *Jewish*.[15] Given this lack of agreement about even such basics as the nature of Jewish experience and identity, the parameters of anti-Semitism, how are Jews supposed to work politically *as Jews*?

America is famous for gobbling up cultures, immigrant and native. But in addition, the nature of the Jewish people on the face of this earth has been totally transformed in the past 45 years by three facts:

- The Holocaust: the partial extermination of European Jewry and the virtual destruction of Ashkenazi culture.
- The expulsion of Jews from the Arab countries and destruction of these centers of Judeo-Arab culture.
- the founding of the state of Israel and the ingathering of many Jews.

We have not yet absorbed these transformations. We don't yet know what it means to be a Jew in the late 20th century.

For many North American Jews (in the US and Canada, half the world's Jews) a key issue is assimilation, a seepage of Jewishness out of Diaspora Jewry, except for those who retain or return to religious practice. Assimilation is often treated, by those who would belittle Jewish issues, as privilege, the *ability* to pass, a ticket out of Jewish oppression.

Anyone who has heard – as I have – Jew-hating remarks said to her face because to the speaker she didn't look Jewish knows both the survival value and the knife twist of passing. (And consider how some Jews came to look non-Jewish: Jewish women raped by gentile men during pogroms; Jewish women with lighter skin, hair, more gentile features, considered prettier, more desirable than their darker, more Semitic-looking sisters.)

But assimilation is a much larger issue than who you do or don't look like. Assimilation is the blurring or erasure of identity and culture. As I have come to recognize Jewish identity and culture not as givens, there for the taking, but as profoundly valuable *and vulnerable*, assimilation has become a source of pain: loss, some of which I can retrieve, some not: gone.

The point is that Jewish identity is not just about oppression, about anti-Semitism and survival, though clearly this is part of our history and we need our history. We also need our culture, need to know *where we grew*. We need *not* to disappear into the vague flesh of America, even if this disappearance were possible.

Those who call resistance to assimilation a luxury might do well to think about calling 'sexual preference' a luxury, or reproductive rights, or access to education or creative expression. None of these is *bread*, but 'Bread *and* Roses' was a demand voiced by Rose Schneiderman, a union organizer and a Jew.

What are the roses? As Jews we need our peoplehood, our culture, history, languages, music, calendar, tradition, literature ... We need these things because they are beautiful and ours, and because the point of struggle is not bare survival but lives full of possibility.

But Rose Schneiderman's metaphor flounders. Our culture is not a rose, it is our backbone. To say it matters that we're Jews; to bond with our people; for a tiny minority, these acts trigger intense fear – fear of being boxed into a perspective that is assumed to be narrow and selfish, fear of being isolated, as we have often historically been isolated.

And the only thing that counters this fear is love for our people, pride in our culture.

*If I am not for myself, who will be?* Hillel could not have predicted the need American Jews in the late 20th century would bring to his first question: the need to know the self, the people, the culture. For several years I have given workshops across the country on anti-Semitism, racism, and more recently, Jewish identity. I have heard Jews talk about gathering as a group, loving the comfort, the opportunity to discuss anti-Semitism, offer support, eat wonderful food, laugh ... but then? uncertain what to do next, as Jews. I have watched Jews sob as they grappled for the first time with the meaning of Jewish resistance, of violence and non-violence in the context of the Holocaust. Jewish radicals are just beginning to tangle with Jewish identity and its relationship to Jewish culture, tradition and politics.

So it's not surprising that we are still, many of us, uncertain in our responses. What *is* a good radical Jewish response? How do we take positions that won't be used against us or where we won't be invisible as Jews? How, for example, do we support the struggle against apartheid, confront the anti-Semitic emphasis on Israel as well as the assumption that as Jews we support the Israeli government's position, do all of this without getting crazed or isolated? What is our position on arms sales to Israel? What's our position on Israel generally? Why do we, as Jews, need a position on Israel – on another country's foreign and domestic policy? What is our relationship to the mainstream Jewish community? How do we look clearly at the strength we have, as a people, without worrying that they'll see us as running the world again?

These questions need to be answered by Jews talking with one another, developing political and emotional clarity and cohesion. And this requires Jewish space in which to piece together a deeply felt Jewish identity and perspective inch by inch from the various threads of tradition, literature, ritual, religion, culture, values, politics, language. Some of us will spend our lives building Jewish identity; others will draw on this work as a strong foundation from which to live our politics. Particularly for those of us who are not religiously observant, much confusion attends our grasping – through anti-Semitism and often prodded by anti-Semitism – for something beyond common danger. We need to figure out how to undo assimilation without being nostalgic or xenophobic: how to reach in and out at the same time.

## III. Guilt vs. Solidarity

Most feminist theory on identity was developed by women of color and focused on fighting racism.[16] I have come to think that had white women fully grasped the nature of this fight and *their own reasons for joining it*, they would now be grasping what Jewish women are trying to do. For the suspicion which greets a developing Jewish identity – from some Jews as well as gentiles – is only partly explained by anti-Semitism (the sense that Jewish identity *in particular* has no value) and by scarcity (the fear that focus on Jews will detract from other pressing issues). The way Jews have been met with 'not you too,' the way anti-Semitism becomes the one issue too many, suggest that many white women are angry and resistant to dealing with racism but are too frightened to express that anger openly;[17] suggest further how little our movement has taught us to see struggles against racism as life-giving, nourishing; as our own.

Most white women have learned, instead, guilt: to oppose racism because it's their – I am tempted to say christian – duty, for they seem to offer two models: the missionary and the crusader.

### Guilt: How Not To Build a Movement
If you join a struggle because you know your life depends on it – even if remotely: because you identify with the people, because people you love are involved – you have one attitude toward the people and their struggle.

But if you join because lucky you, you should help out those less fortunate – you have a different attitude: you consider those you deign to help pathetic victims. (It's no wonder Jews remain outside the paradigm, because Jews are pegged as overprivileged powerhouses: gentiles don't feel guilty about Jews.) The missionary in some way sees herself stooping to pick up the white woman's burden, a dangerous attitude, reeking of condescension, of failure to believe in the value or capacity of other people. Besides, 'the white man's burden' was a polite name for imperialism. I don't imagine that white women in the women's movement are the British Empire, but people who take this attitude are – at best – focused on themselves. They want that rosy do-gooder glow.

They can be harmless. And sometimes they *do* good. Guilt has prompted some white women to act against racism: white teachers who make sure to include books by Third World writers; white women with access to funds, grants, etc., who make sure that women of color get heard, solicited, funded. These acts are not negligible, whatever their motives. And though people acting from guilt may not be reliable allies, they will do in the short run. Sometimes they're all the allies there are.

The crusader, another sort of frail ally, plays on white guilt. She attacks white women whose racism has showed, isolating and shaming them. I have seen her in women's communities all over the US: in crisis centers, in print, in women's studies programs ... Sometimes, I confess, I have been her. And just as crusaders were supposed to gather souls but really killed, so the white knight, I have come to call her, destroys more than she saves.[18]

By doing so, she gains power in her own community – white women are afraid of her – and, besides, she is on to something. The white knight often does useful work: were this not true she would have no credibility – people aren't fools. But instead of enlarging the circle of women doing anti-racist work, fostering an atmosphere in which people believe they can change – by struggling compassionately with other white women (by communicating a vision of why one struggles) the white knight banishes most potential allies, leaving herself and a few others as the only decent white women in town.

Her power thus depends on racism, making her, in the end, no more reliable as an ally than the guilt-responsive missionary, since she has, objectively speaking, a stake in maintaining racism. She can, of course, function overtly as a christian knight and attack other christians who exhibit anti-Semitic behavior, etc.; but since the guilt quotient on Jewish issues is low, she's less likely to get response.

Sometimes acts inspired by guilt or fear of acting wrong have a positive impact. And, for the most cockamamie reasons, people land in situations from which they change and wisen. I did not take the D-train to Harlem when I was 17 with my present consciousness, yet I would not have developed my present consciousness without those formative experiences.

But guilt itself, as a motivating factor, is rooted in a way of thinking which does not promote change. Guilt asks: am I bad or am I good? guilty or innocent? racist or not? Very different from asking 'is this a racist *act*?' which allows me not to commit it, or to do the work that ensures I never commit it again. For in order to change you have to be willing to expose yourself – and observe and examine and understand. This takes time, patience, and a respect for process. Guilt prompts a longing to purge all impure impulses quickly, get it over and done with once and for all. Impulses which seem impure are not examined or transformed; they are stifled while you keep busy trying to act as though you have the right impulses.

We've all seen white women act like corpses around women of color, so afraid of doing the wrong thing: meaning, anything natural, treating a person like a person. For guilt is a freeze emotion: you can't think, you can't feel, you can only knee jerk. This is the infantilizing function of guilt: you lose faith in your own responses because the risk of their being wrong is more than you can handle.

In addition to militating against real change, guilt exercises an uneasy influence over the real difference in resources and options which women may enjoy, leading to downward mobility, pretending to have less, gleefully selecting the most oppressed possible identity: *office worker*, not *daughter of a lawyer and dropout from a prestigious college most office workers never get near (as students)*.

And why does someone embrace an identity of oppression? Because it's groovy? The insult of this must be apparent. Because she feels guilty about what she's got? Are money, power, privilege worthless resources to ignore, bury, pretend away? The insult of this ought to be apparent too.

And besides: behind the guilt, the desire to belong, be one with the people, etc., the resources remain, quietly drawn on or untouched by anyone, but ready to be picked up and used at some future date. So guilt helps people hoard what they've got, because they never come to terms with how to use resources productively.

The thing is: anyone who really wants to hoard her money, power and privilege sooner or later will. She can be targeted for guilt trips – to let go of some of what she wishes no one knew she had – but beneath the guilt had better be fear: fear of exposure, fear of conflict, so she'll stay in line and act right. And how does any sane person react after a while to fear, guilt? Is this a way to build a movement?

Nor can guilt mobilize those who don't feel guilty. Try telling a white working-class woman, for example, to fight racism because of how privileged she is. She may think racism is wrong and may be committed to fight it; she may also think that movement analyses of racism are ridiculous because she is not living the easy life her white skin is supposed to guarantee her. Whatever privilege she may have, she clings to – things are tough – but she hardly feels guilty. Only recognition of a common goal, the possibilities and – I want to say – the joys of solidarity will inspire women who don't feel guilty to join another struggle as their own.

## Solidarity: How To Build a Movement

Solidarity requires the bonding together of a people engaged in common struggle. But solidarity also means standing alongside another struggle, not because you feel guilty but because you recognize it as your own; it means using what you have on behalf of the struggle.

Angela Davis notes, for example, Prudence Crandall, a white woman who risked her life in defense of education for Black girls.[19] Or the strategy suggested by Maria Chapman Weston, a white leader of the Boston Female Anti-Slavery Society; when a white pro-slavery mob burst into a meeting chaired by Weston, she realized that the mob sought to isolate and perhaps violently attack the Black women in attendance, and thus insisted that each white woman leave the building with a Black woman at her side.[20] Or, at the world anti-slavery convention in London, at which the notorious decision was made to bar women from the floor, there were a few men who refused to join the floor but stood with the women in the gallery, silent. Among them was the Black abolitionist Charles Remond, and the white abolitionists William Lloyd Garrison and Nathaniel Rogers.[21] Black leader Frederick A. Douglass, too, at least initially supported the then-radical demand of women's suffrage and used his male privilege on behalf of the emerging women's rights movement.[22] Or, the women workers in the stockyards (mostly Irish and Poles) and in the garment industry (mostly Jews and Italians) who deliberately – and contrary to the practice of the AFL and most of their peers – sought to include and organize with Black women.[23] Or the Women's Trade Union League, upper middle-class college-educated white suffragists who worked in support of immigrant women's unions.[24] Or the Black and white college students – including many Jews – who went south to challenge segregation.

All these actions are examples of informed coalition work. None is a passive giving something up; they are all an aggressive wrapping of two peoples in a cloak only one has. These are acts which build trust between peoples.

But those who performed these acts which build and justify trust – I can't believe that they did not understand that these acts were *also* in defense of *their own freedom*, a freedom without which they, the actors, could not breathe.

*If I am only for myself, what am I?* Lonely. Hungry for sisters, comrades. Listen to the words of the fiery Grinkle sisters, white abolitionists who recognized 'the special bond, linking them with Black women who suffered the pain of slavery ... "They are our countrywomen – they are our sisters." '[25] Or the slogan displayed at the April '85 march in Paris to protest increasing violence against Jews and Arabs (many of whom are also Jews) and to protest increasing racist propaganda about purifying France for the French: *Ne touche pas à mon pote.* 'Keep your hands off my buddy.'

None of the passionless rhetoric which has come to dominate our movement's discussions of race, class. Obviously, if your friends, if your sisters are suffering you put everything you have into the struggle to free them *because you need their freedom as your own.*

Your privilege, insofar as it divides you from others, is *in your way*, unless you resolve how to use it for others, as well as for yourself. This is a non-guilt approach: drawing on what is best in people, not suppressing what is worst.

And let me say something which in this (christian) culture may come as a surprise: what is best in people is not self-abnegation. What is best in people is a sturdy connection between respect for the self and respect for the other: reaching in and out at the same time:

> *If I am not for myself, who will be?*
> *If I am only for myself, what am I?*

# IV. Some Strategies for Action

As we come into our Jewish identity, we feel somehow that to be justified in asserting it, in opposing anti-Semitism, we must be innocent victims, trying to make our oppression palpable to those who don't understand it. My beginning search for Jewish identity focused on the Holocaust and on the immigrant experience only partly because such a search must.

We need our history/herstory, and these are our handles, what we know. These are also all images of greater persecution than most American Jews are subject to today. As Jews, afraid of the myth of Jewish power; as (white?) feminists, guilty about our skin privilege, we are so hungry for innocence that images of oppression come almost as a relief. Innocence, even suffering, seems the only alternative to guilt.

But innocence has its price: while it relieves us of responsibility, it also denies us our strength. The assumption is: since we have been victims, we cannot ever be anything else. Witness Begin, involving the Holocaust to justify the invasion of Lebanon. *How could Jews be oppressive after all we've suffered?* From this perspective, class hostility, for example, has no basis in class distinctions but is only a front for Jewhating. We have to recognize that Jews are relatively well-off economically compared with most people of color in this country, as with the rural white poor; and that Jews endure about the same level of poverty as other ethnic groups who immigrated around the same time. Our job is to untangle class hostility from anti-Semitism, not to pretend the Jewish people still work in the sweatshop.

Non-Jews rely on this innocence too, including people of color. Witness how some excused Farrakhan's description of Hitler as a great German. Was it because support for Jackson's presidential candidacy transcended Jewish danger (which, given Jewish wealth and power, could not possibly be *real* danger)? Or was it because Farrakhan is

Black, and a cry of hatred against Jews carries no threat when the speaker is, by definition, powerless? (Need it be said that this is racist as well as anti-Semitic?) From this perspective, the fears of elderly Jews in racially mixed neighborhoods that they will be mugged and robbed are merely a front for racism, instead of reflecting the reality of urban violence: old people are marks, especially when living in communities no longer theirs. Our job here is to untangle concern for safety from racism, not to come up with justifications for mugging.

How this need for innocence translates politically is a disaster. The attitude that claims we – of any group – are essentially victims and so can't be charged with our behavior is destructive to all of us. If we can't do anything wrong, the fact is we can't do *anything* at all – and how in that state of powerlessness are we to build a vast movement sufficient to transform the exceedingly powerful state we live in? Defensive, protective of that dubious privilege of having our suffering acknowledged, we are at something of a standstill. Can't we look at each other and begin to see what we might build? Can't we extend towards each other so that we can draw on each other's strengths, learn to trust that we can use our power in positive ways?

## Working Alone/Working Together

True coalition is not a smattering of tokens. True coalition forms between groups; the premise is that each group has a strong base in a larger community. Thus Jews who want to work in coalition need not only to know who we are but to be bonded with other Jews.

For feminists, for lesbians, this presents its own complications. Some of us won't work with men. This is not a flawed choice. Some of us will have to be separatist – as Jews, as women, as lesbians, as whoever we are. Separatism gives strength, a base from which coalition is possible. Some of us – because of desire or need – will choose to be with our own. There are different forms of struggle, and separatists often are in the vanguard, creating a strong identity and consciousness for the whole community, including those who are not themselves separatist.

Those of us who choose to work in coalitions can assert that identity and consciousness to others. I know many Jewish women, myself among them, have participated in anti-racist, anti-apartheid, anti-intervention work, but not visibly as Jews. It is time we became visible as Jews, as some are doing.

Yet we need at the same time strategies for combatting anti-Semitism, for Jewish visibility fans the coals of indifference and passive contempt. An individual visible as a Jew simply attracts, like a magnet, all available anti-Jewish prejudice, or gets written off as an exception. And sometimes we even need strategies to ensure visibility. A Jew who travelled to Nicaragua recently tells of her attempts to be visible as a Jew to the Nicaraguan Press, attempts frustrated by her travel group's leader, whose job it was to inform the press about the group members and who kept 'forgetting' to mention the Jewish member. Just as women, as lesbians, need our own groups – for support and as bases for coalitions, a Jewish group travelling to Nicaragua might have had the desired impact, built Jewish pride *and* Jewish-Nicaraguan solidarity. To reach in and out at the same time.

The particular example of Nicaragua offers another possibility for solidarity and coalition. Progressive Jews have something in common with progressive Native Americans who oppose US intervention in Nicaragua, yet are concerned about the status of the Miskito Indians. We might learn from each other ways to express concern about our people without having this concern either used by the right or discredited by the left.

Again, focusing on Nicaragua, there is work to do in the Jewish community, to make sure the justified fear of anti-Semitism is not exploited by the US government, that Jews have access to the facts. There's a need for community education by strongly-identified Jews; there is also a need for honest discussion of liberation theology, of its potential for anti-Semitism (if the revolutionary impulse is christian, where does that leave us?), and of ways we can support the revolution without supporting an unexamined christianity.

## Fears

But there are fears. Mine are that non-Jews won't care about working with us. Who are *we* that they should bother? Our numbers so small, we are so disposable, a liability almost; dislike of us a point of unity among everyone else. And as women, as lesbians, as underemployed professionals or workers at traditional women's jobs, most of us don't even have money to contribute. Sometimes I am simply afraid that radical Jews are on the wrong side of history, trapped between self-respect, love for our people and culture and what we, politically, ideologically would support were it not tangled with Jewhating. I know I am not the only radical Jew whose stomach ties in knots reading the radical press or attending a rally.

Non-Jews, especially people of color, may fear that Jews will deny differences in experience, will aim for the great white American marshmallow of 'you're oppressed/I'm oppressed'.

No doubt on every side there is prejudice, ignorance and mistrust. I think of the Jew who uses the names Palestinian and Lebanese interchangeably, has not bothered to distinguish between the two peoples; the Arab who blames Leon Klinghoffer's death on 'the fact that the whole country of Palestine has been hijacked by the . . . Zionist Jews of Europe, America and elsewhere,' not only condoning the brutal death of an old man in a wheelchair, but also hiding – with the words 'and elsewhere' – the thousands of Jews forced to leave *their* homes in Arab countries.[26] The Jew who says 'We made it, why can't they?' or 'Who cares, they're all *goyim*!' The Black who says '*They* made it on my back.' The Chicana/o who says '*They're* all landlords.' There is work to do on all sides.

263

James Baldwin, in 1967, wrote: 'A genuinely candid confrontation between Negroes and American Jews would certainly prove of inestimable value. But the aspirations of the country are wretchedly middle-class and the middle class can never afford candor.'[27] A genuinely candid confrontation amongst all of us – a genuinely *specific* and candid confrontation – is much needed; and Baldwin is precise, as ever, in indicating that we must be prepared to go further than liberal acceptance, further than maneuvering for our own (larger) slice of the pie. The theme re-emerges: we must *want* equality, and we must grasp that equality does not coexist with class structure.

As a feminist and a Jew, I am asking women of color not to abandon us as we assert our Jewishness, not to hear this assertion as a lowered vigilance against racism.

And I am asking Jews not to withdraw into self-righteousness, not to insist that gentiles understand everything immediately, yesterday. We are not without dignity if we explain our issues. I am also asking Jews not to be so afraid of being trapped with other Jews – including, perhaps, some whose politics or attitudes offend us – that we forget that people can change, including our own people; including ourselves.

## Commonality

I am saying there have got to be many points of unity among us. Even in my fear that non-Jews won't care because we are a small – useless – minority I find a connection – with Native Americans who express the same fear, of irrelevance; and another similar fear, genocide – historical and cultural. And I see difference: the grinding poverty in which most Native American people live.

And in my recognition that Jews are better off economically than most people of color, I find connection with some Asian Americans, not the recent immigrants, from Southeast Asia, who tend to be very poor, but with many Japanese Americans. Looking specifically at the situation of Japanese Americans I see a people also traumatized by events of the past 40 years – internment in camps; the atomic bombs dropped on civilian cities of Hiroshima and Nagasaki; a fear of cultural loss and assimilation; and continued economic discrimination, despite their apparent integration into professional and business life. And I see differences: Japanese – and other Asian-Americans – pressed into the sciences, engineering, computers, pushed away from the humanities, the arts, where much Jewish talent has been channeled.[28]

I could go on. And if I am doing my work, I *will* go on, understanding the ways in which Jewish history and experience are like and unlike the experience of other groups, the ways in which the light skin of some Jews has and has not protected them, the issues *as defined by Jews* and the issues *as defined by other groups*.

We might then, as Jews, offer support to Japanese Americans seeking restitution from the US government for their internment and confiscation of property during World War II, and to those still fighting their convictions for refusing to report for 'relocation.'

We might express – in unison with Japanese American women – our disgust at the stereotype and acronym JAP – a racist name for Japanese people as well as a sexist scapegoating of Jewish middle-class women for the crimes of capitalism.

We might, as Jews, press our religious and community institutions to offer sanctuary to refugees, from El Salvador and other countries, as some are doing, recognizing our own history as refugees. We might, as Jews, support attempts of women garment workers – jobs once held by Jewish and Italian women – to organize for better conditions and pay. We might support bilingual efforts of Chicana, Latina and Francophone communities, grasping through our own linguistic losses the importance of retaining one's language.

We might decide that even in the midst of vitriolic disagreement about peace in the Middle East, we must never accept or leave unchallenged instances of racism against Arabs, remembering our own history of prejudice and stereotypes.

We might even, as Jews, offer support to people whose struggles and issues are different from ours now and in the past simply because we care about justice; because we know that while nothing guarantees allies, callousness guarantees callousness.

Of late, there are positive instances of coalition. An event in NYC of Jews and Latinas/os (including some who are both) reading and performing their work, much of which is bilingual (Spring, 1984). Prior to several of Farrakhan's most recent appearances, coalitions of Black and Jewish leaders joined to denounce him. (In Baltimore, the same group joined to condemn Kahane prior to his appearance there.)[29] In the feminist movement, a Jewish-Arab-Black coalition which prepared for the International Women's Conference at Nairobi has been speaking about this gathering, including information on Jewish-Palestinian dialogue.[30] A workshop for Black-Jewish dialogue was offered at the 1986 Women and the Law conference for the second year. It seems that many of us may have learned something from drawing close to the precipice of total withdrawal and isolation.

If we could start working together *before* we trust, understand, or like each other, we might learn to. Black activist and performer Bernice Reagon says we are stumbling because we have to take the next step.[31] We have gotten entirely too theoretical about these issues, expecting that with words, with ideas, we can work it all out in advance. Perhaps we need to engage, even in uncertainty, and work out issues as they arise. Maulana Karenga, a theorist for the Black movement, has pointed out that a coalition on a specific issue does not create reliable allies: he is critical of what he calls the reliance of middle-class Black movement leaders on alliances with Jews.[32]

But the positive side to Karenga's depressing analysis is that you don't need to be reliable allies to form a coalition. Having formed one, it may be possible to overcome mistrust and establish a larger common ground. It is impossible to do this without some concrete basis of unity, and focusing on the task at hand can help reveal commonality.

The problem is not a lack of common issues, not a lack of desperate need. The problem for us, as Jews, is that we are often afraid, afraid to gather with other Jews, afraid to be visibly Jewish, afraid – too often with reason – to know the extent of anti-Semitism in our comrades, neighbors, co-workers, friends. We are afraid of being or of seeming racist; afraid of our own ignorance of Jewish culture and tradition.

And because, as radicals, we have been taught to see dignity in resistance, in the struggle against oppression, we must remember not to idealize oppression, but to respect the struggles Jews have waged on behalf of their children, who are, sometimes, us. We must remember: what is beautiful is the resistance, and that people can – and must – resist from their own authentic place in the world.

This means we must reach out to Israelis fighting for peace, civil rights, and feminism without secretly feeling the Palestinians are more beautiful, because apparently more besieged. One of the hardest acts of self-love for American radical Jews is to identify in this way with Israelis, and I have come to believe it is a crucial stretch, for the alternative is denial of the Jewish connection. It is from this solid, self-knowing place that we can work towards peace and justice in the Middle East.

It is also from this place of valuing resistance that we are able to reach out to those in the Jewish community who have themselves been fighters for justice, or supporters of this fight, to ask them to continue this tradition; to ask them for what is best in themselves too.

Last Rosh Hashonah I stood with my friend Mitzi Lichtman at the edge of the Atlantic performing (in our own way) the ancient ritual of *tashlekh* – casting our sins into the water, in the form of stones. And among all the sins we hurled into the ocean, the sin of self-hate and the sin of failing to feel compassion for others mingled, as indeed they should, for they are the same sin.

And Hillel had a third question: *If not now, when?*

Portions of this essay were first developed as talks given in Mankato and Minneapolis, MN, on 'Anti-Semitism, Racism, and Coalitions' (1984); a workshop given at the 1985 Women & the Law Conference on 'Dealing with Racism as Jewish Women'; and as a review of *Yours In Struggle* which appeared in *off our backs* (October 1985). I thank the women who attended these events and talked with me about these issues. Much of the essay was also developed in conversation with Irena Klepfisz. I thank Linda Vance for her critical acumen, generous editorial attention, humor and patience. Responsibility for the opinions and analysis is mine alone.

# Notes

1. The Harlem Education Project (HEP) was a branch of the Northern Student Movement (NSM), founded in New Haven as the northern arm of the Student Non-Violent Coordinating Committee (SNCC), the most militant of the southern civil rights activist organizations.
2. The anti-rat campaign consisted of a number of young Black people armed with rifles very visibly hunting rats in Harlem apartment buildings. The sluggish city health department responded immediately to combat the rats.
3. The National Women's Studies Association, pressed by angry Jewish women, agreed to mention opposition 'to anti-Semitism against Arabs and Jews.' Since hatred and discrimination against Arabs are regularly included by the term 'racism' – and since, oddly enough, these same phenomena directed against Jews are often excluded – I wonder why Jews are not allowed to use 'anti-Semitism' to mean anti-Jewish racism, its historic meaning.
4. I have heard this a number of times from women who attended conference planning sessions.
5. Cynthia Kern deserves particular credit for her work. Let me mention that these Jewish events were mostly open to gentiles but were attended almost exclusively by Jews.
6. Flyer for *Not In Our Name*/Women's Resistance Action, Boston Office. See exchange of letters – a critical letter by me and Mitzi Lichtman, and a self-critical response by several *Not In Our Name* women – in *Gay Community News* (17 November 1984).
7. *Heresies.*
8. For a discussion of the queuing effect, see Stanley Lieberson, *A Piece of the Pie: Blacks and White Immigrants Since 1880* (Berkeley, Univ. of Calif., 1980), pp. 296-326; 377-81.
9. See my earlier discussion, 'Anti-Semitism, Homophobia, and the Good White Knight,' *off our backs* (May 1982).
10. Cf. Black activist Bernice Johnson Reagon, on the *discomfort* of working in coalitions: '[Coalition is] a monster. It never gets enough. It always wants more. So you better be sure you got your home someplace for you to go to so that you will not become a martyr to the coalition.' See Reagon's fine discussion, 'Coalition Politics: Turning the Century,' *Home Girls*, ed. Barbara Smith (NY: Kitchen Table/Women of Color Press, 1983), p. 361.
11. The felicitous wording is Linda Vance's.
12. Elly Bulkin, Appendix to 'Hard Ground: Jewish Identity, Racism, and Anti-Semitism,' *Yours In Struggle* (Brooklyn: Long Haul Press, 1984), pp. 194-98. See Bernice Mennis' review, below; also, my review in *off our backs* (October 1985).
13. Adrienne Rich, speaking at the NJA Convention, added another question – 'If not with others, how?' – showing a peculiar failure to note that Hillel's second question already confronts the need for coalition. Her question also places the burden on Jews, as if *we* have refused to work in alliance with Gentiles, whereas in fact the opposite has often been true. The history of Jews engaged in political activity hardly suggests a people unwilling to work with others; what this history reveals, rather, is *erasure* of Jewish

participation, Jews drummed out of movements by anti-Semitism, as well as substantial Jewish contributions to revolutionary activity. See, for example, Elinor Lerner, 'Jewish Involvement in the New York City Woman Suffrage Movement,' *American Jewish History*, LXX (1981), 442-61.

14. See below for Susie Gaynes' moving statement about recognizing how some Jewish women were made to feel unwelcome by just such a reluctance.

15. In this discussion I am drawing heavily on Irena Klepfisz, 'When Jewish Women Disagree,' unpublished (1983).

16. For an early clear statement of identity politics, see the Combahee River Collective, 'A Black Feminist Statement,' reprinted in *Capitalist Patriarchy and the Case for Socialist Feminism*, ed. Zillah R. Eisenstein (NY: Monthly Review Press, 1979).

17. See Susanna Sturgis' analysis of feminist resistance to dealing with fat oppression, 'Is this the new thing I'm going to have to be p c about?' *Sinister Wisdom* 28 (1985).

18. See Kaye/Kantrowitz, '. . . the Good White Knight.'

19. Angela Davis, *Women, Race & Class* (NY: Random House, 1981), pp. 34 ff.

20. Davis, p. 38.

21. Davis, p. 48.

22. Davis, pp. 50 ff.

23. See Eleanor Flexner, *Century of Struggle: A History of the Women's Rights Movement in the US* (Cambridge, MA: Belknap/Harvard Univ., 1978). But also see Rosalyn Terborg-Penn, 'Survival strategies among African-American women workers: A continuing process,' *Women, Work & Protest: A Century of US Women's Labor History*, ed. Ruth Milkman (Boston: Routledge & Kegan Paul, 1985). Terborg-Penn cites the occasional interest of mostly white CIO Unions in organizing with Black women, but the more common lack of interest.

24. Nancy Schrom Dye, *As Equals As Sisters: Feminism, The Labor Movement and The Women's Trade Union League of New York* (Columbia: Univ. of Missouri Press, 1980), p. 93.

25. Quoted in Davis, p. 44.

26. M.T. Mehdi, letter, *NY Times* (17 October 1985).

27. James Baldwin, 'Negroes Are Anti-Semitic Because They're Anti-White,' 1st pub. *NY Times Magazine* (1967); reprinted in *Black Anti-Semitism and Jewish Racism* (NY: Schocken, 1972), p. 11.

28. See Prof. Ronald Takaki's remarks, quoted in the *NY Times* (4 September 1985).

29. See Earl Raab, 'Poisoned Good: Understanding the Farrakhan Factor,' *Moment*, vol. 11, no. 2 (Jan.-Feb. 1986), pp. 13-17.

30. The dialogue was organized by New Jewish Agenda.

31. Reagon, p. 368.

32. Maulana Karenga, 'The Crisis of Black Middle-Class Leadership: A Critical Analysis,' *The Black Scholar* (Fall '82), pp. 16-32.

# Age, Race, Class, and Sex: Women Redefining Difference[1]

Audre Lorde

Much of western European history conditions us to see human differences in simplistic opposition to each other: dominant/subordinate, good/bad, up/down, superior/inferior. In a society where the good is defined in terms of profit rather than in terms of human need, there must always be some group of people who, through systematized oppression, can be made to feel surplus, to occupy the place of the dehumanized inferior. Within this society, that group is made up of Black and Third World people, working-class people, older people, and women.

As a forty-nine-year-old Black lesbian feminist socialist mother of two, including one boy, and a member of an inter-racial couple, I usually find myself a part of some group defined as other, deviant, inferior, or just plain wrong. Traditionally, in american society, it is the members of oppressed, objectified groups who are expected to stretch out and bridge the gap between the actualities of our lives and the consciousness of our oppressor. For in order to survive, those of us for whom oppression is as american as apple pie have always had to be watchers, to become familiar with the language and manners of the oppressor, even sometimes adopting them for some illusion of protection. Whenever the need for some pretense of communication arises, those who profit from our oppression call upon us to share our knowledge with them. In other words, it is the responsibility of the oppressed to teach the oppressors their mistakes. I am responsible for educating teachers who dismiss my children's culture in school. Black and Third World people are expected to educate white people as to our humanity. Women are expected to educate men. Lesbians and gay men are expected to educate the heterosexual world. The oppressors maintain their position and evade responsibility for their own actions. There is a constant drain of energy which might be better used in redefining ourselves and devising realistic scenarios for altering the present and constructing the future.

Institutionalized rejection of difference is an absolute necessity in a profit economy which needs outsiders as surplus people. As members of such an economy, we have *all* been programmed to respond to the human differences between us with fear and loathing and to handle that difference in one of three ways: ignore it, and if that it not possible, copy it if we think it is dominant, or destroy it if we think it is subordinate. But we have no patterns for relating across our human differences as equals. As a result, those differences have been misnamed and misused in the service of separation and confusion.

Certainly there are very real differences between us of race, age, and sex. But it is not those differences between us that are separating us. It is rather our refusal to recognize those differences, and to examine the distortions which result from our misnaming them and their effects upon human behavior and expectation.

*Racism, the belief in the inherent superiority of one race over all others and thereby the right to dominance. Sexism, the belief in the inherent superiority of one sex over the other and thereby the right to dominance. Ageism. Heterosexism. Elitism. Classism.*

It is a lifetime pursuit for each one of us to extract these distortions from our living at the same time as we recognize, reclaim, and define those differences upon which they are imposed. For we have all been raised in a society where those distortions were endemic within our living. Too often, we pour the energy needed for recognizing and exploring difference into pretending those differences are insurmountable barriers, or that they do not exist at all. This results in a voluntary isolation, or false and treacherous connections. Either way, we do not develop tools for using human difference as a springboard for creative change within our lives. We speak not of human difference, but of human deviance.

Somewhere, on the edge of consciousness, there is what I call a *mythical norm*, which each one of us within our hearts knows 'that is not me.' In america, this norm is usually defined as white, thin, male, young, heterosexual, christian, and financially secure. It is with this mythical norm that the trappings of power reside within this society. Those of us who stand outside that power often identify one way in which we are different, and we assume that to be the primary cause of all oppression, forgetting other distortions around difference, some of which we ourselves may be practising. By and large within the women's movement today, white women focus upon their oppression as women and ignore differences of race, sexual preference, class, and age. There is a pretense to a homogeneity of experience covered by the word *sisterhood* that does not in fact exist.

Unacknowledged class differences rob women of each other's energy and creative insight. Recently a women's magazine collective made the decision for one issue to print only prose, saying poetry was a less 'rigorous' or 'serious' art form. Yet even the form our creativity takes is often a class issue. Of all the art forms, poetry is the most economical. It is the one which is the most secret, which requires the least physical labor, the least material, and the one which can be done between shifts, in the hospital pantry, on the subway, and on scraps of surplus paper. Over the last few years, writing a novel on tight finances, I came to appreciate the enormous differences in the material demands between poetry and prose. As we reclaim our literature, poetry has been the major voice of poor, working class, and Colored women. A room of one's own may be a necessity for writing prose, but so are reams of paper, a typewriter, and plenty of time. The actual requirements to produce the visual arts also help determine, along class lines, whose art is whose. In this day

270

of inflated prices for material, who are our sculptors, our painters, our photographers? When we speak of a broadly based women's culture, we need to be aware of the effect of class and economic differences on the supplies available for producing art.

As we move toward creating a society within which we can each flourish, ageism is another distortion of relationship which interferes without vision. By ignoring the past, we are encouraged to repeat its mistakes. The 'generation gap' is an important social tool for any repressive society. If the younger members of a community view the older members as contemptible or suspect or excess, they will never be able to join hands and examine the living memories of the community, nor ask the all important question, 'Why?' This gives rise to a historical amnesia that keeps us working to invent the wheel every time we have to go to the store for bread.

We find ourselves having to repeat and relearn the same old lessons over and over that our mothers did because we do not pass on what we have learned, or because we are unable to listen. For instance, how many times has this all been said before? For another, who would have believed that once again our daughters are allowing their bodies to be hampered and purgatoried by girdles and high heels and hobble skirts?

Ignoring the differences of race between women and the implications of those differences presents the most serious threat to the mobilization of women's joint power.

As white women ignore their built-in privilege of whiteness and define *woman* in terms of their own experience alone, then women of Color become 'other,' the outsider whose experience and tradition is too 'alien' to comprehend. An example of this is the signal absence of the experience of women of Color as a resource for women's studies courses. The literature of women of Color is seldom included in women's literature courses and almost never in other literature courses, nor in women's studies as a whole. All too often, the excuse given is that the literatures of women of Color can only be taught by Colored women, or that they are too difficult to understand, or that classes cannot 'get into' them because they come out of experiences that are 'too different.' I have heard this argument presented by white women of otherwise quite clear intelligence, women who seem to have no trouble at all teaching and reviewing work that comes out of the vastly different experiences of Shakespeare, Molière, Dostoyefsky, and Aristophanes. Surely there must be some other explanation.

This is a very complex question, but I believe one of the reasons white women have such difficulty reading Black women's work is because of their reluctance to see Black women as women and different from themselves. To examine Black women's literature effectively requires that we be seen as whole people in our actual complexities – as individuals, as women, as human – rather than as one of those problematic but familiar stereotypes provided in this society in place of genuine images of Black women. And I believe this holds true for the literatures of other women of Color who are not Black.

The literatures of all women of Color recreate the textures of our lives, and many white women are heavily invested in ignoring the real differences. For as long as any difference between us means one of us must be inferior, then the recognition of any difference must be fraught with guilt. To allow women of Color to step out of stereotypes is too guilt provoking, for it threatens the complacency of those women who view oppression only in terms of sex.

Refusing to recognize difference makes it impossible to see the different problems and pitfalls facing us as women.

Thus, in a patriarchal power system where whiteskin privilege is a major prop, the entrapments used to neutralize Black women and white women are not the same. For example, it is easy for Black women to be used by the power structure against Black men, not because they are men, but because they are Black. Therefore, for Black women, it is necessary at all times to separate the needs of the oppressor from our own legitimate conflicts within our communities. This same problem does not exist for white women. Black women and men have shared racist oppression and still share it, although in different ways. Out of that shared oppression we have developed joint defenses and joint vulnerabilities to each other that are not duplicated in the white community, with the exception of the relationship between Jewish women and Jewish men.

On the other hand, white women face the pitfall of being seduced into joining the oppressor under the pretense of sharing power. This possibility does not exist in the same way for women of Color. The tokenism that is sometimes extended to us is not an invitation to join power; our racial 'otherness' is a visible reality that makes that quite clear. For white women there is a wider range of pretended choices and rewards for identifying with patriarchal power and its tools.

Today, with the defeat of ERA, the tightening economy, and increased conservatism, it is easier once again for white women to believe the dangerous fantasy that if you are good enough, pretty enough, sweet enough, quiet enough, teach the children to behave, hate the right people, and marry the right men, then you will be allowed to co-exist with patriarchy in relative peace, at least until a man needs your job or the neighborhood rapist happens along. And true, unless one lives and loves in the trenches it is difficult to remember that the war against dehumanization is ceaseless.

But Black women and our children know the fabric of our lives is stitched with violence and with hatred, that there is no rest. We do not deal with it only on the picket lines, or in dark midnight alleys, or in the places where we dare to verbalize our resistance. For us, increasingly, violence weaves through the daily tissues of our living — in the supermarket, in the classroom, in the elevator, in the clinic and the schoolyard, from the plumber, the baker, the saleswoman, the bus driver, the bank teller, the waitress who does not serve us.

272

Some problems we share as women, some we do not. You fear your children will grow up to join the patriarchy and testify against you, we fear our children will be dragged from a car and shot down in the street, and you will turn your backs upon the reasons they are dying.

The threat of difference has been no less blinding to people of Color. Those of us who are Black must see that the reality of our lives and our struggle does not make us immune to the errors of ignoring and misnaming difference. Within Black communities where racism is a living reality, differences among us often seem dangerous and suspect. The need for unity is often misnamed as a need for homogeneity, and a Black feminist vision mistaken for betrayal of our common interests as a people. Because of the continuous battle against racial erasure that Black women and Black men share, some Black women still refuse to recognize that we are also oppressed as women, and that sexual hostility against Black women is practiced not only by the white racist society, but implemented within our Black communities as well. It is a disease striking the heart of Black nationhood, and silence will not make it disappear. Exacerbated by racism and the pressures of powerlessness, violence against Black women and children often becomes a standard within our communities, one by which manliness can be measured. But these women-hating acts are rarely discussed as crimes against Black women.

As a group, women of Color are the lowest paid wage earners in america. We are the primary targets of abortion and sterilization abuse, here and abroad. In certain parts of Africa, small girls are still being sewed shut between their legs to keep them docile and for men's pleasure. This is known as female circumcision, and it is not a cultural affair as the late Jomo Kenyatta insisted, it is a crime against Black women.

Black women's literature is full of the pain of frequent assault, not only by a racist patriarchy, but also by Black men. Yet the necessity for and history of shared battle have made us, Black women, particularly vulnerable to the false accusation that anti-sexist is anti-Black. Meanwhile, womanhating as a recourse of the powerless is sapping strength from Black communities, and our very lives. Rape is on the increase, reported and unreported, and rape is not aggressive sexuality, it is sexualized aggression. As Kalamu ya Salaam, a Black male writer points out, 'As long as male domination exists, rape will exist. Only women revolting and men made conscious of their responsibility to fight sexism can collectively stop rape.'[2]

Differences between ourselves as Black women are also being misnamed and used to separate us from one another. As a Black lesbian feminist comfortable with the many different ingredients of my identity, and a woman committed to racial and sexual freedom from oppression, I find I am constantly being encouraged to pluck out some one aspect of myself and present this as the meaningful whole, eclipsing or denying the other parts of self. But this is a destructive and fragmenting way to live. My fullest concentration of energy is available to me only when I integrate all the parts of who I am, openly, allowing power from particular sources of my living to flow back and forth freely through all my different selves, without the restrictions of externally imposed definition. Only then can I bring myself and my energies as a whole to the service of those struggles which I embrace as part of my living.

A fear of lesbians, or of being accused of being a lesbian, has led many Black women into testifying against themselves. It has led some of us into destructive alliances, and others into despair and isolation. In the white women's communities, heterosexism is sometimes a result of identifying with the white patriarchy, a rejection of that interdependence between women-identified women which allows the self to be, rather than to be used in the service of men. Sometimes it reflects a die-hard belief in the protective coloration of heterosexual relationships, sometimes a self-hate which all women have to fight against, taught us from birth.

Although elements of these attitudes exist for all women, there are particular resonances of heterosexism and homophobia among Black women. Despite the fact that woman-bonding has a long and honorable history in the African and African-american communities, and despite the knowledge and accomplishments of many strong and creative women-identified Black women in the political, social and cultural fields, heterosexual Black women often tend to ignore or discount the existence and work of Black lesbians. Part of this attitude has come from an understandable terror of Black male attack within the close confines of Black society, where the punishment for any female self-assertion is still to be accused of being a lesbian and therefore unworthy of the attention or support of the scarce Black male. But part of this need to misname and ignore Black lesbians comes from a very real fear that openly women-identified Black women who are no longer dependent upon men for their self-definition may well reorder our whole concept of social relationships.

Black women who once insisted that lesbianism was a white woman's problem now insist that Black lesbians are a threat to Black nationhood, are consorting with the enemy, are basically un-Black. These accusations, coming from the very women to whom we look for deep and real understanding, have served to keep many Black lesbians in hiding, caught between the racism of white women and the homophobia of their sisters. Often, their work has been ignored, trivialized, or misnamed, as with the work of Angelina Grimke, Alice Dunbar-Nelson, Lorraine Hansberry. Yet women-bonded women have always been some part of the power of Black communities, from our unmarried aunts to the amazons of Dahomey.

And it is certainly not Black lesbians who are assaulting women and raping children and grandmothers on the streets of our communities.

Across this country, as in Boston during the spring of 1979 following the unsolved murders of twelve Black women, Black lesbians are spearheading movements against violence against Black women.

What are the particular details within each of our lives that can be scrutinized and altered to help bring about change? How do we redefine difference for all women? It is not our differences which separate women, but our reluctance to recognize those differences and to deal effectively with the distortions which have resulted from the ignoring and misnaming of those differences.

As a tool of social control, women have been encouraged to recognize only one area of human difference as legitimate, those differences which exist between women and men. And we have learned to deal across those differences with the urgency of all oppressed subordinates. All of us have had to learn to live or work or coexist with men, from our fathers on. We have recognized and negotiated these differences, even when this recognition only continued the old dominant/subordinate mode of human relationship, where the oppressed must recognize the masters' difference in order to survive.

But our future survival is predicated upon our ability to relate within equality. As women, we must root out internalized patterns of oppression within ourselves if we are to move beyond the most superficial aspects of social change. Now we must recognize differences among women who are our equals, neither inferior nor superior, and devise ways to use each other's difference to enrich our visions and our joint struggles.

The future of our earth may depend upon the ability of all women to identify and develop new definitions of power and new patterns of relating across difference. The old definitions have not served us, nor the earth that supports us. The old patterns, no matter how cleverly rearranged to imitate progress, still condemn us to cosmetically altered repetitions of the same old exchanges, the same old guilt, hatred, recrimination, lamentation, and suspicion.

For we have, built into all of us, old blueprints of expectation and response, old structures of oppression, and these must be altered at the same time as we alter the living conditions which are a result of those structures. For the master's tools will never dismantle the master's house.

As Paulo Freire shows so well in *The Pedagogy of the Oppressed*,[3] the true focus of revolutionary change is never merely the oppressive situations which we seek to escape, but that piece of the oppressor which is planted deep within each of us, and which knows only the oppressors' tactics, the oppressors' relationships.

Change means growth, and growth can be painful. But we sharpen self-definition by exposing the self in work and struggle together with those whom we define as different from ourselves, although sharing the same goals. For Black and white, old and young, lesbian and heterosexual women alike, this can mean new paths to our survival.

> *We have chosen each other*
> *and the edge of each others battles*
> *the war is the same*
> *if we lose*
> *someday women's blood will congeal*

upon a dead planet
if we win
there is no telling
we seek beyond history
for a new and more possible meeting.[4]

## Notes

1.  This paper was delivered at the Copeland Colloquium, Amherst Col-
    lege, April 1980.
2.  From 'Rape: A Radical Analysis, An African-American Perspective' by
    Kalamu.
3.  Seabury Press, New York, 1970.
4.  From 'Outlines,' unpublished poem.

# Rage and Desire: Confronting Pornography

Pratibha Parmar

Since the publication in 1981 of *Pornography: Men Possessing Women*
by Andrea Dworkin, feminists, most notably in North America, have
been waging passionate battles and forging new political alliances around
the question of pornography and censorship.[1] Feminists in Britain have
been slower to take on these issues but there is no doubt that the zealous
fervour so predominant in this most recent wave of feminist activity and
debate has wafted across the Atlantic to Britain. This is not to say that
discussions around such issues are a new phenomenon here.

For instance, public debates around issues of sexuality, pornography,
prostitution and birth control have a political history in nineteenth-
century Britain. The work of feminist historians such as Judith Walkowitz
has shown that there has been a history of tension between feminists
involved in the campaign to repeal the Contagious Diseases Acts of
1866 and 1869 and the social purists who too were engaged in the same
campaign for reasons of morality rather than because such acts aimed to
control women's sexuality.[2] The alliances that some feminists made with
such moralists finally led to a further erosion of women's rights and as
Varda Burstyn cautions: 'With the clarity of hindsight we can now see
that many of the early feminists made a number of major errors in their
campaigns on sexual issues, errors that hurt the women's movement as a
whole and undermined its ability to fight for women on other fronts.[3]

One of the characteristics of debates on pornography has been a tendency to make universal generalisations about male power and sexual subjugation. Judging from the books and articles in various magazines that have been published in Britain in the last few years it is clear that it is not only the rhetoric, language and theories of the anti-pornography lobby led by Dworkin that are being adopted almost wholesale, but also that their strategies calling for censorship are being aped. Political critiques of pornography have so far been dominated by feminists who see all men as the perpetrators/collaborators in pornography and all women as their victims.

Debates around pornography and censorship raise complex issues which have significant implications for our daily lives and it is important that we attempt a refinement in the language and concepts we use in our understanding of these issues. It is precisely the particular use of language and the rhetoric of the anti-pornography lobby which is disturbing and which I think reveals their contradictions. It is a language which allows a slide into confusing what the multiple causes and forms of women's oppression are on to a single focus on one manifestation of their oppression.

For example, in the conclusion of her book *Pornography: Men Possessing Women*, Dworkin argues: 'We will know that we are free when the pornography no longer exists. As long as it does exist, we must understand that we are the women in it: used by the same power, subject to the same valuation, as the vile whores who beg for more.'[4]

Fear, rage and frustration are raw emotions which many of the anti-pornography theorists use to incite women to act out of a politics of outrage and anger. This in itself is not necessarily a bad thing. After all, the initial energy of the contemporary Women's Liberation Movements in the west came precisely from such passionate feelings of righteous anger at women's oppression. But the political landscape of the mid 1980s is a bleak one, where repression is a fundamental part of many people's daily lives and anger alone will not bring about the fundamental economic and political changes that are so necessary. Thatcherite Britain is divided dramatically between races, classes and communities. Severe economic pressure and cuts in the health services have greatly reduced many people's access to basic social services. The gap between those housed, fed and in employment and those without any of these basic survival tools has dramatically increased. The rise in racist murders and killings goes unabated. Racist discourses around the origins of AIDS in Africa has been used as a way of justifying stricter immigration controls and increased harassment of Black visitors to Britain.

Women too have been a target of the current backlash. For example, the Alton Bill has attempted to erode what rights women have left to access to legal abortions. All the gains that women have made in the last few decades are slowly being chiselled away not only through legislation but also by the virulent ideology of the moral right.

277

Poverty, racism, violence against women and children have become very much a part of Britain in the 1980s. Increased police powers mean an increase in state control over people's movements and basic rights. The last few years have also seen a dramatic moral and political backlash against the lesbian and gay communities as a direct result of the fear and panic created around AIDS. The media, the government and right-wing forces have not wasted any time. Existing anti-gay prejudices have been mobilised to orchestrate a systematic attack on the lesbian and gay communities. An example of this is the furore caused by a library book, *Jenny Lives with Eric and Martin* – an educational tool to show that gay men too can be parents and live as a family, available under parental control in libraries in Haringey in London: there, local and national right-wing groups joined forces, organised public book burnings, and carried placards which said AIDS = Gays = Death.

The Education Minister ordered the Inner London Education Authority to ban the book because he claimed to 'speak up for parents who want school libraries to contain the best of our children's literature and to emphasise that a normal moral framework is the bedrock of the family'.

The Parents' Rights Group led the main opposition against Haringey Council's progressive policies on lesbians and gays. Leaflets opposing the policy were published by 'Concerned Parents and Citizens of Haringey' in association with 'The New Patriotic Movement'. The latter has been revealed as a far-right group with links to the Moonie World Unification Church. In June 1987, during the General election, Betty Sheridan, a founder member of the Parents' Rights Group, appeared in national newspaper advertisements that said: 'My name is Betty Sheridan. I live in Haringey. I'm married with two children. *And I'm scared.* If you vote Labour they'll go on teaching my kids about Gays & Lesbians instead of giving them proper lessons.' The ads were financed by The Committee for a Free Britain who share an address with the Moonie Unification Church.[5]

The role that the media played in abetting this climate of moral backlash was paramount. The *Sunday Mirror* (26.10.86) interviewed the head of Scotland Yard's Obscene Publications Squad who proclaimed that such books were 'a source for sexual perverts to further their interests'.

The *Daily Telegraph*, an equally right-wing paper defended the censorship of *Jenny Lives with Eric and Martin* and used this as a springboard for a warning of 'the dangers of active, aggressive homosexual proselytising, in which a number of evil people have declared war on marriage and the family'.

The political tensions such a situation created were capitalised on by Mr Wiltshire, Tory MP, who proposed an amendment clause to the 1986 Local Government Bill. Clause 28 would make it illegal for local councils to finance anyone or anything which would 'promote homosexuality' (including publications) or promote the teaching in schools of the acceptability of homosexuality as a 'pretended family relationship' (including publications).

The implications of this clause are worse than horrific: in the area of cultural activity there would be a total ban on any images of lesbians and gay men, any films, videos or photographs that may have been funded directly or indirectly by progressive local councils. It is only in the last five years that there has been a visible growth in lesbian and gay groups, centres, literature and visual materials – all of which has helped enormously to put homosexuality on the political agenda of local government. This has been despite the retrenchment of Thatcherism and largely due to the pressure lesbian and gay activists have put on local Labour councils who have adopted an equal opportunities policy towards issues of homosexuality. So much so that Thatcher's last election campaign focused much energy on discrediting Labour councils for their support of lesbian and gay issues. They issued posters including one with the words: 'Young, gay and proud', 'Policing Classrooms' and 'Sex education taught in schools' and a billboard with the title of a book by an American writer: BLACK LESBIAN IN WHITE AMERICA – plus the words: 'DO YOU WANT YOUR CHILD TO RECEIVE AN EDUCATION LIKE THIS' (VOTE CONSERVATIVE). We were left in no doubt of the Tory Party's not so hidden agenda of eroding any of the progressive policies fought for by the lesbian and gay communities.

In outlining the political landscape of Britain in recent years, my intention is to show that unless we are mindful of the moral backlash around the area of sexual politics and the climate of fear and prejudice, there is every danger that calls for censorship of pornography will coalesce with similar demands coming from the new moral right.

## The language of pornography

Most pornography is about the public depiction of sexual imagery of women which is created, controlled and consumed by men; it is one manifestation of women's oppression but it is not the only one, nor is it *the exclusive* cause of our oppression, as is argued by Dworkin and other anti-pornography supporters. I want to pose several challenges to the contention that pornography plays a major role in the general oppression of women. The prior agenda of such political conclusions is one which is familiar and even may be obvious, but nevertheless it needs to be restated. It is an agenda which sees women as a class oppressed first and foremost by a universal patriarchy unmediated by race, economic class or history. It constructs women as victims, forever silenced and objectified, by a monolithic category of men who become 'them' – an undefined entity, devoid of differences of class, race or access to power. 'All are collapsed into a false unity, the brotherhood of the oppressors, the sisterhood of the victims.'[6]

279

But again this sisterhood of all women assumes that there are no significant differences between women compared to the similarities of our experiences of pornography. I find such analysis both eurocentric and nationalist. It is also insulting in its simplicity. Feminism has a long history of divisions created out of an inability to deal with differences of race, class and sexuality. It is precisely this refusal to recognise the differences amongst us, as well as addressing all theories and campaigns from a supposedly unified female experience that prompted many Black women to organise autonomously in the early 1980s. Central to our experience in Britain has been the racism of the state and this was reflected in our campaigns: for example, against immigration controls, against sub-standard education for Black children, against police brutality, against forced vaginal examinations of Asian women and forced sterilisation. Black women have been at the forefront of initiating analysis and action around the racism within the women's movement and have challenged much of the 'imperialist' theories and practices of white feminism.[7] Most of the writings that I have read on pornography do not in any way show an awareness of this history and acknowledge and/or incorporate an understanding of how racial, class and cultural differences between women shape our subjective experiences of the world, nor do they make any attempts to explore how women may be affected differently by pornography because of their different subjectivities.

The historical processes of European thought and practices *vis-à-vis* images of Black women and men as the Other – i.e., more primitive and therefore more sexual – are deeply rooted and ideologically inscribed within European culture.[8] The way in which images, icons and stereotypes in particular of Black female sexuality are reproduced in contemporary pornography and subsequently received/read by white men and women is and should be an important, indeed necessary, consideration for *all* feminists engaged in unravelling the complex matrix of pornography and representation.

One of the central concerns of the Euro-American women's movement has been understanding the ideological construction of sexuality and developing feminist critiques of sexuality and sexual practices within an overall analysis of the sexual subordination of women. Of course, within this overall scenario, radical-feminist theories of women's subordination have differed from socialist-feminist analyses. While it is no longer tenable to argue that these two perspectives are clearly demarcated on account of the many overlaps between them, nevertheless the dominant thread in much socialist-feminist analysis has been an attempt to locate its arguments within an historically specific framework. Its strength has also been its uncovering of economic and material conditions which give rise to particular forms of women's subjugation. All this is completely absent from the anti-pornography lobby which retreats into presumptuous generalisations about men and male power and about female sexuality.[9] There is an implicit assumption that somewhere and somehow there exists an unchanging and predefined female sexuality which is:

romantic, egalitarian, natural, gentle, free of power dynamics, monogamous, emotional, nurturing and spontaneous. This feminist prescription reflects and reproduces the dominant cultural assumptions about women (and is premissed) on the notion that women are victims of sex and that sex is degrading to women but not to men.[10]

Such a position sees women's sexuality purely in relation to men and ignores the work many feminists have done to create their own sexual agenda, whether in relationship to men or not. It is anti-feminist in its refusal to acknowledge many women's successful attempts to conceptualise and define our sexuality independently of men. Furthermore, it calls on an essentialist notion of women's and men's nature and disregards the social construction of sexuality and fantasies. Women who admit to their contradictory sexual fantasies are accused of being victims of 'politically incorrect early conditioning' . . . contradictory because their responses to pornography evoke at one and the same time feelings of anger, rage, fear and humiliation as well as pleasure, arousal and desire.

Within such a framework, women who engage in discussions or sexual practices which utilise concepts of power, desire and fantasy are made to feel guilty and dismissed as having 'internalised oppressive self-images'. The tragedy is that the spaces which many women have bravely created to continuously question and redefine their sexuality, either in relation to men or to other women, are being eroded by the guilt-inducing moralism of the anti-pornography lobby.[11] It is as if such women are being asked to purge themselves of the 'evil' that has been ingrained into their psyches and which they need to cleanse themselves of in order to emerge as 'good' and 'pure'. Our psyches around sexual desire, pleasure and fantasies are contradictory and problematic. But there is not an inevitable slide from acknowledging or even accepting any one of these fantasies for ourselves, to what we directly do in our everyday life and relationships. Instead, we should welcome them as signals or clues to exploring and discovering our sexual desires and pleasure.

Given the virulent moral overtones of the current right-wing backlash against women and a pressure to reprivatise sexual identity, such formulations around 'evil' and 'pure' are alarming.

## Censorship

While it is crucial to challenge the very basis on which the anti-pornography lobby propagate their arguments by critiquing their political formulations of pornography, it is equally important to confront their call for legal sanctions against pornography.

Censorship of any kind has always had disastrous and repressive effects for communities without access to power. Censorship exists in many different areas and is not only confined to sexuality. The unofficial exclusion of Black women from writing and publishing and from many public spaces is a form of censorship which has existed both within and outside the women's movement. Black people in South Africa speaking out against the apartheid regime experience vicious state censorship, Irish women involved in the struggle for self-determination in Northern Ireland have been imprisoned and harassed by the occupying forces of the British; in effect they have been censored. There are countless other such examples where people have had to bear the brunt of repression arising out of attempts to censor their radical challenges to subjugation and domination. There is no doubt that Clause 28 has been brought in as a way of censoring and silencing many of the positive and combative efforts by lesbians and gay men to become visible and have a voice in the social, cultural and political life of society.

## Dworkin/MacKinnon Ordinance

The Dworkin/MacKinnon ordinance which seeks to pass laws which can enable anyone to bring a civil suit against anything deemed to be 'offensive' and hence 'pornographic' poses several problems. What puzzles me is how women, who have defined all men as the enemy, can ask the 'patriarchal state' to intervene on their behalf and pass laws in the interests of women. Expecting the state to behave in a benevolent manner is naive. Black women and Irish women who have experienced the brutality of the British state first-hand have no such callow notions. The very state that condoned forced vaginal examinations of Asian women at Heathrow airport, a practice which amounted to both sexual and racial harassment, is the same one to which some Dworkin/MacKinnon followers in Britain are appealing.

It is also not very clear who or what they are asking to be censored: is it the consumers, or the porn kings who control the means of production, or is it the imagery itself? There are differences in the strategies that groups such as Women Against Violence Against Women (WAVAW) adopt in their campaigns against pornography and women such as Catherine Itzin who has initiated a legal campaign against pornography in Britain, although they all share the same language. Revolutionary/radical feminists have a history of unthought out and simplistic practices around combatting violence against women on the streets and it is this history which informs and, to this day, shapes their responses to pornography. In the late 1970s many women, mainly white, organised Reclaim the Night demos demanding that the streets be made safe for women – these marches usually went through Black areas, thus reinforcing racist ideas about Black men as perpetrators of sexual crimes against white women. It was also in the late 1970s that the Yorkshire Ripper was brutalising and murdering many women; as a reaction against police calls for women not to venture out at night on their own, some revolutionary feminists, part of WAVAW, called for a curfew on all men. Such a demand in towns and areas where there was a substantial Black population was deeply offensive and racist. It reflected a complete ignorance of the relationship of Black communities to policing, when time and time again Black men had been picked up on the streets for no good reason and harassed by the police.

In a recent interview, Annie Blue from WAVAW said:

We see all pornography as violence against women. We'd like a law that uses this radical-feminist definition of its function in society. It's a double-edged sword because it would give more power to the police and state, but in the present climate, it's the best of two evils. What else have we got?[12]

To pose the police and the state as 'the better of two evils' in such a crass, naive and unpoliticised manner is highly dubious. This throws into question the basis/definition of feminism such women are working with. A position which does not acknowledge, understand or even incorporate an analysis of the state and policing in relation to *all* women should be challenged in its claim to feminism.

The legal lobby is led by Catherine Itzin who has argued that 'pornography was a cause of sex discrimination' and that women who partake in pornography 'are victims, usually poor and exploited'. She then goes on to argue that just as 'negroes were kept in slavery rather than have their full citizenship rights recognised' so it is with the struggle that Dworkin/MacKinnon have had in passing their ordinance in the USA. In arguing for similar anti-pornographic legislation in Britain she uses the example of the Race Relations Act of 1976 as a model to work from: such legislation would incorporate the Dworkin/MacKinnon definition of pornography.[13]

What makes me angry about such formulations is the easy manner in which women such as Itzin use the race analogy to give credence and strength to their arguments. To collapse the denial of basic human rights of slaves with the objectification of women in sexual imagery is not only racist but extremely opportunistic. To attempt to equate the mass genocide of whole nations and communities of African people with the sexual subjugation of women betrays an indecent ignorance of the economic, cultural and political machinations of slavery. It diminishes both African history and women's struggle for control over their sexuality. What I am criticising here is the equation of two historically specific processes of exploitation and oppression. Women are, have been and continue to be, brutalised in and through pornography, but this has to be challenged, changed and critiqued on its own terms and not through emotive recourse to other historical parallels. The fundamental problem lies with the basic presumption of anti-pornographers that pornography is the root of all evil which allows them to make this erroneous and racist equation. The tendency to create such parallels between different struggles comes from a need to give added weight to modernist concerns with historical legacies. But why should this be necessary?

Nor is the Race Relations Act a piece of legislation which has had much effect in safeguarding the interests of Black people in Britain. In fact, it has often worked against our interests. Nor has such legislation stopped the police from contributing to the rise in the murders and street attacks on Black people. Itzin argues that, unlike pornography, at least 'you can't buy racist material in a newsagent's'[14] and this in itself constitutes a powerful statement. But why and how then does she explain the rise in racist murders, assaults and attacks both on the streets and in Black people's homes?

The state is not neutral and this has been demonstrated time and time again not only by Black people's experiences but also by the miners' strike in 1983/4 and by women at Greenham Common. It is suicidal to consider possibilities of strategic alliances with the state. Of course, there is a difference between strategic alliances with the state and progressive demands made of the state. Many social and political movements around the world have made demands of the state as a legitimate and sometimes successful strategy for change. But Catherine Itzin, who is attempting to make 'incitement to sexual hatred' a civil offence does not reveal any sophisticated understanding of such distinctions or strategies.

A second problem is that Dworkin's definition of what is pornographic can be interpreted in a variety of ways depending on who is doing the interpreting. So what a High Court judge, usually a white heterosexual man, believes to be pornographic may be quite different to what any of us interpret or define as pornographic. Indeed when there are so many differences between feminists on this, how can you ask a judge or a judicial system which has itself proved to be anti-women to arbitrate? Having such definitions will also inevitably lead to a policing of everyone's desires, fantasies and sexuality. Who decides what images are permissible and which ones are not?

Anti-pornography theory collapses a variety of sexual images into a generalised statement that all pornography is violence against women. But as Ann Snitow has argued convincingly:

A definition of pornography that takes the problem of analysis seriously has to include not only violence, hatred and fear of women, but also a long list of other elements, which may help explain why we women ourselves have such a mixture of reactions to the genre . . . We need to be able to reject the sexism in porn without having to reject the realm of pornographic sexual fantasy as if that entire kingdom were without meaning or resonance for women . . . Without history, without an analysis of complexity and difference, without a critical eye toward gender and its constant redefinitions, some recognition of the gap – in ideas and feelings – between the porn magazine and the man who reads it, we will only be purveying a false hope to those women whom we want to join us: that without porn, there will be far less male violence, that with less male violence there will be far less male power.[15]

# Power of Imagery

We live in a highly visual culture, controlled by the institutions of the mass media whose primary aim is to increase consumerism through advertising and to present the world through the eyes of a dominant élite. Every day we are presented with images which appear 'natural' and yet bear hardly any resemblance to the reality of most people's lives. The power of images is unquestionable: what is needed is an unmasking of the hidden agenda of the media and the role which representation plays within cultural and political life.

A dominant premise of the pro-censorship lobby is their understanding and/or analysis of the powerful influence that sexual imagery of women has over men. They posit a direct correlation between pornography and violence against women. I do not want to argue this point as to whether such a correlation has a scientific and/or statistical basis; instead I would argue that complex issues around visual representation cannot be reduced to a simple formula of pornography = violence against women.

Much work has been done and is continuing to be done in the women's movement around issues of women's representation in mainstream media, through advertising, films and television. The power of images to inform, misinform, manipulate and feed into notions of female and male roles has long been recognised by feminist cultural activists. Some women have consistently challenged the notion that, although we are influenced by the media, we are not just passive recipients or mere victims.

More recently, such work has been started by many Black women and men concerned with challenging the racist and sexist representations of Black people both within mainstream media and in independent bodies of work. The struggle over imagery and for self-representation and self-definition has been established as a legitimate political struggle by many Black cultural activists.[16] Black photographers, artists, writers and film-makers are not only working to control the content of their representation but also building infrastructures which give us control over the means of production of our work. We are using our respective creative mediums to discover and explore issues around racial, sexual and cultural identities.

This area of work too has suffered from interference and censorship. Take, for example, the film *A People's Account about the Uprisings in Broadwater Farm and Handsworth* about the police shooting of two Black women, namely, Cherry Groce and Cynthia Jarrett made in 1986 by Ceddo, a Black film and video workshop. Channel 4 and the Independent Broadcasting Authority have pulled the film off the screen three times, arguing that it is too one-sided. This film provides a rare forum for the voices of Black people who live on these estates and who experienced police violence. And for once we do not have the overwhelming presence of dominant white voices painting pictures of 'barbaric' and 'savage' Black rioters. The film has still not been seen on

Channel 4 who originally funded it; it has been censored by the channel jointly with the IBA, purely on the grounds of political bias.

Censorship of this kind is clearly about control. When it comes to the visual representation of and by Black people, women, gay men and lesbians, the problem is that when any of us begin to challenge the dominant imagery, whether exploitative, racist, sexist or homophobic, the shackles of censorship are snapped on before any resistance can be mustered up.

To conclude, I want to restate my argument that most women from their different subjectivities will continue to find what they define as pornography both enraging and problematic. What we don't need is a regression to victimisation theories of women's oppression which see women only as sexual victims and passive recipients of authoritarian patriarchal institutions.

What we do need is a greater sophistication in the language and analysis of pornography than has been so far witnessed[17] – an analysis which takes into account the complexity of different subjectivities and their respective relationships to institutions of power and the state. How we fight politically against pornography, violence against women and censorship will ultimately depend not only on how we define and name the problems but also how we wage struggles around other aspects of our political agendas and visions.

## Notes

1. Andrea Dworkin, *Pornography: Men Possessing Women*, The Women's Press, 1981.
2. Judith Walkowitz, *Prostitution and Victorian Society: Women, Class and the State*, Cambridge University Press, 1980.
3. Varda Burstyn, 'Political Precedents and Moral Crusades: Women, Sex and the State' in *Women Against Censorship* edited by Varda Burstyn, Douglas and McIntyre, Vancouver and Toronto, 1985.
4. Andrea Dworkin, *op. cit.*, p. 224.
5. Jan Parker and Chris Baker, 'Association of London Authorities Briefing paper on Clause 29', January 1988 (internal document). My thanks to Jan Parker for useful discussions in this area.
6. Ann Snitow, 'Retrenchment Versus Transformation: The Politics of the Anti Pornography Movement' in *Women Against Censorship, op. cit.*, p. 113.
7. See for example, Hazel Carby, 'White Women Listen! Black Feminism and the boundaries of Sisterhood' in *The Empire Strikes Back, Race and Racism in 70s Britain*, eds., Race and Politics Group, Centre for Contemporary Cultural Studies, Hutchinson, 1982. Also see, 'Many Voices One Chant: Black Feminist Perspectives' *Feminist Review*, Autumn 1984.
8. See Sandra L. Gilman, *Difference and Pathology: Stereotypes of Sexuality, Race and Madness*, Cornell University Press, 1985.
9. See Dworkin, *op. cit.*, in particular, pp. 13–24 where she expounds on the seven tenets of male power and supremacy.
10. Donna Turley, 'The Feminist Debate on Pornography', *Socialist Review*, No. 87–88, May–August 1986.

11. Susan Ardill and Sue O'Sullivan, 'Difference, Desire and Lesbian Sado-masochism' in *Feminist Review*, No. 23, Summer 1986; also this volume.
12. Sarah Baxter, 'Women Against Porn' in which she quotes Annie Blue, *Time Out*, 23–30 March, 1988, No. 918.
13. Catherine Itzin, *London Daily News*, April 20, 1988.
14. Catherine Itzin, Quoted by Sarah Baxter, *op. cit.*
15. Ann Snitow, *op. cit.*, p. 117.
16. See, for instance, 'Black Image, Staying On', Ten:8 photographic maga-zine, No. 16, 1984.
17. Except for the excellent anthology *Women Against Censorship, op. cit.* and a collection of articles titled, *Caught Looking: Feminism, Pornography and Censorship*, eds. Kate Ellis, *et al*, 1987. Unfortunately bookshops in Britain refuse to stock this enjoyable and well-argued collection because of images/illustrations which they deem 'pornographic'.

## Acknowledgements

I would like to thank Vron Ware, Paul Gilroy, Shaheen Haque and Sue O'Sullivan for their constant support, encouragement and useful comments on my earlier drafts and to Gail Chester for her patience.

This article was originally written for and published in Julienne Dickey and Gail Chester (eds) *Feminism and Censorship – The Current Debate* (Prism Press, 1988).

# Making Common Cause: Diversity and Coalitions

Charlotte Bunch

> *This essay is based on a speech that was given at the National Women's Studies Association annual convention in June, 1985, for the panel 'Common Causes: Uncommon Coalitions – Sex, Race, Class & Age'.*

In my twenty years of political organizing, I have been part of numerous coalitions. Some were successful, others disastrous, and most fell somewhere in between. I am not sure that any were really uncommon. For coalitions are one of the most common strategies of creating social change, and the problems that go with them are recurring themes in all movements. Discourse about when, where and how to build coalitions is particularly important when we seek to make change that is inclusive of diverse perspectives. For feminists, especially in a country like the U.S. with so many varied groups, the ability to create a movement that includes and responds to the diversity of women's lives is crucial.

## Diversity and domination

Patriarchy has systematically utilized diversity as a tool of domination in which we learn in childhood that such things as sex and race bring differences in power and privilege, and that these are acceptable. This idea that difference justifies domination is deeply embedded in society and defended as natural. Take, for example, the often heard refrain: 'There will always be poor people' used to perpetuate class privileges. But as women who have challenged the so-called naturalness of male supremacy, feminists must also question it in other areas of domination.

When power hierarchies are accepted as inevitable, people can be manipulated to fear that those who are different are a threat to their position and perhaps even to their survival. We are taught to be afraid that 'they will hurt us – either because they are more powerful or because they want our privileges.' While that fear takes multiple forms depending on where we fit in the various scales of domination, all of us are taught to distrust those who are different. Some aspects of this fear may be necessary to survival – whites do lynch Blacks, men will rape women – and we must watch out for such dangers. But fear and distrust of differences are most often used to keep us in line. When we challenge the idea that differences must be threatening, we are also challenging the patriarchal assignment of power and privilege as birthrights.

Opposing the ways that differences are used to dominate does not mean that we seek to end diversity. Feminist visions are not about creating homogenized people who all look like a blank middle class television ad. Many aspects of diversity can be celebrated as variety, creativity and options in life styles and world views. We must distinguish between creative differences that are not intrinsically tied to domination and the assignment of power and privilege based on the distinct characteristics of some. Diversity, when separated from power to control others, provides valuable opportunities for learning and living that can be missed if one is embedded in an ethnocentric way of seeing reality.

Diversity among feminists today can be a resource for gaining a broader understanding of the world. We see more clearly and our ability to create effective strategies is enhanced if we move beyond the boundaries of our assigned patriarchal slot. Quite specifically, in 1985, white women can look to the growing women of color movement in the U.S. and to feminism in the Third World. But too often we fail to respond to each other's potential for enriching our lives because of unconscious fears of race, class, or national differences. It is not just a matter of learning about race and class – although that is important – but also of understanding women's lives and the world as viewed by others.

Making coalitions does not mean 'watering down' feminist politics as some fear. Rather, it requires engaging in a wider debate about those politics and shaping their expressions to respond to more women's realities. I see this process as reclaiming the radical spirit of feminism that calls for going to the roots of oppression. In the U.S. for example, the present wave of feminism began in the 1960s in close connection to the Black civil rights movement and its demand for recognition of the rights of racially diverse groups. Yet, racism is all too often reflected in the lack of acknowledgment of those origins and the invisibility of women of color who were a part of feminism's resurgence. As Barbara Smith notes in *But Some of Us Are Brave* (Feminist Press, 1982) 'Black women were a part of that early women's movement as were working class women of all races.' This included famous speakers such as Florence Kennedy as well as women like the Welfare Rights mothers who worked in the late '60s in coalition with Washington D.C. Women's Liberation to achieve improvements in the city's health services for women. In the 1970s, efforts to develop diverse coalitions and a broader based agenda were often eclipsed by many factors including intense movement controversies and the media's emphasis on the pursuit of equality within the system. By focusing again on the diversity and depth of women's perspectives and needs in the 1980s, I see feminists reasserting the radical impulse for justice for all and thus strengthening the movement as a force for fundamental change.

There is commonality in the fact that all women are subordinated, but when we examine our diversity, we see that the forms that takes are shaped by many factors. Female oppression is not one universal block experienced the same way by all women, to which other forms of exploitation are then added as separate pieces. Rather, various oppressions interact to shape the particulars of each woman's life. For example, an aging Black lesbian who is poor does not experience oppression as separate packages – one sexism, one poverty, one homophobia, one racism, and one ageism. She experiences these as interacting and shaping each other. Seeing this interaction is vital for coalitions around issues.

Too often analysis of women's oppression isolates single factors such as class or sexual preference in a simplistic manner, trying to show the effects of each separately. But this fails to take account of their inter-relatedness. Further, it often winds up in battles over a hierarchy of seriousness of forms of oppression or over how one really is the cause of the other. But a feminist method suggests the necessity of looking at their interaction – at how race, class, sex, and age oppression shape each other. For example, race and class affect whether an older woman's problem is being abandoned in her house, trapped in an abusive nursing home, or entirely homeless. Or in looking at the exploitation of women's work, we can see the effect of factors such as race, homophobia, or physical disability, as well as class.

Strategies that fail to examine how female exploitation is shaped in different forms often set some women up against others. The interactive approach – taking into account female diversity – is thus essential for effective coalitions. However, it is often difficult to look at all the features of oppression because they are complex and demand continuous re-evaluation of our assumptions. Further, attitudes and emotions around diversity are deeply rooted and often volatile. Systems such as racism, anti-Semitism, classism, nationalism, and homophobia are so much a part of the culture that surrounds us from birth that we often have biases and blind spots that affect our attitudes, behavior, strategies, and values in ways that we do not perceive until challenged by others.

Many problems that arise in coalitions stem from resistance to being challenged about oppressive attitudes and reactions. These need to be approached matter-of-factly, not as moral judgments on someone's personhood, but as negative results of growing up in a patriarchal culture. We must change such attitudes and behavior because they oppress others and interfere with our own humanity as well as impede the process of creating feminist strategies and coalitions. White middle class North Americans are often unaware that their perspectives – which usually coincide with the media's portrayal of reality – are not the only way of seeing the world. Since these ethnocentric biases are reinforced constantly, we must make an extra effort to see other points of view. This does not mean that nothing of this culture is of value. It simply means that we must go beyond its limits to see what can be taken as useful and not oppressive, and what must be challenged.

In looking at diversity among women, we see one of the weaknesses of the feminist concept that the personal is political. It is valid that each woman begins from her personal experiences and it is important to see how these are political. But we must also recognize that our personal experiences are shaped by the culture with all its prejudices. We cannot therefore depend on our perceptions alone as the basis for political analysis and action – much less for coalition. Feminists must stretch beyond, challenging the limits of our own personal experiences by learning from the diversity of women's lives.

## Divisive reactions to diversity

In the 1980s, various groups, such as the women of color movement, are expanding the definitions of and possibilities for feminism. But many women's reactions to diversity interfere with making successful cross-cultural, multi-racial coalitions. Bringing up race or class or lesbianism is not divisive to the movement. Rather I see the reactions to issues of diversity as divisive rather than the issues themselves. I want to outline here some of the reactions that I have seen interfere with efforts at coalition building and suggest ways of getting beyond them.

The most obviously divisive reaction is *becoming defensive* when challenged around an issue of diversity. If you are busy making explanations about how some action or comment was not really what you meant, it is hard to listen to and understand criticism and why it is being made. This does not mean passively accepting every critical comment – for in dealing with such emotional topics, there will be exaggerations, inaccuracies, or injustices that must be worked out. But these problems do not excuse anyone from struggling with the issues. If you remain open, while retaining a sense of your own authenticity, it is usually possible to deal with these by listening and responding constructively. If a critique does not make sense to you, ask about it, or try to figure out what led to it – even if it seems unfair. It is not always easy to listen to criticism first and then sort through what it means, but it is the job of feminists to do just that. To listen carefully, to consider what other views mean for our work, and to respond through incorporating new understandings where appropriate – this is a feminist necessity if we are to make coalitions among diverse women.

Often defensiveness is related to another unhelpful reaction which is *guilt*. It may be appropriate to experience shame over the actions of one's ancestors or at how one has participated in another's oppression. But personal guilt is usually immobilizing, particularly if one sits with it for long. Successful coalitions are not built around feeling sorry for others or being apologetic about one's existence. Coalitions are built around shared outrage over injustice and common visions of how society can be changed. Few of us had control over our origins and the point is not to feel guilt about the attitudes or privileges that we inherited. The question is what we are going to do about them now – how are we going to change ourselves and work to end domination in the world? For example, white women feeling sorry about something like racism is not as useful to women of color as working to eliminate it in society as well as in one's personal life.

Often women are side-tracked by *over-personalization* when dealing with diversity. The issues raised are personal and do require individual change, but it is important not to get stuck there. Sometimes feminists get so involved in trying to be pure and personally free of any oppressive behavior that they become paralyzed and fear taking any political action because it might not be correct. Yet it is through concrete efforts to challenge domination – no matter how small – that we learn and can become more effective and more inclusive in our political work. For example, if a man tells me that he is becoming totally anti-sexist but is not in some way challenging the structures of patriarchal power that continue to oppress women, then his personal changes – if I believe him at all – are of minimal value to me. The same is true for women of color who see some whites talking about racism but not taking action against it in the world.

Another aspect of over-personalization is *withdrawal*. Sometimes feminists have become so personally hurt by criticism or feel so left out when a group is creating its own space, that they withdraw from political engagement. For example, some heterosexual women during the height of lesbian feminist challenges in the 1970s withdrew into their feelings of being attacked or left out rather than working on how they could fight homophobia while still being with men personally. This only reinforced the separation between us. I see similar behavior among some white women today. The hurt is often understandable because there is pain in confrontations around difficult issues, and feminists sometimes spend more energy criticizing women's oppressive behavior than opposing the systems of oppression. Still reacting to this by withdrawing prevents learning from what has happened and growing to the point where coalition is possible. This is sometimes like children who want to be center stage and pout when not in the forefront. Instead we need to see that at any given moment one group may be the creative edge of the movement but that will enrich all of us in the long run.

One of the more infuriating reactions is *acting weary and resentful* when someone brings up 'that issue' again. No one is more tired of homophobia and having to bring it up again than a lesbian like myself. I am sure women of color feel the same way about racism, Jewish women about anti-Semitism, the elderly about ageism etc. But the problems still exist and someone must address them. Until feminists can learn to include the concerns and perspectives of those women whose oppression we do not directly experience, then others will have to keep bringing up those issues. We must strive to become 'one-woman coalitions' – capable of understanding and raising all issues of oppression and seeing our relationship to them – whites speaking about racism, heterosexuals about homophobia, the able-bodied about disabilities, etc. Only as we do this will we be able to build lasting coalitions.

The last divisive reaction that I want to include here is *limiting outspoken 'minority women' to 'their issues.'* When someone speaks out strongly about her group's specific oppression, she often becomes a token whose leadership in other areas is restricted. For example, I have felt pressure either to work only on lesbian issues, or to downplay them if I am involved in other areas of feminist activity. Yet, while I am out of the closet and concerned about homophobia, there are many other topics that I want to address besides lesbianism, just as women of color have much to say about many issues in addition to racism. To counter this tendency, I decided in the late '70s that I would not write any more only about lesbianism, but instead I would address other subjects and include within those my lesbian feminist analysis. Women of all races, classes, ages, and nations have much to say on a whole variety of topics from their particular perspectives. If we limit each to one identity and approach feminism as a string of separate unrelated issues, we narrow the possibilities for insight, growth, and leadership throughout the movement.

Our chances of building successful coalitions are greater if we can avoid divisive reactions such as these and see diversity as a strength. As we struggle to learn from our differences rather than to fear or deny them, we can find our common ground. In this process, we also build the atmosphere of good faith and respect which is necessary for strong coalitions. For while we do not always need to love or even like one another or agree on everything, we do need to be able to challenge each other from the assumption that change is possible. Another requirement when diverse groups coalesce is that each must be clear about its bottom line. We must each know what we need in order to survive in a coalition and how to communicate that to others.

Coalitions that are successful must also be aimed at taking meaningful action in the world. Coalition is not abstract. It functions when groups or individuals are working together around something that each cares about and sees as advancing their goals or vision, or at least protecting the space necessary to develop. When a coalition has some effect then it is worth going through all the trouble and strife of making it work. In any case, it is in the process itself that we often discover the common causes that make it possible to create common coalitions of women in all our diversity working toward both common and varied feminist visions.

# Biographical Notes

**Donna Allegra**: 'I'm thirty-five years old. I work as a construction electrician, write on coffee breaks, in the bathroom, between African dance classes. My life is about writing, dance, music, spiritual growth, peace, greater good. I talk to friends on the phone for fun, for help and for understanding about the process of living. I ride my bike everywhere that I can, buy fruits and vegetables, pray, read, sew, listen to the radio, play African percussion (bell and drum), go to see performance artists, go to the parks, swim.

I studied theater and literature at Bennington College, New York University and Hunter College. I was a producer at WBAI radio, was in Jamaica – a Black lesbian writer's group; Naps, a Black lesbian performance group; Gap Tooth Girlfriends – a writer's workshop: A Piece of the World – a Black women's percussion group.

I'm free of all drugs – including caffein, alcohol, refined sugars and starches. A gentle spirit seeking divinity within myself and others.'

**Gloria E. Anzaldúa** is a Chicana tejana lesbian-feminist poet and fiction writer. She is co-editor of *This Bridge Called My Back: Radical Writings by Women of Color*, winner of the Before Columbus Foundation American Book Award. Gloria has been active in the migrant farm workers movement. She has taught Chicano Studies, Feminist Studies, and Creative Writing at the University of Texas, San Francisco State University, and Vermont College of Norwich University, and has conducted writing workshops around the country. She is currently doing a Distinguished Visiting Professorship at the University of California at Sante Cruz. She has been a contributing editor to *Sinister Wisdom* since 1984. *Borderlands/La Frontera: The New Mestiza*, a book of essays and poems, was released by Spinsters/Aunt Lute in July 1987.

**Susan Ardill** was born in Sydney, Australia in 1955. She is currently working as a television producer and a journalist in London.

**Beth Brant**: Beth started writing at the age of forty after a trip through the Mohawk Valley, when a Bald Eagle flew in front of her car, sat in a tree, and instructed her to write. She has been writing since.

She is the co-founder of Turtle Grandmother, an archive and library for Native American women, and a clearing-house for their manuscripts, published and unpublished. She lives in Detroit with her Diane, her lover of ten years, and two of her daughters.

**Nicole Brossard** was born in Montreal in 1943. Poet, novelist and essayist, she has published more than twenty books since 1965. Seven of them have been translated into English, among them *A Book*, *Daydream Mechanics*, *French Kiss*, *Lovhers* and *The Aerial Letter*. She is co-founder of La Barre du Jour (1965) and co-directed the film *Some American Feminists* (1976). She is twice winner of the Governor General's Award for poetry. Her most recent novel is *Le Desert Mauve*. Nicole Brossard lives in Montreal.

**Charlotte Bunch** is an internationally known writer and organiser, teacher and theorist, speaker and activist, and a leading figure in the women's move-ment for two decades. The first woman resident fellow at the Institute for Policy Studies in Washing-ton, D.C., she was a founder of D.C. Women's Liberation, The Furies, and of *Quest: A Feminist Quarterly*, and served on the Board of the National Gay Task Force for eight years. She has edited seven anthologies of feminist thought, her articles have appeared widely, and her newest book is *Passionate Politics: Feminist Theory in Action, Essays 1968–1986* (St Martin's Press, 1987). She has travelled extensively, working on global feminism and the U.N. Decade for Women through Interfem Consultants, based in Brooklyn, New York. Currently, she is the Laurie New Jersey Chair in Women's Studies at Rutgers University.

**Sandra Butler** is a writer and counselor with a focus on violence against women and children. Author of many articles about sexual abuse, she is now leading workshops for lesbian couples dealing with disabilities and life-threatening illness. 'Reverberations' helped her discover a form in which both she and her partner Barbara could each retain their own unique voice and experience while creating a context in which they as a couple could write of their lives together. *(See photograph of Sandra Butler with Barbara Rosenblum.)*

**Chrystos**: 'Born 7 November. 1946 in San Francisco, of a Lithuanian/Alsace-Lorraine mother and a Menominee father. Self educated. Work appears in *This Bridge called My Back*, *A Gathering of Spirit* and various anthologies and periodicals. Currently working on *Not Vanishing* (prose and poetry) to appear with Press Gang of Canada and writing a play, *Rudey Toot Zoo*. My polical efforts are for the most part devoted to repealing PL 93-531 (Navajo relocation act). My deepest gratitude to the Women of Color Potluck which helps keep me sane.'

**Elana Dykewomon** is the current editor of *Sinister Wisdom*, author of *Riverfinger Woman, They Will Know Me By My Teeth*, and *Fragments from Lesbos*. She is a lesbian separatist, printer, member of the Jewish Lesbian Writers Group, and partner in Diaspora Distribution. After many wanderings she now lives in Oakland, California, where she often feels like a lemming surprised by the reality of the sea.

**Sarah Franklin** is a member of the Birmingham Ladies Indoor Five-a-Side Football League at Aston Villa. She is also attempting to reincorporate the body into social construction theory in her analysis of reproductive technology as a post-graduate research student in Cultural Studies at the University of Birmingham.

**Berta Freistadt**: 'I am a single woman, living alone. I am forty-five and don't seem to have learnt much about life. I like to write, read, study and eat. I love my cat, the garden, the sea and a few special friends. I try to avoid depression, too much responsibility, confrontation and Tesco's on Saturdays.'

**Lorna Hardy**: 'I'm not using my real name because at the time of going to press I'm experiencing some harassment. The perpetrators of Clause 28 have got a lot to answer for.'

©DAVID SMITH 1988

**Kirsten Hearn** is a thirty-two-year-old Scorpio with Aquarius rising, blind lesbian feminist currently working for a local authority as a lesbian and gay officer. Her other career is as a tactile artist. She is active in lesbian and gay politics, the women's movement and disability politics. Her hobbies are swimming, singing, eating and lying in bed listening to the Archers. She is an avid reader of heterosexual trashy romances which take her mind off political struggle.

**Amber Hollibaugh** lives and works in New York.

**Margaret Hunt** was born in Boston, Massachusetts in 1953 and has lived in many parts of the US as well as in the Netherlands and Britain. She is currently assistant professor of History and Women's Studies at Amherst College in Western Massachusetts. She grew up in the women's movement and has worked for many years on projects relating to battered women, low-income women, and women of color, as well as on lesbian and gay concerns and Central American issues. She has written one book, *Life Skills for Women in Transition* (1982) and is currently working on another on eighteenth-century English family history and women's history. She plays softball as often as she can.

**Melanie Kaye/Kantrowitz** is the author of *Some Pieces of Jewish Left* (a collection of short stories); *We Speak in Code: Poems and Other Writings*; and she co-edited *The Tribe of Dina: A Jewish Women's Anthology* (in which her essay in this volume first appeared). From 1983–87 she was editor and publisher of *Sinister Wisdom*, one of the oldest lesbian/feminist literary and political journals in the States (founded 1976). She holds a Ph.D in Comparative Literature from the University of California, Berkeley, and she teaches Writing and Women's Studies in the Adult Degree Program at Vermont College.

Her poems, fiction, essays and reviews have been published widely in the feminist, lesbian and progressive Jewish press and anthologies, including *Jewish Currents*, *Conditions*, *Ikon*, *New America*, *Women of Power*, *Women's Review of Books*, *Blood To Remember: American Poets on the Holocaust*, *Naming the Waves*, *Nice Jewish Girls*, etc.

**Irena Klepfisz** is a poet and author of *Keeper of Accounts* (Sinister Wisdom Books, 1983), *Different Enclosures: The Poetry and Prose of Irena Klipfisz* (Onlywomen Press, 1985) and co-editor of *The Tribe of Dina: A Jewish Women's Anthology* (Sinister Wisdom Books, 1986). An activist in both the Jewish and lesbian/feminist communities, she has lectured, written and led workshops on feminism, office work and class, homophobia, Jewish identity, Yiddish culture, anti-Semitism and the Middle East. She received her Ph.D in English Literature from the University of Chicago in 1970 and has taught literature, creative writing, Yiddish and Women's Studies.

**Alice Lee** was born in Georgetown, Guyana in the year of the Monkey during the hours of the Ox. She enjoys talking, eating and telling stories. She now lives in London.

**Audre Lorde** was born in New York City in 1934. She received her B.A. from Hunter College and did graduate work for an M.L.S. degree at Columbia University. From 1961–1963 she was a librarian for the New York Public Library.

Ms Lorde is the author of twelve books, both non-fiction and poetry. She was poet-in-residence at Tougaloo College in Jackson, Mississippi in 1968. She is currently professor of English at Hunter College in New York City. She is a resident of Staten Island.

**Barbara Macdonald** (born 1913) is author, with Cynthia Rich, of *Look Me in the Eye: Old Women, Aging and Ageism* (Published in USA by Spinsters/Aunt Lute and in GB by The Women's Press). She writes and lectures widely on ageism and other feminist issues. *(See photograph of Barbara Macdonald with Cynthia Rich.)*

**Christian McEwen**: 'Born London, 1956, grew up in Scotland mostly. Moved to the States in 1979, and now live on the Lower East Side of New York. Have worked as a gardener, construction worker, counsellor, editor, creative writing teacher and (currently) literacy advisor. Keep an obsessive journal and depend enormously and passionately on my friends, a number of whom are included in this book.'

**Joan Nestle**: Forty-eight years old, Jewish, feminist, co-founder of the lesbian Herstory Archives in NYC and author of *A Restricted Country*, which tells everything else.

**Sigrid Nielsen**: 'I was born in 1948 and grew up in a small town, as well as the suburbs of large cities. I graduated from college in Santa Fe, New Mexico, travelled, and wrote large numbers of unfinished novels and one biography. After coming to Edinburgh, I co-founded Lavender Menace (now West and Wilde), Scotland's lesbian and gay bookshop and co-edited *In Other Words: Writing as a Feminist* (Hutchinson, 1987) I am now working on a play and a novel.'

**Sue O'Sullivan**: When she works she works very hard but she realizes now that perhaps fancy juggling is not her forte. However, through years of practice she is quite adept and figures it will continue to come in handy in these mean-spirited, poverty-stricken times when money is short and politics more necessary than ever.

**Pratibha Parmar** is a writer, filmmaker and political activist. She has co-edited several books including *The Empire Strikes Back* (Hutchinson 1982), *Many Voices, One Chant: Black Feminist Perspectives*, *Feminist Review 17* (1984), *Through the Break*, (Sheba 1988). Her films and videos include *Emergence* (1986) and *ReFraming AIDS* (1988). She has written for *Marxism Today*, *Women's Review*, *City Limits* and other periodicals.

**Raven** is still living in Maryland State Prison where she has been incarcerated for life. Beth believes that mail no longer reaches her.

**Cynthia Rich** (born 1933) is co-author with Barbara Macdonald of *Look Me in the Eye: Old Women, Aging and Ageism*. They live in a trailer on the Anza Borrego desert in California, and continue to write and organize to end ageism. *(Cynthia Rich is behind Barbara Macdonald in the photo.)*

**Barbara Rosenblum**: April 9, 1943 – February 14, 1988. Barbara was a teacher, a sociologist and a writer. She wrote extensively about many facets of art and culture and after her diagnosis of breast cancer in 1985 added personal non-fiction to her academic writing. Her deep commitment to communicating her experience to others – to making the personal political – was a task that occupied her until her death. 'Reverberations' was the first piece she and her partner Sandy wrote together and began the process of *Cancer in Two Voices*, a book that looks at how life-threatening illness changed their relationship. Barbara Rosenblum died at home on February 14, 1988. A Fellowship she established will assist feminist scholars to study the impact of cancer on the lives of women. Feminists from Britain will be able to apply. Please send contributions to: Barbara Rosenblum Fellowship, c/o Beth Hess, 2 Hampshire Drive, Mendham, New Jersey 07945, USA. *(Barbara Rosenblum is in front in the photo, and Sandra Butler behind.)*

**Joanna Russ** is a science fiction novelist and short story writer, whose recent publications include *Majic Mommas*, *Trembling Sisters*, *Puritans and Perverts*, *Extra (Ordinary) People*, and two collections of short stories: *The Zanzibar Cat* and *The Adventures of Alyx*, as well as a non-fiction study, *How To Suppress Women's Writing*. Her work has been translated into French, German, Italian, Japenese, Dutch, Danish, Spanish, Catalan and Finnish. Her latest book is a new collection of short stories, *The Other Side of the Moon*.

**Lisa Saffron**: 'I am thirty-five years old and live with my daughter in London where I work in the field of women's health information. I am the author of a book called *Getting Pregnant Our Own Way: A Guide to Alternative Insemination* which describes British women's experiences of self-insemination and AID from clinics.'

301

**Sara Scott** has been involved in the Women's Liberation Movement since 1979. She is a member of the editorial collective of *Trouble and Strife* (a radical-feminist magazine) and a counsellor with Manchester Rape Crisis Line.

**Ellen Shapiro** lives in Brooklyn, New York City. She was an editor at Out & Out Books, an independent women's press, and a recipient of a New York State CAPS grant for fiction. Her work has been published in *The Women's Review of Books*, *Ikon* and *Christopher Street*.

© MORGAN GWENWALD

**Linda Smukler** was the 1986 winner of the Katherine Anne Porter Fiction Competition sponsored by *Nimrod* magazine, and has published in various publications including *Conditions* and *Ikon*. A graduate of Yale University, she was a runner-up in the 1985 Narrative Poetry Competition sponsored by the *New England Review/Bread Loaf quarterly*. Linda was a recipient of an Edward Albee Foundation Fellowship in 1985 and has studied with Gloria Anzaldúa, Joseph McElroy and Grace Paley.

**Jackie Stacey** is a post-graduate research student at the Centre for Contemporary Cultural Studies, Birmingham, doing research on women audiences and Hollywood stars in post-war Britain. She also teaches women's studies, film studies and lesbian and gay studies in both adult and higher education.

**Susanna J. Sturgis** is learning to live with the economic (and other) insecurities of taking her creative writing seriously. Among her current projects are *Medea's Daughters*, a multi-genre collection inspired by Euripides' play; a novel; and *One for the Road*, an anthology for past and present teenage alcoholics, which she is co-editing. She lives on the island of Martha's Vineyard, Massachusetts, where her yeast bread regularly wins blue ribbons at the agricultural fair.

302

**Sunna** is an Asian woman who lives in London.

**Jean Swallow** is a lesbian feminist writer and editor currently living in San Francisco. Her work has appeared in *Common Lives/Lesbian Lives*, *Lesbian Inciter*, *Feminary*, *Women: a Journal of Liberation*, *Womenspirit* and *Lesbian Contradictions*. *Out from Under:Sober Dykes and Our Friends* appeared with Spinsters Ink in 1983.

**Lis Whitelaw**: 'I am thirty-seven, a freelance writer and lecturer, much discouraged by late eighties Britain. Nonetheless I continue to write fiction, plays and articles (some published, some not) and to work on a biography of Cicely Hamilton for The Women's Press as part of my contribution to keeping lesbians visible.'

**Marg Yeo** is a Canadian poet, living in London, who is old enough to know better, but still doesn't.